International Poetry of
the First World War

International Poetry of the First World War

An Anthology of Lost Voices

Edited by Constance Ruzich

BLOOMSBURY ACADEMIC
LONDON · NEW YORK · OXFORD · NEW DELHI · SYDNEY

BLOOMSBURY ACADEMIC
Bloomsbury Publishing Plc
50 Bedford Square, London, WC1B 3DP, UK
1385 Broadway, New York, NY 10018, USA
29 Earlsfort Terrace, Dublin 2, Ireland

BLOOMSBURY, BLOOMSBURY ACADEMIC and the Diana logo are
trademarks of Bloomsbury Publishing Plc

First published in Great Britain 2021
This paperback edition published 2022

Selection and editorial matter copyright © Constance Ruzich, 2021

Constance Ruzich has asserted her right under the Copyright,
Designs and Patents Act, 1988, to be identified as Editor of this work.

For legal purposes the Acknowledgments on pp. xi–xiv constitute an
extension of this copyright page.

Cover design: Eleanor Rose
Cover image: 'Solitude: Thiepval after the battles' from the series *Twelve Drypoints of the War 1914–1918*, 1916, by British artist Percy Smith (1882–1948)

All rights reserved. No part of this publication may be reproduced or
transmitted in any form or by any means, electronic or mechanical, including
photocopying, recording, or any information storage or retrieval system,
without prior permission in writing from the publishers.

Bloomsbury Publishing Plc does not have any control over, or responsibility for,
any third-party websites referred to or in this book. All internet addresses given
in this book were correct at the time of going to press. The author and publisher
regret any inconvenience caused if addresses have changed or sites have
ceased to exist, but can accept no responsibility for any such changes.

A catalogue record for this book is available from the British Library.

A catalog record for this book is available from the Library of Congress.

ISBN: HB: 978-1-3501-0644-4
PB: 978-1-3502-2606-7
ePDF: 978-1-3501-0646-8
eBook: 978-1-3501-0645-1

Typeset by Integra Software Services Pvt. Ltd.

To find out more about our authors and books visit www.bloomsbury.com
and sign up for our newsletters.

Contents

Acknowledgments		xi
Introduction		1
1	**Soldiers' Lives**	**17**
	Fragment *Rupert Brooke*	18
	The Transport *John Allan Wyeth*	20
	The Night Patrol *Arthur Graeme West*	22
	In No Man's Land *Ewart Alan Mackintosh*	25
	On Patrol in No Man's Land *James Reese Europe*	27
	War Song (Chanson de Guerre)	
	Albert-Paul Granier, translated by Ian Higgins	31
	Dance of Death 1916 (Totentanz 1916) *Hugo Ball, translated by*	
	Edmund Potts	34
	Trench Poets *Edgell Rickword*	36
	Vigil (Veglia) *Giuseppe Ungaretti, translated by Jonathan Griffin*	38
	The Moles *Cyril Morton Horne*	40
	The Song of the Mud *Mary Borden*	42
	Still Raining… (Il pleut encore…) *Noël Garnier, translated by*	
	Ian Higgins	46
	The Boys Who Live in the Ground *Donald S. White*	48
	A Digger's Disillusion *K.L. Trent*	50
	During the Bombardment *Theodore Percival Cameron Wilson*	53
	Cricket: The Catch *Frederick William Harvey*	56
	The Rainbow *Leslie Coulson*	58
	The Star-Shell *Patrick MacGill*	61
	Back to Rest *William Noel Hodgson*	63
	After the "Offensive" *Theodore van Beek*	65
	Beaucourt Revisited *A.P. Herbert*	67
	Relieved *Frederic Manning*	69
	Picnic: Harbonnières to Bayonvillers *John Allan Wyeth*	71
	The Bathe *A.P. Herbert*	73

	Going In *Henry Lamont Simpson*	75
	A Song of the Air *Gordon Alchin*	78
	To a Taube *Jessie Pope*	80
	The Hill *Mary Borden*	82
	Ammunition Column *Gilbert Frankau*	85
	Unloading Ambulance Train *Carola Oman*	87
	Gramophone Tunes *Eva Dobell*	89
	Quinze Vingt *Helen Mackay*	91
	Little Song of the Maimed (Petite Chanson des Mutilés) *Benjamin Péret, translated by David Gascoyne*	93
2	**Minds at War**	**95**
	Standing To (In Bereitschaft) *Anton Schnack, translated by Patrick Bridgwater*	96
	Night Watch *John Allan Wyeth*	98
	Nothing Much (Peu de chose) *Guillaume Apollinaire, translated by Martin Sorrell*	99
	The Face *Frederic Manning*	101
	III.—Fear *Herbert Read*	103
	Fever (La Fièvre) *Albert-Paul Granier, translated by Ian Higgins*	105
	Prayer before Battle (Gebet vor der Schlacht) *Alfred Lichtenstein, translated by Sheldon Gilman, Robert Levine, and Harry Radford*	107
	Retreat *Wilfrid Wilson Gibson*	110
	There is a healing magic in the night *Colwyn Philipps*	112
	Bivouacs *Gilbert Waterhouse*	114
	Going Over *Charles G.D. Roberts*	116
	Home *Francis Ledwidge*	118
	On the Plains of Picardy *Hugh Stewart Smith*	120
	Picardy Parodies No. 2 (W.B. Y--ts) *William Oliphant Down*	122
	A Lament *Patrick MacGill*	124
	Selections from "Rhymes from a New Nursery" and "Alphabet of Limericks" *Robert Eassie*	126
	Pershing at the Front *Arthur Guiterman*	129
	Left Behind *Harry L. Parker*	132
	A Kiss *Bernard Freeman Trotter*	134
	Albade *Ford Madox Hueffer*	137
	To C.H.V. *Robert Ernest Vernède*	139

	The Raindrops on Your Old Tin Hat *John Hunter Wickersham*	141
	Camouflage *M.G.*	144
	Picnic *Rose Macaulay*	147
	September. 1918 *Amy Lowell*	150
	Home Is Where the Pie Is *Anonymous*	152
	The Soldier Mood *William Kersley Holmes*	154
3	**Noncombatants**	**157**
	The Leaf Burners *Ernest Rhys*	158
	Burning Beehives (Les ruches brûlées) *Edmond Rostand, translated by Ian Higgins*	161
	Going to the Front *Hardwicke Drummond Rawnsley*	164
	Hymn of Hate (Hassgesang gegen England) *Ernst Lissauer, translated by Barbara Henderson*	166
	New Year's Wishes to the German Army *Émile Cammaerts, translated by Tita Brand-Cammaerts*	170
	Regiments (Régiments) *Lucie Delarue-Mardrus, translated by Ian Higgins*	172
	Penelope *Dorothy Parker*	175
	Visé *Maria Dobler Benemann, translated by Margaret R. Higonnet*	177
	Homes *Margaret Widdemer*	179
	After the Retreat *May Sinclair*	181
	A Memory *Margaret Sackville*	184
	May, 1915 *Charlotte Mew*	186
	Any Englishwoman *Evelyn Underhill*	187
	'I know the truth! Renounce all others!' *Marina Tsvetaeva, translated by A.S. Kline*	190
	In Hospital *Edith Nesbit*	192
	Somme Film, 1916 *C.H.B. Kitchin*	194
	The Ballad of Bethlehem Steel *Grace Isabel Colbron*	196
	The Farmer, 1917 *Fredegond Shove*	199
	Spreading Manure *Rose Macaulay*	201
	I Sit and Sew *Alice Moore Dunbar-Nelson*	204
	To the Patriotic Lady across the Way *Zelda*	207
	Portrait of a Mother *Violet Gillespie*	210
	The Mourners *Robert W. Service*	212
	When Will the War Be By? *Charles Murray*	214

	War Time *Mary E. Fullerton*	216
	Gone to the War *Bernard Samuel Gilbert*	218
	Sic Transit— *Vera Brittain*	222
	France *May Wedderburn Cannan*	223
4	**Making Sense of War**	**227**
	I Saw a Man This Morning *Patrick Shaw-Stewart*	228
	A Meditation upon the Return of the Greeks *Ivar Campbell*	230
	A Litany in the Desert *Alice Corbin*	232
	He Went for a Soldier *Ruth Comfort Mitchell*	234
	War *Mary Gilmore*	236
	War (Rhyfel) *Hedd Wyn, translated by Gillian Clarke*	238
	The Falling Leaves *Margaret Postgate*	240
	Eastern Front (Im Osten) *Georg Trakl, translated by Christopher Middleton*	242
	The Camp Follower *Maxwell Bodenheim*	244
	The Other Side *Alec Waugh*	247
	A Letter from the Front *Henry Newbolt*	250
	Singing "Tipperary" *William Kersley Holmes*	252
	O Little David, Play on Your Harp *Joseph Seamon Cotter, Jr.*	254
	To the Memory of Some I Knew Who Are Dead and Who Loved Ireland *A.E.*	257
	America at War *Gertrude Smith*	260
	Violets—April 1915 *Roland Leighton*	262
	High Barbary *James Howard Stables*	264
	Epiphany Vision *Mary-Adair Macdonald*	266
	At Bethlehem—1915 *Egbert T. Sandford*	268
	Veni, Sancte Spiritus! (Deit, Spered Santel!) *Yann-Ber Kalloc'h, translated by Ian Higgins*	269
	Solomon in All His Glory *Geoffrey Studdert Kennedy*	272
	To My Daughter Betty, the Gift of God *Thomas M. Kettle*	274
	'Since they have Died' *May Wedderburn Cannan*	276
	The Gift of India *Sarojini Naidu*	277
	In the Ypres Sector *Carola Oman*	279
5	**Remembering the Dead**	**281**
	Let Us Tell Quiet Stories of Kind Eyes *Geoffrey Bache Smith*	282
	Féri Bekassy *Frances Cornford*	284

Telling the Bees *Katharine Tynan*	286
In Memoriam *Ewart Alan Mackintosh*	288
At the Front (An der Front) *Wilhelm Klemm, translated by Patrick Bridgwater*	291
To L.H.B. (1894–1915) *Katherine Mansfield*	293
To John *William Grenfell*	295
Soldier-Poet *Hervey Allen*	296
Victory *Wilfrid Wilson Gibson*	298
The Son *Clifford Dyment*	299
Out in a Gale of Fallen Leaves *Marian Allen*	302
XX. Jo's Requiem *Ernest Rhys*	303
Anzac Cove *Leon Gellert*	304
To One Dead *Francis Ledwidge*	305
1914 *Ferenc Békássy*	307
Red Cross *John Masefield*	309
Only a Boche *Robert W. Service*	312
"Glad That I Killed Yer" *Joseph Lee*	315
Hallow-e'en, 1915 *Winifred M. Letts*	318
His Latch-Key *John Oxenham*	320
To the Dead *Gerald Caldwell Siordet*	322
Perhaps— *Vera Brittain*	325
New Year, 1916 *Ada M. Harrison*	328
Reported Missing.... *Anna Gordon Keown*	330
An Epilogue *J.C. Squire*	332
Elegy on the Death of Bingo, Our Trench Dog *Edward de Stein*	335

6 Aftermath — 339

November Eleventh *Hilmar R. Baukhage*	340
Paris, November 11, 1918 *May Wedderburn Cannan*	344
Remembrance Day *Marion Angus*	346
Victory, whose calm gaze… (Victoire aux calmes yeux…) *Anna de Noailles, translated by Ian Higgins*	348
To the Survivors *Carola Oman*	350
The Extra *Gladys Cromwell*	352
Recall-Up (Rappel) *Marcel Sauvage, translated by Ian Higgins*	355
Saturdays *E.W. Pigott*	357
The Mascot Speaks *Rags*	359

The Heart of the World *Joshua Henry Jones, Jr.*	362
The Dead (Les Morts…) *René Arcos, translated by Ian Higgins*	365
Reconciliation *Margaret Sackville*	367
Everything's looted, betrayed and traded *Anna Akhmatova, translated by A.S. Kline*	369
The Other Possibility (Die andere Möglichkeit) *Erich Kästner, translated by Walter Kaufmann*	371
High Wood *John Stanley Purvis*	374
Envoie *Edward de Stein*	377
Primary Sources	378
Further Reading	385
Index of Poets, Translators, and Poems	388
Index of Poem Titles and First Lines	393

Acknowledgments

I am grateful to all who have contributed to and assisted in the research and writing of this anthology. My deepest thanks and admiration are due, as always, to my husband, Andy Ruzich, for his research skills in tracing the descendants of lost voices; his insightful work as an editor; his enthusiasm for visiting First World War cemeteries, battle sites, museums, and archives; and his love, patience, and encouragement, without which this project would never have been started, much less completed. I am also grateful to the Fulbright Commission for sponsoring my research in England during the 2014–15 academic year, and to my patient and professional editors at Bloomsbury: David Avital, Lucy Brown, and Ben Doyle. Others who have been invaluable supporters are the wise and wonderful Bess Ruzich, Emily Ruzich, Ian Higgins, Bill Smith, Tim Shortis, and Julie Blake (aka Sherlock Poems). For once, I am at a loss for words, as they are insufficient to express my gratitude.

As well, sincere thanks are due to scholars, librarians, archivists, friends, and twitter colleagues who have supported this project: Neil Adams, Olga Alexeeva, Tess Barry, Richard Batten, Louise Bell, Jennie Benford, Pamela Blevins, Randy Brown, Jessamy Carlson, Alan Clark, Robin Clutterbuck and Lyn Edmonds, Mark Connelly, John Davis, Olga Dermott-Bond, Robin D'Souza, Mark Duffy, Dean Echenberg, Peter Ellis, Steve Enniss, Paul Fitzpatrick, John Garth, Philippa Gregory, Molly Volanth Hall, Patricia Hammond, Marnie Hampton, Mike Hanlon, Marguerite Helmers, Louise Heren, Araceli Hernández-Laroche, Dan Hill, Josie Holford, Andrew Holmes, Lucian Hughes, Andrew J.H. Jackson, Kyla M. Johnson, Jan Jones, Simon Jones, Chris Kempshall, Tim Kendall, Alice Kelly, James Kerr, Katrina Kirkwood, Jackie Klentzin, William J. Kupinse, AnnMarie LeBlanc, Rob Lemmens and Fred van Woerkom, Lucy London, Donal Lowry, Jessica Meyer, Patty and Delvin Miller, Chloe Mills, Sally Minogue, Christine Murray, Debra Myhill, Bradley J. Omanson, Jennifer Orth-Veillon, Cecelia Otto, Judith Palmer, Sylvia Pamboukian, Catriona Pennell, Catherine Perry, Jane Potter, Julia Ribeiro, Gordon Rubenfeld and Sarena Seifer, Jeff Ruzich, Caroline Scott, Dave and Martha Selleck, David Sherman, Hanna Smyth, Dave Siry, Chris Spriet, David Wayne Stanley, Kelly Sultzbach, Jane Tynan, Karen Waddell, Jacqueline Wadsworth, Julian Walker, Sarah Wearne, Susan Werbe, C.J. Whetstone, Lucie Whitmore, Greg and Maggie Wilkinson, Danita Burkett Zanré, and Charlotte Zeepvat.

And a very special thanks to the families and friends of writers who have generously shared their knowledge, family histories, photographs, news clippings, and support: Clara Abrahams, Patrick Aylmer, Carlos (Karlheinz) Benemann, Mark Bostridge, Steve Cooper, Steve Dobell, Judy Greenway, Eileen Griffiths and Elaine Jackson, Karl Jonietz, Adam and A.S. Kline, Alexis and Peter Krasilovsky, Simon Lindley and family, Bairbre O'Hogan and Oriana Conner, John C. Oram, Oliver P. Ramsbotham, James Ritchie, Charlotte Service-Longepe and Anne Longepe, France Sloat and Toby Griggs, Roger Squire, Kate and Lucy van Beek, and John D. Widdemer.

Acknowledgment and thanks are due to the following copyright holders for their permission to include poems and prose excerpts in this anthology:

Anna Akhmatova: with thanks to A.S. Kline for the English translation "Everything's looted, betrayed and traded," copyright © 2012.

Guillaume Apollinaire: Martin Sorrell's English translation "Nothing Much" is reproduced with permission of Oxford Publishing Limited through PLSclear.

René Arcos: Ian Higgins' English translation "The Dead" is included by permission of the translator, Ian Higgins, and publisher, Saxon Books.

Maria Dobler Benemann: with thanks to Margaret Higonnet for her English translation of Benemann's "Visé" and to Carlos (Karlheinz) Benemann for his assistance.

Mary Borden: with thanks to Patrick Aylmer for permission to include the work of Mary (May) Borden.

Vera Brittain: Quotations from Vera Brittain are included by permission of Mark Bostridge and T.J. Brittain-Catlin, Literary Executors for the Estate of Vera Brittain 1970.

Jean-Pierre Calloc'h (Yann-Ber Kalloc'h): Ian Higgins' English translation "Veni, Sancte Spiritus" is included by permission of the translator, Ian Higgins, and publisher, Saxon Books.

Emile and Tita-Brand Cammaerts: "New Year's Wishes to the German Army" and its English translation are reproduced by kind permission of the Senate House Library, University of London.

May Wedderburn Cannan: with thanks to Mrs. Clara Abrahams for permission to include the works of May Wedderburn Cannan.

Cornford, Frances: "Féri Békassy" is reproduced with the permission of the trustees of the Frances Crofts Cornford Will Trust.

Anna de Noailles: Ian Higgins' English translation "Victory, whose calm gaze …" is included by permission of the translator, Ian Higgins, and publisher, Saxon Books.

Edward de Stein: with thanks to Oliver Peter Ramsbotham for permission to include the work of Edward de Stein.

Lucie Delarue-Mardrus: Ian Higgins' English translation "Regiments" is included by permission of the translator, Ian Higgins, and publisher, Saxon Books.

Eva Dobell: with thanks to Steve Dobell, literary executor of the estate of Eva Dobell for permission to include the work of Eva Dobell.

Gilbert Frankau: with thanks to United Agents LLP on behalf of Timothy d'Arch Smith for permission to include the work of Gilbert Frankau.
Noël Garnier: Ian Higgins' English translation "Still Raining" is included by permission of the translator, Ian Higgins, and publisher, Saxon Books.
Wilfrid Wilson Gibson: with thanks to Judy Greenway for permission to include the work of Wilfrid W. Gibson.
Albert-Paul Granier: Ian Higgins' English translations "War Song" and "Fever" are included by permission of the translator, Ian Higgins, and publisher, Saxon Books.
Frederick William Harvey: with thanks to Eileen Griffiths and her daughter Elaine Jackson for permission to include the work of F.W. Harvey.
A.P. Herbert: with thanks to United Agents LLP on behalf of The Executors of the Estate of Jocelyn Herbert, MT Perkins, and Polly MVR Perkins for permission to include the work of A.P. Herbert.
Joshua Henry Jones, Jr.: with thanks to Kim E. Wolfe Moyer for permission to include the work of Joshua Henry Jones, Jr.
Erich Kästner: with thanks to Atrium Verlag for the German rights to "Die andere Möglichkeit," in: Ein Mann gibt Auskunft ©Atrium Verlag AG, Zürich 1930 and Thomas Kästner. With thanks for the English translation "The Other Possibility" by Erich Kästner, from *Twenty-Five German Poets: A Bilingual Collection*, translated and edited by Walter Kaufmann. Copyright © 1975 by Walter Kaufmann Copyright (c) 1962 Random House, Inc. Used by permission of W.W. Norton & Company, Inc.
Anna Gordon Keown: with thanks to Jennifer Gosse for permission to include the work of Anna Gordon Keown.
C.B.H. Kitchin: with thanks to David Higham Associates Limited for permission to include the work of C.B.H. Kitchin.
Wilhelm Klemm: with thanks to Verlagsgruppe Langen Müller Herbig for the German rights to the work of Wilhelm Klemm and to Taylor and Francis for permission to include Patrick Bridgwater's English translation of Wilhelm Klemm, which appeared in *The German Poets of the First World War*, edited and translated by Patrick Bridgwater, St. Martin's, 1985, p. 180.
Winifred Letts: with thanks to Oriana Conner for permission to include the work of Winifred Letts and to Bairbre O'Hogan for her assistance.
Alfred Lichtenstein: with thanks to Robert Levine, Sheldon Gilman, and Harry Radford for their English translation of Ernst Lichtenstein's "Prayer before Battle."
Ernst Lissauer: with thanks to Kimberly Harley Dietz for permission to include Barbara Henderson's English translation of Lissauer's "Hymn of Hate."
Rose Macaulay: with thanks to the Society of Authors as the Literary Representative of the Estate of Rose Macaulay.
Patrick MacGill: with thanks to Knight Features for permission to include the work of Patrick MacGill.
John Masefield: with thanks to the Society of Authors as the Literary Representative of the Estate of John Masefield.
Carola Oman: with thanks to Sir Roy Strong for permission to include the works of Carola Oman.

Dorothy Parker: "Penelope," copyright 1928, renewed © 1956 by Dorothy Parker; and excerpt(s) from *The Portable Dorothy Parker* by Dorothy Parker, edited by Marion Meade, copyright © 1944 by Dorothy Parker; copyright © 1973, 2006 by The National Association for the Advancement of Colored People. Used by permission of Viking Books, an imprint of Penguin Publishing Group, a division of Penguin Random House LLC. All rights reserved.

Benjamin Péret: with thanks to Enitharmon Press for permission to include David Gascoyne's English translation "Little Song of the Maimed."

Margaret Postgate (Cole): with thanks to David Higham Associates Limited for permission to include the work of Margaret Postgate Cole.

Herbert Read: with thanks to David Higham Associates Limited for permission to include the work of Herbert Read.

Edgell Rickword: with thanks to Carcanet Press Limited for permission to include "Trench Poets."

Edmond Rostand: Ian Higgins' English translation "Burning Beehives" is included by permission of the translator, Ian Higgins, and publisher, Saxon Books.

Marcel Sauvage: with thanks to Editions Denoël for the French language rights for "Rappel." Ian Higgins' English translation "Recall-Up" is included by permission of the translator, Ian Higgins, and publisher, Saxon Books.

Anton Schnack: with thanks to Taylor and Francis for Patrick Bridgwater's English translation of "Standing To," which appeared in *The German Poets of the First World War*, edited and translated by Patrick Bridgwater, St. Martin's, 1985, pp. 189–190.

Robert W. Service: with thanks to Charlotte Service-Longepe, Anne Longepe and the Robert W. Service estate.

Gertrude Smith: with thanks to John C. Oram, Jr. for permission to include the work of Gertrude Anna Smith.

J.C. Squire: with thanks to Roger Squire for permission to include the work of J.C. Squire.

Georg Trakl: with thanks to Miranda Middleton and Sarah Poulain for permission to include Christopher Middleton's English translation "Eastern Front."

Marina Tsvetaeva: with thanks to A.S. Kline for the English translation "I know the truth! Renounce all others!" copyright © 2010.

Giuseppe Ungaretti: Italian rights for "Veglia" © Mondadori Libri S.p.A., Milano; with thanks to Anthony Rudolf for permission to include Jonathan Griffin's English translation "Vigil."

Theodore van Beek: with thanks to Stephanie Blaquiere for permission to include the work of Theodore van Beek.

Alec Waugh: "The Other Side" by Alec Waugh reprinted by permission of Peters Fraser & Dunlop (www.petersfraserdunlop.com) on behalf of the Estate of Alec Waugh.

Margaret Widdemer: with thanks to John D. Widdemer for permission to include the work of Margaret Widdemer.

John Allan Wyeth: with thanks to France Sloat and Toby Griggs for permission to include the work of John Allan Wyeth.

Hedd Wyn: with thanks to Gillian Clarke for permission to include her English translation "War."

Introduction

In 1922, just four years after the First World War had ended, W.D. Eaton wrote in the Preface to his edited anthology *Great Poems of the World War*,

> the great storm is gone; the long night that seemed the night of doom is over ... But out of the dark came many voices, voices of lamentation, of home and love and hope and heroism and loftiest ideality, of romance, of strange comedy. These had their inspiration from a gigantic spectacle of elemental passions in cross-play, from the thoughts and emotions not of a single people, but of all that were fighting for the life and light of civilization. Poets great and poets minor followed the war or fought in it, and expressed its spirit with a personal, passionate fidelity impossible to historians. It would not be well were all these voices lost.[1]

And yet many of those voices *have* been lost. This anthology attempts to recover some of those neglected voices and to provide contexts that offer fresh insights into the literature, history, and cultures of the First World War as experienced internationally by both men and women, both soldiers and civilians. Those already familiar with the canonical poetry of the war may discover new poems to enjoy; those who might not typically read poetry may be rewarded by historical details and compelling voices that express diverse experiences of the war.

Poetry is critical to a complete understanding of the First World War because in the years leading up to and including the war, poetry played a central role in public and private life. This specialized use of language was a shared activity, and poetry was not just for the cultural elite, the educated, the romantic, or the bookish. Poetry was an integral part of communal ways of understanding and commenting on social issues, human psychology, and current events. Often poems were regarded less as works of art than as demonstrations of a country's mood and response. Before 1914, the word "bard" was popularly used to refer to poets, reflecting their role as spokespersons for national and cultural concerns.[2]

---

[1] W.D. Eaton, *Great Poems of the World War*, T.S. Denison, Chicago, 1922, pp. 5–6.
[2] Ted Bogacz, "A Tyranny of Words: Language, Poetry, and Antimodernism in England in the First World War," *Journal of Modern History*, vol. 58, no. 3, 1986, p. 653.

Examining international poetry of the First World War allows modern readers to gain a deeper understanding of the various audiences for whom poetry shaped opinion, provided comfort, expressed outrage, constructed meaning, and offered a way to participate in the social and political contexts of the time.

When the First World War began, poems were a regular feature in journals and newspapers, often included in the editorial pages. Poetry held a very different place in society than it does today, so much so that "Before 1914 it was widely held among educated Englishmen that anyone with a 'soul' could write 'poetry'—verse, that is, that 'stirred the heart.'"[3] And in the United States, "just about anyone might consider himself or herself fit to write poetry and even called upon to write it."[4] First World War scholar Randall Stevenson explains, "Though the cinema's popularity was growing rapidly, verbal as well as visual media maintained a strong position in leisure and entertainment during the early years of the century."[5] People were likely to hear or see poetic texts on many public occasions, whether at civic events, educational assemblies, religious meetings, social clubs, or entertainment gatherings.[6] Mike Chasar, author of *Everyday Reading: Poetry and Popular Culture in America*, notes that poetry

> was included in classroom readers, comic books, song books, farmers' almanacs … nature field guides, propaganda, and in a wide variety of advertising media … And it decorated many ephemeral, commemorative, value-added and/or commercial goods, ranging from postcards to greeting cards, calling cards, playing cards, business cards, bookmarks, matchbooks, posters and wall hangings, stickers, calendars, event tickets, notepads, menus, fans, trivets, thermometers, milk bottles, pinup girly posters, bird-food and breath-mint tins, packages for drafting tools, candy boxes, souvenir plates, handkerchiefs, pillows, and table runners.[7]

Poetry was often preserved in scrapbooks; it was common for individuals to create their own anthologies through collecting and arranging poems that were personally meaningful.[8]

It is no surprise then that when war broke out, people responded with poetry—in support of the war, in opposition to the war, or simply describing the ways in which the world seemed to have suddenly shifted. Newspapers across

---

[3] Bogacz, "A Tyranny of Words," p. 653.
[4] Mark W. Van Wienen, *Partisans and Poets*, Cambridge UP, 1997, p. 2.
[5] Randall Stevenson, *Literature and the Great War*, Oxford UP, 2013, p. 123.
[6] Joan Shelley Rubin, *Songs of Ourselves: The Uses of Poetry in America*, Belknap, 2007, p. 4.
[7] Mike Chasar, *Everyday Reading: Poetry and Popular Culture in Modern America*, Columbia UP, 2012, p. 5.
[8] Chasar, *Everyday Reading*, pp. 17–18.

the UK were deluged with poems that commented on the war and the country's response: the London *Times* estimated that it received as many as a hundred such poems a day during August 1914.⁹ Catherine W. Reilly's bibliography of First World War poetry lists over 2,000 poets who were published in England alone. And this outpouring of poetry wasn't limited to England—it is estimated that 50,000 war poems were written daily in Germany in August 1914.¹⁰ In the United States, the military newspaper *The Stars and Stripes* included the regular column "The Army's Poets." In the paper's first year (1918), over 18,000 poems were submitted, and the poetry column was touted as "the most widely read … in the paper."¹¹ Many of the poems first published in newspapers and periodicals were then republished in popular anthologies of war poetry.

Poetry anthologies have long served as a crucial means of preserving and shaping literary, cultural, and social histories, and early anthologists of the First World War approached the task of collecting and publishing war poetry with a variety of interests and agendas. Sally Minogue and Andrew Palmer write, "Perhaps more than another body of literary writing, the poetry of the First World War comes to us through anthologies, each of which makes a claim about which poems are significant, effective and worth preserving."¹² The 1915 collection *The Fiery Cross* aimed "To inspire and to console."¹³ The 1917 *Treasury of War Poetry* sought to be "humanly hospitable, rather than academically critical, especially in the case of some of the verses written by soldiers at the Front," believing these poems to be "psychologically interesting as sincere transcripts of personal experience."¹⁴ The *Muse in Arms* (1917) attempted "to show what passes in the British warrior's soul" and so present "a picture of the visible imagery of battle as mirrored in his mind."¹⁵ Foxcroft's *War Verse* (1918) included "not the work of professional verse writers who have seen in the events of the war stirring and timely literary material; but … the spontaneous expression of sincere feeling,—the feeling of the soldier in the trenches … or the feeling of the wounded man in the hospital or of the nurse who cares for him."¹⁶ Other anthologies were more historically minded: *Valour and Vision* (1920) sought "to present the poet as the historian, and to illustrate the

---

[9] Bogacz, "A Tyranny of Words," p. 647.
[10] Bogacz, "A Tyranny of Words," p. 647.
[11] "Army Poets Submit 18,000 Samples; 384 See Print," *The Stars and Stripes*, 7 Feb. 1919, p. 5.
[12] Sally Minogue and Andrew Palmer, *The Remembered Dead: Poetry, Memory and the First World War*, Cambridge UP, 2018, p. 12.
[13] Herbert Warren, "Preface," *The Fiery Cross*, edited by Mabel C. Edwards and Mary Booth, Grant Richards, 1915, p. 9.
[14] George Herbert Clarke, "Introduction," *A Treasury of War Poetry*, edited by George Herbert Clarke, Houghton Mifflin, 1917, p. xxvii.
[15] E.B. Osborn, "Introduction," *Muse in Arms*, edited by E.B. Osborn, John Murray, 1917, p. v.
[16] Frank Foxcroft, "Preface," *War Verse*, edited by Frank Foxcroft, Thomas Y. Crowell, 1918, p. v.

different aspects and phrase of the war by contemporary poetry,"[17] and Cunliffe's *Poems of the Great War* (1916) included poems that would "give fair representation to various schools of thought and expression as well as to the various phases of the War."[18] Following the Armistice, a number of anthologists began to explicitly comment on the futility of the war. In 1919, the editor of *The Paths of Glory* declared, "The writers whose poems are included in this collection may hold very diverse views on war. But they are nevertheless all agreed in believing that however much individual gallantry and self-sacrifice it may incidentally call forth, war must be regarded to-day as an execrable blot upon civilization."[19] The Foreword to the 1921 collection *Poems of the War and the Peace* asserted,

> in the years which have passed since the armistice, a sense of disillusion, a deepening despair have grown dominant in many men's thought—a doubt expressed in certain of the poems on the victory and the peace. The issue clearly remains unsettled still; the ideal of permanent peace, of great Peace based on justice, appears increasingly doubtful of achievement. And because of this gulf between what men fought for and what their rulers ordained, attention to the poetry which presents the experiences and ideals of men in war seems of pressing significance.[20]

Such anthologies prepared the ground, but Frederick Brereton's 1930 collection, *An Anthology of War Poems*, was the first anthology to focus on the "figure of the archetypal 'war poet' as a battle-traumatized soldier writing in protest against it."[21] Since that time, and particularly over the last fifty years, nearly every anthology of First World War poetry has centered its collection on soldiers' poetry written in protest of the war and has included works by Wilfrid Owen, Siegfried Sassoon, Edward Thomas, Ivor Gurney, Isaac Rosenberg, Charles Sorley, Edmund Blunden, Robert Graves, and, more recently, David Jones.[22]

---

[17] Josephine Trotter, "Prefatory Note," *Valour and Vision*, edited by Josephine Trotter, Longmans, Green, 1920, p. v.
[18] J.W. Cunliffe, "Preface," *Poems of the Great War*, edited by J.W. Cunliffe, Macmillan, 1916, p. v.
[19] Bertram Lloyd, "Preface," *The Paths of Glory*, edited by Bertram Lloyd, George Allen and Unwin, 1919, p. 10.
[20] Sterling Andrus Leonard, "Foreword," *Poems of the War and the Peace*, edited by Sterling Andrus Leonard, Harcourt, Brace, 1921, p. xiii.
[21] Hugh Haughton, "Anthologizing War," *Oxford Handbook of British and Irish War Poetry*, edited by Tim Kendall, Oxford UP, 2007, p. 423. (Brereton was a pseudonym used by Frederick Thomas Smith.)
[22] For example, these writers comprise the majority of poems included in *Up the Line to Death: The War Poets 1914-1918* (edited by Brian Gardener, 1964), *Men Who March Away: Poems of the First World War* (edited by I.M. Parsons, 1965), *The Penguin Book of First World War Poetry* (edited by Jon Silkin, 1979), *Anthem for Doomed Youth: Twelve Soldier Poets of the First World War* (edited by Jon Stallworthy, 2002), *In Flanders Fields: Poetry of the First World War* (edited by George Walter, 2004), *Poetry of the First World War: An Anthology* (edited by Tim Kendall, 2013), and *First World War: Poems from the Front* (edited by Paul O'Prey, 2014).

A sampling of the titles of these anthologies (e.g., *Men Who March Away, Poems from the Front,* and *Up the Line to Death*) demonstrates the general assumption that the best war poetry—some would argue the only war poetry—was written by soldiers (most of whom were British). First World War poetry scholar Jane Potter notes, "the literary landscape of 1914–1918 is firmly rooted in a particular narrative of disillusionment and sorrow, if not protest. The priority accorded to such a resonant body of self-consciously literary work ... has made it difficult to hear different voices."[23] This current anthology, *International Poetry of the First World War,* is intended neither to supplant nor to challenge the value of previous anthologies, the poets, or their work, but rather to supplement the canonical poetry of the war and to be read alongside it.

On July 1, 1923, exactly seven years after the first day's attack at the Somme, Robert Graves published an essay in which he states that the question of literary quality has been "so variously answered that I am inclined to break away altogether from the traditional view that the question can be answered in terms of any particular literary formula ... One age values emotional intensity, another values sophistication and emotional restraint; one age demands a high standard of craftsmanship, another demands an anarchic abandon of grammatical or logical control."[24] To support his point, Graves remarks, "The recent war with its immediate sequel of peace and depression provides an easy example of unusually violent flow and ebb in the sea of literary criticism."[25] According to Graves, the early years of the war had valued Julian Grenfell's "love of battle" and Rupert Brooke's "spirit of sacrifice," but when the mood of the country changed, Siegfried Sassoon "became the spokesman of suffering."[26] Graves predicted there would be yet another change in poetic taste in the years following the war, noting that with the Armistice, "poetry of conflict immediately lost its purpose and now ... the canons of good poetry will select for praise among contemporary writers either the poets of skepticism and cynicism ... or the poets of temporary escape."[27]

As Graves partly foretold, in the years following the First World War, the "canons of good poetry" continued to shift and change. And while the majority of canonical war poems are conventionally Georgian in form, the tenets of

---

[23] Jane Potter, "'A Certain Poetess': Recuperating Jessie Pope (1868–1941)," *Landscapes and Voices of the Great War,* edited by Angela K. Smith and Krista Cowman, Routledge, 2017, p. 97.
[24] Robert Graves, "What Is Bad Poetry?" *The North American Review,* vol. 218, 1923, p. 355.
[25] Graves, "What Is Bad Poetry?" p. 356.
[26] Graves, "What Is Bad Poetry?" p. 356.
[27] Graves, "What Is Bad Poetry?" p. 357.

modernism became increasingly influential. Various dates ranging from 1890 to 1919 are used to mark the beginnings of modernism as a philosophical, cultural, and literary movement. Modernist poetry promoted writing that was experimental, ironic, detached, impersonal, and bluntly realistic. Often hostile to poetry that was perceived as traditional, metaphoric, or overtly expressive, modernists insisted upon direct treatment of the subject.[28] This tended to privilege first-hand accounts written by soldiers.

As editors selected which poems would be anthologized and passed into cultural memory, the poetic experience of the war was largely confined and constrained to that of soldiers fighting on the Western Front. For example, in his 1979 introduction to the *Penguin Book of First World Poetry*, Jon Silkin writes, "A concern with the substance of war, with the terrifying combat, pervades my choices."[29] James Campbell attributes this selection criterion to what he terms an ideology of "'combat gnosticism,' the belief that combat represents a qualitatively separate order of experience that is difficult if not impossible to communicate to any who have not undergone an identical experience."[30] Although this was the experience of many soldiers and ex-servicemen, Campbell argues that the belief "has served both to limit severely the canon of texts that mainstream First World War criticism has seen as legitimate war writing and has simultaneously promoted war literature's status as a discrete body of work with almost no relation to non-war writing."[31]

While there is no single explanation as to why some poetry of the war has endured and other works that had been popular and respected have been largely forgotten, one important reason is that set forth by Santanu Das in *The Cambridge Companion to First World War Poetry*: "it is the poetry of the trenches, as represented by a small group of 'anti-war' soldier poets, that has come to dominate First World War memory."[32] A related reason for the exclusion of some works is that, as Paul Fussell writes, "There seems to be one dominating form of modern understanding; that it is essentially ironic; and that it originates in the application of mind and memory to the events of the Great War."[33] That

---

[28] Sally Minogue and Andrew Palmer provide a fuller discussion of modernism and First World War poetry in "'The World's Worst Wound': Death, Consciousness and Modernism," *The Remembered Dead*, by Minogue and Palmer, Cambridge UP, 2018, pp. 53–80.

[29] Jon Silkin, *The Penguin Book of First World War Poetry*, Penguin, 1979, p. 74.

[30] James Campbell, "Combat Gnosticism: The Ideology of First World War Poetry Criticism," *New Literary History*, vol. 30, no. 1, 1999, p. 203.

[31] Campbell, "Combat Gnosticism," p. 203.

[32] Santanu Das, "Reframing First World War Poetry: An Introduction," *The Cambridge Companion to the Poetry of the First World War*, edited by Santanu Das, Cambridge UP, 2013, p. 4.

[33] Paul Fussell, *The Great War and Modern Memory*, 1975, Oxford UP, 2000, p. 35.

is, after the war, modern understandings of the conflict adopted an increasingly ironic stance, so that writings that were more earnest or emotional came to be labeled as naïve and sentimental.

In his essay "Anthologizing War," Hugh Haughton asserts that "'war poetry' is largely a twentieth-century invention," and "the poets we see as typical of the war … were largely absent from contemporary compilations."[34] Anthologies of poetry that were popular during the war and the years immediately following included voices that were likely to be more patriotic, more emotional, more religious, more traditional and/or more accessible than the better-known poems in the literary canon. Haughton observes, "The modern reader is likely to see such anthologies [those popular during the war] through the eyes of Owen and Sassoon as embodiments of the assembly-line poetry of war they needed to dismantle. Nevertheless, they represent a range of poetic responses greater than the now routine opposition between patriotic rhetoric and realistic anti-war verse allows."[35]

Women's war poetry, which rarely offered a first-hand, realistic account of combat, has also been largely neglected. But as First World War scholar Jane Dowson notes, "Collectively, the diversity and ingenuity of the [women] poets demonstrate that it is fruitless to approach the period with a binary model of modernist or non-modernist art."[36] Instead of measuring poetic texts against an ideal of literary modernism, Dowson contends that it is more helpful to consider "modernisms."[37] Historian Julia Ribeiro extends the argument: "though poetry was seen as a highly intellectual reaction to war when read from the point of view of the *avant-gardes* or of the formal innovations related to irony (Fussell, 1975) or modernism (Sherry, 2003),[38] it was also a more visceral and culturally diverse response to the conflict." Ribeiro advocates not only expanding the literary canon, but also expanding ways in which war poetry might be read and understood. She suggests that a Geertzian anthropological stance "justifies using poetry as a document about war experience" and that poetry can be a valuable historical source, for it provides "not only a potentially accurate model of the experience of the conflict, but also the poetic gesture … [is] capable of changing that experience itself and therefore worthy of study as a practice as well as a discourse."[39]

---

[34] Haughton, "Anthologizing War," p. 422.
[35] Haughton, "Anthologizing War," p. 429.
[36] Jane Dowson, *Women, Modernism, and British Poetry, 1910–1939*, Ashgate, 2002, p. 4.
[37] Dowson, *Women, Modernism, and British Poetry*, p. vii.
[38] Vincent Sherry, *The Great War and the Language of Modernism*, Oxford UP, 2003.
[39] Julia Ribeiro, "'Knowing That You Will Understand': The Usage of Poetry as a Historical Source about the Experience of the First World War," *Alicante Journal of English Studies*, vol. 31, 2018, pp. 121, 117.

Recovering neglected poems that were popular during the war also assists in challenging what Samuel Hynes calls "The Myth of the War," an imagined version of the conflict that developed as the war progressed and that was further shaped in the years following the Armistice. This constructed version of reality presents the war as "a set of abrupt disjunctions—between generations, between fighting soldiers and those who controlled their lives, between the present and the past."[40] Winter further develops the idea, asserting that "the rupture of 1914–1918 was much less complete than previous scholars have suggested," and that there existed instead an "overlap of languages and approaches between the old and the new, the 'traditional' and the 'modern', the conservative and the iconoclastic."[41] As Hynes argues, "The Myth is not the War entire: it is a tale that confirms a set of attitudes, an idea of what the war was and what it meant."[42]

Toni Morrison has written, "Canon building is Empire building. Canon defense is national defense. Canon debate ... is the clash of cultures."[43] Margaret Higonnet applies Morrison's idea to the First World War, writing, "European political imperialism has been tacitly replicated in the practice of literary history, excluding whole regions and types of textual production from view. For most of the twentieth century, the literary canon of Great War literature was restricted by narrow conceptions not only of war but also of the literary."[44] In recent years, there have been increasingly numerous calls to expand the range of voices and perspectives of First World War poetry. Andrew Motion, poet laureate of the UK from 1999 to 2009, reminds readers that "less-familiar voices open up new perspectives," and "our definition of 'war poetry' has become too narrow to be accurate or fair."[45] Seeking to reframe ideas of First World War poetry, Santanu Das argues, "At its expansive best, it is a diffuse category cutting across different genres and nationalities."[46]

There have been anthologies of First World War poetry that have attempted to diversify and expand the canon: Catherine W. Reilly's *Scars upon My Heart*

---

[40] Samuel Hynes, *A War Imagined*, Atheneum, 1991, p. xii.
[41] Jay Winter, *Sites of Memory, Sites of Mourning*, Cambridge UP, 2014, p. 3.
[42] Hynes, *A War Imagined*, p. xi.
[43] Toni Morrison, "Unspeakable Things Unspoken: The Afro-American Presence in American Literature," *Michigan Quarterly Review*, vol. 28, 1989, p. 8.
[44] Margaret Higonnet, "Whose Can(n)on? World War I and Literary Empires," *Comparative Literature*, vol. 57, no. 3, p. vi.
[45] Andrew Motion, "Introduction," *First World War Poems*, edited by Andrew Motion, Faber and Faber, 2003, p. xii and "There Is More to War Poetry than Mud, Wire and Slaughter," *Guardian*, 9 July 2016, web.archive.org/web/20190816200431/https://www.theguardian.com/books/2016/jul/09/andrew-motion-definition-war-poetry-widen-not-just-first-world-war.
[46] Santanu Das, "Reframing First World War Poetry," *Cambridge Companion to the Poetry of the First World War*, edited by Santanu Das, Cambridge UP, 2013, p. 8.

(1981) and Margaret R. Higonnet's *Lines of Fire* (1999) both recover women's war writing. Martin Stephen's *Never Such Innocence* (1988), Vivien Noakes's *Voices of Silence* (2006), and Hibberd and Onions's *The Winter of the World* (2007) offer less-familiar works, although they limit their selections to British writers. Van Wienen's *Rendezvous with Death* (2002) focuses on American poetry of the First World War. And while Tim Cross's groundbreaking *The Lost Voices of World War I* (1989) is international in its scope, it has long been out of print.

This present anthology is deliberately international in its focus, including poems written by authors from America, Australia, Austria-Hungary, Belgium, Canada, France, Germany, Great Britain, India, Ireland, Italy, New Zealand, Russia, and South Africa. And although the present collection includes poems from lesser-known fronts (such as the Eastern Front, the Isonzo, and Mesopotamia), there remains a disproportionate focus on the Western Front and the experiences of writers from English-speaking countries. This is mostly owing to the difficulty of finding translated works from such places as Turkey, Armenia, China, Japan, and Africa. Many of the poems selected have not appeared in print since the decade following the war or have only recently been translated into English. Translating a poem from one language to another means that the original sounds and nuances are lost, but "in good translations, poetry is also found."[47] As translation theorist Susan Bassnett writes, "Translation in the widest sense of the word is an endless process of reshaping, retelling, reworking … Translation offers an afterlife to works that are at risk of vanishing forever."[48] In this anthology, for translated poems, the title of the poem in the original language follows the English translated title. For untitled poems, the first line has been used as the title, and a note specifies this. When poems have disputed titles, the author's title is used, or, if none is given, the earliest title is used and explanatory notes have been added.

As far as is possible, attempts have been made to date each poem. In some cases, the poet has supplied a date as part of the poem. For all other works, the date of first book publication (or first publication, if the poem was not published in a book) follows the author's name. Brief notes attempt to situate each poem in its context. These notes include excerpts from reviews and early critical receptions, authors' biographies, and brief histories relevant to the poem's contents. Such background information is important in appreciating

---

[47] Geoffrey Brock, "Two Tunnels: A Note on Translation," *Italian Poetry: An Anthology*, edited by Geoffrey Brock, Farrar Straus Giroux, 2012, p. xlii.

[48] Susan Bassnett, "Prologue," *Tradition, Translation, Trauma*, edited by Jan Parker and Timothy Mathews, Oxford UP, 2011, pp. 1, 2.

poetry written over a century ago, particularly poetry by writers who are largely unknown or who write from less-familiar perspectives. The interplay between history and poetry is intended to enrich the understanding of each and provide insight into the ways in which men and women of the early twentieth century experienced the First World War. The contextual notes may also provide a starting place for further reading and research.

Rather than organize the poetry by date, gender, or nationality, the poems have been arranged thematically. Interleaving poems in this way allows readers to more readily see and compare the ways in which the war was experienced by various individuals across cultural and national boundaries. As Winter notes, "the very act of imagining the war varies in different countries due to the power of different national assumptions and frameworks."[49] Moving from experience to memory, the sections of the book are arranged topically as follows: "I: Soldiers' Lives," "II: Minds at War," "III: Noncombatants," "IV: Making Sense of War," "V: Remembering the Dead," and "VI: Aftermath."

The collection's first section, "Soldiers' Lives," begins with a work by one of the most familiar of the First World War poets, Rupert Brooke, chiefly known for one poem, his idealistic sonnet "The Soldier" ("If I should die, think only this of me"). Brooke is one of the few canonical poets included in this anthology; he is represented here by his rarely anthologized poem "Fragment," one of two previously unpublished poems found in the notebook he used in the last month of his life. Other poems in "Soldiers' Lives" describe the experience and aftermath of combat on the Western Front, such as West's "Night Patrol" and Horne's "The Moles." Still others reveal life behind the lines, on transport ships, and on other fronts. White's "The Boys Who Live in the Ground" explores the tedium of trench life; Alchin's "Song of the Plane" celebrates one of the new technologies of the war, innovations that held the promise of a breakthrough to victory but were just as likely to increase the level of suffering. Ungaretti's "Vigil" was written on the Isonzo Front, the harsh Alpine terrain that lay between Italy and Austria-Hungary. Some poems in this section are written by women who were eyewitnesses to woundedness, mutilation, and hospital life. There are poems that express abhorrence of war. Yet others, such as Simpson's "Going In," find beauty and wonder in the midst of war.

The poems in the second section of the anthology, "Minds at War," address the psychological traumas of the First World War. Living with the ever-present threat of death, some soldiers vividly imagined their own deaths and dying (e.g.,

---

[49] Jay Winter, *The Great War in History*, p. 197.

Schnack's "Standing To" and Granier's "Fever"), while other writers explored the psychological toll of killing others, such as Apollinaire's "Nothing Much." A significant number of poems depict imaginative escapes from the frontlines, a very different kind of detachment from the tone typically found in the canonical poetry of the war. The soldier in Waterhouse's "Bivouacs" rises while others sleep and dreams that he has "seized a star-beam" to climb far above the mire of Somecourt Wood. Yet there was a danger inherent in surrendering to a world of fantasy, the risk of losing all touch with reality, as described in Gibson's "Retreat," in which a soldier has convinced himself he is home in an English country lane: "Chiming and tinkling in his aching brain, / Until he babbled like a child again— / 'All-heal and willow-herb and meadow-sweet.'" Other soldiers used humor and parody to cope with the stresses of war and to comment on its absurdities. Whether writing war limericks or parodies that transformed well-known poems to commentaries on life in the trenches, many writers turned to comic verse (e.g., Eassie, Down, and Guiterman). Soldiers also found comfort in memories of loved ones at home, while noncombatants wrote of walling off emotions in the struggle to remain sane. Finally, there are poems in this section that describe simple pleasures, such as apple pie and chipped potatoes, that inspired endurance in an alien world at war.

The book's third section, "Noncombatants," includes authors and contexts that are often absent from or underrepresented in more traditional anthologies of First World War poetry. Mark Van Wienen in *Partisans and Poets* indicates the critical importance of the attitudes and ideas held by noncombatants, arguing, "the homefront is important, even more important than the battlefield, because it is there that the cultural energies—political imperatives, social needs, psychological desires and fears, even military necessities—needed to go to war and stay there are defined and maintained."[50] Some of the more popular poems of the time are those that may now seem disturbing in their self-assured nationalism; one of the best-known and most often parodied was the German "Hymn of Hate." Yet other poetry written by those on the home front challenged ideals of nationalism and unexamined patriotism. Writers criticized war supporters for their mercenary motives (as in "The Ballad of Bethlehem Steel") and questioned racial injustice on the home front as men were dying to "make the world safe for democracy" ("To a Patriotic Lady across the Way"). Conscientious objectors were mocked, jailed, and sometimes assigned to agricultural work, the latter as described in Shove's poem "The Farmer, 1917." In addition to the

---

[50] Van Wienen, *Partisans and Poets*, p. 28.

influence of poetry, news accounts and film were key in shaping noncombatants' perceptions of the war. An estimated twenty million people viewed the British documentary film *The Somme* in the months following its premier, and Kitchin's poem "The Somme" relates the experience of watching the war in the dark as "the munition makers clap their hands." Other poems, such as "Homes" by Widdemer, an American poet, and "Visé," by Benemann, a German, ask readers to identify with the emotional upheavals of both civilians and soldiers caught up in the maelstrom of total war. British pacifist Sackville writes of war's seemingly limitless appetite for death and destruction that extended beyond the lines of battle to destroy the lives of civilians. And some noncombatants volunteered for work close to the battle lines. Sinclair wrote "After the Retreat" while working with the Munro Ambulance Corps.

In the 1915 pamphlet *Women and War*, pacifist Helena Swanwick argues, "War is waged by men only, but it is not possible to wage it upon men only. All wars are and must be waged upon women … as well as upon men."[51] The effect of war on women is the subject of Service's poem "The Mourners." American scholar Van Wienen asserts that women should be viewed as "active agents supporting—or resisting—the national mobilizations that undergird nationalist wars … The material contributions of women are indispensable to a nation's capacity for war making, whether that means manufacturing bombs, knitting socks for the 'boys over there,' raising sons to be soldiers, or for that matter, bearing children who might someday be soldiers."[52] On the home front, the war altered even the sounds of daily life. The clacking of knitting needles was a constant backdrop in nearly all public spaces, and Gillespie's "Portrait of a Mother" illustrates the ways in which traditional roles were repurposed to support the war: "Knit two and purl one; / Knit again and stir the fire. / And oh, my son, my only son, / I work for you and never tire." Women also supported the war by taking on agricultural jobs vacated by men who had joined up, as described in "Spreading Manure." Numerous women wrote of their experiences as Voluntary Aid Detachment nurses (VADs). And Murray's Scots dialect poem "When Will the War Be By?" gives voice to the powerlessness of waiting that was experienced not only by soldiers at the front, but by their loved ones at home.

The fourth section of the anthology, "Making Sense of War," includes poems by both soldiers and civilians. Poetry provided a vehicle for writers to shape and communicate responses to the First World War, whether by finding meaning

---

[51] Helena M. Swanwick, "Women and War," *The War in Its Effect upon Women and Women and War*, Garland, 1971, p. 1.
[52] Van Wienen, *Partisans and Poets*, p. 27.

in the conflict, questioning the war's conduct and purpose, or protesting the carnage. Some wrote of the opportunities for greatness that the war promised. Shaw-Stewart appeals to the warriors of the ancient epics for inspiration, while American poet Corbin, assistant editor of America's *Poetry* magazine, hopes that the war will "give us the young men who will make us great." Other writers believed that the war would vanquish tyranny and usher in a better world. Russian Akhmatova acknowledges that "Everything's looted, betrayed, traded," but still trusts that "something miraculous will come / Close to the darkness and ruin." And in Ireland, the writer known as AE (George William Russell) imagines the promise of a united Ireland as he attempts to reconcile the deaths of Irish nationalists killed in the wake of the Easter Rising with those of Irish soldiers who died fighting for the British.

But where some saw hope, others saw only meaningless waste and wanton destruction. Welsh poet Hedd Wyn, posthumous winner of the Welsh National Eisteddfod poetry chair, laments the loss of youth and song: "Ballads of boys blow on the wind, / Their blood is mingled with the rain." Gilmore, an Australian poet, is even more graphic in depicting the waste of young lives: "Out in the dust he lies; / Flies in his mouth, / Ants in his eyes." Austrian poet Trakl envisions nightmarish scenes of apocalyptic horror, and Stables, a British poet who fought and died in Mesopotamia (now modern Iraq), finds it as impossible to tally the numbers of dead as to "gather up the fumes of frankincense." For many, the war was simply incomprehensible, an absurdity that defied rational explanation. At times, even the most articulate of writers admitted themselves hesitant to make definitive comments on the war and skeptical of those who did.

Yet there were those who found meaning in the war, even after millions of deaths and years of deprivation. Despite the common perception that the First World War killed God, or at least belief in God, many poems that were popular during the war expressed belief in a transcendent faith. Writers and readers found comfort in the gospel of a suffering Savior who knew anguish and was thus able to identify with and minister to others in pain. And many refused to believe that so many had died without cause; for them, the dead spoke and affirmed the justness of the war. Indian writer Naidu pleads that the death of nearly 75,000 Indian troops not be forgotten, for the sacrifice itself creates meaning. Survivors often believed that they had received from the dead a personal challenge, that they were obligated to make their own lives count for something, as seen in Cannan's "Since They Have Died" or Oman's "In the Ypres Sector." Writers sought meaning in the millions of deaths, a purpose and significance that some believed the dead had come to know, even if it were still hidden from the living.

What the living could do was honor the dead by eulogizing them, and these poems comprise the fifth section of the book, "Remembering the Dead." Frances Cornford, an English civilian, mourns the loss of Cambridge student Ferenc Békássy, who was killed fighting for Austria-Hungary. In "Jo's Requiem," Welsh civilian Ernest Rhys writes of a dead countryman who had "had the ploughman's strength / in the grasp of his hand" and "could hear the green oats growing." Katharine Tynan dedicates "Telling the Bees" to Edward Tennant, a family friend killed at the Somme, and Edward de Stein, an officer in the King's Royal Rifle Corps, praises the faithful loyalty of one of the millions of animals who served in the First World War in his poem "Elegy on the Death of Bingo, Our Trench Dog." Writers often found solace in memory; G.W. Grenfell, grieving the death of a friend, recalls the years before the war and the careless play of "our little band of brothers" ("To John"). Upon learning that Robert Gilson, one of his closest friends, had died on the first day of the Somme, J.R.R. Tolkien, a young lieutenant on the Western Front, writes, "*Something has gone crack ... I don't feel a member of a little complete body now ... I feel a mere individual.*"[53] Tolkien's friend Geoffrey Bache Smith expresses his sorrow at Gilson's death in "Let Us Tell Quiet Stories of Kind Eyes," recalling the places and occasions when those in their "first fellowship" enjoyed one another's company.

Many were haunted by the prospect of an empty future. Vera Brittain, better known as a memoirist, also wrote war poetry, and in "Sic Transit—," written after the death of her friend Victor Richardson (Brittain's fiancé had been killed earlier in the war), she expresses her hopeless exhaustion: "all I loved the best / Is gone, and every good that I desired / Passes away, an idle hopeless quest." Her fiancé also killed in the war, Marian Allen quietly notes the upheaval of her world: "And the year is dying in which you died / And I shall be lonely this Christmas-tide." Women and civilians were not the only ones haunted by loss: officers had the difficult task of informing families of men's deaths. As he imagines writing to a father to inform him of the death of his only son, Lieutenant Ewart Mackintosh confesses his own guilt and pain in the poem "In Memoriam." The immensity of loss left many feeling powerless.

The First World War also saw a dramatic surge in spiritualism, and in their desperate wish to communicate with the dead, many of the grieving turned to Ouija boards, mediums, and séances. Many poems of the First World War are peopled with ghosts and the imagined return of the dead. These poems include

---

[53] John Garth, *Tolkien and the Great War: The Threshold of Middle-earth*, Houghton Mifflin Harcourt, 2013, p. 176.

Elizabeth Mansfield's "To L.H.B.," written in memory of her younger brother, Leslie Heron Beauchamp, killed in Ploegsteert Wood, and Winifred Lett's "Hallow-e'en, 1915," which invites the dead to return. Other writers envision a future in which they will be reunited with the dead in the afterlife. During the war, the most popular poet of the war was not Wilfred Owen, Siegfried Sassoon, nor any of the trench poets honored in Westminster Abbey, but William Arthur Dunkerley, a teacher writing under the pen name of John Oxenham, who published inspirational Christian verse. In "His Latch Key," Oxenham tells of a family waiting for their soldier's return. When they learn he has been killed in battle, their faith assures them of a reunion with their dead soldier in the next life.

Several poems in this section express concern that anonymous soldiers who died without fame or fanfare will soon be forgotten. Writers of these poems remember "a torn and silent valley … lines of buried bones" (Gellert's "Anzac Cove") or mourn the loss of "Those that go down into silence" (Harrison's "New Year, 1916"). Also included are elegies of a very different kind: those that respond to death with denial or disbelief. Squire's "The Fluke" begins, "For two years you went / Through all the worst of it, / Men fell around you, but you did not fall." The random nature of the death that killed Squire's friend William Smith was almost too absurd to be believed. But perhaps more difficult for survivors was the agony of not knowing. Over 70,000 British and Commonwealth men were never found after the battle of the Somme, and nearly 55,000 were missing in action after battles in the Ypres Salient. Outside the city of Verdun, the Douaumont Ossuary contains the bones of over 130,000 French and German men who were never identified. Keown's "Reported Missing" recalls past scenes of shared simple pleasures, closing with the lines, "Of these familiar things I have no dread / Being so very sure you are not dead." Such poems remind us that remembering those who died did not require acceptance of the loss.

The poems included in the anthology's final chapter, "Aftermath," capture the mix of emotions that anticipated and accompanied the end of the war. British writer Carola Oman celebrates the joys of homecoming in "To the Survivors." Others lament those who will never return—the dead and the missing. French writer René Arcos describes enemies joined by their shared suffering and loss, "The bannerless, unhating dead." Joshua Henry Jones, Jr., an African American writer inspired by the speech of American President Woodrow Wilson during the peace conference in 1919, hears a new call arising "that will banish all hatred and wrong." Other poets express a less optimistic view of the prospects for a lasting peace. In "Reconciliation," Margaret Sackville acknowledges the hard work of forgiveness that remains. German poet Erich Kästner imagines an alternative past with a chilling future in "The Other Possibility": if Germany had won the war, "then everyone / would be a soldier; the entire / land would be run by goon and gun." In 1917, having fought at the Somme with the British, Lieutenant J.S. Purvis foretold the throngs of tourists who would visit the battlefields of the First World War. In "High Wood," Purvis juxtaposes the sacrifices of those who fought and died with the callousness of visitors who scatter trash and seek out souvenirs of the battle.

Over one-hundred years later, these poems underscore the point that despite efforts to research and remember the First World War, we can never fully comprehend the multitude of ways in which "the men, women, and children who lived through the war composed their own experiences of the ordeal. They all faced the challenge of making sense of the war's impact on people like themselves."[54] As the poems in this anthology demonstrate, there was no single representative experience of the Great War, nor was there a typical response to the conflict. The present collection may assist in recovering the complexity of the time, the people, and the poetry of the First World War.

---

[54] Roger Chickering, "Why Are We Still Interested in This Old War?" *Finding Common Ground: New Directions in First World War Studies,* edited by Jennifer D. Keene and Michael S. Neiberg, Brill, 2011, p. 16.

1
Soldiers' Lives

Poems in this chapter describe patrols, raids, and attacks; assess the aftermath of assaults; contrast the perspectives of fresh troops with those of veterans; relate the tedium of life in the trenches; and respond to the new technologies of war. Some poems describe the experiences of the wounded and the horrors of mutilation; others tell of finding laughter, beauty, and wonder at the front. The experiences and moods of military life during the First World War were more varied than has been fully represented by the war's canonical poetry.

Fragment

I strayed about the deck, an hour, to-night
Under a cloudy moonless sky; and peeped
In at the windows, watched my friends at table,
Or playing cards, or standing in the doorway,
Or coming out into the darkness. Still
No one could see me.

                   I would have thought of them
—Heedless, within a week of battle—in pity,
Pride in their strength and in the weight and firmness
And link'd beauty of bodies, and pity that
This gay machine of splendour'ld soon be broken,
Thought little of, pashed, scattered....

                        Only, always,
I could but see them—against the lamplight—pass
Like coloured shadows, thinner than filmy glass,
Slight bubbles, fainter than the wave's faint light,
That broke to phosphorus out in the night,
Perishing things and strange ghosts—soon to die
To other ghosts—this one, or that, or I.
     April 1915

—Rupert Brooke

Rupert Brooke is best known for his poem "The Soldier" and its memorable first lines, "If I should die, think only this of me: / That there's some corner of a foreign field / That is for ever England." That poem was published in the *London Times Literary Supplement* in March of 1915 and read by the Dean of St. Paul's Cathedral in London on Easter Sunday, April 4, 1915. During the sermon, a war protestor objected so loudly that he had to be removed from the church (as reported in the *London Times* the following day).[1] Three weeks later, Brooke died en route to Gallipoli. "The Soldier" appeared in his posthumously published collection *1914 and Other Poems* (1915), which by the end of the war was in its twenty-fourth reprinting. Brooke's "Fragment," titled as such by Edward

---

[1] "Dean Inge at St. Paul's: Spirit of the Martyr-Patriot," *London Times*, 5 Apr. 1915, p. 8.

Marsh, was one of only two "coherent fragments found in the notebook which he [Brooke] used in the last month of his life."[2] Published in 1918, it appears in the Appendix of *The Collected Poems of Rupert Brooke: With a Memoir*. In "The Soldier," Brooke speculates on his own death. In his lesser-known poem "Fragment," he imagines the future of other soldiers as he writes from a troopship headed for the Dardanelles and the attack at Gallipoli.

Brooke never reached the Turkish coast, dying on the island of Skyros on April 23, 1915. His early death transformed the soldier-poet into an iconic figure. The man was far more complicated than the myth, however, and scholars argue that neither Brooke nor his poetry is as naïve or idealistic as often assumed.[3] In 1918, Bertrand Russell reflected on Rupert Brooke and his early death:

> Rupert and his brother ... and lots of others—in whom one foolishly thought at the time that there was hope for the world—they were full of life and energy and truth—Rupert himself loved life and the world—his hatreds were very concrete, resulting from some quite specific vanity or jealousy, but in the main he found the world lovable and interesting. There was nothing of humbug in him.[4]

An early reviewer wrote, "Rupert Brooke not only lived in perpetual interrogation of the unknowable; he made poetry of his questionings."[5]

---

[2] Edward Marsh, "Note," *The Collected Poems of Rupert Brooke: With a Memoir*, Sidgwick and Jackson, 1918, p. 148.
[3] See for example Tim Kendall, "Rupert Brooke," *Poetry of the First World War*, Oxford UP, 2013, pp. 102–104.
[4] Bertrand Russell, *The Autobiography of Bertrand Russell: 1914–1944*, Little, Brown, 1967, p. 122.
[5] "A Peace Unshaken," *Times Literary Supplement*, no. 705, 22 July 1915, p. 244.

The Transport

I.

A thick still heat stifles the dim saloon.
The rotten air hangs heavy on us all,
and trails a steady penetrating steam
of hot wet flannel and the evening's mess.
Close bodies swaying, catcalls out of tune,
while the jazz band syncopates the *Darktown Strutters' Ball*,
we crowd like minnows in a muddy stream.
O God, even here a sense of loneliness ...
I grope my way on deck to watch the moon
gleam sharply where the shadows rise and fall
in the immense disturbance of the sea.
And like the vast possession of a dream
that black ship, and the pale sky's emptiness,
and this great wind become a part of me.

—John Allan Wyeth[6] (1929)

When America entered the First World War on April 6, 1917, many politicians and members of the public assumed that the United States would simply continue to send armaments and aid, with no direct military involvement. Shortly after war was declared, Virginia senator Thomas S. Martin expressed stunned surprise upon learning that President Wilson intended to send American troops overseas: "Good Lord! You're not going to send soldiers over there, are you?"[7] On June 14, 1917, a little more than two months after the United States entered the war, the first American troops sailed for France—14,000 soldiers of the First Division. By August of 1918, the United States had sent nearly 1,500,000 men overseas.[8] Willard Newton, a doughboy sailing with the 105th Engineers of North Carolina, describes his outbound voyage:

> As the transport steams slowly out of Hoboken it passes the Statue of Liberty, and though we are all supposed to be below deck several of us fellows slip up and take a last look at the statue and then go back below. The fellows congregate in small groups, some singing songs that have become popular since the war, and

---

[6] See also Wyeth's "Picnic: Harbonnières to Bayonvillers" and "Night Watch."
[7] Frederick Palmer, *Newton D. Baker: America at War*, vol. 1, Dodd, Mead, 1931, p. 120.
[8] Leo P. Hirrel, *Supporting the Doughboys: US Army Logistics and Personnel During World War I*, Combat Studies Institute, 2017, p. 63.

others are discussing the journey that lays before them. We are leaving the States to return no more until our task "over there" is finished.[9]

John Allan Wyeth served as a staff officer and language translator with the 33rd Division of the American Expeditionary Forces (AEF). His only volume of poetry, *This Man's Army: A War in Fifty-Odd Sonnets,* was published in 1929. Wyeth's use of modernist forms, especially his "mixed meters and disjunctive syntax"[10] may be attributed to Ezra Pound's influence. The men formed a friendship in the years after the war; both lived in Rapallo, Italy, in the mid-1920s and socialized in a literary circle that included Max Beerbohm and W.B. Yeats.[11] Yet from the 1930s to the present, not one of Wyeth's poems has appeared in an anthology of First World War poetry. "Of all the writers of the Lost Generation, there was perhaps none quite so lost as John Allan Wyeth," writes B.J. Omanson, the military historian and poet who, together with Dana Gioia, rediscovered Wyeth and his work.[12] Since the republishing of *This Man's Army* in 2008, scholars have remarked on the craftsmanship of Wyeth's sonnets, praising them for their "clarity of perspective and … emotional detachment,"[13] and comparing them to "quick, on-the-spot sketches, struck down on paper with no objective beyond capturing the fleeting essence of the moment."[14] Tim Kendall, editor of *Poetry of the First World War: An Anthology* (Oxford, 2013), describes Wyeth's sonnet sequence as "the great forgotten book of the War."[15] Dana Gioia argues that *This Man's Army* "is the most ambitious, representative, and successful poetic venture by an American combatant in the Great War, and it is also probably the only volume that stands comparison with the work of the best British soldier poets."[16]

In 1932, a review of *This Man's Army* appeared in *Poetry* magazine. The book was described as "A group of sonnets, strung with slang and soldiers' *patois,* telling of the poet's experiences in the war. They are scrupulously exact descriptions with little comment, and they ring with vivid reality. They are probably not poetry but they are good stuff."[17]

---

[9] Willard Newton, 28 May 1918 diary, "Chapter 2—Crossing the Atlantic," *Over There for Uncle Sam: Private Willard Newton's Diary* published serially in the *Charlotte Observer,* 22 Aug. 1920, p. 4.
[10] Dana Gioia, "The Unknown Soldier: An Introduction to the Poetry of John Allan Wyeth," *This Man's Army: A War in Fifty-Odd Sonnets,* by John Allan Wyeth, U of South Carolina P, 2008, p. xv.
[11] B.J. Omanson, *Before the Clangor of the Gun: The First World War Poetry of John Allan Wyeth,* Monongahela, 2019, pp. 99–100.
[12] Omanson, *Before the Clangor,* p. 3.
[13] Gioia, "The Unknown Soldier," p. xv.
[14] Omanson, *Before the Clangor,* p. 24.
[15] Tim Kendall, qtd in interview with *World War I Bridges,* 1 Sept. 2015, web.archive.org/save/www.worldwarone.it/2015/09/an-interview-with-tim-kendall-about.html.
[16] Gioia, "The Unknown Soldier," p. xxii.
[17] "Brief Notices," *Poetry,* vol. 41, no. 3, Dec. 1932, pp. 165–166.

The Night Patrol
France, March 1916

Over the top! The wire's thin here, unbarbed
Plain rusty coils, not staked, and low enough:
Full of old tins, though—"When you're through, all three,
Aim quarter left for fifty yards or so,
Then straight for that new piece of German wire;
See if it's thick, and listen for a while
For sounds of working; don't run any risks;
About an hour; now, over!"
      And we placed
Our hands on the topmost sand-bags, leapt, and stood
A second with curved backs, then crept to the wire,
Wormed ourselves tinkling through, glanced back, and dropped.
The sodden ground was splashed with shallow pools,
And tufts of crackling cornstalks, two years old,
No man had reaped, and patches of spring grass.
Half-seen, as rose and sank the flares, were strewn
With the wrecks of our attack: the bandoliers,
Packs, rifles, bayonets, belts, and haversacks,
Shell fragments, and the huge whole forms of shells
Shot fruitlessly—and everywhere the dead.
Only the dead were always present—present
As a vile sickly smell of rottenness;
The rustling stubble and the early grass,
The slimy pools—the dead men stank through all,
Pungent and sharp; as bodies loomed before,
And as we passed, they stank: then dulled away
To that vague fœtor, all encompassing,
Infecting earth and air. They lay, all clothed,
Each in some new and piteous attitude
That we well marked to guide us back: as he,
Outside our wire, that lay on his back and crossed
His legs Crusader-wise; I smiled at that,
And thought on Elia and his Temple Church.
From him, at quarter left, lay a small corpse,
Down in a hollow, huddled as in bed,
That one of us put his hand on unawares.
Next was a bunch of half a dozen men

All blown to bits, an archipelago
Of corrupt fragments, vexing to us three,
Who had no light to see by, save the flares.
On such a trail, so lit, for ninety yards
We crawled on belly and elbows, till we saw,
Instead of lumpish dead before our eyes,
The stakes and crosslines of the German wire.
We lay in shelter of the last dead man,
Ourselves as dead, and heard their shovels ring
Turning the earth, then talk and cough at times.
A sentry fired and a machine-gun spat;
They shot a flare above us, when it fell
And spluttered out in the pools of No Man's Land,
We turned and crawled past the remembered dead:
Past him and him, and them and him, until,
For he lay some way apart, we caught the scent
Of the Crusader and slid past his legs,
And through the wire and home, and got our rum.

—Arthur Graeme West

Arthur Graeme West was described by friends as "quiet, tranquil, and unassuming."[18] When he first attempted to enlist in the British army in 1914, he was rejected for his "defective eyesight." Determined to join up, he consulted a private physician who passed his records, "more or less by ruse."[19] West arrived at the front lines in France in November of 1915, and in February of 1916 wrote a friend,

> Also I had rather an exciting time myself with two other men on a patrol in the 'no man's land' between the lines. A dangerous business, and most repulsive on account of the smells and appearance of the heaps of dead men that lie unburied there as they fell, on some attack or other, about four months ago. I found myself much as I had expected in the face of these happenings: more interested than afraid, but more careful for my own life than anxious to approve any new martial ardour ... For the Hun I feel nothing but a spirit of amiable fraternity that the poor man has to sit just like us and do all the horrible and useless things that we do, when he might be at home with his wife or his books.[20]

---

[18] C.J. (C.E.M. Joad), "Introduction," *Diary of a Dead Officer*, by Arthur Graeme West, George Allen and Unwin, [1918?], p. xi.
[19] Arthur Graeme West, *Diary of a Dead Officer*, p. 2.
[20] West, *Diary,* pp. 11, 12–13.

"Night Patrol" is West's poetic description of that "exciting time," a ghastly twist on the fairy tale story of "Hansel and Gretel."

West grew increasingly disillusioned with the war, at one point considering desertion or suicide as preferable to returning to the Western Front. In September of 1916, he wrote, "There was but one way for me, and I have seen it only when it was too late to pursue it … To defy the whole system, to refuse to be an instrument of it—this *I* should have done."[21] He was killed by a sniper's bullet on April 3, 1917.

---

[21] West, *Diary*, p. 59.

In No Man's Land

The hedge on the left, and the trench on the right,
And the whispering, rustling wood between,
And who knows where in the wood to-night
Death or capture may lurk unseen,
The open field and the figures lying
Under the shade of the apple trees—
Is it the wind in the branches sighing,
Or a German trying to stop a sneeze?

Louder the voices of night come thronging,
But over them all the sound is clear,
Taking me back to the place of my longing
And the cultured sneezes I used to hear,
Lecture-time and my tutor's "handker"
Stopping his period's rounded close,
Like the frozen hand of the German ranker[22]
Down in a ditch with a cold in his nose.

I'm cold, too, and a stealthy snuffle
From the man with a pistol covering me,
And the Bosche[23] moving off with a snap and a shuffle
Break the windows of memory—
I can't make sure till the moon gets lighter—
Anyway shooting is over bold.
Oh, damn you, get back to your trench, you blighter,[24]
I really can't shoot a man with a cold.
       Hammerhead Wood
       Thiepval, 1915

—Ewart Alan Mackintosh[25]

Ewart Alan Mackintosh, though born in Brighton, spent childhood holidays in his father's native Scotland, where the family stayed at Alness. He embraced his Scottish heritage, played the pipes, spoke Gaelic, and was nicknamed "Tosh." When war broke out in August of 1914, Mackintosh tried to enlist, but was

---

[22] Slang term used for an enlisted man of the lower classes.
[23] *Boche* was a derogatory term used to refer to Germans, originating from the shortening of the nineteenth-century French slang *Alboche*. It is variously spelled *Bosche* and *Bosch*, perhaps in attempts to make the word look and/or sound more German.
[24] Slang term used for a man who is contemptibly unlucky.
[25] See also Mackintosh's "In Memoriam."

initially rejected for poor eyesight (there's evidence he wore pince-nez, removing them for photographs).[26] Joining the Seaforth Highlanders in December of 1914, he served in France from July 1915 until August of 1916, when he was wounded and gassed at the Somme. He returned to active duty in France in October of 1917 and was killed by enemy fire on the second day of the Battle of Cambrai, November 21, 1917. The death notice of the 24-year-old Military Cross recipient appeared in the *London Times* in early December. Titled "A New Heroic Poet," the obituary commented on Mackintosh's recently published book, *A Highland Regiment* (which included "In No Man's Land"):

> It has in it all the stern tenderness of the Gaelic folksong, plus the mighty exaltation of the Flanders front, where men march out to die without external glory, cheerfully, wearily, muddied to the eyes, smiling to the last moment, because the thing that they purchase with their death has become so immensely worth while. What Lieutenant E. A. Mackintosh sang about in his poems he has at last accomplished. The war created him; the war has taken him away."[27]

---

[26] Colin Campbell and Rosalind Green, *Can't Shoot a Man with a Cold,* Argyll, 2004, p. 82.
[27] "Roll of Honour, 143 Casualties to Officers, Personal Notes: A New Heroic Poet," *The Times*, no. 41652, 4 Dec. 1917, p. 4.

On Patrol in No Man's Land

What's the time, nine, all in line,
Alright, boys, now take it slow—
Are you ready? steady! very good, Eddy,[28]
Over the top let's go—
Quiet, sly it, else you'll start a riot,
Keep your proper distance, follow 'long—
Cover, smother, when you see me hover,
Obey my orders and you can't go wrong—

There's a minnenwerfer[29] coming, look out (Bang!)
Hear that roar, there's one more.
Stand fast, there's a Vary Light—[30]
Don't gasp or they'll find you alright—
Don't start to bombing with those hand grenades
There's a machine gun, Holy Spades—
Alert, Gas, put on your masks—
A-just it correctly and hurry up fast—

Drop, there's a rocket for the Boche Barrage,
Down hug the ground close as you can, don't stand,
Creep and crawl, follow me that's all—
What do you hear? nothing near, all is clear, don't fear,
That's the life of a stroll when you take a patrol—
Out in No Man's Land!
Ain't it grand?
Out in No Man's Land.

—James Reese Europe (1919)

James Reese Europe, more commonly known as Jim Europe, was the first black bandleader to record in the United States and the first to conduct a black orchestra performing ragtime/jazz music on the concert stage of New York's Carnegie Hall. He was also the first black American officer to enter the trenches of the First World War, the first to lead troops in combat in the war, and the first black American to be given a public funeral in New York City. Yet James Reese

---

[28] Reference to popular 1915 Broadway musical *Very Good Eddie*.
[29] *Minenwerfer* ("mine launcher") was a German short-range artillery weapon that fired explosive shells.
[30] *Very light*, *Vary light*, and *Very pistol* refer to the flare gun named after Edward W. Very, a nineteenth-century US naval officer. The flares were used for signaling and to briefly illuminate night scenes.

Europe is virtually unknown today, both for his contributions to music and for his service in the First World War.

In 1916, before the United States entered the war, Jim Europe joined the 15th Infantry Regiment of the New York National Guard, explaining to his friend Noble Sissle, "there has never been such an organization of Negro men that will bring together all classes of men for a common good. And our race will never amount to anything, politically or economically, in New York or anywhere else unless there are strong organizations of men who stand for something in the community."[31] Europe was commissioned as a lieutenant in the 15th Infantry Regiment of the National Guard in December of 1916. Before Jim Europe left for the war, John Love, personal secretary to the wealthy Wanamaker family of Philadelphia and a professional acquaintance of Europe, had tried to dissuade him from overseas service. In the summer of 1917, Europe had undergone emergency surgery for health complications related to Graves' disease, and Love argued that Europe would be entitled to a medical exemption. Jim Europe replied, "if I could, I would not. My country calls me and I must answer; and if I live to come back, I will startle the world with my music."[32]

Europe's regiment (which became the 369th, known as the Harlem Hellfighters) was attached to the 93rd Division, one of only two black military divisions that the segregated US Army allowed to participate in combat. Europe trained as a machine-gunner, but because he was one of the most popular bandleaders in America before the war, he was also charged with forming the best military band in the US Army.[33] Music was key to military morale:

> It was the belief that every man became a better warrior for freedom when his mind could be diverted from the dull routine of camp life by arousing his higher nature by song, and that he fared forth to battle with a stouter heart when his steps were attuned to the march by bands that drove out all fear of bodily danger and robbed "grim-visaged war" of its terrors.[34]

Recruiting musicians from New York, Chicago, and Puerto Rico, Europe put together a military band that some described as the best in the world.[35] It is

---

[31] Noble Sissle, *Memoirs of Lieutenant 'Jim' Europe*, qtd. in *A Life in Ragtime*, by Reid Badger, Oxford UP, 1995, p. 142.
[32] From John Love's letter to Noble Sissle dated 28 Jan. 1920 and included in Sissle's *Memoirs*, qtd. in *A Life in Ragtime*, p. 154.
[33] Badger, *A Life in Ragtime*, p. 143.
[34] Emmett J. Scott, *Scott's Official History of the American Negro in the World War*, Homewood, 1919, p. 301.
[35] "Loss of an American Musician," *New York Times*, 12 May 1919, p. 12.

estimated that the Harlem Hellfighters regimental band traveled over 2,000 miles in France, performing for foreign dignitaries and military commanders, wounded soldiers in hospitals, troops on recreational leave, French citizens, and American Army Headquarters in Paris. In between concerts, Lieutenant Europe was assigned to machine gun duty in the trenches on the Western Front. Charles Welton, writing for the *New York Age,* said that in addition to Europe "sowing jazz selections over the agricultural terrain and bunching bits of it in the cantons *en route,*" the officer also "did solo work with a machine gun forty times heavier than a trombone, and actually got it to working in syncopated time."[36]

In the spring of 1918, Europe participated in a French raid on German trenches. He described the night raid to Sissle, the drum major of the Harlem Hellfighters regimental band. Europe's description is rich with the sounds of war as he remembers the din of artillery shells whirring overhead that sounded "like a thousand pheasants," the exploding shrapnel "hizzing hither and thither," the crack of an officer's pistol firing a red flare from his Very pistol, and "the excited yelling of our men, as they darted first up one trench and down another, bombarding every nook and corner with hand grenades." Europe told Sissle, "I found everything last night that I ever heard existed out there."[37] Injured in a gas attack just weeks later, Europe used his time in the hospital to compose music; among the songs he wrote while recuperating was "On Patrol in No Man's Land." The sheet music credits the song to James Europe, Noble Sissle, and Eubie Blake. Blake has said he had no part in writing the music but was credited for the song "because that's the kind of partners they were."[38] Sissle's memoir recounts visiting Jim Europe in the hospital and hearing Europe's greeting: "Gee, I am glad to see you boys! Sissle, here's a wonderful idea for a song that just came to me, in fact it was [from the] experience that I had last night during the bombardment that nearly knocked me out."[39]

"On Patrol in No Man's Land" was recorded on the Pathé label in March 1919 by Jim Europe and members of the 369th Infantry Hellfighters band, shortly after they returned to America. It's probable that the composition had been performed in France. With band instruments simulating the sounds of machine-gun fire, artillery explosions, and gas raid sirens, the song communicates the danger of battle while assuring its listeners that action on the front lines is a

---

[36] Qtd. in *Scott's Official History,* pp. 305–306.
[37] Sissle's *Memoirs,* qtd. in *A Life in Ragtime,* pp. 181–182.
[38] Qtd. in *A Life in Ragtime,* p. 174.
[39] Qtd. in *A Life in Ragtime,* p. 187.

grand adventure not to be missed. Advertisements for the recording included personal testimonials:

> One of the boys in our office went to war. On his return I asked him what American effort most impressed him and he answered JIM (Lieut.) EUROPE'S BAND. He said that the French and British bands would play, and one would say to himself, "what beautiful music!" But when Europe's band came along no one, whatever his race, could keep still. There was that pep, that something of life and animation that made everybody want to do something.[40]

Sergeant Noble Sissle wrote, "Who would think that little U.S.A. would ever give to the world a rhythm and melodies that, in the midst of such universal sorrow, would cause all students of music to yearn to learn how to play it? ... I sometimes think if the Kaiser ever heard a good syncopated melody he would not take himself so seriously."[41]

In early May of 1919, just months after the New York City homecoming parade, Jim Europe was killed backstage during a concert in Boston by a disgruntled musician who was later declared mentally unfit to stand trial. Noted jazz musician Eubie Blake was Jim Europe's business partner and friend. Recalling the legacy of James Reese Europe, Blake said,

> People don't realize yet today what we lost when we lost Jim Europe. He was the savior of Negro musicians. He was in a class with Booker T. Washington and Martin Luther King. I met all three of them. Before Europe, Negro musicians were just like wandering minstrels ... Before Jim, they weren't even supposed to be human beings. Jim Europe changed all that. He made a profession for us out of music. All of that we owe to Jim. If only people would realize it.[42]

---

[40] *Talking Machine World*, 15 June 1919, qtd. in *Lost Sounds: Blacks and the Birth of the Recording Industry, 1890–1919*, by Tim Brooks, U of Illinois P, 2004, p. 285.
[41] Qtd. in *Scott's Official History*, p. 309.
[42] From *Eubie Blake* by Al Rose, Macmillan, 1983, qtd. in *Lost Sounds*, p. 291.

War Song (Chanson de Guerre)

Dame Death is joyously dancing,
a drunken, hip-swinging jig,
never a word, just wriggling
and playfully juggling skulls
like so many knucklebones.

Dame Death is glad, and very drunk—
for there's blood in full flow out there,
a heavy red brookful in every ravine.

Accompanying her weird dancing
is the tom-tom of guns in the distance:
"Tom-tom-tom! tom-tom-tom! Come then, White Lady,
come dance to the sound of the drums!"

Dame Death's getting drunker and splashing
her sweet little face with blood,
like a child who's been eating the jam.

Dame Death is paddling in blood,
and slapping down into it with her long hands,
as though she were washing her shroud;
wallowing, and silently sniggering.
Dame Death is flushed, writhing, dancing
like a girl who's had too much drink.

"Hey, Death, get your hopping in time
with the tom-tom of guns in the distance!"

—Tomtomtom-tomtomtom!
          The guns in the distance
quicken their murderous presto,
guns laughing together in rhythm;
the guns in the band force the tempo,
whipping her up for The Jubilation Ball:

"Spin on those dainty thin heels,
squirm the meat off those sinuous hips,
get waltzing and whirling, White Lady!
dancing and skipping! waving your arms!

> Here's blood, here's blood!
> And here's some more, to keep you busy!
> Come on now, drink up! totter and reel!
> This is the start of the Orgy in Red!"
>
> Dame Death is dancing, insanely drunk,
> to the tom-tom of guns in the distance.
> *1914*
>
> —Albert-Paul Granier,[43] translated by Ian Higgins

How much blood? How much death? During the duration of the First World War, on average, nearly 900 French soldiers were killed every day; of the 8.4 million French soldiers who were mobilized, an estimated 1.35 million died and 4.2 million were wounded. Over 73 percent of the French troops who enlisted became casualties of the war.[44]

French artillery officer Albert-Paul Granier was born in the Atlantic coastal village of Le Croisic in September of 1888. He was raised in a home where he was surrounded by music; Gabriel Fauré was a family friend. Although Granier studied law and qualified as a solicitor, he was also a composer and accomplished pianist. In the years before the war, he also wrote poetry and met with other artists who read and shared their work. Joining the French army in August of 1914, Granier was assigned to the 116th Heavy Artillery regiment; in 1916, his unit was stationed at Verdun in support of some of the fiercest fighting of the war. By 1917, Granier had volunteered and been reassigned as an aerial observer, accompanying pilots on reconnaissance missions in the Verdun sector. Less than three weeks before his twenty-ninth birthday, on August 17, 1917, Albert-Paul Granier was killed while flying over the Verdun battlefield. His plane was hit by a shell; no trace of his body was ever found.[45] He is honored in the Pantheon in Paris, his name appearing with those of 560 French writers who died in the Great War.

Granier's only book of poems, *Les Coqs et les Vautours* (*Cockerels and Vultures*), was published in Paris in 1917. Even his earliest poems, written in 1914, evoke

---

[43] See also Granier's "Fever" (La Fièvre).
[44] Ingrid P. Westmoreland, "Casualties," *The European Powers in the First World War: An Encyclopedia*, edited by Spencer Tucker, Laura Matysek Wood, and Justin D. Murphy, Taylor and Francis, 1999, p. 172.
[45] Biographical information from Claude Duneton, "Préface," *Les Coqs et les Vautours*, by Albert-Paul Granier, Des Equateurs, 2008, pp. 7–22 and from Ian Higgins, "Foreword," *Cockerels and Vultures*, by Albert-Paul Granier, Saxon Books, 2014, pp. 7–9.

the surreal violence of war: "And so, then, for all in time of war, here / are the cockerels, clamouring defiance, / and the vultures, ponderous with hate, / talons stained with the blood of memories."[46] Despite receiving a commendation from the Académie française in 1918,[47] Granier's volume of poetry was soon forgotten and only rediscovered in 2008 after a copy was found at a French flea market.

---

[46] Granier, epigraph from *Cockerels and Vultures,* translated by Higgins.
[47] *Anthologie des Écrivains Morts a la Guerre, 1914–1918,* E. Malfére, 1925, p. 329.

Dance of Death 1916 (Totentanz 1916)

So we die, we die
And die every day,
For it is so comfortable to let ourselves slip away.
The morning, stuck in sleep and dream,
By midday already there,
Come evening deep within our graves.

The battle is our pleasure-house,
Our sun is made of blood,
Death our emblem and our password.
Child and wife we leave behind:
What use have we for them!
When we can only rely upon ourselves!

So we kill, we kill,
And every day we kill
Our comrades in the dance of death.
Brother, present yourself before me!
Brother, your breast!
Brother, that you must fall and die.

We don't grumble, we don't groan,
Every day we hold our tongue
'Til our leg wrenches from the hip.
Hard is our resting place,
Dry is our bread,
The dear Lord bloodied and soiled.

We thank you, we thank you,
Herr Kaiser for your mercy,
In choosing us to die.
Sleep, sleep softly and still,
Till you are woken
By our poor bodies, shrouded beneath your lawn.

—Hugo Ball, translated by Edmund Potts

Twenty-eight-year-old German poet and playwright Hugo Ball greeted the outbreak of the First World War with enthusiasm, declaring in his early poem "Splendor of the Flag" ("Glanz um die Fahne") that the corrupt world could be renewed by "abandoning itself to the primitive energy released by the conflict."[48] In the early months of the war, Ball repeatedly tried to volunteer for the German army, but was turned down three times due to a heart condition. Wanting to see the war first-hand, Ball traveled to Belgium, where his ideals were shattered. In his diary, he protested, "the war ... is based on a stupid mistake; men have been mistaken for machines; it is the machines that should be decimated, not the men."[49] In November of 1914, he wrote from Belgium that "the world had fallen prey to diabolical madness."[50] Upon returning to Berlin, Hugo Ball's anti-war stance made life nearly impossible, and in May of 1915, he emigrated to Switzerland. Less than a year later, he and a group of fellow writers and artists opened Zurich's Cabaret Voltaire, a nightclub that mixed avant-garde entertainment with politics, giving rise to the Dada movement. One of the cabaret numbers was a musical performance of Ball's poem "Totentanz 1916" ("Dance of Death"), which parodied a German marching tune with references to the popular cabaret song "That's How We Live." With a chorus of soldiers' voices, the performance scathingly described soldiers "engaged in an erotic dance of mutual slaughter as they thank the Kaiser for the privilege of dying."[51]

Patrick Bridgwater has remarked, "If Ball had been living in Germany at the time, 'Totentanz 1916' would have been treasonable."[52] Two years later, "Dance of Death 1916" was used by Germany's enemies for their own propagandist purposes. The Allies printed copies of this poem and other German literature that criticized the war and dropped the leaflets behind German lines in August of 1918, hoping to break morale.[53] Even poetry was weaponized in the First World War.

---

[48] Hugo Ball, qtd. in *Everything to Nothing: The Poetry of the Great War, Revolution and the Transformation of Europe*, by Geert Buelens, Verso, 2015, p. 207.
[49] Hugo Ball, qtd. in *The German Poets of the First World War*, by Patrick Bridgwater, St. Martin's, 1985, p. 73.
[50] Ball, qtd. in *Everything to Nothing*, p. 207.
[51] Timothy Shipe, "Hugo Ball," *Encyclopedia of German Literature,* edited by Matthias Konzett, Routledge, 2000, p. 68.
[52] Bridgwater, *The German Poets*, p. 74.
[53] Bridgwater, *The German Poets*, pp. 74–75.

Trench Poets

I knew a man, he was my chum,
But he grew blacker every day,
And would not brush the flies away,
Nor blanch however fierce the hum
Of passing shells; I used to read,
To rouse him, random things from Donne;
Like "Get with child a mandrake-root,"
But you can tell he was far gone,
For he lay gaping, mackerel-eyed,
And stiff and senseless as a post
Even when that old poet cried
"I long to talk with some old lover's ghost."

I tried the Elegies one day,
But he, because he heard me say
"What needst thou have more covering than a man?"
Grinned nastily, and so I knew
The worms had got his brains at last.
There was one thing that I might do
To starve the worms; I racked my head
For healthy things and quoted "*Maud*."
His grin got worse and I could see
He laughed at passion's purity.
He stank so badly, though we were great chums
I had to leave him; then rats ate his thumbs.

—Edgell Rickword (1921)

In *The Great War and Modern Memory*, Paul Fussell describes the entertainment world of 1914: "Except for sex and drinking, amusement was largely found in language formally arranged, either in books and periodicals or at the theater and music hall, or in one's friends' anecdotes, rumors, or clever structuring of words."[54] Language was entertainment, and books were the immortal companions of the soldiers in the trenches. For one of the first times in warfare, most soldiers were literate, and reading offered an escape to worlds far removed from the mud and blood, as well an antidote to the boredom of trench life. Fussell argues that "the *Oxford Book of English Verse* presides over the Great War in a way that has

---

[54] Paul Fussell, *The Great War and Modern Memory*, 1975, Oxford UP, 2000, p. 158.

never been sufficiently appreciated."[55] Soldiers tried to make sense out of the senselessness of the war, and when ordinary language failed, they often turned to the language of literature, recycling words and images from traditional sources.

Just shy of his sixteenth birthday when the war began, Edgell Rickword is one of the youngest of the soldier poets. Joining the Artists' Rifles in 1916, he took with him to the front a two-volume edition of the poetry of John Donne, the seventeenth-century English metaphysical poet. The excerpts from Donne that Rickword uses in "Trench Poets" tell their own story: the recitation begins with an invitation to accomplish the impossible ("Get with child" from Donne's "Song,"), then moves to the frustration of unrequited love ("I long to talk" from "Love's Deity"), and ends with a reference to nakedness and seduction (from "To His Mistress Going to Bed"). The continued unresponsiveness of his dead friend causes the poem's speaker to abandon the sensual immorality of the last Donne reference, and so he reaches for "wholesome lines" and settles upon *Maud*, Tennyson's romantic poem of doomed love. But the putrefying body "sneers" at these ideals of purity; his reality is better expressed by Marvell: "The grave's a fine and private place, / But none, I think, do there embrace." Ironically, the body of the dead soldier addressed in Rickword's poem has been deprived the dignity of a private grave. The last two lines of "Trench Poets" abandon the noble tradition of literary poetry, closing with a final clumsy couplet that sounds as if it belongs in a limerick rather than a sonnet. Minogue and Palmer write, "Faced with the grotesque reminders of what happens to the body in sudden, violent death, First World War poets grappled with a poetic inheritance which didn't seem to fit their current experience … we can see poets asking questions of the traditions, disrupting formal certainties, and struggling to find new forms and languages to fit new modes of consciousness."[56] Rickword himself later described the effort required of poets who tried to wrestle the First World War into words while writing from the trenches:

> It was a hard task these men had, writing under a precariously suspended sentence of death, and inheriting a technique of verse from which the impressive crudity of the actual had been long since refined away. In their struggle towards honesty of speech we find one of the few scattered evidences of those dark times that the human intellect was not prepared to succumb to the bestiality in which it had unwittingly involved itself.[57]

---

[55] Fussell, *The Great War*, p. 159.
[56] Sally Minogue and Andrew Palmer, *The Remembered Dead: Poetry, Memory and the First World War*, Cambridge UP, 2018, p. 5.
[57] Edgell Rickword, "War and Poetry: 1914–1918 (1940)," *Edgell Rickword: Literature in Society*, edited by Alan Young, Carcanet, 1978, p. 146.

Vigil (Veglia)

A whole night long
crouched close
to one of our men
butchered
with his clenched
mouth
grinning at the full moon
with the congestion
of his hands
thrust right
into my silence
I've written
letters filled with love

I have never been
so
coupled to life.

Cima Quattro, 23 December 1915

— Giuseppe Ungaretti, translated by Jonathan Griffin

Despite her alliances with Germany and Austria-Hungary, when the First World War began, Italy remained neutral. But in the secret Treaty of London of April 1915, the Allies promised Italy significant territory held by the Austria-Hungarian Empire, including parts of Tyrol and Dalmatia, as well as the port of Trieste. On May 23, 1915, Italy declared war on Austria-Hungary and fired the first shells on what would become one of the harshest fronts of the war: the Isonzo. Italian and Austro-Hungarian troops fought in the Dolomite mountains, a section of the Alps that traversed the border between the two countries, both armies attacking on impossibly steep mountain passes where trenches were dug into the rocks and glaciers of the Alps at altitudes of nearly 10,000 feet. Soldiers were shot, gassed, and shelled, but they also froze to death, and in a one-month stretch, an estimated 10,000 men from both armies were killed in avalanches, "the white death."[58] By November of 1915, after the first four battles of the Isonzo (there would be twelve), nearly 25 percent of the mobilized Italian soldiers had either been killed (over 70,000) or wounded (over 80,000).[59] "The Italian

---

[58] Mark Thompson, *The White War*, Basic Books, 2009, p. 204.
[59] John Gooch, *The Italian Army and the First World War*, Cambridge UP, 2014, pp. 109–118.

Front: In the Trenches," a 1916 essay appearing in *The Living Age*, commented, "What heroism to maintain a stout heart in such a woeful atmosphere!"[60]

Before the war, Giuseppe Ungaretti had spent three years in Paris, where he became friends with French writer Guillaume Apollinaire. Glauco Cambon notes, "The parallelism between Ungaretti's early experiments in verse and Apollinaire's own ventures is certainly a marked one. Both poets modernized diction, simplified syntax, and abolished punctuation, to give a sense of suspended flow to their free rhythm, with the consequence that their vivid imagery stood out the better."[61] Both men joined the war, Apollinaire serving with the French and Ungaretti with the Italians on the Isonzo front.

In notes that accompanied a later poetry volume, Ungaretti said that he began his war poetry collection, *Il porto sepolto*, on Christmas Day of 1915, the day he arrived in the trenches of Mount San Michele in the Carso. He writes,

> From the moment that I became a man who makes war, it wasn't the idea of killing or being killed that tormented me: I was a man who wanted nothing for himself but the absolute, the absolute that was represented by death, not by danger, that was represented by the tragedy that man brought to man to meet himself in massacre. In my poetry there is no trace of hatred for the enemy, nor for anyone: there is the grip of consciousness of the human condition, of the fraternity of mankind in suffering, of the extreme precariousness of its condition. There is the will to expression, the necessity of expression ... that almost savage elation of vital impulse, of the appetite for living, that is multiplied in the proximity and daily company of death.[62]

Ungaretti was in Paris at the Armistice. He arrived at Apollinaire's house, bringing the French poet his favorite Tuscan cigars, only to learn that Apollinaire, weakened by his war wounds, had died shortly before, a victim of the 1918 influenza pandemic.[63] In an essay written in 1966 near the end of his life, Ungaretti declared, "After the war we witnessed a change in the world that separated us from what we used to be and from what we once had made and done, as if at one blow millions of years had passed."[64]

---

[60] Herbert Vivian, "The Italian Front: In the Trenches," *The Living Age*, vol. 289, 1916, p. 178.
[61] Glauco Cambon, *Giuseppe Ungaretti*, Columbia UP, 1967, p. 9.
[62] Giuseppi Ungaretti, *Giuseppe Ungaretti: Selected Poems*, translated by Andrew Frisardi, Farrar, Straus and Giroux, 2002, p. 264.
[63] Allen Mandelbaum, *Selected Poems of Giuseppe Ungaretti*, Cornell UP, 1975, p. xviii.
[64] Ungaretti, *Giuseppe Ungaretti: Selected Poems*, p. xxvii.

The Moles

I've been in a trench for fifteen days,
  I'm choked for the want of air;
It's harvest-time where my mother stays,
  And I'm wishing that I was there.

I've ceased to count in the scheme of things,
  My courage has waned and set;
It's trysting-time where the mavis sings
  And I'm wishing I could forget.

With straightened shoulders and hearts that sang
  "For Freedom and Liberty!"
That was the battle-cry that rang
  From the men-that-we-used-to-be.

We've learnt the law of shot and shell,
  We've learnt the law of steel;
But the Law of the Trench is a cultured Hell,
  For it stifles the power to feel.

Death we have ventured many times
  Nor flinched at the sacrifice,
But if this be the debt of our youthful crimes—
  Lord God we have paid the price!

We have used our youth and lost the strength
  That the spirit of youth controls;
We have become no more at length
  Than partially human moles.

We're growing inanimate: Bit by bit
  We're getting inert—decayed;
The score of our sins was boldly writ
  But Mother of God—we've paid!

And this is our Fate: When the Gods are kind
Our existence shall simply cease—
A sniper's bullet—a trench that's mined—
God-speed, and a quick release!

—Cyril Morton Horne (1916)

Before Irish-born Cyril Morton Horne was commissioned in the King's Own Scottish Borderers in 1915, he had sung and danced in musical comedies in London's West End and on New York's Broadway. In Horne's last role before joining the British Army, he appeared as the romantic lead in the operetta *Mlle. Modiste*, playing a French army captain in love with a shop-girl. In that role, he'd sung in the finale, "Alas to part, how great the sorrow, to leave the friends grown fond with years, to know perchance that on the morrow, for love and smiles comes doubts and tears." Horne found himself in a very different drama in 1915, one of the few officers from his company who survived the Battle of Loos unwounded. Sometime after the battle, in late 1915, he wrote what is considered to be one of the earliest poems describing the realities of the trench life, "The Moles."

Horne was killed on January 27, 1916, when he and a fellow officer ignored "The Law of the Trench" and attempted to rescue a wounded comrade lying in No Man's Land. The preface to his posthumously published book of poems states, "A shrapnel shell exploded overhead just as his comrades were ready to cheer him [Horne] for his heroic rescue. Both men were killed instantly."[65] Horne's wife, Marie, chose as the epitaph for his grave the first two lines from his posthumously published poem "Aftermath":

> A grim gray tribute of memory
>   Is all we have left to give
> To those who have fought and fallen
>   From those who sorrow and live.
> Memory lives; and we wonder
>   If the law of the Gods was kind,
> For the hardest battle was fought by
>   The Somebody-left-behind.

---

[65] "Foreword," *Songs of the Shrapnel Shell*, by Cyril Morton Horne, Harper and Brothers, 1916, p. viii.

The Song of the Mud

This is the song of the mud,
The pale yellow glistening mud that covers the hills like satin;
The grey gleaming silvery mud that is spread like enamel over the valleys;
The frothing, squirting, spurting, liquid mud that gurgles along the road beds;
The thick elastic mud that is kneaded and pounded and squeezed under the
 hoofs of the horses;
The invincible, inexhaustible mud of the war zone.

This is the song of the mud, the uniform of the poilu.
His coat is of mud, his great dragging flapping coat, that is too big for him and
 too heavy;
His coat that once was blue and now is grey and stiff with the mud that cakes
 to it.
This is the mud that clothes him.
His trousers and boots are of mud,
And his skin is of mud;
And there is mud in his beard.
His head is crowned with a helmet of mud.
He wears it well.
He wears it as a king wears the ermine that bores him.
He has set a new style in clothing;
He has introduced the chic of mud.

This is the song of the mud that wriggles its way into battle.
The impertinent, the intrusive, the ubiquitous, the unwelcome,
The slimy inveterate nuisance,
That fills the trenches,
That mixes in with the food of the soldiers,
That spoils the working of motors and crawls into their secret parts,
That spreads itself over the guns,
That sucks the guns down and holds them fast in its slimy voluminous lips,
That has no respect for destruction and muzzles the bursting shells;
And slowly, softly, easily,
Soaks up the fire, the noise; soaks up the energy and the courage;
Soaks up the power of armies;
Soaks up the battle.
Just soaks it up and thus stops it.

This is the hymn of mud—the obscene, the filthy, the putrid,
The vast liquid grave of our armies.

It has drowned our men.
Its monstrous distended belly reeks with the undigested dead.
Our men have gone into it, sinking slowly, and struggling and slowly disappearing.
Our fine men, our brave, strong, young men;
Our glowing red, shouting, brawny men.
Slowly, inch by inch, they have gone down into it,
Into its darkness, its thickness, its silence.
Slowly, irresistibly, it drew them down, sucked them down,
And they were drowned in thick, bitter, heaving mud.
Now it hides them, Oh, so many of them!
Under its smooth glistening surface it is hiding them blandly.
There is not a trace of them.
There is no mark where they went down.
The mute enormous mouth of the mud has closed over them.

This is the song of the mud,
The beautiful glistening golden mud that covers the hills like satin;
The mysterious gleaming silvery mud that is spread like enamel over the valleys.
Mud, the disguise of the war zone;
Mud, the mantle of battles;
Mud, the smooth fluid grave of our soldiers:
This is the song of the mud.

—Mary Borden[66] (1929)

Few know of Mary Borden—nurse, memoirist, novelist, and poet—but the mud she writes about is one of the most iconic images of the war. Wilfred Owen wrote to his mother, "In 2 ½ miles of trench which I waded yesterday there was not one inch of dry ground. There is a mean depth of two feet of water"; another soldier's diary recorded, "Water knee deep and up to the waist in places."[67]

The daughter of a wealthy Chicago industrialist, Borden graduated from Vassar in 1907 and in 1908 married George Douglas Turner, a Scottish lay minister who was working with the YMCA in India. When Turner joined the British army in 1914, Borden volunteered her services with the Red Cross and, with income from her family inheritance, helped to establish a military hospital in Belgium.

---

[66] See also Borden's "The Hill."
[67] Owen and Mitchell, qtd. in *The Great War and Modern Memory*, by Paul Fussell, Oxford UP, 2000, p. 48.

For four years, she worked in hospitals attached to the French Army, moving from Flanders to the Somme, to Champagne, and then back to Belgium. While at the Somme, Borden served at a field hospital that was targeted by German artillery. In a series of richly descriptive short vignettes, Borden recorded her experiences. She attempted to publish her writing in 1917 as a short memoir titled *The Forbidden Zone*, but British authorities censored the book and halted publication, concerned that it would damage morale. *The Forbidden Zone* was eventually published in 1929. In one excerpt, Borden describes the implacable character of military command:

> It is all carefully arranged. Everything is arranged. It is arranged that men should be broken and that they should be mended. Just as you send your clothes to the laundry and mend them when they come back, so we send our men to the trenches and mend them when they come back again … And we send our men to the war again and again, just as long as they will stand it; just until they are dead, and then we throw them into the ground.[68]

In another, she describes her work at the hospital:

> There was a man stretched on the table. His brain came off in my hands when I lifted the bandage from his head. When the dresser came back I said: "His brain came off on the bandage."
> "Where have you put it?"
> "I put it in the pail under the table."
> "It's only one half of his brain," he said, looking into the man's skull. "The rest is here."
> I left him to finish the dressing and went about my business. I had much to do … Life was leaking away from all of them; but with some there was no hurry, with others it was a case of minutes. It was my business to create a counter-wave of life, to create the flow against the ebb. It was like a tug of war with the tide. The ebb of life was cold.[69]

Minogue and Palmer compare Borden's writing to that of Isaac Rosenberg, for both writers "show the same determination to hold an unflinching gaze on the dying or about-to-die man in circumstances which threaten to render that man *only* an animal," and both insist "on seeing the *man*."[70] More than ten years

---

[68] Mary Borden, *The Forbidden Zone*, William Heinemann, 1929, p. 117.
[69] Borden, *The Forbidden Zone*, pp. 142–143.
[70] Sally Minogue and Andrew Palmer, *The Remembered Dead: Poetry, Memory and the First World War*, Cambridge UP, 2018, p. 42.

after the war had ended, following the publication of *The Forbidden Zone*, a critic for the London *Times* expressed concern that Borden's writing might still threaten morale:

> The scenes [Borden describes] inside the operating room during a battle are dreadful, and all the more so because they are described with considerable power. It is perhaps right that this aspect of war should be made clear to the public which knows nothing of it; but there is some risk that the fashion in which the subject is handled will make it appear that the hospital was for the wounded a place of horror rather than of relief.[71]

In the preface to *The Forbidden Zone*, Borden explains that the fragmentary quality of her impressions was intended to reflect the brokenness and confusion of the war and that "any attempt to reduce them to order would require artifice on my part and would falsify them."[72]

---

[71] "Shorter Notices: The Forbidden Zone," *Times Literary Supplement*, no. 1453, 5 Dec. 1929, p. 1030.
[72] Borden, *The Forbidden Zone*.

Still Raining… (Il pleut encore…)
To my father, whose 'motherly' letters were always 'fine weather'

'How like the dead we look, in the glisten
of early, inevitably raining, dawn…
It rained all yesterday, and the day before,
it's been raining, day and night, the whole War!
We look so like the dead, in their misery.'

'The sun was out…' —When? I can't remember…
last year… or the year before, perhaps?
Yesterday? —Rained harder than ever!
Or else I've just forgotten… Can't remember:
         I didn't get a letter.

How lucky you are to have a mother—
the weather's always fine in mothers' letters,
and, in your replies, it's always sunny;
the poor dear things would be so upset
if you didn't always say 'It's sunny.'

'No, I've not been cold, and today
there's a swallow twittering away.
I tell you, spring has well and truly come—
Yes, that naughty winter's gone away,
that worried you so much, my dearest Mum!'

—Sweet pleasure, so to lie to those you love,
with the words of every day, the only ones
we truly understand, which never change
and never lose, as they journey on, the love
they bring from the lips that gave them shape.
         —Noël Garnier (1920), translated by Ian Higgins

The term *weather front* was first used in 1918, the name being a metaphorical extension of the battle-fronts of the war.[73] Soldiers on all sides fought the weather, and at times it seemed as if the rain would never end. French soldier Louis Barthas wrote that it was as if "God was unleashing a second Deluge to extinguish the madness of his creatures," and described the rain as "another enemy … against which we had no defense at all."[74] The weather was a formidable foe, as torrents

---

[73] Andrew Ross, *Strange Weather*, Verso, 1991, p. 228.
[74] Louis Barthas, *Poilu: The World War I Notebooks of Corporal Louis Barthas,* translated by Edward M. Strauss, Yale UP, 2014, p. 27.

transformed trenches into open sewers and collapsed trench walls. German soldier Erich Maria Remarque describes the constant downpour in his novel *All Quiet on the Western Front:* "Behind us lay rainy weeks—grey sky, grey fluid earth, grey dying. If we go out, the rain at once soaks through our overcoat and clothing; —and we remain wet all the time we are in the line. We never get dry ... Our hands are earth, our bodies clay and our eyes pools of rain."[75] British writer Edmund Blunden describes a world engulfed by rain: "Mute misery lapses into trickling rain, / That wreathes and swims and soon shuts in our world."[76] Men suffered the agonies of trench foot, died of exposure, and drowned in the mud.

French soldier Noël Garnier was awarded military honors for his actions during the war. During his time on *permission* and on *repos*, he wrote poems, "but he kept them to himself."[77] It wasn't until 1920 that Garnier published his volume of pacifist war poetry, *Le don de ma Mère*. The French Minister of War responded by issuing an edict to withdraw the Cross of Chevalier of the Legion of Honor and the Croix de Guerre from the veteran soldier, "because of certain socialistic tendencies which have been evident in his verse of late."[78] Following the French decision to strip Garnier of his military medals, an editorial appeared in the American periodical *The Nation* that reprinted Garnier's war-time citation for exceptional bravery:

> M. Garnier, Noël, second lieutenant in the 11th regiment of hussars, attached to the 15th battalion of chasseurs, is named to the order of the Legion of Honor, with the rank of knight: A young second lieutenant transferred at his own request from the cavalry to a battalion of chasseurs. Volunteered to establish communication between two companies placed, on September 14, in a very delicate position; struck by three bullets in the thigh and one in the arm, very seriously wounded, he succeeded in dragging himself across the ground to fulfil his mission. Had himself carried on a stretcher to his *chef de corps* and before mentioning his wounds gave a detailed report on his reconnaissance. Proved a heroism which will never be surpassed. Two citations. [signed] PETAIN

The editorial concluded, "It is not required of patriotism that it be always and ever patriotic, but poetry, it seems, must be patriotic, or else past action is forgotten. Fortunately, there are others besides Ministers of War to judge of both."[79]

---

[75] Erich Maria Remarque, *All Quiet on the Western Front*, translated by A.W. Wheen, Ballantine, 1982, pp. 286–287.
[76] Edmund Blunden, "Third Ypres," *The Poems of Edmund Blunden*, Cobden-Sanderson, 1930, p. 153.
[77] The Drifter, "In the Driftway," *The Nation*, vol. 111, 10 Nov. 1920, p. 532.
[78] "First Aid to Socialism," *Life Magazine*, vol. 76, no. 1974, 2 Sept. 1920, p. 410.
[79] The Drifter, "In the Driftway," p. 532.

The Boys Who Live in the Ground

Some sing the glory of the war,
   Of the heroes who die in the fight,
Of the shock of battle, the roar of guns,
   When armies clash by night.

Some mourn the savagery of war,
   The shame and the waste of it all,
And they pity the sinfulness of men
   Who heard not the Master's call.

They may be right and they may be wrong,
   But what I'm going to sing
Is not the glory nor sin of war,
   But the weariness of the thing.

For most of the time there's nothing to do
   But to sit and think of the past,
And one day comes and slowly dies
   Exactly like the last.

It's the waiting that's seldom talked about;
   Oh, it's very rarely told
That most of the bravery at the front
   Is just waiting in the cold.

It is not the dread of the shrapnel's whine
   That sickens a fighting soul,
But the beast in us comes out sometimes
   When we're waiting in a hole.

Just sitting and waiting and thinking,
   As the dreary days go by,
Takes a different kind of courage
   From marching out to die.

And I often think when the thing is done,
   And the praises are all passed around,
If, with all their words, they'll say enough
   For the boys who lived in the ground.

—Donald S. White (1918)

"The Boys Who Live in the Ground" appeared in *Songs from the Trenches: The Soul of the A.E.F.*, published in September of 1918, when masses of American troops were arriving in France and preparing for battle. The anthology chose poems from the thousands submitted to the *New York Herald's* Literary Competition, and the collection was dedicated to the memory of Alan Seeger, "The First American Soldier Poet who gave his life in France." The book's foreword states that the poems were "a message from the American soldiers abroad to the home folks, written on the decks of transports, in French villages, in muddy camps, in the trenches, beside cannon or camion, in hospitals. Each writer speaks for thousands of his fellows."[80]

Donald S. White graduated from Bowdoin College in 1916. The class yearbook notes that his devotion to ragtime music had earned him the nickname "Raggy," and that he also enjoyed "writing fond verses to the probable and improbable feelings of himself and others."[81] He did not wait for the United States to enter the war, but instead, early in 1917, joined the American Field Service (AFS) as an ambulance driver attached to the French army. When America declared war later that year, White resigned from his position with the AFS, enlisted in the American army, and served as a pilot on the Western Front with the 20th Air Squadron. The young lieutenant was cited for "exceptional devotion to duty"; an article in his university magazine reported that "he had served in a day-bombing squadron in every raid since the squadron had been called into active work during the severe fighting in the Argonne." The article went on to say that of the American aviators who flew over enemy lines in the war, "only fifteen percent ... were left after the signing of the armistice."[82] Donald S. White survived the war.

---

[80] Herbert Adams Gibbons, editor, *Songs from the Trenches, the Soul of the A.E.F.*, Harper and Brothers, 1918, p. xi.
[81] Bowdoin College, *Bowdoin Bugle*, 1916, p. 85.
[82] "Lieut. Donald S. White, '16, Cited," *Bowdoin Orient*, vol. 48, no. 18, 14 Jan. 1919, p. 176.

A Digger's Disillusion

When I first thought of enlisting,
And courageously assisting
In this game the poet calls the sport of Kings,
   I had dreams of martial glory,
   Dashing charge with bayonet gory,
And a host of other brave and stirring things:

Of attacks with bugles sounding,
Banners everywhere abounding,
With the gen'ral on his charger in the lead;
   Then triumphant, lusty shouting,
   As, the issue never doubting,
Fritz flies panic-stricken with his utmost speed.

Then the feasting and the revels
When we've beaten back the devils,
And the cheering, and vociferous hurrahs;
   Then the lights from hollows peeping,
   When, on beds of soft grass sleeping,
We sink wearily to rest beneath the stars.

But, alas! for dreams deceiving,
And imagination weaving
Such a web of utter falsehood in my brain!
   For my visions all are shattered,
   And I've just become a tattered,
Weary digger, working knee-deep in a drain.

For the war is but a sequence
Of fatigues of dismal frequence,
Digging holes and straightway filling them again;
   While the subaltern aspiring,
   Turns his energies to wiring—
(I.e., supervises wiring by his men).

Day by day we dig new trenches,
Bury war-created stenches,
Build up castles in the mud, and drain the floor;
   Night by night the big guns thunder,
   Trench and castle rend asunder,
And at dawn we start to dig and build once more.

So farewell to old romances,
Childhood's tales of glistening lances,
Naked sword-blades flashing gaily in the sun;
  Let the spade replace the sabre;
  Let the poet sing of labour,
Never ceasing till the day of war is done.

— K.L. Trent (1918)

At the outbreak of the war, New Zealand was a Dominion of the British Empire, and many New Zealanders were eager to join the British war effort. When recruitment opened in Auckland on the morning of August 6, 1914, over 1,000 men had signed up by 11:00 a.m., and by day's end, more than 3,000 had volunteered for active duty. Across the country over the following week, nearly 15,000 men enlisted (the total population of New Zealand was just over one million).[83] As troops prepared to leave for overseas, each soldier was reminded of his duty:

> Every New Zealander, when leaving his native shores for active service on land or sea, was given a printed slip having upon it special messages from Earls Roberts and Kitchener, the latter's last message to the British troops, and the following words from the New Zealand Minister for Defence:—"Remember that you will hold the Dominion's honour in your keeping. Remember that both the friends you meet and the enemies you fight will form their opinions of New Zealanders from you; therefore see that you are brave as you are honourable, and modest and courteous as you are brave."[84]

Ready to prove themselves, soldiers from New Zealand referred to themselves as "Diggers," and an estimated 100,000 served overseas. A 1923 account of New Zealand's participation in the war states, "42 per cent of New Zealand's male population of military age actually embarked for active service ... Of those who left on the Great Adventure, 16,554 were destined never to see their beloved country again."[85] As for those who did return, researchers have found that men who left for combat in 1914 and who survived the war lost on average eight years of life, dying earlier than their comparable non-military cohort, suggesting that the impact of the war "continued to lower their lifespan in subsequent years."[86]

---

[83] Imelda Bargas and Tim Shoebridge, *New Zealand's First World War Heritage*, Exisle, 2015, p. 12.
[84] Lt. H.T.B. Drew, editor, *The War Effort of New Zealand*, Whitcombe and Tombs, 1923, p. 86.
[85] *War Effort of New Zealand*, p. 21.
[86] Nick Wilson et al., "Mortality of First World War Military Personnel: Comparison of Two Military Cohorts," *BMJ*, 16 Dec. 2014, DOI: https://doi.org/10.1136/bmj.g7168.

"The Digger's Disillusionment" appeared in the 1918 magazine *New Zealand at the Front: Written and Illustrated in France by Men of the New Zealand Division*. The publication also featured the "Digger's Dictionary," which provided a tongue-in-cheek definition for "Digger":

> These curious animals are exported from New Zealand in large numbers, and frequently in custody. There are two great primary classes: a) Aucklanders. b) Others … The DIGGER is of a sporting nature … He has marked social tendencies, and select societies for "spiritual uplift" may be met with at any *estaminet* between the hours of 6 and 8 p.m. He is usually well-educated, speaks several languages, including Australian, is fond of rum, children, military police, fatigues, Red tabs, and White Label …
>
> P.S.—Since the foregoing was written a strong rumour (straight from the best sources) is afloat to the effect that a new type of DIGGER has been seen on the Western Front. This variety salutes officers. Confirmation of this is required, as no previous report of this nature has been received. [87]

The editor of *New Zealand at the Front* writes,

> When it is remembered that this book is the work of the men of but one Division, representing a small Dominion of only a million people all told, and that by far the greater part of it has been written and drawn under fire during the most critical stage of the War, allowances will no doubt be made for its imperfections.[88]

The author K.L. Trent is most likely a pseudonym. Neither the Imperial War Museum's *Lives of the First World War* nor the Auckland Museum's *Online Cenotaph* records a First World War soldier who matches the name. The pseudonym may allude to Trentham, one of the largest military training camps in New Zealand; men who trained there were known as the "noble Trents."

---

[87] "Digger's Dictionary," *New Zealand at the Front*, Cassell, 1918, p. 32.
[88] "Editor's Note," *New Zealand at the Front*, Cassell, 1918, p. xi.

During the Bombardment

What did we know of birds?
Though the wet woods rang with their blessing,
And the trees were awake and aware with wings,
And the little secrets of mirth, that have no words,
Made even the brambles chuckle, like baby things
Who find their toes too funny for any expressing.

What did we know of flowers?
Though the fields were gay with their flaming
Poppies, like joy itself, burning the young green maize,
And spreading their crinkled petals after the showers—
Cornflower vieing with mustard; and all the three of them shaming
The tired old world with its careful browns and greys.

What did we know of summer,
The larks, and the dusty clover,
And the little furry things that were busy and starry-eyed?
Each of us wore his brave disguise, like a mummer,
Hoping that no one saw, when the shells came over,
The little boy who was funking—somewhere inside!

— Theodore Percival Cameron Wilson (1919)

A wall of sound. A deafening roar. A ceaseless rain of shells. These were soldiers' impressions as they described one of the greatest artillery actions the world had yet seen: the bombardment that preceded and accompanied the British attack at the Somme on July 1, 1916. "The din of hundreds of shells whizzing over our heads was like several ghost-like express trains hurtling through the sky," said Corporal George Ashurst of the Lancashire Fusiliers.[89] There are reports that the shelling was heard over 240 miles away on London's Hampstead Heath.[90] For seven days before the attack, more than 1,500 heavy guns, often spaced at intervals of less than thirty yards, fired over 1,500,000 artillery and gas shells at German positions. British General Sir Henry Rawlinson is reported to have said, "nothing could exist at the conclusion of the bombardment in the area covered by it."[91]

[89] George Ashurst, *My Bit: A Lancashire Fusilier at War 1914–18*, edited by Richard Holmes, Crowood, 2001, p. 97.
[90] Nicholas J. Saunders, "Materiality, Space and Distance in the First World War," *Modern Conflict and the Senses*, edited by Paul Cornish and Nicholas J. Saunders, Taylor and Francis, 2017, p. 35.
[91] Martin Samuels, *Command or Control?* Taylor and Francis, 2013, pp. 128–129, 138.

Yet while it was possible to survive prolonged artillery fire, bombardments were a horrific torture to endure. In a letter dated April of 1916, T.P. Cameron Wilson wrote, "a real bombardment where the sky is one screaming sheet of metal is hell indescribable."[92] How loud is a bombardment that can be heard over 200 miles away? First World War bombardments were estimated to reach noise levels of at least 140 decibels (dBs), louder than a jackhammer at fifty feet (95 dBs), louder than a power mower at three feet (107 dBs), louder than sandblasting or a rock concert (115 dBs), and well past the point of pain that begins at 125 dBs. Even with hearing protection (which was not issued to men at the Front), 140 dBs is the loudest recommended noise exposure, and short-term exposure at this level is likely to result in permanent damage.[93] In 1917, Macleod Yearsley, former Senior Surgeon to the Royal Ear Hospital, wrote, "A large number of cases illustrating the effects of modern high explosives upon the organ of hearing are being collected from the Front and present features varying from shock to permanent injury."[94] And research published in 2016 investigating the effects of chronic blast exposure suggests that exposure to concussive explosions may be related to post-traumatic stress disorder (PTSD).[95]

Theodore Percival Cameron Wilson, who preferred to be called "Jim," was a writer, teacher, and son of a clergyman from rural England. He volunteered for the British Army in August of 1914 and was later commissioned an officer with the 10th Battalion Sherwood Foresters. After his own experience enduring an artillery bombardment, Wilson wrote,

"As to my own feelings under fire, I was horribly afraid—sick with fear—not of being hit, but of seeing other people torn in the way that high explosive tears. It is simply hellish. But, thank God, I didn't show any funk. That's all a man dare ask, I think."[96] In April of 1916, he wrote to his aunt,

> War is about the most unclean thing on earth. There are certain big clean virtues about it—comradeship and a whittling away of non-essentials, and sheer

---

[92] Captain Theodore Percival Cameron Wilson, letter dated 27 Apr. 1916, *War Letters of Fallen Englishmen,* edited by Laurence Housman, E.P. Dutton, 1930, p. 297.

[93] Robert Traynor, "Hearing Loss in the Trenches of World War I," 1 Apr. 2014, *Hearing Health and Technology Matters,* web.archive.org/save/https://hearinghealthmatters.org/hearinginternational/2014/hearing-loss-trenches-wwi.

[94] Macleod Yearsley, "An Air Raid Case," *Journal of Laryngology, Rhinology and Otology,* vol. 32, no. 9, Sept. 1917, p. 18.

[95] Sharon Baughman Shively et al., "Characterisation of Interface Astroglial Scarring in the Human Brain after Blast Exposure: A Post-Mortem Case Series," *The Lancet Neurology,* vol. 15, Aug. 2016, pp. 944–953.

[96] T.P.C. Wilson, qtd. in "Introduction," by Robert Norwood, in *Waste Paper Philosophy, to Which Has Been Added Magpies in Picardy,* by T.P.C. Wilson, George H. Doran, 1920, p. vii.

stark triumphs of spirit over shrinking nerves, but it's the calculated death, the deliberate tearing of fine young bodies—if you've once seen a bright-eyed fellow suddenly turned to a goggling idiot, with his own brains trickling down into his eyes from under his cap—as I've done, you're either a peace-maker or a degenerate.[97]

Wilson did not live to see the peace; he was killed in the German spring offensive of 1918, his body never found. In the introduction to Wilson's posthumously published book of poems, *Magpies in Picardy*, Harold Monro wrote that Wilson was "extremely shy about his verse, and, unlike most youthful poets, was always disinclined to let it be seen, or discussed, by his friends … The question whether the poems which follow are, or are not, important contributions to the literature of our time will be decided by their readers. As the expression of a personality, they are, at any rate, remarkable."[98]

---

[97] *War Letters of Fallen Englishmen*, p. 298.
[98] Harold Monro, "Introduction," *Magpies in Picardy*, by T.P. Cameron Wilson, The Poetry Bookshop, 1919.

Cricket: The Catch

Whizzing, fierce, it came
  Down the summer air,
Burning like a flame
  On my fingers bare,
And it brought to me
As swift—a memory.

Happy days long dead
  Clear I saw once more.
Childhood that is fled:—
  Rossall on the shore,
Where the sea sobs wild
Like a homesick child.

Oh, the blue bird's fled!
  Never man can follow.
Yet at times instead
  Comes this scarlet swallow,
Bearing on its wings
  (Where it skims and dips,
  Gleaming through the slips)
Sweet Time-strangled things.

—Frederick William Harvey (1916)

In 1897, Henry Newbolt published a poem comparing the violence of war with school sport: "The river of death has brimmed his banks, / And England's far, and Honour a name, / But the voice of schoolboy rallies the ranks, / 'Play up! play up! and play the game!'"[99] At the time of the First World War, it was commonly believed that experience and ability in athletics would translate directly to success on the battlefield—Americans were reputed to be better than the French at tossing grenades, due to Americans' love of baseball. The British Army encouraged sporting competitions to improve troops' physical fitness, boost morale, and strengthen bonds between officers and their men. Numerous First World War poems make reference to one of the most English of sports: cricket.

---

[99] Henry Newbolt, "Vitaï Lampada," *Admirals All, and Other Verses,* John Lane, 1898, p. 23.

F.W. Harvey, the "Laureate of Gloucestershire," typically wrote light-hearted poems; his best known is "Ducks." He was a key contributor to the first British trench newspaper, the *Fifth Gloucester Gazette*, and a close friend of the soldier-poet-composer Ivor Gurney (Gurney would later set several of Harvey's poems to music). Harvey dedicated his 1916 volume of poetry, *A Gloucestershire Lad at Home and Abroad*, "To all comrades of mine who lie dead in foreign fields for love of England, or who live to prosecute the war for another England." During a night reconnaissance mission on August 17, 1916, he was captured by Germans and spent the remaining years of the war in prison camps, making several failed escape attempts. Harvey survived the war and returned to Gloucestershire, dying in 1957. A memorial to him in Gloucestershire Cathedral reads, "He loved the vision of this world and found it good."[100]

---

[100] Lines from F.W. Harvey's poem "F.W.H. (A Portrait)," *A Gloucestershire Lad*, p. 50.

The Rainbow

I watch the white dawn gleam,
    To the thunder of hidden guns.
I hear the hot shells scream
Through skies as sweet as a dream
    Where the silver dawnbreak runs.
    And stabbing of light
    Scorches the virginal white.
But I feel in my being the old, high, sanctified thrill,
And I thank the gods that the dawn is beautiful still.

    From death that hurtles by
        I crouch in the trench day-long,
    But up to a cloudless sky
    From the ground where our dead men lie
        A brown lark soars in song.
    Through the tortured air,
    Rent by the shrapnel's flare,
Over the troubleless dead he carols his fill,
And I thank the gods that the birds are beautiful still.

    Where the parapet is low
        And level with the eye
    Poppies and cornflowers glow
    And the corn sways to and fro
        In a pattern against the sky.
    The gold stalks hide
    Bodies of men who died
Charging at dawn through the dew to be killed or to kill.
I thank the gods that the flowers are beautiful still.

    When night falls dark we creep
        In silence to our dead.
    We dig a few feet deep
    And leave them there to sleep—
        But blood at night is red,
    Yea, even at night,
    And a dead man's face is white.

And I dry my hands, that are also trained to kill,
And I look at the stars—for the stars are beautiful still.
France, August 8th, 1916

—Leslie Coulson

For many British soldiers, ideals of home and national identity were embodied in nature and rural country scenes. John Lewis-Stempel has analyzed the major themes of over 200 First World War soldier poets and found that although "Pity was well-nigh absent, affinity with nature was everywhere, as metaphor, as subject."[101] The effects of the First World War on the countryside where battles once raged are still felt today: over 100 years after the end of the war, farmers in France and Belgium continue to unearth bodies and weapons, and children are instructed to avoid unexploded shells and grenades that remain in forests and fields. The Interior Ministry of France estimates that "12 million unexploded shells [from the First World War] ... still sleep in the soil near Verdun."[102] In 1991, thirty-six farmers died when their machinery detonated buried shells, and since 1946, over 600 French *démineurs* (weapon disposal experts) have died in the line of duty.[103] *Démineur* Henry Belot has said, "I doubt we'll ever clear these forests completely ... We haven't even gotten to the big shells yet. They're still deep in the ground."[104]

Coulson was a journalist like his father. Enlisting in September of 1914 with the 2/2nd London Royal Fusiliers, he served in Malta, Egypt, and Gallipoli before being sent to the Western Front in April of 1916. In the summer of 1916, billeted near one of the devastated villages of France, Leslie Coulson wrote, "I have seen men shattered, dying, dead—all the sad tragedy of war. And this murder of old stone, and lichened thatches, this shattering of little old churches and homesteads brings the tragedy home to me more acutely. I think to find an English village like this would almost break my heart."[105] Coulson spent five months on the Somme in 1916. On October 7, his company was ordered to attack the German lines near Lesboeufs. In the first wave of the assault, Coulson was shot in the chest. Carried to a nearby first aid station, he "thanked the stretcher

---

[101] John Lewis-Stempel, *Where Poppies Blow*, Weidenfeld and Nicolson, 2016, p. xxiv.
[102] Donovan Webster, *Aftermath: The Remnants of War*, Vintage, 1998, p. 18.
[103] Webster, *Aftermath*, p. 19.
[104] Webster, *Aftermath*, pp. 25–26.
[105] Leslie Coulson, qtd. in "Introduction," by F.R.C. [Coulson's father, Frederick Raymond Coulson], *From an Outpost and Other Poems*, by Leslie Coulson, Erskine MacDonald, 1917, pp. 5–6.

bearers and sent a last message home to his family."[106] He died the next day at Grove Town casualty clearing station; Coulson was twenty-seven years old. No trace of the first aid station remains, except the British cemetery where 1,395 men are buried. Coulson's only book of poetry, *From an Outpost,* was published by his father in 1917. In the early fall of 1916, Coulson had written home, "If I should fall, do not grieve for me. I shall be one with the wind and the sun and the flowers."[107] The epitaph that the family chose to have inscribed on his headstone reads, "Nothing but well and fair and what may quiet us in a death so noble."[108]

---

[106] Anne Powell, *A Deep Cry,* Palladour, 1993, p. 172.
[107] Leslie Coulson, qtd. in "Introduction," *From an Outpost,* p. 8. Researcher Sarah Wearne has noted that the father of British soldier Henry James Bezer (killed 22 Aug. 1918) must have read Coulson's book, as he chose a variation of these lines for his son's epitaph.
[108] The opening lines from Milton's "Samson Agonistes."

The Star-Shell
(Loos.)

A star-shell holds the sky beyond
Shell-shivered Loos, and drops
In million sparkles on a pond
That lies by Hulluch[109] copse.

A moment's brightness in the sky,
To vanish at a breath,
And die away, as soldiers die
Upon the wastes of death.

—Patrick MacGill[110] (1917)

On September 25, 1915, the British launched their greatest offensive to date of the First World War. By the time the Battle of Loos had ended on October 15, they had lost over 50,000 men, at least 16,000 of them dead or missing. The Germans called the battle *Der Leichenfeld von Loos,* or "the Corpse Field of Loos," and a German regimental diary recorded the slaughter:

> Dense masses of the enemy, line after line, came into sight on the ridge, some of their officers even mounted on horseback, and advancing as if carrying out a field-day drill in peacetime. Our artillery and machine guns riddled their ranks as they came on. As they crossed the northern front of Bois Hugo, the machine guns positioned there caught them in the flank and whole battalions must have been utterly destroyed.[111]

Patrick MacGill was wounded at Loos. An Irish soldier from County Donegal, MacGill served with the London Irish Rifles and wrote of his experiences in *The Great Push: An Episode of the Great War* (1916). His war novel recounts an interlude during the Battle of Loos as men watch a bombardment:

> A momentary lull followed, and a million sparks fluttered earthwards from a galaxy of searching star-shells.
> "Why are such beautiful lights used in the killing of men?" I asked myself. Above in the quiet the gods were meditating, then, losing patience, they again burst into irrevocable rage, seeking, as it seemed, some obscure and fierce retribution.

---

[109] Hulluch is a town near Loos, the scene of heavy fighting throughout the war.
[110] See also MacGill's "A Lament."
[111] Philip Warner, *The Battle of Loos*, Wordsworth, 1976, p. 48.

> The shells were loosened again; there was no escape from their frightful vitality, they crushed, burrowed, exterminated; obstacles were broken down, and men's lives were flicked out like flies off a window pane ... We crouched under the bomb-shelter, mute, pale, hesitating. Oh! the terrible anxiety of men who wait passively for something to take place and always fearing the worst![112]

During a break in the shelling, the narrator, working as a stretcher bearer, attempts to give aid to the wounded:

> Men and pieces of men were lying all over the place. A leg, an arm, then again a leg, cut off at the hip. A finely formed leg, the latter, gracefully putteed ...
>
> The tortured things lying at my feet were symbols of insecurity, ominous reminders of danger from which no discretion could save a man.[113]

In the aftermath of the battle, he describes the scene: "Nature, vast and terrible, stretched out on all sides; a red star-shell in the misty heavens looked like a lurid wound dripping with blood."[114] Wandering the battlefield in his search for the wounded and survivors, he comes upon a dead body: "The corpse was a mere condensation of shadows with a blurred though definite outline. It was a remainder and a reminder."[115] MacGill was one of the casualties of Loos. Although he was wounded, his injury sent him home, and he survived the war.

---

[112] Patrick MacGill, *The Great Push*, pp. 33–34.
[113] MacGill, *The Great Push*, p. 77
[114] MacGill, *The Great Push*, p. 210.
[115] MacGill, *The Great Push*, pp. 210–211.

Back to Rest
(Composed while marching to Rest Camp after severe fighting at Loos.)

A leaping wind from England,
   The skies without a stain,
Clean cut against the morning
   Slim poplars after rain,
The foolish notes of sparrows
   And starlings in a wood—
After the grime of battle
   We know that these are good.

Death whining down from Heaven,
   Death roaring from the ground,
Death stinking in the nostril,
   Death shrill in every sound,
Doubting we charged and conquered—
   Hopeless we struck and stood.
Now when the fight is ended
   We know that it was good.

We that have seen the strongest
   Cry like a beaten child,
The sanest eyes unholy,
   The cleanest hands defiled,
We that have known the heart blood
   Less than the lees of wine,
We that have seen men broken,
   We know man is divine.

—William Noel Hodgson (1916)

Nearly 10,000 British soldiers attacked on the first day of the Battle of Loos: over 8,000 were killed or wounded.[116] A British commander writing after the assault said, "From what I can ascertain, some of the divisions did actually reach the enemy's trenches, for their bodies can now be seen on the barbed wire."[117]

---

[116] Martin Gilbert, *The First World War: A Complete History*, Henry Holt, 1994, p. 201.
[117] General Henry Rawlinson, qtd. in *The Little Field-Marshal*, by Richard Holmes, Jonathan Cape, 1981, p. 304.

William Noel Hodgson, youngest child of a vicar and known to his regiment as "Smiler," was among those who fought at Loos. He wrote his account of the battle in the third person, as if to distance himself from the experience. Finding a group of men killed by artillery fire, Hodgson describes seeing "a white hand with a ring on the little finger" and "thinking of some girl or wife at home, [he] bends down to recover the ring, and finds that the hand ends abruptly at the wrist. There is no sign of the owner about."[118] Less than a year later, on the opening day of the Somme offensive, Hodgson and the men of the 9th Devonshires were ordered to attack German trenches near Mametz. By the end of the day, 159 men of the battalion lay dead in No Man's Land, including Hodgson, who had been shot through the throat. The soldiers were buried together in the trench they had left that morning. The unit's survivors erected a wooden cross above the graves that reads, "The Devonshires held this trench. The Devonshires hold it still."

---

[118] Qtd. in *Before Action: William Noel Hodgson and the 9th Devons,* by Charlotte Zeepvat, Pen and Sword, 2015, p. 127.

After the "Offensive"

This is the end of it, this the cold silence
Succeeding the violence
That rioted here.
This is the end of it—grim and austere.

This is the end of it—where the tide spread,
Runnels of blood,
Débris of dead.
This is the end of it: ebb follows flood.

Waves of strong men
That will surge not again,
Scattered and riven
You lie, and you rot;
What have you not given?
And what—have you got?

—Theodore van Beek (1919)

The Battle of the Somme lasted for four months and eighteen days, from July 1 to November 18, 1916. During that time, 481,842 British soldiers were either killed or wounded, while French casualties numbered over 250,000 and German over 235,000.[119] On the first day of the Somme offensive, the bloodiest day in the history of the British Army, British troops suffered 57,470 casualties; 19,240 British men died.

What was it like to survive the Somme? Theodore van Beek was a junior officer with the Royal Field Artillery; his poem "After the 'Offensive'" expresses the shock and loss of those who were left to soldier on.[120] Born in South Africa, van Beek published his first book, *Poems and a Drama*, in Johannesburg in 1907. He wrote nostalgically about his boyhood home and family farm in Mistley, Kwazulu–Natal: "There are some things I always shall remember— / The ring-dove croodling in the old gum tree, / The silvering of the maize as the wind passes."[121] Van Beek left South Africa in 1908 to attend Edinburgh University, and during the First World War, he served as a subaltern in the Royal Field Artillery.

---

[119] John F. Williams, *ANZACS, the Media and the Great War*, U of New South Wales P, 1999, p. 183.
[120] According to Partridge's *Dictionary of Slang*, the expression 'to soldier on' ("to persevere against peril and/or hardship") came into use 1916–1918.
[121] Theo van Beek, "To the Farm of My Boyhood (Mistley, Natal)," *The Day of Love and Other Poems*, Heathvale Press, 1986.

At some point during the war, van Beek, attired in his military uniform, stood in London and publicly recited his anti-war poetry, and for this act, he was "severely reprimanded by his Army superiors."[122] Given the strong anti-war sentiment of "After the 'Offensive'" and its challenge to military authority, it is not surprising that the poem was not published until after the war had ended, appearing in April of 1919 in *The English Review*. After the war, writing under the pseudonym of Martyn Mayne, van Beek turned his talents to popular music, composing the lyrics for "I Remember the Cornfields," recorded by Anne Shelton, and "A Kiss in the Night," recorded by Benny Goodman and his orchestra. In 1986, van Beek's son published a limited edition of his father's selected works, *The Day of Love*. The introduction provides further information about van Beek's war experience, stating, "his contemporaries and friends at that time included Siegfried Sassoon, Wilfred Owen, Stephen Black and his fellow South African poet, John Runcie."[123]

---

[122] Dominic Hibberd and John Onions, "Biographical Notes," *Poetry of the Great War: An Anthology*, Macmillan, 1986, p. 213.
[123] T.R. van Beek, "Introduction," *Day of Love*.

Beaucourt Revisited

I wandered up to Beaucourt; I took the river track,
And saw the lines we lived in before the Boche went back;
But peace was now in Pottage, the front was far ahead,
The front had journeyed Eastward, and only left the dead.

And I thought, How long we lay there, and watched across the wire,
While guns roared round the valley, and set the skies afire!
But now there are homes in HAMEL and tents in the Vale of Hell
And a camp at Suicide Corner, where half a regiment fell.

The new troops follow after, and tread the land we won,
To them 'tis so much hill-side, re-wrested from the Hun;
We only walk with reverence this sullen mile of mud;
The shell-holes hold our history, and half of them our blood.

Here, at the head of Peche Street, 'twas death to show your face;
To me it seemed like magic to linger in the place;
For me how many spirits hung round the Kentish Caves,
But the new men see no spirits—they only see the graves.

I found the half-dug ditches we fashioned for the fight,
We lost a score of men there—young James was killed that night;
I saw the star shells staring, I heard the bullets hail,
But the new troops pass unheeding—they never heard the tale.

I crossed the blood-red ribbon, that once was No-Man's Land,
I saw a misty daybreak and a creeping minute-hand;
And here the lads went over, and there was Harmsworth shot,
And here was William[124] lying—but the new men know them not.

And I said, "There is still the river, and still the stiff, stark trees,
To treasure here our story, but there are only these";
But under the white wood crosses the dead men answered low,
"The new men know not BEAUCOURT, but we are here—we know."

—A.P. Herbert (1918)[125]

---

[124] Believed to refer to Herbert's friend Lieutenant William Ker (see also Herbert's "The Bathe" in this volume).
[125] The poem was first published in September of 1917 in Herbert's divisional magazine, *The Mudhook*. The version included here appears in Herbert's *The Bomber Gipsy*, published in 1918.

From November 13–18 of 1916, British troops launched their final offensive of the Somme: the Battle of Ancre. The week-long bombardment before the attack was staggering; artillery fire was twice as heavy as that preceding the July 1 offensive. Although the attack was considered a success—the towns of St. Pierre Divion, Beaumont Hamel, and Beaucourt were taken—the gains came at great cost: over 22,000 British troops were killed or wounded.[126]

Alan Patrick Herbert was a young officer with the Royal Naval Division (RND). His unit was virtually obliterated in the fighting at Beaucourt: of the 435 men who attacked the village, only twenty escaped serious injury or death and were able to continue the fight the following day. Herbert was one of the twenty; his poem "Beaucourt Revisited" recounts the memories of a survivor. One of the stories that haunted Herbert was that of a fellow officer who was court-martialed for failing in his duty in the attack at Beaucourt. After the war, Herbert published *The Secret Battle*, a novel that drew heavily upon his own experiences. The central character is Harry Penrose, a young officer whose nerves fail him during an attack. Court-martialed for desertion, Penrose is found guilty and shot at dawn for cowardice. The story is almost certainly based upon the true account of 21-year-old Edwin Dyett, also an officer of the RND who was shot by men from his own unit. Blindfolded and tied to a stake, Dyett's last words reportedly were, "Well, boys, goodbye. For God's sake, shoot straight."[127] In his war novel, Herbert writes,

> And if the Court had been able to imagine themselves in Harry's condition of mind and body, crouching in the wet dark under that bank, faint with weariness and fear, shaken with those blinding, tearing concussions, not knowing what they should do, or what they *could* do, perhaps they would have said in their hearts, 'I will believe that story.' But they could not imagine it. For they were naturally stout-hearted men, and they had not seen too much war. They were not young enough.[128]

---

[126] William James Philpott, *Bloody Victory: The Sacrifice on the Somme and the Making of the Twentieth Century*, Little, Brown, 2009, p. 416.
[127] Robert King, *Shot at Dawn*, History Press, 2014, p. 66.
[128] A.P. Herbert, *The Secret Battle*, Methuen, 1919, p. 228.

Relieved
For S.J. Kimm

We are weary and silent,
There is only the rhythm of marching feet;
Tho' we move tranced, we keep it,
As clock-work toys.

But each man is alone in this multitude;
We know not the world in which we move,
Seeing not the dawn, earth pale and shadowy,
Level lands of tenuous grays and greens;
For our eye-balls have been seared with fire.

Only we have our secret thoughts,
Our sense floats out from us, delicately apprehensive,
To the very fringes of our being,
Where light drowns.

—Frederic Manning[129] (1917)

When published in Clarke's 1919 *A Treasury of War Poetry,* Frederic Manning's original dedication was removed and replaced by the subtitle "Guillemont."[130] In peacetime, the rural French village of Guillemont was home to less than 100 farmers and their families. But by the summer of 1916, the small hamlet had become an object lesson that demonstrated the relentless character of the First World War. Guillemont was a key military objective for Allied forces during the months-long Battle of the Somme, and from July to early September of 1916, repeated attacks were made on the village. Assaults were largely uncoordinated and unsupported, resulting in over 300,000 combined casualties from both sides, and heavy rains turned the area into a swamp, adding to the misery of the men. In a letter dated September of 1916 after the village of Guillemont had finally been taken, British officer P.F. Story writes, "Guillemont was blotted right out, not one brick standing on another—nothing but a sea of crump holes of all sorts and sizes."[131]

---

[129] See also Manning's "The Face."

[130] The dedication to S.J. Kimm appears in Manning's *Eidola*; when reprinted in Clarke's *A Treasury of War Poetry,* the dedication was replaced by "(Guillemont)." Manning's biographers make no mention of an S.J. Kimm. Private Samuel J. Kimm served with the King's Shropshire Light Infantry, and it is likely this is the person to whom Manning dedicated the poem.

[131] Lt. Col. P.F. Story qtd in *Somme 1916: A Battlefield Companion,* by Gerald Gliddon, Sutton, 2006, p. 240.

Before the war, Australian writer Frederic Manning had emigrated to England, where he joined a literary circle that included Ezra Pound, T.E. Hulme, and Richard Aldington. In October of 1915, Manning enlisted in the British Army as a private with the King's Shropshire Light Infantry, and by 1916, he was fighting at the Somme. In 1917, he was commissioned as a second lieutenant with the Royal Irish Regiment. According to biographer Jonathan Marwil, while at the Somme, Manning was attached to the signal section of his battalion, but "his primary duty was as a relay runner between the trenches and brigade," carrying messages in the dark of night along roads that were often shelled.[132] The solitary experience may have heightened in Manning a "highly developed sense of his own separateness as well as a longing to immerse himself in the world of men and experience,"[133] echoes of which can be heard in "Relieved." In 1929, Manning anonymously published a novel based on his war experiences, *The Middle Parts of Fortune*. In 1930 an expurgated version was republished, again anonymously, as *Her Privates We*. Manning was named as the book's author only in 1943, seven years after his death. In one passage from the novel, Manning writes of his protagonist, Bourne, "He was not of their county, he was not even of their country … He felt like an alien among them."[134] Ernest Hemingway included an excerpt from the novel in *Men at War: The Best War Stories of All Time*, saying of Manning's work, "It is the finest and noblest book of men in war that I have ever read. I read it over each year to remember how things really were so that I will never lie to myself nor to anyone else about them."[135]

---

[132] Jonathan Marwil, *Frederic Manning: An Unfinished Life*, Duke UP, 1988, p. 166.
[133] Marwil, *Frederic Manning*, p. 170.
[134] Frederic Manning, *The Middle Parts of Fortune*, Penguin, 1990, p. 54.
[135] Ernest Hemingway, editor, "Introduction," *Men at War: The Best War Stories of All Time*, Crown, 1942, p. xvi.

Picnic: Harbonnières to Bayonvillers

A house marked 𝔒rtskommandantur—a great
sign 𝕂aiserplatz on a corner of the church,
and German street names all around the square.
Troop columns split to let our sidecar through.
"Drive like hell and get back on the main road—it's getting late."
"Yessir."
        The roadway seemed to reel and lurch
through clay wastes rimmed and pitted everywhere.
"You hungry?—Have some of this, there's enough for two."
We drove through Bayonvillers—and as we ate
men long since dead reached out and left a smirch
and taste in our throats like gas and rotten jam.
"Want any more?"
        "Yes sir, if you got enough there."
"Those fellows smell pretty strong."
        "I'll say they do,
but I'm too hungry sir to care a damn."

        —John Allan Wyeth[136] (1929)

The Battle of Amiens began on August 8, 1918. By the close of the day, the Germans had lost an estimated 27,000 men, 12,000 of whom had surrendered. German Commander-in-Chief Erich Ludendorff described it as "the black day of the German Army." By the end of the battle, German casualties totaled 75,000, but Allied losses were also staggeringly high: 44,000 men had been killed or wounded.[137] As Allied troops pushed forward in the heat of summer, they moved through a charnel house of corpses. In his memoir *I Remember the Last War*, AEF Sergeant Bob Hoffman writes,

> Three weeks these men had lain in the sun and our troops set out to bury them … Did you ever smell a dead mouse? This will give you about as much idea of what a group of long dead soldiers smell like as will one grain of sand give you an idea of Atlantic City's beaches … It was hard to touch these dead men at first. My people at home, hearing of what I was passing through, expected me to come back hard, brutal, callous, careless. But I didn't even want to take a dead mouse out of a trap when I was home. Yet over there I buried seventy-eight men one morning … They were shot up in a great variety of ways, and it was not pleasant,

---

[136] See also Wyeth's "The Transport" and "Night Watch."
[137] Saul David, *100 Days to Victory*, Hodder and Stoughton, 2013, pp. 447–449.

but I managed to eat my quota of bread and meat when it came up with no opportunity to wash my hands.[138]

In "Picnic: Harbonnières to Bayonvillers," John Allan Wyeth narrates the account of American soldiers riding through the scene of an earlier battle. The poem's title names two small villages, approximately three miles apart, both taken by the Allies on August 8, 1918. Eyewitness accounts describe a landscape littered with bodies and wreckage left in the wake of the attack. It's a disturbing setting for a picnic, and the poem's title is an ironic play on words, as *picnic* is an American slang term used since the 1870s to refer to something as "easy or straightforward ... a pushover."[139]

Although Wyeth was a staff officer and interpreter, his work as an intelligence courier brought him near the front lines, where he came under fire from artillery and aerial bombardment.[140] Wyeth's war writings reveal him to be "an astute witness"—whether of natural phenomena, the peripheries of battle, or the idiosyncrasies of soldiers.[141] Kendall notes that Wyeth's war sonnets alter the traditional form, "with a rhyme scheme of Wyeth's own invention (abcdabcdabecde) and an extraordinarily acute ear for the pentameter-busting rhythms of everyday conversation ... Among his contemporaries, perhaps only Robert Frost matches that nuanced appreciation of the speaking voice."[142] Although Wyeth has been described as "perhaps the finest American soldier poet of World War I,"[143] he left the army after the war and did not pursue a career as a writer. He briefly taught French at St. Paul's School in New Hampshire, then left teaching to spend the remainder of his life as a painter. Wyeth lived in Europe for most of the 1930s and 1940s, and historian B.J. Omanson suggests he may have worked a spy, reporting to British and American intelligence communities on Nazi activities.[144] In later life, he returned to America; Wyeth died at age eighty-six in Princeton, New Jersey.

---

[138] Bob Hoffman, *I Remember the Last War*, Strength and Health Publishing, 1940, pp. 161, 162, 165–166.
[139] "Picnic, *n, adj, and adv*, 3. colloquial." *Oxford English Dictionary Online*, Oxford UP, Mar. 2019, www.oed.com/view/Entry/143450.
[140] B.J. Omanson, *Before the Clangor of the Gun: The First World War Poetry of John Allan Wyeth*, Monongahela, 2019, p. 70.
[141] Omanson, *Before the Clangor*, p. 70.
[142] Tim Kendall, "John Allan Wyeth's Dead Landscapes," *Dead Ground 2018–1918*, edited by Andrew McNeillie and James McNeillie, Clutag, 2018, p. 192.
[143] Dana Gioia, "This Man's Army by John Allan Wyeth, Jr.," *War, Literature, and the Arts*, vol. 16, no. 1/2, 2004, p. 269.
[144] Omanson, *Before the Clangor*, pp. 75–91.

The Bathe

Come friend and swim. We may be better then,
    But here the dust blows ever in the eyes
And wrangling round are weary fevered men,
    For ever mad with flies.
I cannot sleep, nor even long lie still,
    And you have read your April paper twice;
To-morrow we must stagger up the hill
    To man a trench and live among the lice.

But yonder, where the Indians have their goats,
    There is a rock stands sheer above the blue,
Where one may sit and count the bustling boats
    And breathe the cool air through;
May find it still is good to be alive,
    May look across and see the Trojan shore
Twinkling and warm, may strip, and stretch, and dive.—
    And for a space forget about the war.

Then will we sit and talk of happy things,
    Home and 'the High' and some far fighting friend,
And gather strength for what the morrow brings,
    For that may be the end.
It may be we shall never swim again,
    Never be clean and comely to the sight,
May rot untombed and stink with all the slain.
    Come, then and swim. Come and be clean to-night.

—A.P. Herbert (1916)

The Gallipoli campaign was the Allies' attempt to establish a sea route between Russia and the Mediterranean and was launched on April 25, 1915, when troops landed on the shores of the Turkish peninsula. By early June, Allied troops had twice attacked Turkish positions on the high ground just beyond the village of Krithia, failing in both attempts. The Third Battle of Krithia was launched at noon on June 4, 1915, as part of British command's attempt to maintain "ceaseless initiative," an ironic description of a campaign that resulted in an estimated 500,000 total casualties. On May 24 of 1915, the stench of bodies decaying between the lines caused a truce to be called so that the dead of both sides could be buried. One of the men assigned to the burial detail recalls,

> Some of the bodies were rotted so much that there were only bones and part of the uniform left. The bodies of the men killed on the nineteenth (it had now been five days) were awful. Most of us had to work in short spells as we felt very ill. We found a few of our men who had been killed in the first days of the landing.[145]

Most likely at some time in the next ten days, just before the attack of early June, A.P. Herbert wrote "The Bathe." Herbert had swum off the coast of Turkey with his friends before the battle. His friend and fellow Oxford graduate Lieutenant William Ker described the experience in a letter home dated May 30, 1915:

> You never saw such a conglomeration of strange troops. You should have seen me and A. P. Herbert the other evening bathing in the Dardanelles near some Frenchmen and Senegalese, with the Turkish lines (or, rather, the place where they were) in sight on a ridge to our left beside some dismantled forts, the Plain of Troy before us on the other side, some guns on the Asiatic side sending an occasional shrapnel shell over on our right, and a French battery immediately behind us having shots at them ... I took a bathing party down to the beach yesterday. The scene was a cross between Blackpool in the season and the Ganges ... The men think it a fine picnic, but we are going into the firing line to-morrow night.[146]

On June 4, Herbert joined the attack with his unit, the Hawke Battalion. He survived Gallipoli and other battles on the Western Front, but was seriously wounded in April of 1917 and invalided back to England. His friend William Ker also survived Gallipoli, but was killed on November 13, 1916, at Beaucourt.[147]

---

[145] A.B. Facey, *A Fortunate Life*, Viking Penguin, 1984, p. 269.
[146] Qtd. in *The Hawke Battalion*, by Douglas Jerrold, Ernest Benn, 1925, p. 51 [ellipsis in original text].
[147] It is believed that William Ker is the "William" referenced in Herbert's poem "Beaucourt Revisited" (included in this anthology): "And here the lads went over, and there was Harmsworth shot, / And here was William lying—but the new men know them not."

Going In

   We went down to the lake
Yesterday, half a hundred friends and I,
   And laughed and sang to shake
The clouds in the sky.

   The golden sunlight splashed
Through the half-asleep contented trees,
   To where sun-brown bodies flashed
And sprawled at ease....

   There are three things of worth
(Let me say this much before all ends)—
   Loveliness, and mirth,
These, and friends.

   I have had my fill of these three;
The earth is very full of lovely things—
   Trees, and hills, and the sea
Full of gulls' wings.

   I have had my fill of these three;
The earth is very full of mirthful things—
   Thank God for all there be
Whence laughter springs.

   I have had my fill of these three;
Friendship is the greatest gift God sends—
   All men were brothers to me,
Most were my friends....

   God, take my life to-day
Before the leaves of loveliness are shed,
   And mirth is hid away,
And friends are dead.
          (Ypres, August 1917 and Carlisle, November 1917)
                        —Henry Lamont Simpson

Numerous war poems describe soldiers bathing; Paul Fussell in *The Great War and Modern Memory* explains,

> Watching men (usually "one's own" men) bathing naked becomes a set-piece scene in almost every memory of the war. And this conventional vignette of soldiers bathing under the affectionate eye of their young officer recurs not because soldiers bathe but because there's hardly a better way of projecting poignantly the awful vulnerability of mere naked flesh ... the stark contrast between beautiful frail flesh and the alien metal that waits to violate it.[148]

In Simpson's poem, it is not only men's bodies that are vulnerable, but their minds and emotions. Worse than the fear of dying in battle is that of watching one's friends die.

Lieutenant Henry Lamont Simpson was the son of a tailor from Newcastle. Raised in Carlisle, he attended Carlisle Grammar School (now Trinity School) and won numerous prizes in maths, reading, French, and classics. Awarded a scholarship to Cambridge at Pembroke College, Simpson deferred admission and instead joined the Lancashire Fusiliers in 1917. By July of that year, he was planning a book of poetry and sending drafts of his manuscript to his former teacher H.C. Duffin. Wounded in September of 1917, Simpson composed an epitaph for himself while in hospital:

> R.I.P.
> ---
> H.L.S.
> HE MADE SOME BAD VERSE AND MANY
> GOOD FRIENDS, BUT HE HAD AN
> ABSOLUTE GENIUS FOR FALLING
> ON HIS FEET[149]

In a letter to his former teacher, the young lieutenant wrote,

> I believe with all my heart that man is, in the main, a loveable, and, at bottom, a good creature. (Curse the word good! but you know what I mean—worthy, sterling, right, true, real.) He sings dirty songs and swears, and is altogether a sensual drunken brute at times; but get to know him, start by loving him, believe in him through thick and thin, and you will not go unrewarded.[150]

---

[148] Paul Fussell, *The Great War and Modern Memory*, Oxford UP, 2000, p. 299.
[149] Henry Lamont Simpson, *Moods and Tenses*, Erskine Macdonald, 1919, p. 9.
[150] Simpson, *Moods and Tenses*, pp. 8, 10.

Simpson's poetry was published in 1919 in the volume *Moods and Tenses*, and Duffin's introductory note states that it is "obvious from his poems that Simpson was a worshipper at the shrine of that brightest of youth's ideals, friendship."[151] The majority of poems had been written before Simpson joined up or during his military training, but ten poems were composed after he arrived at the front. One of these—"Going In"—was started while Simpson was fighting in the Ypres sector and revised while Simpson recovered from his wounds at Carlisle. Elizabeth Vandiver in *Stand in the Trench, Achilles* argues that Simpson's "poetic trajectory is an almost textbook example of the traditional paradigm for a Great War poet; direct experience of the front hurtled him out of his mannered and old-fashioned poetry into new forms and new vocabulary."[152]

Less than three months after his twenty-first birthday, in August of 1918, Henry Lamont Simpson was killed by a sniper while reconnoitering in No Man's Land. His father wrote to the Master of Pembroke, "It is my painful duty to notify you that my son 2nd Lieut, HL Simpson, for whom you were holding a scholarship, was killed in action in France on August 28th."[153] Duffin, Simpson's former teacher, ensured that Simpson's poems were published, noting, "On the whole, the grisly experience of the Western Front—though he hated it, as all good men must hate such hateful things—was good for his verse … the shock of war—though for a time it killed in him all desire to write—sent his power along new channels."[154] His body was never recovered: Henry Lamont Simpson's name is one of 9,847 listed on the Vis-en-Artois memorial to the missing.

---

[151] H.C. Duffin, "Introductory Remarks," *Moods and Tenses*, p. 8.
[152] Elizabeth Vandiver, *Stand in the Trench, Achilles*, Oxford UP, 2010, p. 92.
[153] Henry C. Simpson, qtd. in "Henry Lamont Simpson," *Trinity School War Memorials*, web.archive.org/web/20190824185743/https://www.trinity.cumbria.sch.uk/warmemorials/henry-lamont-simpson/.
[154] Duffin, "Introductory Remarks," p. 7.

A Song of the Air

This is the song of the Plane—
  The creaking, shrieking plane,
  The throbbing, sobbing plane,
And the moaning, groaning wires:—
  The engine—missing again!
  One cylinder never fires!
      Hey ho! for the Plane!

This is the song of the Man—
  The driving, striving man,
  The chosen, frozen man:—
The pilot, the man-at-the-wheel,
  Whose limit is all that he *can*,
  And beyond, if the need is real!
      Hey ho! for the Man!

This is the song of the Gun—
  The muttering, stuttering gun,
  The maddening, gladdening gun:—
That chuckles with evil glee
  At the last, long dive of the Hun,
  With its end in eternity!
      Hey ho! for the Gun!

This is the song of the Air—
  The lifting, drifting air,
  The eddying, steadying air,
The wine of its limitless space:—
  May it nerve us at last to dare
  Even death with undaunted face!
      Hey ho! for the Air!

—Gordon Alchin (1916)

Flight was in its infancy at the start of the First World War. The Wright brothers' first successful attempt had occurred just over ten years earlier in December of 1903, and it wasn't until September of 1904 that they managed to maneuver their plane in a circle. Before that, flights had been limited to short, straight lifts over a flat field. Yet the military was relatively quick to recognize and develop the killing power of the flying machine: the first use of massed airplane squadrons for strategic bombing occurred in September of 1914, and the first time a machine gun was mounted to a plane for aerial combat was in the spring of 1915.[155] During the course of the war, the speed of airplanes and the maximum altitude at which they could fly doubled, while their load-bearing capacity increased many times over.[156] Airplanes came to serve an important role in reconnaissance missions, bombing raids, enemy aircraft attacks, and support of infantry, but it is the glamour and adventure of the men and their flying machines that have persisted, recounted in story and song.

Captain Gordon Alchin was a classical scholar at Oxford (Brasenose) when war was declared. An early volunteer, he was commissioned in August of 1914 with the Royal Field Artillery, and by January of 1915 he was at the Western Front. He saw action in the Ypres Salient at St. Eloi and was gassed in April at the Second Battle of Ypres. In June of 1915, Alchin volunteered as an observer; he trained flying BE2c's and was appointed flying officer/observer in late November of 1915. Just days after Christmas of that year, while taking off for a reconnaissance flight, Alchin's plane failed to clear the trees and crashed. His injuries sent him back to England to recover, and during his time in hospital, he wrote many of the poems published in *Oxford and Flanders*; the volume was published in June of 1916 anonymously (its author identified only as "Observer, R.F.C."). Alchin rejoined the RAF in May of 1916 and returned to service in the Ypres Sector. That he survived the war is remarkable, as he logged "some 2000 hours flying as Observer, Flying Officer, Flt Cdr [Flight Commander] and Squadron Cdr."[157] He was awarded the Air Force Cross for his service. Returning to civilian life in 1919, Alchin completed his studies at Oxford and pursued a career in law. When England entered the Second World War, he rejoined the RAF Volunteer Reserve Force as a pilot officer, but was assigned to Intelligence before being appointed as a judge of County Courts, a position he held until his death in 1947.

---

[155] Aaron Norman, *The Great Air War*, Macmillan, 1968, pp. 41, 55–56.
[156] Lee Kennett, *The First Air War: 1914–1918*, Free Press, 1991, p. 93.
[157] Ronald Dixon, "Captain Gordon Alchin, AFC, RFA, RFC, RAF," *Cross and Cockade International*, vol. 17, no. 3, 1986, pp. 114–120.

To a Taube

Above the valley, rich and fair,
    On flashing pinions, glittering, gay,
You hover in the upper air,
    A bird of prey.

Snarling across the empty blue
    You curve and skim, you dip and soar,
A dove in flight and shape and hue—
    The dove of war.

Above the soldier and the slain,
    An armoured bird, you hang on high,
Directed by a human brain,
    A human eye.

A thirsty hunter out for blood—
    Drinking adventure to the dregs—
Where hidden camps the country stud
    You drop your eggs.

Thus, man, who reasons and invents,
    Has inconsistently designed
The conquest of the elements
    To kill his kind.

—Jessie Pope (1915)

The Taube was the first military airplane to be mass-produced in Germany, its name translated in English as *dove*. A 1914 military journal wrote that the plane in flight "gives the impression of a pigeon resting on its wings," but it was heavy and slow, as well as being "badly designed for bomb-dropping, as the pilot cannot see directly below, but only straight ahead."[158] Although Taubes were more commonly used for German reconnaissance, the sight of any enemy aircraft overhead was likely to inspire fear and panic. During the First World War, German airplanes dropped over 300 tons of explosives on England; it is estimated that British pilots dropped over 660 tons of explosives on Germany.[159]

---

[158] "On Varied Ground: The German Taube Monoplane," *Infantry Journal,* vol. 11, United States Infantry Association, 1915, p. 526.

[159] Earl H. Tilford, Jr., "Air Warfare: Strategic Bombing," *The European Powers in the First World War,* edited by Spencer Tucker, Laura Matysek Wood, and Justin D. Murphy, Taylor and Francis, 1999, p. 15.

Before the war, Jessie Pope was a popular British writer of comic and light verse. The three volumes of war poems that she published during the conflict were "very popular with the troops, and Pope received letters of appreciation from soldiers all over the world."[160] Her work offered readers narratives of purpose and patriotism, and it is likely that she reflected public opinion as much as she shaped it. Over 100 years later, she may be one of the best known and most disliked of the female war poets: this is largely due to Wilfred Owen's draft inscription to "Dulce et Decorum Est," in which he caustically dedicates the poem to her. Jane Potter writes that Owen's "original dedication has in many ways damned Pope: her fate as a woman who seemingly ignored the suffering of soldiers was sealed when Owen achieved canonical status."[161] Seldom is it noted that Pope's writing often raised money for war charities or that she volunteered at St. Dunstan's hospital for blind soldiers and the Great Ormond Street Children's Hospital.[162] Potter argues, "Pope's reputation as an ultra-jingoistic supporter of the war is a one-sided characterisation that has obscured a more multi-faceted, popular writer, who was a successful brand in her day."[163] Comparing Pope and Owen, Potter explains that the two writers "were indeed opposites. Owen was a serious young man who longed for literary immortality; Pope was a professional writer who was more concerned with earning a living through her work as a humourist."[164] Other scholars have also argued that Pope's writings are "more double-edged than they first appear."[165]

---

[160] Nosheen Khan, *Women's Poetry of the First World War*, UP of Kentucky, 1988, p. 19.
[161] Jane Potter, "'A Certain Poetess': Recuperating Jessie Pope (1868–1941)," *Landscapes and Voices of the Great War*, edited by Angela K. Smith and Krista Cowman, Routledge, 2017, p. 98.
[162] Vivien Newman, *Tumult and Tears*, Pen and Sword, 2016, p. 185.
[163] Potter, "Rehabilitating," p. 98.
[164] Potter, "Rehabilitating," p. 109.
[165] Andrew Maunder, *The Short Story and the Novella*, Pickering and Chatto, 2011, p. 173.

The Hill

From the top of the hill I looked down on the beautiful, the gorgeous, the super-human and monstrous landscape of the superb exulting war.
There were no trees anywhere, nor any grasses or green thickets, nor any birds singing, nor any whisper or flutter of any little busy creatures.
There was no shelter for field mice or rabbits, squirrels or men.
The earth was naked and on its naked body crawled things of iron.
It was evening. The long valley was bathed in blue shadow and through the shadow, as if swimming, I saw the iron armies moving.
And iron rivers poured through the wilderness that was peopled with a phantom iron host.
Lights gleamed down there, a thousand machine eyes winked.
The sun was setting, gilding the smooth crests of the surging hills. The red tents clustering on their naked yellow sides were like scarlet flowers burning in a shining desert of hills.
Against the sunset, along the sharp edge of a hill, a strange regiment was moving in single file, a regiment of monsters.
They moved slowly along on their stomachs,
Dragging themselves forward by their ears.
Their great encircling ears moved round and round like wheels.
They were big and very heavy and heavily armoured.
Obscene crabs, armoured toads, big as houses,
They moved slowly forward, crushing under their bellies whatever stood in their way.
A flock of aeroplanes was flying home, a flight of wild ducks with iron wings.
They passed over the monstrous regiment with a roar and disappeared.
I looked down, searching for a familiar thing, a leaf, a tuft of grass, a caterpillar; but the ground dropped away in darkness before my feet, that were planted on a heap of stones.
A path, the old deserted way of cattle, showed below beyond the gaping caverns of abandoned dug-outs, where men had once lived underground. And along the path a German prisoner was stumbling, driven by a black man on a horse.
The black man wore a turban, and he drove the prisoner before him as one drives an animal to market.
These three—the prisoner, the black man and the horse—seemed to have wandered into the landscape by mistake. They were the only creatures of their kind anywhere.
Where had they come from and where were they going in that wilderness of iron with night falling?

> The German stumbled on heavily beneath the nose of his captor's horse. I could see the pallid disc of his face thrust forward, and the exhausted lurching of his clumsy body.
> He did not look to the right or left, but watching him I saw him trip over a battered iron helmet and an old boot that lay in his way.
> Two wooden crosses showed just ahead of him, sticking out of the rough ground.
> The three passed in silence.
> They passed like ghosts into the deepening shadow of the valley, where the panorama of invisible phantom armies moved, as if swimming.
> And as I watched I heard the faint music of bagpipes, and thought that I heard the sound of invisible men marching.
> The crests of the naked hills were still touched with gold.
> Above the winking eyes of the prodigious war the fragile crescent of the moon floated serene in the perfect sky.
>
> —Mary Borden[166] (1929)

On September 15, 1916, the British Army recorded the first use in battle of a newly developed weapon: the tank. Originally known as a land battleship, the term *tank* was adopted to preserve secrecy during the development of the armored vehicles (factory workers had noted their resemblance to steel water tanks). Writing shortly after the war's end in 1919, historian Francis March explains, "Originally this was a caterpillar tractor invented in America and adopted in England. At first these were of two varieties, the male, carrying heavy guns only, and the females, equipped with machine guns … All the tanks were heavily armored and had as their motto the words 'Treat 'Em Rough.'"[167] March comments, "Never since the dawn of time had there been such a perversion of knowledge to criminal purposes; never had science contributed such a deadly toll to the fanatic and criminal intentions of a war-crazed class."[168]

While serving at a French field hospital at the Somme, Anglo-American nurse Mary Borden witnessed the newly introduced "regiment of monsters"; her description of the scene resembles a medieval vision painted by Hieronymus Bosch. Borden's poem "The Hill" appears in her war memoir, *The Forbidden Zone*, in which she describes the nightmarish world that the war has created:

> The great gun down by the river is roaring, is shouting. What a relief! That I understand—that giant's voice. He is a friend—another familiar, monstrous

---
[166] See also Borden's "Song of the Mud."
[167] Francis A. March, *History of the World War,* United Publishers, 1919, p. 217.
[168] March, *History of the World War,* p. 217.

friend. I know him. I listen every night for his roar. I long to hear it. But it is dying away now. The echo goes growling down the valley, and again the trees and the grasses begin that murmuring and whispering. They are lying. It is a lie they are saying. There are no lovely forgotten things. The other world was a dream. Beyond the gauze curtain of the tender night there is War, and nothing else but War. Hounds of war, growling, howling; bulls of war, bellowing, snorting; war eagles, shrieking and screaming; war fiends banging at the gates of Heaven, howling at the open gates of hell. There is War on the earth—nothing but War, War let loose in the world, War—nothing left in the whole world but War—War, world without end, amen.[169]

---

[169] Mary Borden, *The Forbidden Zone,* William Heinemann, 1929, pp. 57–58.

Ammunition Column

I am only a cog in a giant machine, a link of an endless chain:—
And the rounds are drawn, and the rounds are fired, and the empties return again;
Railroad, lorry, and limber, battery, column, and park;
To the shelf where the set fuze waits the breech, from the quay where the shells embark.
We have watered and fed, and eaten our beef: the long dull day drags by,
As I sit here watching our "Archibalds"[170] *strafing* an empty sky;
Puff and flash on the far-off blue round the speck one guesses the plane—
Smoke and spark of the gun-machine that is fed by the endless chain.

I am only a cog in a giant machine, a little link of the chain,
Waiting a word from the wagon-lines that the guns are hungry again:—
Column-wagon to battery-wagon, and battery-wagon to gun;
To the loader kneeling 'twixt trail and wheel from the shops where the steam-lathes run.
There's a lone mule braying against the line where the mud cakes fetlock-deep;
There's a lone soul humming a hint of a song in the barn where the drivers sleep;
And I hear the pash of the orderly's horse as he canters him down the lane—
Another cog in the gun-machine, a link in the self-same chain.

I am only a cog in a giant machine, but a vital link of the chain;
And the Captain has sent from the wagon-line to fill his wagons again:—
From wagon-limber to gunpit dump; from loader's forearm at breech,
To the working party that melts away when the shrapnel bullets screech.
So the restless section pulls out once more, in column of route from the right,
At the tail of a blood-red afternoon; so the flux of another night
Bears back the wagons we fill at dawn to the sleeping column again—
Cog on cog in the gun-machine, link on link in the chain!

—Gilbert Frankau (1917)

Over thirty million artillery shells were fired during the battle of Verdun, and over 3,000 artillery guns were used by the Allies during the Third Battle of Ypres. During the battle of High Wood on August 24, 1916, it is estimated that ten British machine guns fired over one million rounds in twelve hours. The death toll was staggering: over thirty-five million men were killed or wounded, and on

---

[170] British slang term for anti-aircraft fire.

average, 230 soldiers died each hour of every day during a conflict that lasted over four years.[171]

Gilbert Frankau joined the British Army in 1914 and was transferred to the Royal Field Artillery in early 1915. He fought at Loos, Ypres, and the Somme, but left the army "on account of ill-health contracted on active service" in February of 1918.[172] His younger brother Paul was killed in early November of 1917 during an attack on Gaza, part of the Sinai and Palestine Campaign.

In the years following the war, Frankau became a popular writer. He was described in 1926 as "one of the most widely read novelists of the present day," and a 1940 review for *Punch* praised him as "perhaps as good a storyteller as we have in England at this moment."[173] But today, Frankau is best remembered for his racial and political views. Raised as an Anglican, he had a "vexed and obsessive relation to his own Jewishness" (Frankau wasn't told he was Jewish until he was sixteen).[174] His post-war fiction frequently draws contrasts between "good Jews" (those with money and education who are not discernably Jewish) and "bad Jews" (left-wing socialists from Eastern Europe).[175] Many of his novels present one-dimensional racial stereotypes and assert that character traits based on race and ethnicity are genetically determined.[176] Frankau was an early supporter of Mussolini, but the main source of his notoriety is his 1933 article that appeared in the *Daily Express*, "As a Jew I Am Not against Hitler." As more information about Nazi Germany reached England, Frankau recanted his earlier position. In his 1939 memoir he described the Nazi regime "as a 'virus' and admitted he had been 'too intolerant, too intransigeant, too much the diehard' 15 years earlier."[177] Shortly before his death in 1952, Frankau converted to Roman Catholicism.

---

[171] Scott Addington, *The Great War 100*, History Press, 2014.
[172] *Supplement to the London Gazette*, 21 Feb. 1918, p. 2286.
[173] Todd M. Endelman, "The Frankaus of London: A Study in Radical Assimilation, 1837–1967," *Jewish History*, vol. 8, nos. 1/2, 1994, p. 137.
[174] Caroline Gonda, "'A Roller-coaster of a Life with Everything in It': Pamela Frankau (1908–1967)," *Jewish/Christian/Queer: Crossroads and Identities*, edited by Frederick Roden, Routledge, 2016, p. 183.
[175] Endelman, "The Frankaus of London," p. 139.
[176] Endelman, "The Frankaus of London," p. 138.
[177] Endelman, "The Frankaus of London," p. 142.

Unloading Ambulance Train

Into the siding very wearily
She comes again:
Singing her endless song so drearily,
The midnight winds sink down to drift the rain.

So she comes home once more.

Is it an ancient chanty
Won from some classic shore?
The stretcher-bearers stand
Two on either hand.
They bend and lift and raise
Where the doors open wide
With yellow light ablaze.
Into the dark outside
Each stretcher passes. Here
(As if each on his bier
With sorrow they were bringing)
Is peace, and a low singing.

The ambulances load,
Move on and take the road.
Under the stars alone
Each stretcher passes out.
And the ambulances' moan
And the checker's distant shout
All round to the old sound
Of the lost chanty singing.
And the dark seamen swinging.
Far off some classic shore…

So she comes home once more.
Wimereux, Sept. 1918

—Carola Oman[178]

In addition to the nine million soldiers who died in the First World War, over twenty million men were seriously wounded. Complex challenges were involved in transporting men who had suffered the effects of artillery shelling, grenade

---

[178] See also Oman's "In the Ypres Sector" and "To the Survivors."

explosions, machine-gun fire, gas attacks, frostbite, and shell shock to places where they could receive medical care. The wounded either crawled behind the lines or were carried there by stretcher bearers or comrades-in-arms. Taken to advanced dressing stations or *postes des secours*, those fortunate enough to survive were then driven by ambulance to casualty clearing stations. From there, the most common means of transporting the wounded was the ambulance train. Stretching for as long as one-third of a mile, a typical ambulance train was equipped with a kitchen, rows of bunks for the most seriously wounded, carriages with seats for the injured who could sit upright, an operating and pharmaceutical carriage, and housing quarters for orderlies, nurses, and doctors. The diary of a nurse assigned to an ambulance train describes a typical scene:

> We had 368; a good 200 were dangerously and seriously wounded, perhaps more; and the sitting-up cases were bad enough … nearly all the men had more than one wound—some had ten; one man with a huge compound fracture above the elbow had tied on a bit of string with a bullet in it as a tourniquet above the wound himself … They were bleeding faster than we could cope with it; and the agony of getting them off the stretchers on to the top bunks is a thing to forget. We were full up by about 2 a.m., and then were delayed by a collision up the line, which was blocked by dead horses as a result. All night and without a break till we got back to Boulogne at 4 p.m. next day (yesterday) we grappled with them … The head cases were delirious, and trying to get out of the window, and we were giving strychnine and morphia all round. Two were put off dying at St Omer, but we kept the rest alive to Boulogne.[179]

On July 1, 1916, as British troops in France were suffering tremendous casualties on the first day of the Battle of the Somme, twenty-year-old Carola Oman joined the British Red Cross as a nurse without pay and served until April of 1919. She dedicated her book of war poetry, *The Menin Road and Other Poems* (1919), to four of her friends and fellow volunteer nurses: Lillian Chapman, Janet Dundas Allen, Una Barron, and May Wedderburn Cannan.

---

[179] Katherine Luard [published anonymously], *Diary of a Nursing Sister on the Western Front,* William Blackwood and Sons, 1915, pp. 89–90.

Gramophone Tunes

Through the long ward the gramophone
   Grinds out its nasal melodies:
"Where did you get that girl?" it shrills.
   The patients listen at their ease,
Through clouds of strong tobacco-smoke:
   The gramophone can always please.

The Welsh boy has it by his bed,
   (He's lame—one leg was blown away.)
He'll lie propped up with pillows there,
   And wind the handle half the day.
His neighbor, with the shattered arm,
   Picks out the records he must play.

Jock with his crutches beats the time;
   The gunner, with his head close-bound,
Listens with puzzled, patient smile:
   (Shell-shock—he cannot hear a sound.)
The others join in from their beds,
   And send the chorus rolling round.

Somehow for me these common tunes
   Can never sound the same again:
They've magic now to thrill my heart
   And bring before me, clear and plain,
Man that is master of his flesh,
   And has the laugh of death and pain.

—Eva Dobell (1919)

Popular music provided the soundtrack of the First World War. Troops sang "It's a Long Way to Tipperary" as they marched toward rail stations that would take them far from their homes; mothers, wives, and sweethearts promised to "Keep the Home Fires Burning"; and many tunes encouraged soldiers to laugh at the war, from "Pack Up Your Troubles in Your Old Kit Bag" to "Mademoiselle from Armentieres." The recently invented portable phonograph brought the melodies of the music halls into hospitals crowded with wounded and dying men. The song "Where Did You Get That Girl" referenced in "Gramophone Tunes" was a comic tune that charted at #6 in 1913. Its lyrics tell of a lonely lad whose luck turns, causing all who meet him to exclaim,

Where did you get that girl? Oh! you lucky devil.
Where did you get that girl? Tell me on the level
Have you ever kissed her? If she has a sister
Lead me, lead me, lead me to her mister![180]

Volunteer Aid Detachment (VAD) nurse Vera Brittain hated the "blaring, blatant gramophones" of the hospital wards, commenting that "though the men found them consoling—perhaps because they subdued more sinister noises—they seemed to me to add a strident grotesqueness to the cold, dark evenings of hurry and pain."[181]

The author of "Gramophone Tunes," Eva (Eveline Jesse) Dobell, lived in Charlton Kings, Gloucestershire, before joining the British Red Cross as a volunteer nurse in early November of 1914. She worked thirty-six hours a week without pay for over three years until she received a discharge in November of 1917. The dedication to her 1919 volume of poetry, *A Bunch of Cotswold Grasses*, reads, "Part of the proceeds from this book will be devoted to 'St. Martin's,' Glos. Red Cross Hospital for Disabled Soldiers."[182]

---

[180] Bert Kalmar and Harry Puck, "Where Did You Get That Girl?" Kalmar and Puck Music Company, 1913.
[181] Vera Brittain, *Testament of Youth,* Virago, 2014, p. 196.
[182] Eva Dobell, *A Bunch of Cotswold Grasses,* Arthur H. Stockwell, 1919.

Quinze Vingt

Their last sight was the red sight of battle,
and they will see no other thing,
down all their lives.
They sit in darkness,
and are very silent.
They are all young,
and all their lives they must sit still,
in darkness.

At the door of their house is hopelessness.
Hopelessness waits at the door of their house.

Hopelessness is thick and dense.
It has no wet of tears.
One could take hopelessness in one's hands,
and make a bandage of it
to bind about one's eyes.

It would be dry and stiff,
and hurt one's eyes.

They are all young and strong.
They will have long to live,
and to be blind.

—Helen Mackay (1916)

The poem's title, "Quinze Vingt," refers to the National Ophthalmology Hospital in Paris: *Les Quinze-Vingts: Centre Hospitalier National d'Ophtalmologie*. Founded by French king Louis IX in 1260, the Quinze Vingt was transformed into a military hospital for the blind during the First World War.

American writer Helen Mackay was in France when the war began. She kept a diary, later published as *Journal of Small Things*, which shares "random memories of a sympathetic friend of France" and records her observations as she visited Paris and rural towns.[183] Struck by the human cost of the conflict, Mackay describes a *dépôt d'éclopés* (literally translated as a *depot for the lame*):

> The dépôt d'éclopés is just beyond the town, on the Roman road ... All day long, and every day, as many of the éclopés as can get about, and do not mind that the

---

[183] W.L. Courtney, "Preface," *Journal of Small Things*, by Helen Mackay, Duffield, 1917.

road see them, and can find space in the shade of the plane tree, sit there, and look up and down the sunshine and the dust.

Some of them have one leg, and some of them have one arm. There is one of them who is packed into a short box on wheels. He sits up straight in the box, and he can run it about with his hands on the wheels. There is another in such a little cart, but that one has to lie on his back, and cannot manage the wheels himself. There is one who lies on a long stretcher, that they fix on two hurdles. There are two who are blind. The two blind men sit, and stare and stare ...

The two blind men at the gate who stare and stare, they cannot see the golden town or the golden mountains. They cannot see the compassion and the kindness that there is for them in the faces of all those who look upon them.[184]

Mackay lived much of her life in France, writing in both French and English (her novel *Patte Blanche* won a French Academy literary prize in 1929). She is most noted, however, for her humanitarian work during both world wars, for which the French government awarded her the Chevalier Legion of Honour. During the Second World War, her rural home in France was requisitioned for the safeguarding of the treasures of the Louvre.[185] Despite publishing her 1915 journal and a 1916 volume of war poetry, Mackay struggled with the incomprehensibility of the First World War, confessing at one point, "I try not to write. The only things worth saying are the things I do not know how to say."[186]

---

[184] Helen Mackay, *Journal of Small Things*, pp. 42–43, 44.
[185] "French Hail Novel by American Woman," *New York Times*, 10 Nov. 1929, p. E45; "Helen G. Mackay, Author and Poet," *New York Times*, 19 May 1961, p. 31.
[186] Mackay, *Journal*, p. 35.

Little Song of the Maimed (Petite Chanson des Mutilés)

Lend me your arm
to replace my leg
The rats ate it for me
at Verdun
at Verdun
I ate lots of rats
but they didn't give me back my leg
and that's why I was given the CROIX DE GUERRE
and a wooden leg
and a wooden leg

—Benjamin Péret (1936) translated by David Gascoyne

Germans called the battle of Verdun "the Meat Grinder"; the French named it "the Cauldron." At Verdun, the Germans attempted to goad the French into a fight that was beyond the point of rational calculation, a battle that would "bleed France white." Lasting from February 21, 1916 to December 18, 1916, the battle of Verdun produced horrific conditions that drove men mad. Over twenty-three million artillery shells were fired; entire villages were destroyed, and an estimated 650,000 men were killed.[187] French cubist artist Fernand Léger, the victim of a mustard gas attack at Verdun, describes his impressions of the battlefield:

> I could see out over an area of ten square kilometers that had been turned into a uniform desert of brown earth. The men were all so tiny and lost in it that I could hardly see them. A shell fell in the midst of these little things, which moved for a moment, carrying off the wounded—the dead, as unimportant as so many ants, were left behind. They were no bigger than ants down there. The artillery dominates everything. A formidable, intelligent weapon, striking everywhere with such desperate consistency.[188]

Benjamin Péret is one of the preeminent poets of Surrealism. At the age of sixteen, he joined the French army at his mother's urging and served as a *cuirassier* from 1917–1919.[189] When later asked how he had gotten his start in life, Péret replied, "The 1914 war, which made everything easy!"[190] For the

---

[187] Martin Gilbert, *The First World War: A Complete History*, Henry Holt, 1994, pp. 299–300.
[188] Fernand Léger, letter to Louis Poughon, 7 Nov. 1916, qtd. in *Fernand Léger: Une Correspondance de Guerre à Louis Poughon, 1914-1918*, edited by Christian Derouet, Centre Georges Pompidou, 1997, p. 68.
[189] Julia Field Costich, *The Poetry of Change*, U of North Carolina P, 1979, p. 109.
[190] J.H. Matthews, *Benjamin Péret*, Twayne, 1975, p. 19.

remainder of his life, Péret's art was shaped by his contempt for and rejection of nationalism, the military establishment, and the Church and State, which had, in his view, conspired together to lead France to war. "Petite Chanson des Mutilés" was published in his collection *Je ne mange pas de ce pain-là*. Together with "Hymne des anciens combattants patriotes," and "Epitaphe pour un monument aux morts de la guerre," the three poems appear as a veteran's trilogy, poems that express "compassion along with contempt for those who have willingly sacrificed themselves to the chimera of military glory."[191]

---

[191] Costich, *Poetry of Change*, p. 109.

2

Minds at War

Poetry expressed the psychological traumas of the First World War, but it also served as a way of coping with those traumas. Living with the ever-present threat of death, some writers imagined their own deaths and dying; others examined the psychological toll of killing. Numerous poems depict imaginative escapes from the front-lines of battle, blurring the lines between reality and fantasy, sanity and shell shock. Humor and parody were also used to cope with the stresses of war, and soldiers found comfort in memories of mothers, sweethearts, and wives. Both soldiers and civilians also attempted to distance themselves from emotional response. Concluding this section, poems tell of simple pleasures such as apple pie and chipped potatoes that inspired endurance in an alien world at war.

Standing To (In Bereitschaft)

I shall go into death as into a doorway filled with summer coolness, the scent of
    hay, and cobwebs: I shall never return
To colourful butterflies, flowers and girls, to dancing and violin music.
Somewhere or other I shall fall on stones, shot in the heart, to join someone
    else who fell wearily earlier;
I shall have to wander through much smoke and fire and have beautiful eyes
    like the godly, inward-looking,
Dark as velvet, incredibly ardent ...What is death? A long sleep? Sleeping
    eternally deep down beneath grass and plants
Among old gravel? Trumpery. Maybe I shall go to Heaven and enter the snow-
    white night of God's stars, His silken gardens,
His golden evenings, His lakes ... I shall lie beneath the open sky, looking
    strange, ancient, portentous,
My mind once again filled with days out in the Tyrol, fishing in the Isar,
    snowfields, the noise and excitement of the annual fair
In prosperous villages in Franconia, prayers, songs, cuckoos calling, woods,
    and a train journey along the Rhine by night.
Then I shall become like evening, secret, dark, puzzling, mysterious, benighted;
    then I shall be like earth, lifeless and void,
And totally removed from the things around me: days, animals, tears, deep
    blue dreams, hunting, merrymaking,
I shall go into death as into the doorway of my house, with a shot in the heart,
    painless, strangely small.

—Anton Schnack (1920), translated by Patrick Bridgwater[1]

In front-line trenches of the First World War, armies developed the early morning ritual of *stand-to* (in English, a shortening of the command "Stand to Arms"). At the order, every man stood at attention and stared in the half-light toward the enemy's lines, for dawn was "zero hour"—the time scheduled for over-the-top attacks on the enemy's trenches. When it became clear that an attack was not imminent, troops were allowed to "stand down" and prepare their breakfasts. In German, the poem's title "In Bereitschaft" can be translated as "standing to" as well as "being in a state of preparedness (for death)."[2] Paul Fussell describes stand-to as "a daily routine of quiet terror."[3]

---

[1] Bridgwater's English prose translation has been formatted to follow the line breaks in the original German poem.
[2] Patrick Bridgwater, *The German Poets of the First World War,* St. Martin's, 1985, p. 117.
[3] Paul Fussell, *The Great War and Modern Memory,* 1975, Oxford UP, 2000, p. 60.

In 1915, Anton Schnack was a 22-year-old journalist and junior member of the philosophy faculty at the University of Munich when he was conscripted into the German Army. In charge of munitions, Schnack served at the Somme and Verdun between November 1915 and February 1916 until he was injured in an accident while unloading ammunition.[4] In 1920, by then identified as an Expressionist poet, Schnack published sixty war sonnets in *Tier rang gewaltig mit Tier (Beast Strove Mightily with Beast)*. Stretching the formal constraints of the sonnet, he uses long, uneven lines to relate the horrors of war with dispassionate detachment, an approach that works "to diminish the 'I,' to reduce the individual human to a tiny helpless figure in the landscape."[5] Schnack's realistic depictions of battle and his questions about the purpose of the war would likely have prevented publication of his poems during the conflict.

Thirteen years after publication of *Tier rang gewaltig mit Tier*, in 1933 Schnack was among the eighty-eight writers who signed the Oath of Allegiance in support of Adolph Hitler. In 1944, he was again required to enlist in the German army as a member of the Home Guard; for a brief time, he was imprisoned by American forces.[6] Schnack's poetry has largely been forgotten, even in Germany, despite scholar Patrick Bridgwater's claim that "he is one of the two unambiguously great poets of the war on the German side and is also the only German-language poet whose work can be compared with that of Wilfred Owen."[7]

---

[4] Chris Waller, "Anton Schnack (1892–1973): The First World War and the Fate of the Self," *Oxford German Studies*, vol. 42, no. 1, Apr. 2013, p. 57.
[5] Waller, "Anton Schnack," pp. 74, 68.
[6] Waller, "Anton Schnack," p. 58.
[7] Bridgwater, *The German Poets*, p. 96.

Night Watch
(Tronville-en-Barrois)

Autumn and dusk—a band far off plays *I—*
ain't got nobo—dy and nobo—dy cares for me.
Already autumn here in this new part
of France—the garden has a bitter reek!
How lonely stars look in a changing sky—
I turn the lights on so as not to see.
Already late for my night watch to start.
Silence too strong for anything to creak.
The night is very wide—the room turns sly,
and things keep still to watch what there may be
back of my tight shut eyes and secret smile.
Are you there?—and like the heart of God my heart
is vast with love and pain and very bleak—
O France, be still in here a little while.

—John Allan Wyeth[8] (1929)

Many soldiers valued the comradeship they developed with their fellow soldiers in the war. Henry Lamont Simpson writes, "Friendship is the greatest gift God sends— / All men were brothers to me, / Most were my friends."[9] Yet war also intensified soldiers' sense of estrangement and alienation. The song that Wyeth references in "Night Watch"—"I ain't got nobody" (also known as "I'm so sad and lonely")—was recorded by Marion Harris in 1916 and quickly became a popular hit during the war.

John Allan Wyeth wrote "Night Watch" sometime between August 25 and September 5 of 1918, while training with the American First Army in France, about forty miles south of Verdun. Wyeth's autobiographical war sonnets mix tones, textures, languages, and dialects as they describe his own isolation as well as the "cultural dislocation of the AEF in its trek across Western Europe."[10]

---

[8] See also Wyeth's "The Transport" and "Picnic: Harbonnières to Bayonvillers."
[9] See Simpson's "Going In" in this anthology.
[10] Dana Gioia, "The Unknown Soldier: An Introduction to the Poetry of John Allan Wyeth," *This Man's Army*, by John Allan Wyeth, U of South Carolina P, 2008, p. xxv.

Nothing Much (Peu de chose)

How many d'you reckon we've killed
Christ
It's weird it doesn't affect us
Christ
A slab of chocolate for our German friends
Fire by Christ
A camembert for their gunners
Fire by Christ
Each time you say fire! the word becomes steel
   that explodes far off
Christ
Take cover
Christ
Kra
The bastards are answering back
Strange language by Christ

              —Guillaume Apollinaire (1915),[11] translated by Martin Sorrell

Born as the illegitimate son of a Russo-Polish woman who lived in Rome's Vatican, Guillaume Apollinaire moved to Paris in his twenties, was arrested (wrongly) in 1911 for the theft of the *Mona Lisa* from the Louvre, and counted among his friends and collaborators Marc Chagall, Marcel Duchamp, Gertrude Stein, and Pablo Picasso. A defender of Cubism, Apollinaire coined the term *surrealism*; his creativity was not confined to a single movement, but instead embraced the freedoms of avant-garde modernism.

In December of 1914, Apollinaire volunteered for military service with the French army. In letters sent to friends he explained, "Soldiering is my true profession," and "I love art so much, I have joined the artillery."[12] Many of Apollinaire's war poems, including "Nothing Much," reflect an "aesthetic of surprise, expressing pervasive unpredictability, the spurting adrenalin and libertarian irreverence of gunners in the combat zone."[13] In a poem composed

---

[11] Writing to his fiancée Madeleine Pagès, Apollinaire included the poem in a letter dated 13 Oct. 1915. Along with most of his other poems to Madeleine, the poem was published posthumously in *Tendre comme le souvenir* (Gallimard, 1952).

[12] Tony Hoagland, "I Seem to Be at a Great Feast: The War Poems of Guillaume Apollinaire," *American Poetry Review,* July/Aug. 2014, p. 15.

[13] Peter Read, "Guillaume Apollinaire 1880–1918," *The Lost Voices of World War I,* edited by Tim Cross, Bloomsbury, 1998, p. 203.

shortly after war broke out, Apollinaire expresses his enthusiasm for what he viewed as an archetypal drama of primeval forces: "Nations hurled together so they might learn to know one another" (from "The Little Car"). Tony Hoagland comments, "Apollinaire's definition of war as a kind of terrible blind date is comic, cosmic, and, on one level, terribly true."[14]

In November of 1915, Apollinaire transferred to the infantry. Just four months later while in the trenches at Bois-des-Buttes, a shrapnel fragment pierced his helmet and entered his skull just above his right temple. Efforts were made to remove the shell fragment at a field hospital, and Apollinaire was invalided back to Paris. Despite another operation, he suffered from confusion, dizzy spells, and loss of the use of his left arm. Apollinaire never fully recovered from his war injury, but died in Paris on November 9, 1918, a victim of the influenza pandemic. His friend André Billy recorded his last words: "Sauvez-moi, docteur, sauvez-moi! J'ai tant à donner" ("Save me, doctor, save me! I have so much yet to give").[15]

---

[14] Hoagland, "I Seem to Be," p. 15.
[15] Qtd. in *Lost Illusions: Paul Léautaud and His World*, by James Harding, Farleigh Dickinson UP, 1974, pp. 117–118.

The Face

Out of the smoke of men's wrath,
The red mist of anger,
Suddenly,
As a wraith of sleep,
A boy's face, white and tense,
Convulsed with terror and hate,
The lips trembling....

Then a red smear, falling....
I thrust aside the cloud, as it were tangible,
Blinded with a mist of blood.
The face cometh again
As a wraith of sleep:
A boy's face, delicate and blond,
The very mask of God,
Broken.

—Frederic Manning[16] (1917)

Distance plays a key role in the trauma of taking another life: "if one does not have to look into the eyes when killing, it is much easier to deny the humanity of the victim."[17] A mental health counselor from the US Department of Veterans Affairs explains, "When your friends are dead, it's a real loss. It's a loss of your friend that you trusted and you loved in a very intense way. When you personally take another life and you go up to that lifeless body with a hole in it and you look down on it, and you say, 'I did that,' I think it is a loss of yourself at the same time."[18] In *On Killing: The Psychological Cost of Learning to Kill in War and Society*, Grossman writes, "The dead soldier takes his misery with him, but the man who killed him must forever live and die with him. The lesson becomes increasingly clear: Killing is what war is all about, and killing in combat, by its very nature, causes deep wounds of pain and guilt."[19]

Frederic Manning served with the King's Shropshire Light Infantry and the Royal Irish Regiment. He saw action at the Somme and survived the war. In 1929,

---

[16] See also Manning's "Relieved."
[17] Dave Grossman, *On Killing: The Psychological Cost of Learning to Kill in War and Society*, Little, Brown, 1995, p. 128.
[18] Jim Dooley, "The Soldier's Heart: Interview Jim Dooley," *PBS Frontline*, 1 Mar. 2005, web.archive.org/web/20190825183743/https://www.pbs.org/wgbh/pages/frontline/shows/heart/themes/prep.html.
[19] Grossman, *On Killing*, p. 93.

Manning published a novel that drew heavily upon his own war experiences: *The Middle Parts of Fortune* (later expurgated and republished as *Her Privates We*). In the book's preface, Manning writes, "War is waged by men; not by beasts, or by gods. It is a peculiarly human activity. To call it a crime against mankind is to miss at least half its significance; it is also the punishment of a crime."[20]

---

[20] Frederic Manning, *The Middle Parts of Fortune,* Penguin, 1990, p. xv.

III.—Fear

Fear is a wave
Beating through the air
And on taut nerves impingeing
Till there it wins
Vibrating chords.

All goes well
So long as you tune the instrument
To simulate composure.

(So you will become
A gallant gentleman.)

But when the strings are broken....
Then you will grovel on the earth
And your rabbit eyes
Will fill with the fragments of your shattered soul.

—Herbert Read (1919)

In the First World War, 346 men who fought with the British Army were executed, typically by men in their own unit, after court martials found them guilty of desertion, cowardice, or other serious violations of military conduct. France executed over 600 of its soldiers (many think this number is actually much higher, due to the French practice of *decimation*—shooting every tenth man in units that mutinied or refused orders to attack). Italians shot an estimated 750 of their own men; Austria-Hungary shot over 1,100 of its soldiers, and the Germany army executed 48 of their own during the war.[21] It is now believed that many of the men convicted of desertion, cowardice, and refusing to follow military orders suffered from shell-shock or post-traumatic stress disorder (PTSD), but at the time of these executions, military authorities may have been more concerned about setting an example and maintaining discipline than they were about attending to the specifics of individual cases.

Herbert Read was a Yorkshire farmer's son whose studies at the University of Leeds were interrupted by the war. He served in France and Belgium with the Yorkshire Regiment, his conduct in battle earning him the Military Cross and Distinguished Service Order. But Read was no stranger to fear. In his essay "The

---

[21] Gerard Oram, *Military Executions during World War I,* Palgrave Macmillan, 2003, p. 18.

Cult of Sincerity," Read writes, "I have never written about the real horror of fighting, which is not death nor the fear of mutilation, discomfort or filth, but a psychopathic state of hallucination in which the world becomes unreal and you no longer *know* whether your experience is valid—in other words, whether you are any longer sane."[22] "Fear" is one of Read's six short imagist poems collected under the title "The Scene of War." According to Hugh Cecil,

> Survival, as he [Read] said elsewhere, came through the members of a community being *with* each other in real communion … His concern to show courage was not just so as to prove himself, but because that quality was essential for the survival and success of the whole group. Read was obsessively determined not to betray his own men through cowardice.[23]

In the preface to his 1919 poetry collection, Read sharply rebuked anyone who might seek to romanticize the war or to ignore the toll it had taken on men who had endured the unimaginable: "We, who in manhood's dawn have been compelled to care not a damn for life or death, now care less still for the convention of glory and the intellectual apologies for what can never be to us other than a riot of ghastliness and horror, of inhumanity and negation."[24]

---

[22] Herbert Read, "What Is There Left to Say?" *The Cult of Sincerity,* Faber and Faber, 1968, p. 54.
[23] Hugh Cecil, "Herbert Read and the Great War," *Herbert Read Reassessed*, edited by David Goodway, Liverpool UP, 1998, p. 34.
[24] Herbert Read, "Preface," *Naked Warriors,* Art and Letters, 1919.

Fever (La Fièvre)

"Heartbeat, heartbeat, why the rush?
Whither the headlong dash,
where are you taking me,
where is this punishing mad gallop
dragging my disheveled life?"

My heart is racing off, up through the clouds,
over the mountains, across the plains—
not Pécopin[25] himself, on Satan's thoroughbred,
flew as swift through all those haunted years
as me, on this runaway heart
careering like a wild stallion.

   "Where are you rushing me, heart?"
   "To a white hospital, in a quiet garden,
women softly rustling through the wards,
and, at nightfall, distant tranquil bells
murmuring a call to evensong;
to a white hospital, and a peaceful death,
a woman's white hand on your pale brow,
and precious words of comfort on her lips."
   "No, rampaging heart! No!"

   "Fetch my horse!"
—Sooner the fierce alarm-cry of guns
announcing torrents of thunder-strikes;
and sooner than the nurses' soft footsteps,
give me merciless flying splintered steel
whizzing invisible just above our heads!

No, heart…
           Let me die beside rearing guns,
in the mad triumph of this great Epic,
die lying here, in the mud and the blood,
my eyes filled with sky, my heart with stars,

---

[25] Pécopin, a character in the Victor Hugo novel *The Story of the Bold Pécopin*, makes a deal with the Devil in hopes of returning to his lover, but the Devil keeps Pécopin from his lover for 100 years, compelling him to race around the world on a ghostly horse.

here, soothed by the moon's affectionate caress,
with a great chunk of steel in my chest!
1916

—Albert-Paul Granier,[26] translated by Ian Higgins

Albert-Paul Granier was killed on August 17, 1917, when his plane was shot down over Verdun; his poetry collection *Les Coqs et les Vautours* was published in Paris that same year. Forgotten for over ninety years, the poems were rediscovered in 2008 at a rummage sale in Brittany. In the foreword to the English edition published in 2014, translator Ian Higgins attributes the power of Granier's poetry to the "paradoxical child-like vulnerability and gritty toughness of a generous mind attempting to encompass and express the unimagined new sorts of nightmare that the war was flinging at ordinary people day by day."[27]

---

[26] See also Granier's "War Song" (Chanson de Guerre).
[27] Ian Higgins, "Foreword," *Cockerels and Vultures,* by Albert-Paul Granier, edited and translated by Ian Higgins, Saxon, 2014, p. 9.

Prayer before Battle (Gebet vor der Schlacht)

The troops are singing fervently, each for himself:
God, protect me from misfortune,
Father, Son and Holy Spirit,
That no grenades strike me,
That the bastards, our enemies,
Do not catch me, do not shoot me,
That I don't die like a dog
For the dear fatherland.

Look, I would like to go on living,
Milk cows, bang girls
And beat the bastard, Sepp,
Get drunk often
Until my blessed death.
Look, I eagerly and gladly recite
Seven rosaries daily,
If you, God, in your grace
Would kill my friend Huber or Meier,
And not me.

But if the worst should come,
Let me not be too badly wounded.
Send me a slight leg wound,
A small injury to the arm,
So that I may return as a hero,
With a story to tell.

—Alfred Lichtenstein (1919), translated by Sheldon Gilman,
Robert Levine, and Harry Radford

When war broke out in Germany in August of 1914, a German Jewish newspaper urged men to volunteer:

> To all German Jews! At this hour we must again show we Jews, proud of our heritage, belong to the best sons of the Fatherland. The nobility of our thousands of years of history demands this of us. We expect that our youth will volunteer for the flag with joy in their hearts. German Jews! We call up on you, in the sense of our old Jewish commandments, to devote yourselves with all your heart, soul and property to the service of the Fatherland.[28]

---

[28] Editorial appearing in *Jüdische Rundschau*, 7 Aug. 1914, qtd. in *Loyal Sons: Jews in the German Army in the Great War*, by Peter C. Appelbaum, Vallentine Mitchell, 2014, p. 49.

An estimated 96,000 Jewish soldiers joined the German army, and for every eight of those who enlisted, one was killed—12,000 died in the First World War.[29] Much as Israel's King David had asked God in the imprecatory Psalms to punish his enemies, Jewish rabbis led prayers for the destruction of Germany's foes:

> Our Father Our King: Oppose the evil ones of the earth who are fighting against us. Send against them calamity upon calamity, breach upon breach. Destroy them utterly by your wrath and your anger each time they attack us ... Weaken their armies and swallow up their thoughts and let both them and their ships go down together into the uttermost depths ... Many fight against us but we will overcome them because You, O Lord, are our Shield and Aid ... Therefore harm will not come to our country, because You will bring destruction to our foes.[30]

But as casualties mounted and Germans faced starvation on the home front, some began to blame Jews for Germany's psychological and economic collapse, charging that Jews were war profiteers who shirked military service. In 1916, Germany imposed the *Judenzählung,* a Jewish military census intended to expose Jewish perfidy. For Jewish soldiers, "the census represented a catastrophe as well as a direct insult. It showed clearly that neither society, nor the military nor the government recognized their patriotism or their sacrifice."[31] In the years following the war, the situation worsened dramatically for German Jews as the Jewish people became the scapegoat for their nation's military losses: Germans came to believe the invented argument that their army had not lost the war, but "had been betrayed by communists, Jews, and other dissidents."[32]

Alfred Lichtenstein, a Prussian Jew born in Berlin, graduated with a law degree in October of 1913 and planned to become a writer. His friends knew him as "a clown, a wit, a man apart, possessed by a profound sense of the absurdity of the world."[33] He was less than two months from finishing his year of compulsory military service when the war began, and in August of 1914, Lichtenstein was ordered to the Western Front with the 2nd Bavarian Infantry Regiment. Niall Ferguson asserts, "Lichtenstein has a good claim to have been the first of the anti-war poets. His 'Prayer before Battle' predates Sassoon's change of style by a year and a half."[34] Lichtenstein did not return as a hero with a story to tell. Shot in the stomach in German action near the Somme, he died several days later on

---

[29] Appelbaum, *Loyal Sons,* pp. 271–272.
[30] Appelbaum, *Loyal Sons,* pp. 49–50.
[31] Appelbaum, *Loyal Sons,* p. 261.
[32] Jay Winter, "Foreword," *Loyal Sons,* p. xxiv.
[33] Patrick Bridgwater, *The German Poets of the First World War,* St. Martin's, 1985, p. 63.
[34] Niall Ferguson, *The Pity of War,* Penguin, 1999, p. xxvii.

September 25, 1914.³⁵ He is buried in one of fifteen mass graves in the German War Cemetery at Vermandovillers, the largest German war cemetery in France and the final resting place of 22,632 German soldiers. Lichtenstein was killed fighting for Germany in September of 1914; his mother and two of his siblings were killed by the Nazis twenty-eight years later.³⁶

---

[35] Ray Ockenden, "The Neglected Voice of Alfred Lichtenstein," *Oxford German Studies,* vol. 41, no. 3, 2012, p. 364.
[36] Sheldon Gilman, Robert Levine, and Harry Radford, "Introduction," *The Prose and Verse of Alfred Lichtenstein,* Xlibris, 2000, p. 13.

Retreat

Broken, bewildered by the long retreat
Across the stifling leagues of southern plain,
Across the scorching leagues of trampled grain,
Half-stunned, half-blinded, by the trudge of feet
And dusty smother of the August heat,
He dreamt of flowers in an English lane,
Of hedgerow flowers glistening after rain—
All-heal and willow-herb and meadow-sweet.

All-heal and willow-herb and meadow-sweet—
The innocent names kept up a cool refrain—
All-heal and willow-herb and meadow-sweet,
Chiming and tinkling in his aching brain,
Until he babbled like a child again—
"All-heal and willow-herb and meadow-sweet."

—Wilfrid Wilson Gibson[37] (1916)

"The Great Retreat" is the name given to the British Army's forced march from Mons to the outskirts of Paris in late August and early September of 1914. The summer of 1914 was one of the hottest of the century, and the retreat was grueling as exhausted British troops attempted to escape the pursuing German Army. Men slept as they marched, some regiments covering nearly 250 miles in thirteen days. Over 15,000 men were casualties of the march, either captured, wounded, or killed. Describing the scene, John Lewis-Stempel writes, "Some units lost all cohesion, some men lost all reason. One officer was so spooked he started firing his revolver at imaginary Germans in the street."[38] Although many have written of the tactics and topography of the Retreat from Mons, Wilfrid Wilson Gibson's short poem captures the interior landscapes of the mind.

Gibson was born in Northumberland, though for a time he lived in Gloucestershire, where he joined the Dymock Poets (whose members included Lascelles Abercrombie, Rupert Brooke, John Drinkwater, Robert Frost, and Edward Thomas). Gibson himself never served at the front (due to poor vision and ill health), but he was close friends with both Brooke and Thomas. When

---

[37] See also Gibson's "Victory."
[38] John Lewis-Stempel, "The Battle of Mons," *Express*, 24 Aug. 2014, web.archive.org/save/https://www.express.co.uk/news/world-war-1/502649/WWI-The-Battle-of-Mons.

Gibson learned that Rupert Brooke had enlisted, he declared, "Such people as Rupert [i.e. poets] must run no risks," for Gibson strongly believed that poetry needed to be written and published during the war, to "keep our flag flying during the triumph of barbarism."[39] Gibson feared "that war would kill not just poets but poetry itself."[40] His poem "Retreat" appeared in his collection *Friends*, published in 1916 and dedicated "To the memory of Rupert Brooke."

---

[39] Wilfrid Gibson, qtd. in "'War Is a Business of Innumerable Personal Tragedies': Wilfrid Gibson, Elizabeth Gibson Cheyne and the First World War," by Judy Greenway, *Dymock Poets and Friends*, no. 15, 2016, p. 50.

[40] Greenway, "'War Is a Business,'" p. 50.

There is a healing magic in the night[41]

There is a healing magic in the night,
The breeze blows cleaner than it did by day,
Forgot the fever of the fuller light,
And sorrow sinks insensibly away
As if some saint a cool white hand did lay
Upon the brow, and calm the restless brain.
The moon looks down with pale unpassioned ray—
Sufficient for the hour is its pain.
Be still and feel the night that hides away earth's stain.
Be still and loose the sense of God in you,
Be still and send your soul into the all,
The vasty distance where the stars shine blue,
No longer antlike on the earth to crawl.
Released from time and sense of great or small
Float on the pinions of the Night-Queen's wings;
Soar till the swift inevitable fall
Will drag you back into all the world's small things;
Yet for an hour be one with all escaped things.
Found in his note-book when his kit came home

—Colwyn Philipps (1915)

A captain in the Royal Horse Guards, Colwyn Philipps arrived in the Ypres Salient in early November of 1914. Less than six months later, at the age of twenty-six, he was killed in an attack on German lines. Several months before his death, in November of 1914 Philipps wrote to his mother and described his first battle experience:

> As we went through the first village, we got heavily shelled by the famous Black Marias; they make a noise just like an express train and burst like a clap of thunder, you hear them coming for ten seconds before they burst. It was very unpleasant, and you need to keep a hold on yourself to prevent ducking—most of the men duck.[42]

A few weeks later, he wrote of another lesson he had learned at the front: "All officers should know how to stop an artery in any part … iodine and stopping

---

[41] Untitled in first publication (*Colwyn Erasmus Arnold Philipps*, 1915); later titled "Release" by E.B. Osborn when included in *The Muse in Arms*, 1917.
[42] Colwyn Philipps, "Nov. 10, 1914," *Colwyn Erasmus Arnold Philipps*, Smith, Elder, 1915, p. 91.

bleeding are essential. I advise all to carry some pain-deadening pills, as a man screaming will shake a company's nerves more than shells."[43]

Colwyn Philipps has no known grave: his name is one of the 54,896 listed on the Menin Gate memorial. When his belongings were sent home to his parents in Wales, "There is a healing magic in the night" was found among his possessions. The poem's repetition of the phrase "Be still" recalls Psalm 46 and its meditation on God and war: "He makes wars cease to the end of the earth; He breaks the bow and shatters the spear; He burns the chariots with fire. Be still, and know that I am God."[44] The introduction to Philipps's posthumously published book of poetry begins, "There may be differences of opinion as to the literary merits of these little verses: there can be none as to their sincerity." The introduction concludes, "what he freely sacrificed was not life alone, but the prospect of a happy and a brilliant future."[45]

---

[43] Philipps, "Nov. 27, 1914," 1915, p. 99.
[44] *The Bible*, English Standard Version, Crossway, 2001.
[45] "Introduction," *Colwyn Erasmus Arnold Philipps*, pp. v, vii.

Bivouacs

In Somecourt Wood, in Somecourt Wood,
The nightingales sang all night,
The stars were tangled in the trees
And marvellous intricacies
Of leaf and branch and song and light
Made magic stir in Somecourt Wood.

In Somecourt Wood, in Somecourt Wood,
We slithered in a foot of mire,
The moisture squelching in our boots;
We stumbled over tangled roots,
And ruts and stakes and hidden wire,
Till marvellous intricacies
Of human speech, in divers keys,
Made ebb and flow thro' Somecourt Wood.

In Somecourt Wood, in Somecourt Wood,
We bivouacked and slept the night,
The nightingales sang the same
As they had sung before we came.
'Mid leaf and branch and song and light
And falling dew and watching star.
And all the million things which are
About us and above us took
No more regard of us than
We take in some small midge's span
Of life, albeit our gunfire shook
The very air in Somecourt Wood.

In Somecourt Wood, in Somecourt Wood,
I rose while all the others slept,
I seized a star-beam and I crept
Along it and more far along
Till I arrived where throbbing song
Of star and bird and wind and rain
Were one—then I came back again—
But gathered ere I came the dust
Of many stars, and if you must
Know what I wanted with it, hear,

I keep it as a souvenir
Of that same night in Somecourt Wood.

In Somecourt Wood, in Somecourt Wood,
The cuckoo wakened me at dawn.
The man beside me muttered, "Hell!"
But half a dozen larks as well
Sang in the blue—the curtain drawn
Across where all the stars had been
Was interlaced with tender green,
The birds sang, and I said that if
One didn't wake so cold and stiff
It would be grand in Somecourt Wood.

. . . . .

And then the man beside me spoke,
But what *he* said about it broke
The magic spell in Somecourt Wood.

—Gilbert Waterhouse (1916)

Gilbert Waterhouse served with the Essex Regiment. His poem "Bivouacs" recalls Romantic poet John Keats's "La Belle Dame sans Merci," for in both poems, a wandering warrior loses his illusions and must confront his final journey into the unknown. Waterhouse was last seen midmorning on the first day of the battle of the Somme as he led his men in the attack on Serre. It is almost certain that he died of his wounds sometime during that chaotic day, but as the Germans held the ground where he lay, his body was not recovered until the summer of 1917. His story is not unique: in his regiment alone on July 1 of 1916, 22 of the 24 officers and 414 of the 606 men of other ranks were killed or wounded.

Going Over

A girl's voice in the night troubled my heart.
Across the roar of the guns, the crash of the shells,
Low and soft as a sigh, clearly I heard it.

Where was the broken parapet, crumbling about me?
Where my shadowy comrades, crouching expectant?
A girl's voice in the dark troubled my heart.

A dream was the ooze of the trench, the wet clay slipping,
A dream the sudden out-flare of the wide-flung Verys.
I saw but a garden of lilacs, a-flower in the dusk.

What was the sergeant saying? —I passed it along.—
Did *I* pass it along? I was breathing the breath of the lilacs.
For a girl's voice in the night troubled my heart.

Over! How the mud sucks! Vomits red the barrage.
But I am far off in the hush of a garden of lilacs.
For a girl's voice in the night troubled my heart.
Tender and soft as a sigh, clearly I heard it.

—Charles G.D. Roberts (1919)

Sometimes referred to as the "Father of Canadian poetry," Charles G.D. Roberts was one of the older poets to serve in the war. His full name was Charles George Douglas Roberts, but his middle initials led to the nickname "Charles God Damn Roberts," the phrase used variously as a mnemonic, an expression of jocular affection, or a curse.[46] Born in New Brunswick in 1860, Roberts had to lie about his age to join the army, enlisting as a private in September of 1914 with the Legion of Frontiersmen. In early October of 1914 he wrote to his son, "I have lost ten pounds in weight, and more than half my sleep, since war began; & I am coming to the feeling that it would be actual relief and blessed comfort to lie in the trench with my cheek to the rifle, & just give oneself, give oneself utterly, for all that we stand for in this war."[47] Roberts was commissioned as a first lieutenant in December 1914 with the 16th Battalion of the King's (Liverpool) Regiment,

---

[46] John Coldwell Adams, *Sir Charles God Damn: The Life of Sir Charles G.D. Roberts,* U of Toronto P, 1986, p. ix.

[47] Charles G.D. Roberts to Douglas Roberts, 4 Oct. 1914, *The Collected Letters of Sir Charles G.D. Roberts,* edited by Laurel Boone, Goose Lane Editions, 1989, p. 301.

serving first as a troop instructor in Britain, and later attached to the Canadian Corps as Special Press Correspondent on the Western Front. From December of 1916 he spent long periods of time in France, but wrote only three war poems: "To Shakespeare, 1916," "Cambrai and Marne," and "Going Over" (which he subtitled "The Somme, 1917," when it was republished in 1941).

Amanda Frank suggests that in "Going Over," Roberts "may have emulated McCrae by writing a French-form war poem." She notes,

> Roberts's villanelle, like McCrae's rondeau ["In Flanders Fields"], contrasts the images of pastoral with the images of trench warfare; also like "In Flanders Fields," a pre-war form seems to offer the poet a safe harbor of nostalgia from which to cautiously venture into new moral waters. In "Going Over," however, Roberts goes farther than McCrae with formal experimentation and not nearly so far with moral imperative.[48]

Roberts was knighted by King George V in 1935 for his contributions to literature; he died of heart failure in 1944 at the age of eighty-three.

---

[48] Amanda Lowry French, *Refrain, Again: The Return of the Villanelle,* 2004, U of Virginia, PhD dissertation, pp. 141, 142.

Home

A burst of sudden wings at dawn,
Faint voices in a dreamy noon,
Evenings of mist and murmurings,
And nights with rainbows of the moon.

And through these things a wood-way dim,
And waters dim, and slow sheep seen
On uphill paths that wind away
Through summer sounds and harvest green.

This is a song a robin sang
This morning on a broken tree,
It was about the little fields
That call across the world to me.
Belgium, July 1917

—Francis Ledwidge (1918)[49]

An Irishman from County Meath, Francis Ledwidge was a poet before the war. In November of 1914, shortly after enlisting, he wrote a friend, "This life is a great change to me, and one which somehow I cannot become accustomed to. I have lived too much amongst the fields and the rivers to forget that I am anything else other than the 'Poet of the Blackbird.'"[50] Stationed at the front with the Royal Inniskilling Fusiliers, Ledwidge continued to write of folklore, fairies, and country scenes; his war poems are linked to the land and legends of Ireland. From Gallipoli, he wrote to Lord Dunsany, his mentor and a fellow Irish writer, explaining,

> It is surprising what silly things one thinks of in a big fight. I was lying one side of a low bush on August 15th, pouring lead across a little ridge into the Turks and for four hours my mind was on the silliest things of home. Once I found myself wondering if a cow that I knew to have a disease called "timber-tongue" had really died. Again a man on my right who was mortally hit said: "It can't be far off now," and I began to wonder what it was could not be far off. Then I knew it was death and I kept repeating the dying man's words: "It can't be far off now."[51]

---

[49] See also Ledwidge's "To One Dead."
[50] Ledwidge letter to Bobby Anderson, 9 Nov. 1914, qtd. in *Francis Ledwidge, a Life of the Poet*, by Alice Curtayne, Martin Brian and O'Keefe, 1972, p. 87.
[51] Ledwidge letter to Lord Dunsany, Aug. 1915, qtd. in *Francis Ledwidge*, p. 127.

In 1917, writing to Irish poet Katharine Tynan, Ledwidge confessed,

> I am a unit in the Great War, doing and suffering, admiring great endeavour and condemning great dishonour. I may be dead before this reaches you, but I will have done my part. Death is as interesting to me as life. I have seen so much of it, from Sulva to Serbia and now in France. I am always homesick. I hear the roads calling, and the hills, and the rivers wondering where I am. It is terrible to be always homesick.[52]

Ledwidge wrote the poem "Home" in mid-July of 1917, during a pause in the bombardment that preceded the Third Battle of Ypres. He was killed two weeks later on July 31. Virginia Woolf reviewed his posthumous book of poetry in 1918, writing, "Most of Mr. Ledwidge's poems are about those little things that only few hold dear not because they are rare or remote, but because they lie all about us, as common as grass and sky ... And you come to believe in the end that you, too, hold these things dear."[53]

---

[52] Ledwidge letter to Tynan, 6 Jan. 1917, qtd. in *Francis Ledwidge,* p. 170.
[53] Virginia Woolf, "Two Irish Poets," *Times Literary Supplement,* 2 May 1918, no. 850, p. 206.

On the Plains of Picardy[54]

On the Plains of Picardy
Lay a soldier, dying
Gallantly, with soul still free
Spite the rough worlds' trying.
Came the Angel who keeps guard
When the fight has drifted,
"What would you for your reward
When the Clouds have lifted?"
Then the soldier through the mist
Heard the voice and rested
As a man who sees his home
When the hill is breasted—
This his answer and I vow
Nothing could be fitter—
Give me Peace, a dog, a friend
And a glass of bitter!

—Hugh Stewart Smith (c. 1916)

An abundance of light verse was written during the First World War, but little has been reprinted or remembered. According to various sources,[55] the above short poem was found in Captain Hugh Stewart Smith's personal effects after he was killed on August 18, 1916, in an attack on the German trenches at High Wood, part of the offensive of the Battle of the Somme.

The provenance of the poem is a mystery. Smith wrote poems while at university (Oxford's Corpus Christi), during which time he "gained a reputation in College ... as a wit."[56] Much of this poetry is included in his posthumously published book, *Verses*. The volume is credited to "H.S.S.," although a frontispiece photography of Smith in uniform, as well as a brief introduction, confirms that he is the author. Curiously, the untitled poem "On the Plains of Picardy" does not appear in *Verses*, Smith's only published volume of poetry, and Reilly's bibliography *English Poetry of the First World War* lists *Verses* as the sole

---

[54] The poem is untitled in Powell's *A Deep Cry*.
[55] The first mention of the poem appears to occur in Anne Powell's *A Deep Cry* (Palladour, 1993), which lists Smith's *Verses* among its primary sources and states that the poem was found in Smith's pocketbook. Martin Gilbert's *The Somme* (McClelland and Stewart, 2006) makes a similar reference to Smith and the poem.
[56] P.J.P, "Roll of Honour: H.S. Smith," *The Pelican Record*, vol. XIII, no. 4, Dec. 1916, pp. 161–162.

published source of Smith's poems. It is possible that Smith did not compose the poem, but rather copied it in his journal, a common practice among soldiers. However, the poem's style is in keeping with his other work. If Smith did write "On the Plains of Picardy," it may be that whomever compiled *Verses* thought it too irreverent or frivolous to include.

Smith had been a district officer in Northern Nigeria for two years before the war, but returned to England to join the Army in March 1915 and was commissioned an officer in the Argyll and Sutherland Highlanders. In his poem "The Incorrigibles: Written from the Front to a Friend," Smith gently pokes fun at himself for once believing those who told him that war "was Glory, Triumph and Trumpet-call":

> For us, foot-slogging sadly, it is clear
> That War is fleas, short rations, watered beer,
> Noise and mismanagement, bluster and foreboding,
> Triumph but the sequel to enough exploding.
> Yet like a ray across a storm-torn sea
> Shines through it all the glint of Comedy,
> And pompous Death, whose table they have messed at,
> Has given the Men another butt to jest at![57]

Smith, an only son, was twenty-seven when he died. He is buried at Caterpillar Valley Cemetery, Longueval, France.

---

[57] Hugh Stewart Smith, "The Incorrigibles," *Verses*, [publisher not identified], [1916?], p. 38.

Picardy Parodies No. 2 (W.B. Y--ts)

I will arise and go now, and go to Picardy,
    And a new trench-line hold there, of clay and shell-holes made,
No dug-outs shall I have there, nor a hive for the Lewis G.,
    But live on top in the b. loud glade.

And I may cease to be there, for peace comes dropping slow,
    Dropping from the mouth of the Minnie[58] to where the sentry sings;
There noon is high explosive, and night a gunfire glow,
    And evening full of torpedoes' wings.

I will arise and go now, though always night and day
    I'll feel dark waters lapping with low sounds by the store,
Where all our bombs grow rusty and countless S.A.A.;[59]
    I'll feel it in my trench-feet sore.

                                —William Oliphant Down (1921)

William Oliphant Down was a West Country man, born in Somerset and raised in Dorset. Before the war, he had achieved recognition for a play "as iridescent as a soap bubble,"[60] *The Maker of Dreams,* a one-act fantasy that asserts that "the greatest thing that dreams are made of is love."[61] Caught up in the patriotic fervor of 1914, Down volunteered and was commissioned an officer in the British infantry, first joining the 15th Royal Hussars, then the Royal Berkshire's 1st/4th Battalion. He was awarded the Military Cross for action at the Somme in July of 1916. Leading a night patrol mission, Down commanded an attack during which he and his men killed eleven Germans in hand-to-hand combat and captured two.[62] While rotating in and out of the front lines of battle, Down continued writing plays and poetry. Three of his trench poems are parodies that reshape popular songs and poems. In "Picardy Parodies No. 2," he turns his wry humor to W.B. Yeats's poem "The Lake Isle of Innisfree." In "War, Passive Suffering, and the Poet," Jonathan Allison comments,

---

[58] The slang term for *minenwerfer,* a German short-range artillery trench mortar.
[59] S.A.A. is the military acronym for Small Arms Ammunition.
[60] "The Maker of Dreams: Some Press Opinions," *The Maker of Dreams,* by Oliphant Down, Gowans and Gray, 1917, p. 42.
[61] "Lecture Given on 'Maker of Dreams,'" *Columbia Daily Spectator,* 27 Mar. 1915, p. 1.
[62] C.R.M.F. Cruttwell, "Chapter X: The July Fighting at Pozières," *The War Service of the 1/4 Royal Berkshire Regiment,* Oxford Basil Blackwell, 1922, p. 53.

Down's parody ... mingles wonderfully the intoxicating rhythms of antimodern, Celtic Twilight pastoral with the precise diction of the trenches ... Clearly, some soldiers had read Yeats and carried him with them to Flanders, though he scarcely returned the compliment: when considering the poetry of the trenches, he judged it unfit for a "country newspaper" (as he said of Wilfred Owen's poems). He condemned what he called its "passivity": Yeats preferred his war heroes to be active ... Standing up to announce your imminent departure for Innisfree, after all, is the impulse of a free man ... As the war-time parody suggests, such freedom to choose, to act freely, was not an option for a soldier on the Western Front, surrounded by the weapons of mass slaughter that made a mockery of nineteenth-century ideals of individual heroism.

William Oliphant Down died of wounds on May 23, 1917. He was most likely shot by enemy machine gun fire on the night of May 22 as his unit was relieving the Glosters near Demicourt, France. In the foreword to Down's posthumously published book of poems, Harold Veasey writes, "His was a nature that abhorred war and its attendant horrors; it is, therefore, remarkable that this dreamer and idealist should have developed into such a very gallant and capable soldier."[63]

---

[63] Harold Veasey, "Foreword," *Poems,* by Oliphant Down, Gowans and Gray, 1921, p. v.

A Lament
(The Ritz-Loos Salient.)

I wish the sea were not so wide
   That parts me from my love;
I wish the things men do below
   Were known to God above.

I wish that I were back again
   In the glens of Donegal,
They'll call me coward if I return,
   But a hero if I fall.

"Is it better to be a living coward,
   Or thrice a hero dead?"
"It's better to go to sleep, my lad,"
   The Colour Sergeant said.

—Patrick MacGill[64] (1917)

Known as "The Navvy Poet" before the war, Patrick MacGill published *Soldier Songs* in 1917. A reviewer said of MacGill's war poetry, "he does not edge the raw and haggard facts of war with any light from heaven. An unflinching realist, he paints the thing as he saw it, and whatever of charm is in his lines comes of the love of comrades, of joy in their stubborn courage, of some incongruous glimpse of beauty in the sky over him or in the desolated scene around him."[65] Close bonds of comradeship caused many of the soldiers of the First World War to reflect, without irony, that their experiences in military service were some of the happiest of their lives. Shortly before his death, Wilfred Owen reassured his mother of his own contentment:

> So thick is the smoke in this cellar that I can hardly see by a candle 12 ins. away, and so thick are the inmates that I can hardly write for pokes, nudges & jolts. On my left, the Coy. Commander snores on a bench: other officers repose on wire beds behind me ... It is a great life ... I hope you are as warm as I am; as serene in your room as I am here ... I am certain you could not be visited by a band of friends half so find as surround me here.[66]

---

[64] See also MacGill's "The Star-Shell."
[65] A. St. John Adcock, "Poets in Khaki," *Bookman*, vol. 55, Dec. 1918, p. 97.
[66] Wilfred Owen, *Collected Letters*, Oxford UP, 1967, p. 591.

Edgar Jones, in "The Psychology of Killing: The Combat Experience of British Soldiers during the First World War," writes, "The intensity of the soldiers' experience was often so great that it is difficult to imagine anything in civilian life that came anywhere close to these bonds."[67]

In the Preface to *Soldier Songs,* Patrick MacGill recalls a lyric that "echoed in billets and dug-outs from Le Harve to the Somme."[68] It is a lullaby of sorts, an ironic reminder of the bonds of comradeship and snatches of song that got men through the war.

Sing Me to Sleep

Sing me to sleep where bullets fall,
Let me forget the war and all;
Damp is my dug-out, cold my feet,
Nothing but bully and biscuits to eat.
Over the sandbags helmets you'll find
Corpses in front and corpses behind.

Chorus.
Far, far from Ypres I long to be,
Where German snipers can't get at me,
Think of me crouching where the worms creep,
Waiting for the sergeant to sing me to sleep.

Sing me to sleep in some old shed,
The rats all running around my head,
Stretched out upon my waterproof,
Dodging the raindrops through the roof,
Dreaming of home and nights in the West,
Somebody's overseas boots on my chest.

---

[67] Edgar Jones, "The Psychology of Killing: The Combat Experience of British Soldiers during the First World War," *Journal of Contemporary History,* vol. 41, no. 2, 2006, p. 245.
[68] MacGill, *Soldier Songs,* p. 12.

Selections from "Rhymes from a New Nursery"

Jack and Bill, they stuck it till
Their knees were under water;
Jack fell down, and said to Bill
Some words he didn't oughter!

Fritzie-Witzie sat on a bomb,
Fritzie-Witzie went up pom-pom!
All Bill's Herr Doktors and medicine men
Couldn't put Fritzie together again!

—Robert Eassie (1917)

Selections from an "Alphabet of Limericks"

A
There was a young hero of Aire
Who was hit, but he couldn't say where,
    Till a comrade close by
    Said, "Just sit down and try,"
And he did, and he shouted, "It's there!"

N
There was a brave girl of Nieppe
Who was full of sand, ginger, and pep;
    With Taube or Fokker
    The Huns couldn't shock her
And she'd smile when she spotted a Zepp!

O
There was a sweet thing at Olhain
Whose kisses were hard to obtain;
    But, once they were snatched,
    They couldn't be matched
From the Salient down to the Aisne.

V
There was a young fellow of Vimy
Who said, "If my sweetheart could see me

> Accepting the kisses
> Of these here French misses,
> I guess I would rather not be me!"
>
> —Robert Eassie (1917)

Recovering in hospital from a war wound, Canadian soldier Tom Johnson wrote his sweetheart, "I begin to think that the gift of humor is as priceless as the gift of physical courage."[69] In his essay on Canadian soldiers' humor in the First World War, Tim Cook writes, "Comedy and humour allowed for the soldiers to exert some control over their wartime experience, which was profoundly discombobulating, unsettling, and terrifying .... In this war of endurance, laughter was armour, the joke was a crutch, and the song was a shield. Gentle or jagged, humour was everywhere."[70] Yet not everyone appreciated war humor. The satirical cartoons of Bruce Bairnsfather, immensely popular with the soldiers of the First World War, were initially criticized by many on the home front, including a member of the British Parliament who condemned them as "vulgar caricatures of our heroes."[71] Cook explains, "Antiheroic jokes were among the most transgressive forms of humour as they seemingly undermined the patriotic and heroic discourse of the war," allowing soldiers to "distance themselves from those at home, and reinforce the bonds that strengthened their own insulated society."[72]

War limericks offer an example of this transgressive humor, as they invite soldiers to mock traditional notions of war's glory, while affirming British cultural values. A post-war collection of limericks asserts, "Whenever two or three of our countrymen are gathered together in rough parts of the world, there you will find these verses; it is limericks that keep the flag flying, that fill you with a breath of old England in strange lands, and constitute one of the strongest sentimental links binding our Colonies to the mother-country."[73]

Robert M. Eassie served with the Canadian 5th Battalion and published his comic verses in his 1917 volume of poetry, *Odes to Trifles*. A review in *The Literary Digest* supposed that the author "must be the most cheerful man in all

---

[69] Thomas William Johnson, Letter to Lulu, 11 Oct. 1917, *Canadian Letters and Images Project*, web.archive.org/web/20190825215312/https://www.canadianletters.ca/content/document-11797?position=47&list=6TXF2wK8atAw6ICrL7KFnnAuJ4EwSB-IKb7tOtFy8DA.

[70] Tim Cook, "'I Will Meet the World with a Smile and a Joke': Canadian Soldiers' Humour in the Great War," *Canadian Military Studies*, vol. 22, no. 2, 2015, p. 50.

[71] Bevis Hillier, *Cartoons and Caricatures*, Studio Vista, 1970, p. 114.

[72] Cook, "I Will Meet the World," pp. 57–58.

[73] Norman Douglas, "Introduction," *Some Limericks*, 1929, Grove, 1967, pp. 16–17.

the Canadian Expeditionary Forces," an "incurable optimist [who] beguiles his time in the trenches by bringing the Nursery Rimes up to date."[74] Eassie also co-edited the Fifth Canadian Infantry Battalion's annual magazine, *Christmas Garlands from the Front,* published between 1915 and 1918. A satirical advertisement in the 1917–1918 issue encouraged soldiers to contact the Poetry Bureau to purchase custom-made verses for impressing sweethearts, offering "a smart quatrain to suit any reasonable female." The Poetry Bureau ad promised to deliver "The Cheapest Poetry on the Market ... Our Poetry Is Guaranteed. No Short Feet. No Gassed Metres."[75]

---

[74] "Current Poetry," *Literary Digest,* vol. 56, 30 Mar. 1918, p. 42.
[75] F.B. Bagshaw and R.M. Eassie, editors, *Another Garland from the Front, Mark III,* G. Pulman, 1917–1918, p. 128.

Pershing at the Front

The General came in a new tin hat
To the shell-torn front where the war was at;
With a faithful Aide at his good right hand
He made his way toward No Man's Land,
And a tough Top Sergeant there they found,
And a Captain, too, to show them round.

Threading the ditch, their heads bent low,
Toward the lines of the watchful foe
They came through the murk and the powder stench
Till the Sergeant whispered, *"Third-line trench!"*
And the Captain whispered, *"Third-line trench!"*
And the Aide repeated, *"Third-line trench!"*
And Pershing answered,—not in French—
"Yes, I see it. Third-line trench."
Again they marched with wary tread,
Following on where the Sergeant led
Through the wet and the muck as well,
Till they came to another parallel.
They halted there in the mud and drench,
And the Sergeant whispered, *"Second-line trench!"*
And the Captain whispered, *"Second-line trench!"*
And the Aide repeated, *"Second-line trench!"*
And Pershing nodded: *"Second-line trench!"*

Yet on they went through mire like pitch
Till they came to a fine and spacious ditch
Well camouflaged from planes and Zeps
Where soldiers stood on firing steps
And a Major sat on a wooden bench;
And the Sergeant whispered, *"First-line trench!"*
And the Captain whispered, *"First-line trench!"*
And the Aide repeated, *"First-line trench!"*
And Pershing whispered, *"Yes. I see.
How far off is the enemy?"*
And the faithful Aide he asked, asked he,
"How far off is the enemy?"
And the Captain breathed in a softer key,
"How far off is the enemy?"

> The silence lay in heaps and piles
> And the Sergeant whispered, *"Just three miles."*
> And the Captain whispered, *"Just three miles."*
> And the Aide repeated, *"Just three miles."*
> *"Just three miles!"* the General swore,
> *"What in hell are we whispering for?"*
> And the faithful Aide the message bore,
> *"What in hell are we whispering for?"*
> And the Captain said in a gentle roar,
> *"What in hell are we whispering for?"*
> "Whispering for?" the echo rolled;
> And the Sergeant whispered, *"I have a cold."*
>
> —Arthur Guiterman (1927/1929)[76]

In 1937, *The Saturday Evening Post* published a list of its most popular poems, explaining, "Of the three poems most often asked for, two are serious, Alfred Noyes' 'A Victory Dance' and Arthur Guiterman's 'Pershing at the Front,' the latter printed in 1927. The third is Newman Levy's burlesque of Hamlet, printed on the humor page in 1923."[77] "Pershing at the Front" is not a typical "serious" poem; it uses humor to lampoon military hierarchy and protocol. The lowest-ranking soldier, the whispering Sergeant, is the man who is most informed about the realities of war in the front-line trenches. With its concluding twist, the poem mocks the limited information possessed by those in command and their estrangement from the men they order into battle. Part of the poem's popularity may be explained by its use of humor to make a serious point. One American student remembers his history teacher Wilbur Kirwan explaining to the class, "things that seemingly contradict each other—such as humor and horror—can coexist."[78] Each Memorial Day, Kirwan would recite to his class Wilfred Owen's "Dulce et Decorum Est," followed by Guiterman's "Pershing at the Front."

Arthur Guiterman wrote and published over 4,000 verses in his lifetime and co-founded the Poetry Society of America, serving as its president from 1925

---

[76] Although published in 1927 in the *Saturday Evening Post,* the version included here is from Guiterman's *Song and Laughter* (1929).
[77] *A Short History of the Saturday Evening Post,* Curtis Publishing, 1937, p. 42.
[78] Gary E. Frank, "Education, Transformation, Transcendence," *The Colgate Scene,* vol. 31, no. 5, Mar. 2003.

to 1926. In a 1916 article, American poet Joyce Kilmer called Guiterman "The Most American of Poets," explaining,

> The rich humor which permeates his verse is American—American of Mark Twain and Artemus Ward and Josh Billings … Kindness, and shrewdness, and common sense lit by idealism—these are qualities we like to consider American. And Arthur Guiterman has them.[79]

---

[79] Joyce Kilmer, "The Most American Poet," *The Independent*, 20 Nov. 1916, p. 312.

Left Behind

I got a letter from
My girl. She said,
"I love you.
When the mud is
Thick, and
You have a large pack on
Your back
And you are hungry
And tired
Think of me.
I love you."
And one day we were
On the march.
The mud was
Thick. And
I had a large
Pack
On my back
And I was
Hungry
And tired, when
I fell to thinking
Of her.
And
A lieutenant
Gave me
A swift kick
And set me to
Double timing
To
Catch up.

—Harry L. Parker (1919)

Women have frequently motivated men to enlist, to march, and to fight. Elsie Janis was one of the most famous entertainers of the First World War, a comedian who sang, danced, and cartwheeled her way into the hearts of American soldiers. The "Sweetheart of the AEF," Janis visited hospitals and military camps, sharing laughter and music with thousands of doughboys, and by March of 1918 she had given over 400 performances.[80] Her act included song, dance, handsprings, and impersonations of Charlie Chaplin; Elsie Janis touched her audiences with "an American performance, by an American girl, done in an American way, the first of its kind to be seen by most of the audience in many months."[81] She would frequently call out to the troops, "Do I come from Ohio? By damn yes!" Championing the young entertainer as "an oasis of color and vivacity in the midst of a dreary desert of frock-coated and white-tied legislators and lecturers," the American military newspaper *The Stars and Stripes* proclaimed, "Elsie Janis is as essential to the success of this Army as charge of powder is essential to the success of a shell. More entertainment by her and 'the likes of her' and less instruction by people who take themselves seriously—that's one formula for winning the war!"[82] Idealized views of women strongly influenced the morale of soldiers, and letters from women back home were important to the troops. One soldier wrote to his sweetheart, "I get a lot of peace thinking about you. I like to think of the good times we used to have and dream of the good times to come when I get home again."[83]

Lieutenant Harry L. Parker (later promoted to Captain) was a South Carolinian who had attended Clemson College, where he was voted "Wittiest" and "Most Original" in his graduating class. Joining the American Expeditionary Force, Parker served in the supply department of *The Stars and Stripes,* the American military newspaper. Following the war, in 1924 Parker earned a doctorate from the University of Paris and began a long and distinguished career as an etymologist and expert in the control of biological pests. Parker died in Cannes in 1979, and colleagues remembered his intelligence, quick wit, and "joie de vivre." Harry Parker's obituary also reveals that he did not return home to a sweetheart in South Carolina, but rather in 1923 he married Henriette Charraire, a young French girl.[84] Their marriage lasted for over fifty-five years, until Henriette was left behind at his death.

---

[80] "Elsie One of Us While War Lasts," *The Stars and Stripes,* 29 Mar. 1918, p. 7.
[81] "Elsie Janis Here to Delight AEF," *The Stars and Stripes,* 8 Mar. 1918, p. 6.
[82] "Elsie," *The Stars and Stripes,* 15 Mar. 1918, p. 4.
[83] Elmer Lewis to Goldie Little, personal letter qtd. in *Pershing's Crusaders: The American Soldier in World War I,* by Richard S. Faulkner, UP of Kansas, 2017, p. 536.
[84] John J. Drea, "Obituary: Harry Lamont Parker, 1893–1979," *Bulletin of the Entomological Society of America,* vol. 26, no. 1, 15 Mar. 1980, p. 89.

A Kiss

She kissed me when she said good-bye—
A child's kiss, neither bold nor shy.

We had met but a few short summer hours;
Talked of the sun, the wind, the flowers,

Sports and people; had rambled through
A casual catchy song or two,

And walked with arms linked to the car
By the light of a single misty star.

(It was war-time, you see, and the streets were dark
Lest the ravishing Hun should find a mark.)

And so we turned to say good-bye;
But somehow or other, I don't know why,

—Perhaps 't was the feel of the khaki coat
(She'd a brother in Flanders then) that smote

Her heart to a sudden tenderness
Which issued in that swift caress—

Somehow, to her, at any rate
A mere hand-clasp seemed inadequate;

And so she lifted her dewy face
And kissed me—but without a trace

Of passion,—and we said good-bye....
A child's kiss,... neither bold nor shy.

My friend, I like you—it seemed to say—
Here's to our meeting again some day!
      Some happier day....
    Good-bye.
      (August 1916)

—Bernard Freeman Trotter

Known as the "Canadian Rupert Brooke," Bernard Freeman Trotter was a 25-year-old graduate student at the University of Toronto when he volunteered for the Canadian Overseas Expeditionary Force in February of 1916. Serving as a second lieutenant with the 11th Leicestershire Regiment, he trained as a transport officer on the Western Front. Trotter was happy with the assignment, assuring his parents back home, "I find shell fire far less trying on the nerves when on horseback in charge of a convoy than when crouching in a trench."[85] His letters home also revealed the ways the war was changing him: "One is inclined, I am afraid, to lose perspective very badly, and give no thought to what happens to anyone save your own little party." He explained, "You watch shells bursting over the other people's areas with the most perfect equanimity."[86] The year before war broke out, Trotter had written a poem titled "The Songs We Need." Its last stanza reveals his determined good cheer: "Sing of Sorrow? All men know it. / Share with them their tears; / Then—ah! then, forget not, poet— / Sing the Hope that cheers."

Trotter wrote "The Kiss" while stationed in England as he trained for war; he had been at the front less than six months when he was killed on May 7, 1917. His commanding officer wrote to his father with details of the young lieutenant's death and burial:

> [He] was returning to the stables when a High Explosive Shell burst quite close to him. It must have killed him instantaneously as he dropped off his horse and was past all help when one of his corporals went over to him about half a minute afterwards ... We buried him here in the Military Cemetery alongside two of his brother officers who have been killed quite recently here ... We are putting up a simple oak cross and a wooden curb on his grave and shall get it planted with violets and other flowers, and in due course of time you will receive a photo of it I hope from the Graves Commissioners (the only people allowed to take photos) ... I am afraid this is a very incomplete sort of letter to write but we get very hard hearted and rough with these constant casualties, (I have lost eight officers this last month alone), so I must ask you to excuse it, I and all the officers do feel your son's loss very much and we offer you and his mother our deepest sympathies.[87]

---

[85] Bernard Freeman Trotter, "Trotter, Bernard Freeman Letter: 1917 May 5th," *Canadian Letters and Images Project*, web.archive.org/web/20190825221903/https://www.canadianletters.ca/content/document-2637?position=67&list=ZKH7VCKW2VOcyJ7JUnIQC2YZHWE30w87yF8__B3nxCg.

[86] Bernard Freeman Trotter, "Trotter, Bernard Freeman Letter: 1917 January 28th," *Canadian Letters and Images Project*, web.archive.org/web/20190825222030/https://www.canadianletters.ca/content/document-2619?position=51&list=-9DwzlpEq4xphUfTF5BRZu7NEsug7Hpf6-1Ec1eZt1o.

[87] Lieutenant Colonel C. Turner, "Letter, 8 May 1917," *McMaster University Library*, web.archive.org/web/20190825222228/http://digitalcollections.mcmaster.ca/pw20c/turner-lt-col-c-letter-8-may-1917.

Bernard Trotter's father chose as the inscription for his son's headstone, "How, dying, smotest thou the one full chord ere thy lute broke," the first lines from Gertrude Moffat's "In Appreciation of Bernard Freeman Trotter," a poem written to honor the young soldier-poet.[88]

A review of Trotter's poetry in the *Times Literary Supplement* said, "Never to have grown old and disillusioned is a kind of immortality ... What he would have written, had he lived to know the full significance of war, cannot be guessed at. But it would have been well worth hearing, for this young poet had the courage to think as well as feel for himself."[89]

---

[88] Gertrude McGregor Moffat, "In Appreciation of Bernard Freeman Trotter," *McMaster University Monthly,* Feb. 1918, p. 195.

[89] "A Canadian Soldier Poet," *Times Literary Supplement,* no. 852, 16 May 1918, p. 230.

Albade

The little girls are singing, *"Rin! Ron! Rin!"*
The matin bell is ringing *"Din! Don! Din!"*
Thirty little girls, while it rains and shrapnel skirls
By the playground where the chapel bells are ringing.

> The stout old nuns are walking,
> *Dance, little girls, beneath the din!*
> The four-point-ones are talking,
> *Form up, little girls, the school is in!*
> Seven stout old nuns and fourteen naval guns
> All around the playground go on talking.

And, my darling, you are getting out of bed
Where the seven angels watched around your head,
With no shrapnel and no Huns
And no nuns or four-point-ones …
Getting up to catch the train,
Coming back to tea again
When the Angelus is sounding to the plain
And the statue shells are coming from the plain
And the little girls have trotted home again
In the rain….

Darling, darling, say one funny prayer again
For your true love who is waking in the rain.
    The Salient, 7/9/16

—Ford Madox Hueffer (Ford Madox Ford)[90]

Ford Madox Ford is one of the most respected novelists of the First World War: numerous critics argue that *The Good Soldier* and *Parade's End* deserve a place among the great novels of the twentieth century. He joined the Welch infantry when he was forty-one, in July of 1915. At the Somme in 1916, Ford was injured by the blast of a nearby artillery shell, but rejoined his battalion at the Ypres Salient in early September. In a letter to Joseph Conrad, his friend and sometime literary collaborator, Ford attempted to describe the sounds of the Western Front:

---

[90] Born Ford Hermann Hueffer, he used the pen name Ford Madox Hueffer until 1919, when, wishing to sound less Germanic, he changed it to Ford Madox Ford.

> In woody country heavy artillery makes *most* noise, because of the echoes—and most prolonged in a *diluted* way. On marshland—like the Romney Marsh—the *sound* seems alarmingly close: I have seldom heard the *Hun* artillery in the middle of a strafe except on marshy land ... On dry down land the sound is much *sharper*; it hits *you* & shakes *you*. On clay land it shakes the ground & shakes you thro' the ground ... Shells falling on a church: these make a huge "*corump*" sound, followed by a noise like crockery falling off a tray—as the roof tiles fall off. If the roof is not tiled you can hear the stained glass, sifting mechanically until the next shell. (Heard in a church square, on each occasion, about 90 yds away). Screams of women penetrate all these sounds—but I do not find that they agitate me as they have done at home.[91]

The day after writing his letter to Conrad, Ford composed the poem "Albade." The title refers to an early morning love song, specifically a love ballad sung from a window or doorway to a sleeping woman.

The poem is rich with the soundscape of war as it creates a curious grouping: celibate religious women, young school girls, German gunners, a sheltered Englishwoman, and a British soldier in the trenches. Despite their differences, all share one thing in common: a deep and heart-felt desire to survive the war. In the preface to his war poetry collection, *On Heaven, and Poems Written on Active Service* (1918), Ford writes,

> But I think that, in these sad days and years, we have got to believe in a Heaven—and we shall be all the happier if it is a materialist's Heaven. I know at least that I would not keep on going if I did not feel that Heaven will be something like Rumpelmayer's tea shop, with the nice boys in khaki, with the haze and glimmer of the bright buttons, and the nice girls in the fashions appropriate to the day, and the little orchestra playing, "Let the Great Big World ...." For our dead wanted so badly their leave in a Blighty, which would have been like that—they wanted it so badly that they *must* have it. And they must have just that. For haven't we Infantry all seen that sort of shimmer and shine and heard the rustling and the music through all the turmoil and the mire and the horror? ... And dying so, those images assuredly are the last things that our eyes shall see: that imagination is stronger than death. For we *must* have some such Heaven to make up for the deep mud and the bitter weather and the long lasting fears and the cruel hunger for light, for graciousness and for grace![92]

---

[91] Ford Madox Ford, letter 6 Sept. 1916, *Letters of Ford Madox Ford,* edited by Richard Ludwig, Princeton UP, 2015, p. 73.

[92] Ford Madox Hueffer, *On Heaven and Poems Written on Active Service,* John Lane, 1918, pp. 7–8 [ellipses in original text].

To C.H.V.

What shall I bring to you, wife of mine,
    When I come back from the war?
A ribbon your dear brown hair to twine?
    A shawl from a Berlin store?
Say, shall I choose you some Prussian hack
    When the Uhlans[93] we o'erwhelm?
Shall I bring you a Potsdam goblet back
    And the crest from a Prince's helm?

Little you'd care what I laid at your feet,
    Ribbon or crest or shawl—
What if I bring you nothing, sweet,
    Nor maybe come home at all?
Ah, but you'll know, Brave Heart, you'll know
    Two things I'll have kept to send:
Mine honour for which you bade me go
    And my love—my love to the end.

—Robert Ernest Vernède (1917)

Robert E. Vernède, "of the dark eyes and the unforgettable smile,"[94] was a married man of thirty-nine, a published novelist, and an enthusiastic gardener when he enlisted with the British army. Between November of 1915 and September of 1916, he served in some of the most dangerous locations on the Western Front: in the Ypres Salient and at the Somme. Wounded in the thigh, he spent a brief period of recovery in England, returning to the front lines of Flanders in late 1916. A friend of the writer G.K. Chesterton (they had attended school together), Vernède wrote hundreds of letters home. His correspondence reveals him as an officer who cared deeply about his men, a writer with a dry wit and self-deprecating sense of humor, and a husband who was devoted to his wife, Caroline Howard Vernède. In his last letter to his wife, written on Easter Sunday of 1917, the day before he was killed, Robert Vernède closes with these lines: "I think it will be summer soon, and perhaps the war will end this year and I shall see my Pretty One again."[95] Remembering Vernède, his close friend F.G. Salter said,

---

[93] British term for German cavalry units.
[94] H.D. Rawnsley, "Vernède, Poet and Soldier," *The Living Age*, vol. 296, p. 469.
[95] Robert Ernest Vernède, "Easter Sunday, April 8," *Letters to His Wife*, W. Collins Sons, 1917, p. 219.

> He loved life, with a solid, English love; he loved his garden, his art, his friends; above all, he loved the wife who for all the years since their betrothal had been the inspirer and encourager of everything he did, and who was so in this decision also, and to the end. He very greatly desired to come back alive after the war. But it seemed to him that such a desire was, for the present, simply irrelevant.[96]

Vernède's poems were published posthumously in 1917, and in the introduction Gosse writes,

> The circumstances of his death repeat the story of a thousand such events in this prodigious war. Vernède was in charge of his platoon on the advance, and was in front with a couple of his men when they suddenly came upon a concealed enemy machine gun. He was hit, and it was immediately seen that the wound was serious. His men carried him back alive to the aid station, but he died upon the further journey. He was buried in the French cemetery at Lechelle.[97] His friend Captain F. E. Spurling put up a cross and planted around it a large bowl of daffodil bulbs which had been the joy of the poet when they flowered in the company mess. They now, in their long sleep, watch over his rest.[98]

Vernède's last words were "Send my love to my wife."[99]

---

[96] F.G. Salter, qtd. in "Introduction," by Edmund Gosse, *War Poems and Other Verses*, by Robert Vernède, Heinemann, 1917, p. 16.
[97] During burial concentrations, his remains were moved to the Lebucquière Communal Cemetery Extension.
[98] Edmund Gosse, "Introduction," *War Poems*, pp. 12–13.
[99] Robert Vernède, *Letters to His Wife*, p. xiii.

The Raindrops on Your Old Tin Hat

The mist hangs low and quiet on a ragged line of hills,
    There's a whispering of wind across the flat,
You'd be feeling kind of lonesome if it wasn't for one thing—
    The patter of the raindrops on your old tin hat.

An' you just can't help a-figuring—sitting there alone—
    About this war and hero stuff and that,
And you wonder if they haven't sort of got things twisted up,
    While the rain keeps up its patter on your old tin hat.

When you step off with the outfit to do your little bit,
    You're simply doing what you're s'posed to do—
And you don't take time to figure what you gain or lose—
    It's the spirit of the game that brings you through.

But back at home she's waiting, writing cheerful little notes,
    And every night she offers up a prayer
And just keeps on a-hoping that her soldier boy is safe—
    The Mother of the boy who's over there.

And, fellows, she's the hero of this great big ugly war,
    And her prayer is on the wind across the flat,
And don't you reckon maybe it's her tears, and not the rain,
    That's keeping up the patter on your old tin hat?
                                     —John Hunter Wickersham (1920)

Many American soldiers of the First World War were poets, but only 119 were awarded America's highest military decoration, the Congressional Medal of Honor (CMH). John Hunter Wickersham was both a poet and a CMH hero. One of the first to volunteer when America entered the war, Wickersham attended Officers' Training Camp in May of 1917 and was assigned to the 353rd Infantry 89th Division as a second lieutenant. In the first week of September 1918, American forces prepared to attack German positions in the St. Mihiel sector of northeastern France. The historian of the 353rd Regiment recalls,

> Each day had brought increasing signs of "something doin'" in the near future … Big guns were being pulled into place day and night … At dusk [Sept 11, 1918] the different outfits began to move to their jumping off places. The roads were

crowded with men ... It was a dark night; a cold rain was falling—now a drizzle, now a downpour; the bottom of the trenches held water ankle deep.[100]

Perhaps crouched in a mud-filled trench waiting for Zero-Hour (the term originated in the First World War), John Wickersham wrote his last letter home. In the note to his mother, he included a poem, most probably untitled. By the time his mother received his letter, her son was dead. The poem first appeared in a small Oregon newspaper the *St. Helen's Mist* on December 13, 1918. The paper noted that the poem had been contributed by the aunt and uncle of a soldier who had been killed in battle and published it under the title "Its Patter Touches the Heart." In later publications, the poem appears as "The Raindrops on Your Old Tin Hat."[101]

The historian of the 353rd Infantry Regiment writes of the events of September 12, 1918, the morning of the attack:

> crouched down in the mud-filled trenches with thousands of fellow Americans, we waited for the Zero hour. All surplus clothing except raincoats had been stored and it seemed that Zero was upon us while we shivered and waited for the hour ... It was impossible to remember all the instructions. One warning, however, stuck fast—"No one goes to the rear" ... So we waited for the time to go "Over the Top" ...
>
> Some losses occurred, too, from our own artillery. "Follow the barrage," were the orders. As soon as the barrage had lifted from an objective ahead the men moved up, not realizing that the artillery would roll back almost to their own position before moving forward again to the next objective ... While Lieutenant Wickersham was advancing with his platoon a shell burst at his feet and threw him into the air with four mortal wounds. He dressed the wounds of his orderly, improvised a tourniquet for his own thigh and then ordered the advance to continue. Although weakened by the loss of blood he moved on with his pistol in his left hand until he fell and died before aid could be administered to him. Everywhere action was heroic.[102]

By the end of the first day of the St. Mihiel offensive, the 353rd had lost nearly 250 men, 39 killed in action. For his actions on September 12, 1918, John Hunter Wickersham was posthumously awarded the Medal of Honor. He is buried in

---

[100] Charles Franklin Dienst et al., *History of the 353rd Infantry Regiment, 89th Division*, 353rd Infantry Society, 1921, pp. 69, 72.
[101] There are slight variations in punctuation in published versions; the version included in this anthology is from *The American Legion Weekly*, vol. 2, no. 33, 10 Sept. 1920, p. 3.
[102] Dienst, *History of the 353rd*, pp. 72–74.

France at St. Mihiel American cemetery, where overlooking the graves, the sculpted figure of a young American officer stands. The inscription above the stone soldier reads, "*Il dort loin des siens dans la douce terre de France*" (He sleeps far away from his family in the gentle lands of France), and at his feet is inscribed, "Blessed are they that have the home longing for they shall go home."[103]

---

[103] *The Soldiers Monument* by Paul Manship (best known for his statue of Prometheus at Rockefeller Center in New York City).

Camouflage

They tell us tales of camouflage,
The art of hiding things;
Of painted forts and bowered guns
Invisible to wings.
    Well, it's nothing new to us,
    To us, the rank and file;
    We understand this camouflage
    —We left home with a smile.

We saw the painted battleships
And earthen-colored trains,
And planes the hue of leaden skies,
And canvas-hidden lanes.
    Well, we used the magic art
    That day of anxious fears;
    We understand this camouflage
    —We laughed away your tears.

They say that scientific men
And artists of renown
Debated long on camouflage
Before they got it down.
    Well, it came right off to us,
    We didn't have to learn;
    We understand this camouflage
    —We said we'd soon return.

We understand this camouflage,
The art of hiding things;
It's what's behind a soldier's jokes
And all the songs he sings.
    Yes, it's nothing new to us,
    To us, the rank and file;
    We understand this camouflage,
    —We left home with a smile.

—M.G. (1919)[104]

---

[104] Although the unsigned poem was first printed in *The Stars and Stripes* on 28 June 1918, this version appears in *Yanks: A.E.F. Verse*, G.P. Putnam's Sons, 1919, pp. 52–53.

Visiting the Western Front in July of 1917, British monarch King George V toured a camouflage unit in Belgium. A special correspondent for the *Times* described the workshop as "a magician's palace in a Belgium farm, where nothing is what it seems ... where bushes are men and things dissolve when you look at them and the earth collapses ... It is the grown-up home of make-believe."[105] Armies had previously used tactics to hide themselves from the enemy, but the conditions of the First World War made concealment more necessary than ever before. Enemy trenches were often only yards apart, and planes, balloons, and dirigibles flew overhead to photograph positions and gather intelligence.

In 1915, the French were the first to establish a military camouflage unit (their section's badge featured a silver chameleon).[106] Other armies quickly followed suit. The military use of the word *camouflage* entered English during the First World War, its origins in the French word *camoufler* (to make up for the stage). Theatrical set designers, sculptors, painters, and other artists served in these units. Their job was not only to conceal, but to deceive. Paper mâché dummy heads were used to draw fire and expose the position of enemy snipers; fake trees fashioned from bullet-proof steel and encased in hammered iron plates served as observation posts in No Man's Land (the simulated bodies of dead horses and human corpses served the same function), and tanks and ships were painted in bold, abstract designs based upon the principles of Cubist art, breaking up silhouettes and confusing observers' sense of perspective. One merchant ship captain who objected to the "vivid painting of his vessel" received the following response from a camouflage officer: "Dear Sir, — The object of camouflage is not, as you suggest, to turn your ship into an imitation of a West African parrot, a rainbow in a naval pantomime, or a gay woman. The object of camouflage is rather to give the impression that your head is where your stern is."[107]

Camouflage officers were not the only ones who sought to give false impressions, nor were enemy soldiers the only ones deceived. From his position in front line trenches in 1918, Private Ollie Hankins wrote home to his father in Richmond, Virginia:

> Hello Pop! Guess you thought it was about time I was writing. I am feeling exubrious at present and hope this will find you all well. This is the 4th of July and we have just finished a lovely dinner. We had real dishes to eat out of &

---

[105] *London Times*, qtd. in *A Genius for Deception*, by Nicholas Rankin, Oxford UP, 2009, p. 141.
[106] Rankin, *A Genius for Deception*, p. 25. The French society portrait painter Lucien-Victor de Scévola is often credited with devising the first modern camouflage; in September of 1914, he used painted canvas to disguise the position of a French artillery battery (Rankin, p. 24).
[107] Rankin, *A Genius for Deception*, p. 131.

sat at a table in real chairs. Just think of it! I haven't heard a word from you all yet, but you need not feel bad about that as there is a reason for my mail being delayed at present, and I expect to get it very soon. We have holiday today and are endeavoring to make the most of it.[108]

Six months later just after the Armistice, Ollie Hankins sent another letter home that revealed the actual occurrences of that Independence Day:

Dear Papa, I have your letter dated Oct. 28th. I know that my being over here has caused you a lot of worry, but I hope that from now on you will not worry any more about me ... My letter to you all dated July 4th was written just a few yards behind the front line trench and large shells were bursting close by while we ate that 4th of July dinner that I told you about. While on this front I got caught in a barrage, which is not the pleasantest thing in the world to get caught in. Also had some real use for my gas mask on this front and went to sleep in the blooming thing on several occasions.[109]

Many soldiers like Ollie Hankins hid the truth of the war from their families and loved ones, some never talking about what they had encountered. When *The Stars and Stripes* poem was reprinted in the 1920 *Yearbook of Newspaper Poetry*, it was retitled to reflect a truth soldiers in the rank and file had learned: "We Understand Camouflage."

---

[108] Private C.O. Hankins, letter dated 4 July 1918, "War Letters, Diaries, and Incidents," Box 80, Library of Virginia Archives.
[109] Private C.O. Hankins, letter dated 16 Nov. 1918, "War Letters, Diaries, and Incidents," Box 80, Library of Virginia Archives.

Picnic
July 1917

We lay and ate sweet hurt-berries
    In the bracken of Hurt Wood.[110]
Like a quire of singers singing low
    The dark pines stood.

Behind us climbed the Surrey hills,
    Wild, wild in greenery;
At our feet the downs of Sussex broke
    To an unseen sea.

And life was bound in a still ring,
    Drowsy, and quiet, and sweet …
When heavily up the south-east wind
    The great guns beat.

We did not wince, we did not weep,
    We did not curse or pray;
We drowsily heard, and someone said,
    "They sound clear to-day."

We did not shake with pity and pain,
    Or sicken and blanch white.
We said, "If the wind's from over there
    There'll be rain tonight."

      * * * * *

Once pity we knew, and rage we knew,
    And pain we knew, too well,
As we stared and peered dizzily
    Through the gates of hell.

But now hell's gates are an old tale;
    Remote the anguish seems;
The guns are muffled and far away,
    Dreams within dreams.

And far and far are Flanders mud,
    And the pain of Picardy;

---

[110] Hurt Wood is an actual location in rural Surrey; *hurt berries* is a folk term used for whortleberries.

And the blood that runs there runs beyond
    The wide waste sea.

We are shut about by guarding walls:
    (We have built them lest we run
Mad from dreaming of naked fear
    And of black things done.)

We are ringed all round by guarding walls,
    So high, they shut the view.
Not all the guns that shatter the world
    Can quite break through.

* * * * *

Oh, guns of France, oh, guns of France,
    Be still, you crash in vain....
Heavily up the south wind throb
    Dull dreams of pain,...

Be still, be still, south wind, lest your
    Blowing should bring the rain....
We'll lie very quiet on Hurt Hill,
    And sleep once again.

Oh, we'll lie quite still, not listen nor look,
    While the earth's bounds reel and shake,
Lest, battered too long, our walls and we
    Should break… should break….

—Rose Macaulay[111]

By the time the war ended in November of 1918, an estimated 80,000 men serving in the British Army had been treated for shell shock, although the actual number of sufferers was undoubtedly much higher.[112] Rose Macaulay's 1916 novel, *Non-combatants and Others,* vividly relates the psychological impact of the war on both soldiers and civilians. It tells the story of Alix, a young art student who becomes violently ill after witnessing the night terrors of a shell-shocked soldier. The soldier repeatedly relives finding the leg of a friend, "thinking it led on to the entire friend, finding it didn't."[113] Alix is admonished by her cousin Dorothy,

---

[111] See also Macaulay's "Spreading Manure."
[112] Suzie Grogan, *Shell Shocked Britain,* Pen and Sword, 2014, p. 2.
[113] Rose Macaulay, *Non-combatants and Others,* 1916, Methuen, 1986, p. 21.

"After all, what they can bear to go through, we ought to be able to bear to hear about."[114] But lying awake, Alix is tortured by the memory of the man's moans and sobs, her mind circling around the memories of the haunted man: "'What they can bear to go through …. But they can't, they can't, they can't … we can bear to hear about … but we can't, we can't, we can't ….' It was like the intolerable ticking of a clock, and beat itself away at last into a sick dream."[115]

In her Poem "Picnic," written a year after the publication of *Non-combatants*, Rose Macaulay again explores civilians' attempts to cope with the mental sufferings of the war. Patriotism and support for the men at the front seemed to demand a stoic continuation of daily life, but the pretense of normalcy often gave the impression that civilians were naïve or insensitive. As Grogan asks in *Shell-Shocked Britain*, "How far can the term [shell-shocked] be applied not just to the soldiers on the front line, but to the country as a whole? To the communities those soldiers belonged to and the families who had to live through four years of ever more desperate warfare?"[116] Macaulay's "Picnic" can be compared to poems written by soldiers in its "retreat into disengagement … a defining response to the horror of being surrounded by death."[117]

---

[114] Macaulay, *Non-combatants*, p. 19.
[115] Macaulay, *Non-combatants*, p. 19 (ellipses in original text).
[116] Grogan, *Shell Shocked Britain*, p. 4.
[117] Sally Minogue and Andrew Palmer, *The Remembered Dead: Poetry, Memory and the First World War*, Cambridge UP, 2018, p. 59.

September. 1918

This afternoon was the colour of water falling through sunlight;
The trees glittered with the tumbling of leaves;
The sidewalks shone like alleys of dropped maple leaves,
And the houses ran along them laughing out of square, open windows.
Under a tree in the park,
Two little boys, lying flat on their faces,
Were carefully gathering red berries
To put in a pasteboard box.

Some day there will be no war,
Then I shall take out this afternoon
And turn it in my fingers,
And remark the sweet taste of it upon my palate,
And note the crisp variety of its flights of leaves.
To-day I can only gather it
And put it into my lunch-box,
For I have time for nothing
But the endeavour to balance myself
Upon a broken world.

—Amy Lowell

America did not enter the First World War until April 1917, and AEF troops were not sent in significant numbers until May of 1918. Two-thirds of American military deaths of the war occurred between September of 1918 and the Armistice.[118] That same autumn, the country and the world reeled from the effects of one of the deadliest pandemics in history: the Spanish flu killed more than fifty million people between 1918 and 1920, an estimated 2.5–5 percent of the world's population.[119]

It is no easy task to balance upon a broken world. In early September of 1918, Lowell received a letter from author D.H. Lawrence, who related news of their mutual friend, British soldier and poet Richard Aldington (the three writers were leading innovators in Imagist poetry). Lawrence reported that Aldington was "still all right—in France, back of the firing lines" and then confessed to

---

[118] Carol R. Byerly, "War Losses (USA)," *1914–1918 Online, International Encyclopedia of the First World War,* 8 Oct. 2014, web.archive.org/web/20190825230014/https://encyclopedia.1914-1918-online.net/article/war_losses_usa.

[119] Laura Spinney, *Pale Rider: The Spanish Flu of 1918 and How It Changed the World,* Public Affairs, 2017, p. 4.

feeling overwhelmed in a world spiraling out of control: "I can't do anything in the world today—am just choked. —I don't know how on earth we shall get through another winter—how we shall ever find a future. Humanity as it stands, and myself as I stand, we just seem mutually impossible to one another. The ground dwindles under one's feet—what next, heaven knows."[120] Lowell also felt unmoored, set adrift by the violent changes accompanying the war. She wrote a friend,

> The war has shaken us out of an eddy into the main stream of the centuries, and has given me the sensation of swirling along on a rapidly moving current, passing woods and water-plants and shores almost too fast to glimpse them, realizing as I pass that many other shingles like me have rushed down this same river, rushed toward something which I cannot now see.[121]

For Lowell, poetry became an anchor.

Convinced that it had the power to comfort, inspire, and change the world, Lowell set to convincing the American public of the value of contemporary poetry. When she learned that American Army training camps were requesting books for their libraries, she arranged to supply poetry books to thirty-four military bases across the United States and also donated funds to supply books to military hospitals. Writing to British poet Richard Aldington, she explained,

> Here we have had a most curious experience. Each of the training camps has a library, and they tell me that the demand for poetry in these libraries is phenomenal. Of course, the kind of poetry is not always what you and I would choose, for they like Kipling and Robert Service as well as a lot of other things; but that a lot of private soldiers that come from every walk in life should loudly demand poetry is such an extraordinary thing.[122]

Nina Sankovitch writes, "By the summer of 1918, Amy Lowell had placed poetry in the hands of just about any United States soldier asking for it. Modern or classics: they wanted poems and she answered their need."[123]

---

[120] D.H. Lawrence, "To Amy Lowell, 11 Sept. 1918," *The Letters of D.H. Lawrence: Volume III, October 1916–June 1921*, Cambridge UP, 2007, p. 280.

[121] Amy Lowell to Franz Rickaby, qtd. in *Amy Lowell Anew*, by Carl Rollyson, Rowman and Littlefield, 2013, p. 113.

[122] Amy Lowell to Richard Aldington, 7 Dec. 1917, qtd. in *Amy Lowell: A Chronicle*, by S. Foster Damon, Archon, 1966, pp. 435–436.

[123] Nina Sankovitch, "Amy Lowell: Making the World Safe for Poetry," *The History Reader: Dispatches in History from St. Martin's Press*, 25 May 2017, web.archive.org/web/20190825230213/http://www.thehistoryreader.com/modern-history/amy-lowell/.

Home Is Where the Pie Is

"Home is where the heart is" —
    Thus the poet sang;
But "home is where the pie is"
    For the doughboy gang.
Crullers in the craters
    Pastry in abris—[124]
Our Salvation Army lass
    Sure knows how to please.

Watch her roll the pie crust
    Mellower than gold;
Watch her place it neatly
    Within its ample mold;
Sniff the grand aroma
    While it slowly bakes—
Though the whine of Minnie shells
    Echoes far awakes.

Tin hat for a halo!
    Ah, she wears it well!
Making pies for homesick lads
    Sure is "beating hell";
In a region blasted
    By fire and flame and sword,
Our Salvation Army lass
    Battles for the Lord!

Call me sacrilegious,
    And irreverent, too;
Pies? They link us up with home
    As naught else can do!
"Home is where the heart is"—
    True, the poet sang;
But "home is where the pie is"
    To the Yankee gang!

    —Anonymous (1919)

---

[124] Dugouts or bomb shelters.

Over a century ago, charitable organizations such the Salvation Army, the Jewish Welfare Board, and the Young Men's Christian Association (YMCA) mobilized to support the soldiers of the American Expeditionary Forces. The YMCA was responsible for 90 percent of the welfare work that supported American troops in Europe,[125] but it was Salvation Army volunteers who first served doughnuts to homesick soldiers (at Montier-sur-Saulx, France in September of 1917). The Salvationists, all of whom had been given the rank of military private by General Pershing and ordered to wear regulation uniforms, "with the addition of the red Salvation Army shield on the hats, red epaulets, and with skirts for the women,"[126] did more than feed the hungry bodies of the troops. They also ministered to the souls and spirits of the soldiers, offering doughnuts and pies in a rite of comfort and communion. A historian of the Salvation Army during the war explains,

> The Salvation Army hut was home to the boys over there. They came to it in sorrow or joy. They came to ask to scrape out the bowl where the cake batter had been stirred because mother used to let them do it; they came to get their coats mended and have their buttons sewed on. Sometimes it seemed to the long-suffering, smiling woman who sewed them on, as if they just ripped them off so she could sew them on again; if so, she did not mind. They came to mourn when they received no word from home; and when the mail came in and they were fortunate they came first to the hut waving their letter to tell of their good luck before they even opened it to read it. It is remarkable how they pinned their whole life on what these consecrated American women said to them over there.[127]

We will likely never know the name of the writer who composed an ode praising the most American of desserts and the women who ministered to the troops; the unsigned poem first appeared in the military newspaper *The Stars and Stripes* on April 26, 1918.

---

[125] *Summary of World War Work of the American YMCA,* International Committee of YMCA, 1920, p. 26.
[126] Evangeline Booth and Grace Livingston Hill, *The War Romance of the Salvation Army,* J.B. Lippincott, 1919, p. 55.
[127] Booth and Hill, *The War Romance,* pp. 113–114.

The Soldier Mood

We were eating chip potatoes underneath the April stars
That glittered coldly and aloof from earth and earthly wars;
We were three good pals together, and the day's hard work was done,
So we munched our chip potatoes, half for food and half for fun.

Half the world was war's dominion, but the mutter of the strife
Had come to seem accustomed as the undertone of life;
We were fit and hard and happy, and the future was unknown,
The past—all put behind us; but the present was our own.

We were doing our plainest duty, meant to end what we'd begun;
Why worry for to-morrow till to-day's big job was done?
So we walked and laughed together like three modern musketeers—
Defying indigestion and the Germans and the years.

We were eating chip potatoes with our fingers, like a tramp,
And the unseen owls were hooting in the trees around the camp;
We were happy to be hungry, glad to be alive and strong;
So—to-morrow might be terror, but to-night could be a song!

—William Kersley Holmes[128] (1915)

In *The Great War and Modern Memory,* Fussell describes the growing sense contemporaries held that the First World War "would literally never end and would become the permanent condition of mankind. The stalemate and attrition would go on infinitely, becoming, like the telephone and the internal combustion engine, a part of the accepted atmosphere of the modern experience."[129] Because it seemed as if the war might last forever, those caught in its grip became increasingly aware of the evanescent quality of human life. In her memoir *Testament of Youth,* Vera Brittain explains, "France was the scene of titanic, illimitable death, and for this very reason it had become the heart of the fiercest living ever known to any generation. Nothing was permanent; everyone and everything was always on the move; friendships were temporary, appointments were temporary, life itself was the most temporary of all."[130]

---

[128] See also Holmes's "Singing 'Tipperary.'"
[129] Paul Fussell, *The Great War and Modern Memory,* 1975, Oxford UP, 2000, p. 71.
[130] Vera Brittain, *Testament of Youth,* Virago, 2014, pp. 338–339.

For some, fiercely living in the present meant savoring whatever small and simple pleasures could be found in the existing circumstances. In another of his poems "The Neutral," W. Kersley Holmes acknowledges that the war has put at risk not only men's lives, but their sense of themselves: "War, like a restless fever, haunts the air, / Changing the world we knew; / The men we are forget the men we were / In all we think and do." Grasping at simple pleasures that were part of life before the war—"eating chip potatoes"—gave soldiers a tangible way of preserving personal identities that many felt were slipping away with each day the war dragged on.

William Kersley Holmes was a banker who joined the Lothians and Border Horse Yeomanry regiment and was promoted to the rank of second lieutenant with the Royal Field Artillery. Holmes published two volumes of poetry: *Ballads of Field and Billet* and *More Ballads of Field and Billet* (which includes "The Soldier Mood"). A reviewer for the *Morning Post* praised Holmes's poems, writing, "We find their simplicity and sincerity very refreshing … as a change from the superheated, pumped-up patriotism of the average war poet."[131]

---

[131] Review qtd. in the front matter of *More Ballads of Field and Billet,* by W. Kersley Holmes, Alexander Gardner, 1915.

3

Noncombatants

The energies and attitudes of the home front are critical in waging war, as demonstrated in the writing of noncombatants. Some of the more popular poems of the First World War may now seem disturbing in their self-assured nationalism; others served as vehicles for dissent and anti-war protest. Writers called attention to the plight of civilians who were victims of war, and they described the experience of noncombatants who volunteered close to the battle lines. On the home front, the war reshaped gender roles, and as women became indispensable in munitions factories and agricultural work, they wrote poetry that both celebrated their contributions and chafed at societal restrictions. The war cast a spotlight on injustice, intolerance, and racism in nations "fighting to make the world safe for democracy," and writers explored these tensions. And like soldiers, noncombatants also struggled with experiences of isolation and powerlessness.

The Leaf Burners

Under two oak trees
   on top of the fell,[1]
With an old hawthorn hedge
   to hold off the wind,
I saw the leaf burners
   brushing the leaves
With their long brooms
   into the blaze.
Above them, the sky
   scurried along
Pale as a plate,
   and peered thro' the oaks,
While the hurrying wind
   harried the hedge.
But fast as they swept
   feeding the leaves
Into the flame
   that flickered, and fumed,
The wind, the tree-shaker,
   shaking the boughs,
Whirled others down
   withered and wan—
Summer's small folk,
   faded, and fain
To give up their life;
   earth unto earth,
Ashes to ashes,
   life unto death.

Far on the fell,
   where the road ran,
I heard the men march,
   in the mouth of the wind:
And the leaf burners heard
   and leaned down their heads,
Brow upon broom,
   and let the leaves lie,

---

[1] *Fell* is a dialect word used to refer to a hill or area of high land.

And counted their kin
    that crossed over sea,
And left wife and wean,[2]
    to fight in the war.

Forth over fell,
    I fared on my way;
Yet often looked back,
    when the wind blew,
To see the flames coil
    like a curl of bright hair
Round the face of a child—
    a flower of fire,
Beneath the long boughs
    where, lush and alive,
The leaves flourished long,
    loving the sun.

Much I thought then
    of men that went forth,
Or dropt like the leaves,
    to die and to live;
While the leaf burners
    with their long brooms
Drew them together
    on the day of their death.
I wondered at that,
    walking the fell—
Feeling the wind
    that wafted the leaves
And set their souls
    free of the smoke,
Free of the dead,
    speeding the flame
To spire on the air—
    a spark that should spring
In me, man of men;
    last of the leaves.

—Ernest Rhys[3] (1918)

---

[2] *Wean* is a dialect word used to refer to an infant.
[3] See also Rhys's "Jo's Requiem."

"The Leaf Burners" uses alliterative sounds and kennings—compound words used to rename nouns, such as "tree-shaker" for the wind—to recall the meditative poetry of the Anglo-Saxons, a distant warrior culture that sought meaning and solace in the natural world. The phrase "ashes to ashes," although describing the burned leaves, also recalls the Anglican burial rite: "Then shall the dust return to the earth as it was: and the spirit shall return unto God who gave it" (Ecclesiastes 12:7).

Born in London in 1859, Ernest Rhys grew up in Wales. Writer, editor, and reviewer, he established the Rhymer's Club with W.B. Yeats in 1890, and in 1906, Rhys began the work for which he is best known: he was the founding editor of *Everyman's Library.* He was fifty-five years of age and an established author when the war began. Rhys's war poetry appears in his 1918 collection *The Leaf Burners and Other Poems*; several of his pre-war ballads are included in the 1917 anthology *Welsh Poets: A Representative English Selection from Contemporary Writers.* The preface to that book situates Welsh war poetry within a historic tradition:

> Wales has made her sacrifices in war—from Evesham to Mametz Wood and Pilckem Ridge. She has never flinched from the ordeal by battle. Her sword will never be scabbarded while Justice cries wearily from the hills. But the soul of her is the soul of peace … The real Wales dwells amid fellowship of art and culture, by the hearth-fire, with the strong comradeship of humanity.[4]

---

[4] A.G. Prys-Jones, *Welsh Poets,* Erskine Macdonald, 1917, pp. 7–8.

Burning Beehives (Les ruches brûlées)[5]

How pleasing: straight away, they burned some beehives…

O bees, tumbling, buzzing gold in the blue air,
As long as you're aloft they haven't triumphed,
O last little glimmer from the golden age!

'But why ever are you burning my bees?'
The curé of Fraimbois asked the German brute.
'That's war!' replied the General. —Yes, war as waged
By the horde on the buzz and pride of freedom.
Why, then, did they burn this hive of straw?
Because the hive at work intoned a psalm
As it fashioned what resembled sunbeams.
And earlier, remember, on entering Brussels,
The Chiefs had issued orders to their thugs
To trample the flowerbeds underfoot.
As janissaries rush to please their vizier,
So the soldiers joyed to stamp down the flowers.
That they should blithely now be burning beehives
Is simple logic: it is but one short step,
One goose-step, from trampled flowers to bees in flames.
How they flared and crackled in the blue air,
And dropped! A fine sight; and the perfumed wax
Streaming black! And then, burn a beehive,
And up in smoke go famous names as well—
Plato, Vergil, La Fontaine, Maeterlinck—
Alongside the bees, as if to fade away,
A further fading out of humanism
To mark the triumph of the feldgrau lout.

The bee is spirit visible in light,
A drop of honey risen on two wings!
How might it ever find forgiveness from
Such clods? The bee is instant choice, sureness
Of touch and taste: briefly floating, exploring—
Then aim, effort, balance, judgement, skill!
And when the human mind in wonderment

---

[5] This is an excerpt (ll. 1–40, 70–95) from the longer poem, which can be read in its entirety in *French Poems of the Great War*, translated by Ian Higgins, Saxon Books, 2016, pp. 20–23.

Sees, deep in a hive, its own destiny
Mysteriously sketched out by pure instinct,
To serve the Hun it is disinclined! —Rather
This sweet, free order than their Discipline!
Yes, hives murmur. —All murmuring will
At once be shriven, purged and burnt alive!
....

'But why,' the poor priest asked, 'why burn my beehives?'
Pleasing, then, that to the bees' good shepherd
The Burner of bees said 'That's war'. —Their war, yes,
But what of ours?

                In those first, tragic days,
When our troops were moving north to Belgium,
It is told that French armoured cavalry
Rode through a Flemish village—I forget
The name—their horses festooned with roses,
Singing, as they rode, the Marseillaise—
But through their teeth, mouths closed, simply humming;
And it was magnificent. And this hum
Of Latin anger from across all those flowers,
Wordless, and gestureless, was the growl
Of mind and soul, it was conscience, and reason;
The sound of storm and oratory, pious,
Threatening, and with a fierce, golden
Calm. Not a single mouth was seen to move,
As though it were the flowers themselves that hummed.
And those who heard it, eyes filled with tears, thought
To hear, in the reddening evening dust,
Some kind of strange Marseillaise hummed by bees…
Thus, with purity and purpose, did our men
Transmute their warlike anthem into a swarm's hum,
As north they rode, prepared for ambush, prepared to die
For beehives and to save the honey of the world!
                    —Edmond Rostand (1919), translated by Ian Higgins

In August of 1914, the Germany army invaded Belgium and pushed into France. Almost immediately, reports of German war atrocities spread, including accounts of rape, massacre, and the burning of villages. The French Commission to Establish Acts Committed by the Enemy in Violation of the Law of Nations published these accounts in *Documents Relating to the War* (1915). The book was translated numerous times and was reprinted in English as *The New York Times Current History of the European War* (1917). In one eye-witness account of the invasion, a curé was arrested by Germans in the village of Fraimbois. Confronting German officers, the village priest asked why the troops had burned his beehives and received the reply, "What do you expect? It is war!"[6]

French writer Edmond Rostand, best known for his play *Cyrano de Bergerac*, shaped the story of the burning bees into a poem that merges history, fable, and patriotic political commentary. Rostand associates bees with religious martyrs and the enchantment of the natural world, but more importantly he recognizes bees as a symbol of French royalty and power, dating from the Merovingian rulers of the fifth century and later adopted by Napoleon as the emblem of his reign. The poem links industrious, selfless bees with France and its army, arguing that to burn a hive is to annihilate the ideals expressed by philosophers and authors who have written of the winged insects: bees settled on Plato's lips when he was a child; Virgil describes his hopes for Rome's political renewal in "The Bees"; La Fontaine's fable "The Hornets and the Bees" praises bees for their practical approach to conflict resolution, and Maeterlinck's *Life of the Bee* celebrates their "harmonious concord." Rostand died in December 1918, a victim of the influenza pandemic.

---

[6] "French Official Report on German Atrocities," *The New York Times Current History of the European War,* vol. 1, no. 2, New York Times, 1917, p. 1153.

Going to the Front

I had no heart to march for war
    When trees were bare and fell the snow;
To go to-day is easier far
    When pink and white the orchards blow,
While cuckoo calls and from the lilac bush
Carols at peace the well-contented thrush.

For now the gorse is all in flower,
    The chestnut tapers light the morn,
Gold gleam the oaks, the sun has power
    To robe the glittering plain with corn;
I hear from all the land of hope a voice
That bids me forward bravely and rejoice.

So merry are the lambs at play,
    So cheerfully the cattle feed,
With such security the May
    Has built green walls round every mead,
O'er happy roofs such grey old church-towers peep,
Who would not fight these dear, dear homes to keep?

For hawthorn wreath, for bluebell glade,
    For miles of buttercup that shine,
For song of birds in sun and shade
    That fortify this soul of mine,
For all May joy beneath an English sky,
How sweet to live—how glad and good to die!

                          —Hardwicke Drummond Rawnsley (1919)

Many were willing to fight and die for the lands they loved. One soldier who was inspired to fight by his deep love of home is Irish poet Francis Ledwidge; another is the British soldier-poet Edward Thomas. When Thomas was asked by his friend Eleanor Farjeon why he had enlisted, he paused, bent for a handful of soil, and answered, "Literally, for this."[7] Yet by 1916, the British government realized that the army's demand for soldiers was outstripping the rate of

---

[7] Matthew Hollis, *Now All Roads Lead to France: The Last Years of Edward Thomas,* Faber and Faber, 2011, p. 287.

voluntary enlistment. In January of 1916, the British introduced conscription to supplement the hundreds of thousands of men who had been killed and wounded in the first eighteen months of the conflict.[8] Beginning on March 2, 1916, single men between the ages of eighteen and forty-one were required to serve if called up, and married men were added to the conscription lists on May 25, 1916.

Canon Hardwicke Drummond Rawnsley was a 64-year-old clergyman in the spring of 1916; he served as Honorary Chaplain to George V from 1912 to 1917. Although Rawnsley was far too old to go to war himself, his only son, Noel, enlisted shortly after war was declared. Noel Rawnsley first joined the British Red Cross, then once in France, worked to be transferred to the Royal Engineers, where he served as a dispatch rider. Promoted to lieutenant, the younger Rawnsley "was invalided out having contracted pleurisy in the terrible conditions of the 1916 Winter."[9] Noel Rawnsley survived the war, but Noel's youngest son, Derek, died in 1943 while on active service in the Second World War.

H.D. Rawnsley was a prolific writer and active clergyman, but his chief legacy rests in fighting for the countryside he loved. He was a tireless campaigner for the environment, and in 1883, he founded the Lake District Defense Society. Rawnsley battled railway proposals that would have cut through scenic wilderness areas, and he organized protest marches to advocate for the opening of public footpaths. In 1895, he and two friends (Octavia Hill and Robert Hunter) met to strategize the formation of a national organization that would protect Britain's countryside and history. Today, Rawnsley is best known as one of the founders of the National Trust.

---

[8] When American joined the war, they referred to conscription as "Selective Service" or the "Selective Draft."
[9] "Noel Hardwicke Rawnsley," *Queensland Family Trees*, 21 May 2013, web.archive.org/web/20191120220428/https://www.queenslandfamilytrees.com/getperson.php?personID=112307&tree=5.

Hymn of Hate (Hassgesang gegen England)[10]

French and Russian, they matter not,
A blow for a blow and a shot for a shot;
We love them not, we hate them not,
We hold the Weichsel and Vosges-gate,
We have but one and only hate,
We love as one, we hate as one,
We have one foe and one alone.

He is known to you all, he is known to you all,
He crouches behind the dark gray flood,
Full of envy, of rage, of craft, of gall,
Cut off by waves that are thicker than blood.
Come, let us stand at the Judgment place,
An oath to swear to, face to face,
An oath of bronze no wind can shake,
An oath for our sons and their sons to take.
Come, hear the word, repeat the word,
Throughout the Fatherland make it heard.
We will never forego our hate,
We have all but a single hate,
We love as one, we hate as one,
We have one foe and one alone—
    ENGLAND!

In the Captain's Mess, in the banquet-hall,
Sat feasting the officers, one and all,
Like a sabre-blow, like the swing of a sail,
One seized his glass and held high to hail;
Sharp-snapped like the stroke of a rudder's play,
Spoke three words only: "To the Day!"
Whose glass this fate?
They had all but a single hate.
Who was thus known?
They had one foe and one alone—
    ENGLAND!

---

[10] When first published in the *New York Times*, Henderson's translation was titled "A Chant of Hate against England."

Take you the folk of the Earth in pay,
With bars of gold your ramparts lay,
Bedeck the ocean with bow on bow,
Ye reckon well, but not well enough now.
French and Russian they matter not,
A blow for a blow, a shot for a shot,
We fight the battle with bronze and steel,
And the time that is coming Peace will seal.
You we will hate with a lasting hate,
We will never forego our hate,
Hate by water and hate by land
Hate of the head and hate of the hand,
Hate of the hammer and hate of the crown,
Hate of seventy millions, choking down.
We love as one, we hate as one,
We have one foe and one alone—
    ENGLAND!

—Ernst Lissauer (1914), translated by Barbara Henderson

Internationally, the most famous poem of the war is likely that written by Ernst Lissauer, a German-Jewish poet who had tried to enlist in the German army but was "deemed unfit for service."[11] His "Hymn of Hate" was composed shortly after war broke out in 1914 and published in the pamphlet "Words for our Times." The poem became an immediate success in Germany: it was set to music, reprinted in school books, and distributed to German soldiers. In January 1915, the Kaiser awarded Lissauer the Order of the Red Eagle, Fourth Class, with Crown, an honor normally reserved for military service.[12] As early as December of 1914, however, a German anti-Semitic publication attacked Lissauer and his poem, claiming that it was un-German in its tone and that Jews resembled the hated English—as both were characterized by "pettiness and greed."[13]

Within two months of the poem's first publication, Barbara Henderson's English translation appeared in the *New York Times*.[14] The *Times* editors

---

[11] Richard Millington and Roger Smith, "'A Few Bars of the Hymn of Hate': The Reception of Ernst Lissauer's 'Hassgesang gegen England' in German and English," *Studies in 20th and 21st Century Literature*, vol. 41, no. 2, Article 5, p. 5.
[12] Millington and Smith, "A Few Bars," p. 6.
[13] Millington and Smith, "A Few Bars," p. 8.
[14] Henderson's translation, originally titled "A Chant of Hate Against England," appeared in the *New York Times*, 15 Oct. 1914, p. 12. In nearly all subsequent publications, it was retitled "Hymn of Hate."

admired Lissauer's technical skill as a writer, but described the poem as "simply abominable," and "a brutal and wicked production."[15] That did not stop Henderson's translation from being quickly republished "in the leading magazines throughout the English-speaking world—in the *Outlook* of October 28; the *London Daily Mail* of October 28; the *London Times* of October 29; the *Independent* of November 2; the *Literary Digest* of November 4, and virtually all leading English newspapers. It was also widely copied in Japan."[16] Newspapers in England republished the translated text of the poem with an accompanying musical score, and the choir at the Royal College of Music performed it as a farce. A review of the performance noted that although the 100-member British choir was instructed to sing "with plenty of snarl," their laughter made this difficult, and "when they came to the word *England*, they rolled it out in fine style."[17] The eminent author Sir Arthur Conan Doyle wrote a response to the Hymn in his 1914 essay "Madness," arguing that the poem's tone "is indicative of a German lack of manliness, as if 'we were really fighting with a furious, screaming woman,'" and claiming that the poem exposed a crucial difference between Germany and the British: the Germans are unsportsmanlike.[18] The poem was so familiar with Allied soldiers that its title was used as a slang term for artillery bombardments. A New Zealand soldier in the Gallipoli campaign wrote, "We are all living in dug-outs close to the beach, and have plenty of swimming until the Turks start with their Hymn of Hate, as we call their shells."[19]

Ernst Lissauer grew to regret writing the poem. In 1926, he stated that instead of composing a poem of hatred against England, he should have written a poem of love for Germany. In 1936, living in Vienna, he wrote, "To the German I am a Jew masked as a German; to the Jew a German faithless to Israel."[20] Lissauer died of pneumonia in 1937, a forgotten poet, "even, perhaps particularly, in Germany."[21] If he is remembered at all, it is solely for his "Hymn of Hate": its international notoriety persisted well after the end of the First World War. As Millington and Smith note,

---

[15] C.C. Aronsfeld, "Ernst Lissauer and the Hymn of Hate," *History Today*, vol. 37, no. 12, Dec. 1987, p. 49.
[16] "Contributions to Periodicals: Henderson, Barbara," *Proceedings and Addresses of the Fifteenth Annual Session of the State Literary and Historical Association of North Carolina*, Edwards and Broughton, 1915, p. 121.
[17] Aronsfeld, "Ernst Lissauer," p. 49.
[18] Millington and Smith, "A Few Bars," p. 12.
[19] Millington and Smith, "A Few Bars," p. 16.
[20] Aronsfeld, "Ernst Lissauer," p. 50.
[21] Aronsfeld, "Ernst Lissauer," p. 48.

In both themes and form, the poem diverges radically from modern assessments of the most important literary responses to the First World War. Yet the breadth and depth of its contemporary reception single it out as a monument of its time, and if for no other reason, it warrants continued attention for the sake of accurate historical understanding. As a literary document, it is remarkable because it traversed so many social and political boundaries, provoked so many and such varied responses, and became an internationally recognizable symbol of the German national outlook and temperament.[22]

---

[22] Millington and Smith, "A Few Bars," p. 17.

New Year's Wishes to the German Army
(Voeux de Nouvel An à l'Armée Allemande)

I wish that every hour of life
May wound your heart.
I wish each step you take in strife
May burn your feet.
I wish that you may be both blind and deaf
Unto all lovely things,
That you may walk all day and night
Beneath a sky bereft of light,
Seeing no flowers in the fields,
Hearing no word, no bird's sweet song
To mind you of the wives and children left
Alone at home so long.
I wish the soil—our country's soil—
May open and become
A quicksand 'neath your ranks,
And that the streams—our country's streams—
May overflow their banks
And drown your hosts.
I wish your nights may poisoned be
By all our martyrs' ghosts,
That you may neither watch nor sleep,
But ever breathe the smell of blood
By our Holy Innocents shed.
I wish the ruins of our homes
May crash above your head,
That your brain with anguish reel,
That doubt confound your rage,
That you may wander like lost beasts
Before the wild storm flying ...

I wish that you may live to feel
All we have suffered of late,
So that God may spare you the punishment supreme—
His eternal vengeance and hate.

(London, January 1915)

—Émile Cammaerts, translated by Tita Brand-Cammaerts

Numerous popular poems written during the First World War inflamed support for the war and advocated violence as the means of balancing the scales of justice. Émile Cammaerts, a 36-year-old Belgian writer living in London, had tried to enlist when he heard of the invasion of his country, but his application was denied due to his age. In her biography of her father, Cammaerts's youngest daughter writes that in 1914 her father "already had a slight academic stoop, [and] was painfully thin."[23] Émile Cammaerts turned to poetry to express his patriotism and to gain public support for Belgians who had suffered during the German invasion of their country. His poem "To My Country in Bondage" ("À Ma Patrie Enchaînée") concludes, "How long, oh how long, / My own country, / Wilt thou stretch out towards me / Patiently / Thy bruised hands?" Cammaerts's first volume of war poetry, *Belgian Poems: Patriotic Songs and Other Poems*, was written in French and translated into English by his British wife. A review in the *London Times* praised the volume: "We have come to know him as the limpid singer of Belgium victorious in defeat ... and a poet whose imaginative simplicity is ordered after the fashion of William Blake." The *Pall Mall Gazette* concurred: "Here, again, we have the note of hate—not in the doggerel of a Lessauer [sic], but in the reasoned stanzas of a man who can, and does, give chapter and verse for his anger ... 'New Year's Wishes to the Germany Army' ... will take an honoured place in the literature of malediction."[24]

The Cammaerts had six children: their son Pieter was killed in the Second World War while serving with the British Royal Air Force in 1941. Pieter's older brother, Francis, was a pacifist and conscientious objector in the Second World War, but after the death of his brother he joined British Special Operations, organizing resistance groups in occupied France to sabotage German military operations. The Cammaerts' grandson is Michael Morpurgo, the British Children's Laureate and author of the novels *War Horse* and *Private Peaceful*.

---

[23] Jeanne Lindley, *Seeking and Finding: The Life of Émile Cammaerts*, S.P.C.K, 1962, p. 100.
[24] "Press Opinions of Belgian Poems by Emile Cammaerts," *Belgian Poems: Chants Patriotiques et Autres Poèmes par Émile Cammaerts,* by Émile Cammaerts and translated by Tita Brand-Cammaerts, John Lane, 1916 edition.

Regiments (Régiments)

    All those boys who have left,
These soldiers reared to abominate war,
      Were little babies once, held
Snug and swaddled in a mother's arms.

    All a-swagger in steel helmets,
They march towards the crack of flung lightning,
      And leave behind that other hell,
The sorry female hell of tears and silence.

    Mothers, in your inmost being, deep
Flesh of your flesh, you carried your children;
      For you, victory and defeat
Are one: you hold your children's deaths a crime.

    But I just watch these lads march away,
And think in stupefaction of their birth;
      And deep inside myself I say:
'All these men's heads have torn women with pain.'
                —Lucie Delarue-Mardrus (1918), translated by Ian Higgins

On August 27, 1914, just weeks after war was declared, German mother and artist Käthe Kollwitz wrote in her diary that she had read in her local newspaper "a piece by Gabriele Reuter in the *Tag* on the tasks of women today. She spoke of the joy of sacrificing—a phrase that struck me hard." Kollwitz questioned Reuter's joy in the sacrifice: "Where do all the women who have watched so carefully over the lives of their beloved ones get the heroism to send them to face the cannon? … Those who now have only small children … seem to me so fortunate. For us, whose sons are going, the vital thread is snapped."[25] Kollwitz's two sons, Hans and Peter, had recently joined the German army. Peter was killed on October 22, 1914, less than two months after leaving for war. Today, Kollwitz is best known for her sculpture *Trauerndes Elternpaar (Grieving Parents)*, a memorial to her son and to the countless family tragedies of the First World War.

Nearly all nations used idealized images of motherhood to recruit soldiers and marshal support for the war. In Britain, one of the best-known letters of

---

[25] Käthe Kollwitz, *The Diary and Letters of Kaethe Kollwitz*, edited by Hans Kollwitz and translated by Richard Winston, Northwestern UP, 1989, p. 62.

the First World War was titled "A Mother's Answer to 'A Common Soldier'" and signed simply, "A Little Mother." Addressed to "Pacifists," "the Bereaved," and "the Trenches," the letter purportedly was written by "a mother of an only child—a son who was early and eager to do his duty" and explains "what the mothers of the British race think of our fighting men." Originally printed in August of 1916 in the *Morning Post,* the letter was reprinted as a pamphlet, and 75,000 copies were sold the first week. The Little Mother writes,

> We women pass on the human ammunition of 'only sons' to fill up the gaps, so that when the 'common soldier' looks back before going 'over the top' he may see the women of the British race at his heels, reliable, dependent, uncomplaining ... Women are created for the purpose of giving life, and men to take it. Now we are giving it in a double sense.[26]

After the war, British trench poet Robert Graves dismissed the letter as an example of civilians' "war-madness" and "newspaper language."[27] More recently, Jean Bethke Elshtain in *Women and War* has condemned the Little Mother for expressing "bloodcurdling patriotism coated in vapid and lifeless pieties."[28] At the time of its publication, however, the letter was enormously popular, and advertisements for its sale reported that "The Queen was deeply touched at the 'Little Mother's' beautiful letter."[29]

The French tried to boost military morale by matching isolated soldiers with *marraines,* godmothers who would send letters and gifts. The scheme was very popular with women old and young, until suspicions arose that the program encouraged immoral romantic relationships.[30] In her essay "Mothers, Marraines, and Prostitutes: Morale and Morality in First World War France," Susan R. Grayzel writes,

> Women, seen both as a guarantee of and as a potential threat to conventional morality and the social order, were recognized to be the key to keeping up morale. The quality of their morality and maternity would either lead the nation to victory against Germany or to ignominious defeat ... At the heart of the debate about the role of French women in the First World War can be heard the patriotic call to motherhood.[31]

---

[26] "A Mother's Answer to a 'Common Soldier,'" *Morning Post,* 14 Aug. 1916, qtd. in *Goodbye to All That,* by Robert Graves, Penguin, 1975, pp. 188–190.

[27] Robert Graves, *Goodbye to All That,* p. 188.

[28] Jean Bethke Elshtain, *Women and War,* U of Chicago P, 1987, p. 193.

[29] Qtd. in *Goodbye to All That,* p. 189.

[30] Susan R. Grayzel, "Mothers, Marraines, and Prostitutes: Morale and Morality in First World War France," *The International History Review,* vol. 19, no. 1 Feb. 1997, pp. 70–75.

[31] Grayzel, "Mothers, Marraines, and Prostitutes," p. 67.

In September of 1914, *Le Petit Journal* published "Pour les Mères de France," comparing the sacrifice of soldiers with that of mothers: "Since their sons left, the sun does not shine, the flowers have lost their scent, the day is without joy … Mothers of France, for your sacrifice there is no reward except that of the duty accomplished. Under your humble bodices beats the very heart of your son's country."[32] By the war's end, 1,393,000 soldiers had died for France, an estimated 20 percent of men under fifty years of age.[33]

Lucie Delarue-Mardrus was a journalist, novelist, and poet who in the early months of the war worked as a Red Cross nurse before resigning to devote her time and energies to writing. In her memoir, she recalls, "The absurdity of this war, of all wars, seemed to me like that of a vandal who furiously smashes piles of china plates, then dreamily steps back to gaze at the debris with consternation."[34]

---

[32] André Lichtenberger, "Pour Les Mères de France," *Le Petit Journal*, 20 Sept. 1914 (my trans.).
[33] "Veuves et orphelins de la Première Guerre mondiale," *Chemins de Mémoire*, web.archive.org/save/https://www.cheminsdememoire.gouv.fr/fr/veuves-et-orphelins-de-la-premiere-guerre-mondiale.
[34] Lucie Delarue-Mardrus, *Mes Memoires*, Gallimard, 1938, p. 196 (my trans.).

Penelope

In the pathway of the sun,
   In the footsteps of the breeze,
Where the world and sky are one,
   He shall ride the silver seas,
      He shall cut the glittering wave.
I shall sit at home, and rock;
Rise, to heed a neighbor's knock;
Brew my tea, and snip my thread;
Bleach the linen for my bed.
   They will call him brave.

—Dorothy Parker (1928)

In her examination of French, English, and German poetry of the First World War, Marsland notes that English criticism has privileged "realism as a protest device" so that "poems that do not present the 'observable realities' of the Front" have been dismissed and ignored.[35] While soldier-poets often wrote of the physical realities of the front lines, women were more likely to describe the psychological effects of war.

The writings of American author Dorothy Parker are rarely discussed in the context of the First World War. Dorothy Rothschild married Edwin Pond Parker II in the spring of 1917, and shortly after the wedding, her husband joined the American Expeditionary Force, enlisting with the 33rd Ambulance Company. Eddie Parker, a heavy drinker before the war, returned home addicted to morphine. After a four-year separation, Dorothy Parker was granted a divorce in 1928 on the grounds of "intolerable cruelty."[36] Eddie Parker remarried within months, but died five years later of what was deemed an accidental drug overdose. The title of Parker's poem "Penelope" alludes to Odysseus's wife, who waited twenty years for her husband to return from the Trojan War.

Over fifteen years after the break-up of her first marriage, as the Second World War was drawing to a close and her second husband was serving with

---

[35] Elizabeth A. Marsland, *The Nation's Cause: French, English and German Poetry of the First World War*, Routledge, 1991, p. 177.
[36] "Dorothy Parker Granted Divorce," *Boston Globe*, 9 Apr. 1928, p. 5.

US Army Intelligence in Europe, Parker published a short story about another waiting wife. "The Lovely Leave" tells of a woman's desperate attempts to bridge the impassable gulf that war has erected between the couple:

> To keep something, you must take care of it. More, you must understand just what sort of care it requires. You must know the rules and abide by them. She could do that. She had been doing it all the months, in the writing of her letters to him. There had been rules to be learned in that matter, and the first of them was the hardest: never say to him what you want him to say to you. Never tell him how sadly you miss him, how it grows no better, how each day without him is sharper than the day before. Set down for him the gay happenings about you, bright little anecdotes, not invented, necessarily, but attractively embellished. Do not bedevil him with the pinings of your faithful heart because he is your husband, your man, your love. For you are writing to none of these. You are writing to a soldier.[37]

The fictional story likely draws from both Parker's experience as a 23-year-old abandoned bride during the First World War and her second husband's absence in the Second World War.

By the end of the 1920s, Dorothy Parker was frequently applauded as the wittiest woman in America. Alexander Woollcott describes her writing as a mixture of "pure gold and prussic acid" and the author as "so odd a blend of Little Nell and Lady Macbeth."[38] Parker died in June of 1967, naming Lillian Hellman as her executor and leaving her entire estate to Martin Luther King, Jr. She left no instruction as to what should be done with her ashes (she wished to be cremated). They remained in an attorney's filing cabinet until 1988, when they were buried in a memorial garden at NAACP headquarters in Baltimore, marked by a plaque that reads, "Here lie the ashes of Dorothy Parker, 1893–1957, humorist, writer, critic, defender of human and civil rights. For her epitaph she suggested, 'Excuse my dust.'"

---

[37] Dorothy Parker, "The Lovely Leave," *Portable Dorothy Parker*, Viking, 1944, p. 24.
[38] Qtd in "The Cream of the Crop," by Lincoln Kirstein, *Virginia Quarterly Review*, vol. 10, no. 1, Jan. 1934, p. 148; Alexander Woolcott, "Our Mrs. Parker," *While Rome Burns*, Grosset and Dunlap, 1934, p. 149.

Visé
After a Letter from the Field
(Visé, Nach einem Feldpostbrief)

Smoke-black the air, the city in rubble,
buildings reduced to beams all charred
that strew the streets like barricades.
No roof shields the weary, just distant stars.

On paving stones troops take hard rest,
barely covered by a coat.
Around, fatigue-dulled men breathe deep,
while you alone lie awake so late.

Behind, a heap of ashes haunts you,
an elegant house that you transformed
when hunting for a sniper's nest.

One room still held an instrument,
above it a fearful Virgin hung:
the quiet greeting and silent respite
caught you in their sudden embrace.

As light waned you plucked some chords,
hollow echoes of the home's dead souls.
The Queen you salvaged in your coat
to bring her to me, when you make peace.

Then set fresh flames: you do your duty,
blow this house up like all the rest.
…Was that a cry? or just a broken string?
Music, music behind you has collapsed.

—Maria Dobler Benemann (1915), translated by Margaret R. Higonnet

It was called the bloodbath of Liège—the first battle of the Great War. When German troops invaded Belgium in early August of 1914, as part of the initial step in their plan to bypass strong French defenses, one of their first military objectives was the town of Visé. To delay the German advance, Belgians destroyed the town's bridge over the river Meuse and resisted German attacks. When German troops finally took Visé, they executed civilians in reprisal for the deaths of German soldiers who had been killed by Belgian snipers. They also burned two-thirds of the town's homes and rounded up its citizens, sending men to prison camps and exiling women and children.

Maria Dobler Benemann was a German writer and associate of the poet Rainer Maria Rilke. Her husband, Ernst Gerhard Benemann, fought with the German army and kept a diary account of his time in Visé. When Ernst's friends returned home on leave, they told Maria that while in the devastated town, her husband had found a piano in a ruined home and sat down briefly to play. She used these accounts as material for "Visé." Ernst Benemann was killed sometime in 1914 on the Western Front. Margaret Higonnet writes that after his death, due to economic circumstances, Maria was forced to send her two children to live with other families, and yet, "Apolitical, she nonetheless stood publicly against the war in its final phases and was courted by communists and reviled by right-wing patriots, who tried to deny her access to ration cards."[39] In addition to poetry, Benemann wrote children's books and short fiction; her autobiography, *Leih mir noch einmal die leichte Sandale* (*Lend me once again the light sandal*) was published in 1978.

---

[39] Margaret R. Higonnet, *Lines of Fire: Women Writers of World War I*, Plume, 1999, p. 484.

Homes

The lamplight's shaded rose
On couch and chair and wall,
The drowsy book let fall,
The children's heads, bent close
In some deep argument,
The kitten, sleepy-curled,
Sure of our good intent,
The hearth-fire's crackling glow:
His step that crisps the snow,
His laughing kiss, wind-cold....

Only the very old
Gifts that the night-star brings,
Dear homely evening-things,
Dear things of all the world,
And yet my throat locks tight...

Somewhere far off I know
Are ashes on red snow
That were a home last night.

—Margaret Widdemer (1918)

British journalist, feminist, and pacifist Helena Swanwick argued in 1915, "War is waged by men only, but it is not possible to wage it upon men only. All wars are and must be waged upon women and children as well as upon men."[40] Civilians whose homes were in the path of armies or who lived in enemy-occupied territories "lived both at home and, to an extent, on the front line."[41] Air raids and long-range artillery fire killed thousands of civilians, destroyed homes, and heavily damaged towns and cities. Over 700 bombs were dropped on Paris during the war; over 2,300 civilians in London were the casualties of German air-raids between 1917 and 1918; and in a single attack on June 22, 1916, 120 women and children were killed when a French air raid targeted the town of Karlsruhe, Germany.[42]

---

[40] Helena M. Swanwick, "Women and War," *The War in Its Effect upon Women and Women and War*, Garland, 1971, p. 1.
[41] Susan R. Grayzel, "The Role of Women in the War," *Oxford Illustrated History of the First World War*, edited by Hew Strachan, Oxford UP, 2014, p. 153.
[42] Martin Gilbert, "The War in the Air," *Atlas of the First World War*, Oxford UP, 1994, pp. 64–73.

American writer Margaret Widdemer was awarded the Pulitzer Prize in 1919, sharing the honor with Carl Sandburg. Reviewing Widdemer's war poetry, the *Christian Advocate* wrote, "These lines ... are among the war verse destined to survive the conflict."[43] Widdemer was a prolific writer and an associate of Ezra Pound, F. Scott Fitzgerald, and T.S. Eliot, but she is chiefly remembered today for popularizing the word *middlebrow* in a 1933 essay.[44] The essay, like its author, has been largely forgotten. In "Message and Middlebrow," Widdemer argues that literary critics and intellectual elites have coerced the reading public into accepting a narrow and truncated view of literary merit, one that attempts to exclude works that address morality and ideals.

---

[43] Madeleine Sweeny Miller, "Poems of the Great War," *The Christian Advocate*, vol. 93, 18 Apr. 1918, p. 489.

[44] Margaret Widdemer, "Message and Middlebrow," *The Saturday Review*, vol. 9, no. 31, 18 Feb. 1933, pp. 433–434.

After the Retreat

If I could only see again
The house we passed on the long Flemish road
That day
When the Army went from Antwerp, through Bruges, to the sea;
The house with the slender door,
And the one thin row of shutters, grey as dust on the white wall.
It stood low and alone in the flat Flemish land,
And behind it the high slender trees were small under the sky.

It looked
Through windows blurred like women's eyes that have cried too long.

There is not anyone there whom I know,
I have never sat by its hearth, I have never crossed its threshold, I have never
    opened its door,
I have never stood by its windows looking in;
Yet its eyes said: "You have seen four cities of Flanders:
Ostend, and Bruges, and Antwerp under her doom,
And the dear city of Ghent;
And there is none of them that you shall remember
As you remember me."

I remember so well,
That at night, at night I cannot sleep in England here;
But I get up, and I go:
Not to the cities of Flanders,
Not to Ostend and the sea,
Not to the city of Bruges, or the city of Antwerp, or the city of Ghent,
But somewhere
In the fields
Where the high slender trees are small under the sky—

If I could only see again
The house we passed that day.

—May Sinclair (1915)

One month after Britain declared war on Germany, 51-year-old English novelist May Sinclair (the pseudonym of Mary Amelia St. Clair) volunteered to join the Munro Ambulance Corps in Belgium. The early months of the war were chaotic, and Sinclair, along with the ambulance unit to which she'd been assigned, was caught up in the Allied retreat and forced to flee the German advance while attempting to assist the wounded. Sinclair's journal records an episode outside the village of Melle:

> There were no more wounded. Only two Germans lying in a turnip-field. The three of us—Mrs. Torrence and Janet and I—tried to bring pressure to bear on M.—[the Commandant]. We meant to go and get those Germans.
>
> But M.— was impervious to pressure. He refused either to go with the car himself or to let us go … He said that for two Belgians, or two French, or two British, it would be worth while taking risks. But for two Germans under German fire it wasn't good enough.
>
> But Mrs. Torrence and Janet and I didn't agree with him. Wounded were wounded. We said we were going if he wasn't … The Commandant … absolutely forbade the expedition.
>
> It took place all the same.[45]

The women had persuaded a Belgian army medical officer to allow them to proceed with an ambulance and an armed Belgian soldier to protect them, when the Commandant ordered Sinclair down from the car's running board. She writes,

> What happened then was so ignominious, so sickening, that, if I were not sworn to the utmost possible realism in this record, I should suppress it in the interests of human dignity.
>
> Mrs. Torrence, having the advantage of me in weight, height, muscle and position, got up and tried to push me off the step. As she did this she said: "You can't come. You'll take up the place of a wounded man."
>
> And I found myself standing in the village street, while the car rushed out of it, with Janet clinging on to the hood, like a little sailor to his shrouds. She was on the side next the German guns.
>
> It was the most revolting thing that had happened to me yet, in a life filled with incidents that I have no desire to repeat. And it made me turn on the Commandant in a way that I do not like to think of. I believe I asked him how he could bear to let that kid [Janet] go into the German lines, which was exactly what the poor man hadn't done.[46]

---

[45] May Sinclair, *A Journal of Impressions in Belgium*, Hutchinson, 1915, pp. 245–246.
[46] Sinclair, *Journal*, pp. 247–248.

They waited for what Sinclair describes as "a whole dreadful lifetime," and she recalls,

> We were dreadfully silent now. We stared at objects that had no earthly interest for us as if our lives depended on mastering their detail. We were thus aware of a beautiful little Belgian house standing back from the village street down a short turning … This house and its tree were vivid and very still. They stood back in an atmosphere of their own, an atmosphere of perfect but utterly unreal peace. And as long as our memories endure, that house which we never saw before, and shall probably never see again, is bound up with the fate of Mrs. Torrence and Janet McNeil.[47]

The ambulance eventually returned safely with the two women and the wounded Germans. Sinclair confesses, "The Commandant was entirely right to forbid the expedition, and we were entirely wrong in disobeying him. But it was one of those wrong things that I would do again to-morrow."[48] What she did not realize at the time was that because of her insubordination, the Commandant requested that she be forbidden to continue with the Ambulance Corps. Evacuated to England for her safety, Sinclair ends her journal, "Well—there are obsessions and obsessions. I do not know whether I have done the right thing or not in leaving Flanders (or, for that matter, in leaving Ghent). All that I know is that I love it and that I have left it. And that I want to go back."[49]

Charlotte Jones, writing for the *Guardian* in 2013, says that despite "her central role in the modernist revolution, May Sinclair remains shrouded in obscurity." Sinclair coined the literary term "stream of consciousness"; was an early reviewer of T.S. Eliot's poetry; served as a patron to Ezra Pound and a good friend to Thomas Hardy, Henry James, H.G. Wells, and Rebecca West; but "was never a self-promoter (unlike most of her contemporaries) and seems to have suffered the consequences."[50]

---

[47] Sinclair, *Journal*, p. 249.
[48] Sinclair, *Journal*, p. 248.
[49] Sinclair, *Journal*, p. 332.
[50] Charlotte Jones, "May Sinclair: The Readable Modernist," *The Guardian Books Blog*, 1 Aug. 2013, web.archive.org/save/https://www.theguardian.com/books/booksblog/2013/aug/01/may-sinclair-readable-modernist.

A Memory

There was no sound at all, no crying in the village,
    Nothing you would count as sound, that is, after the shells;
Only behind a wall the low sobbing of women,
    The creaking of a door, a lost dog—nothing else.

Silence which might be felt, no pity in the silence,
    Horrible, soft like blood, down all the blood-stained ways;
In the middle of the street two corpses lie unburied,
    And a bayoneted woman stares in the market-place.

Humble and ruined folk—for these no pride of conquest,
    Their only prayer: "O! Lord, give us our daily bread!"
Not by the battle fires, the shrapnel are we haunted;
    Who shall deliver us from the memory of these dead?

—Margaret Sackville[51] (1916)

While it is difficult to precisely account for noncombatant deaths in the First World War, it is thought that between 6.5 and 7 million civilians died as a result of the war.[52] These deaths include those who were executed in reprisals or killed in military actions, as well as those who were the victims of genocide, famine, and disease that were directly related to the war (the statistic does not include those who died as a result of the Spanish flu, the Russian Revolution, or the Turkish War of Independence). While many know that nearly 20,000 British soldiers were killed on the first day of the Somme, few realize that an estimated 750,000 German civilians died as a result of the Allied naval blockade, or that more Serbian civilians were killed in the war (82,000) than Serbian soldiers (45,000).[53] And these numbers are dwarfed by civilian deaths in Africa, Russia, Poland, Lithuania, and the Ottoman Empire.

The First World War spilled beyond the boundaries of the combat zone, yet the civilian dead of the war have been largely forgotten. The last line of Sackville's poem asks in grim irony, "Who shall deliver us from the memory of these dead?" In ceremonies, cemeteries, poems, and monuments, most commemorations of

---

[51] See also Sackville's "Reconciliation."
[52] The number of civilian casualties is difficult to determine and estimates vary widely. These figures are from Michael Clodfelter, *Warfare and Armed Conflicts—A Statistical Reference to Casualty and Other Figures, 1618-1991*, vol. 2, McFarland, 1992, pp. 781–782.
[53] Martin Gilbert, *The First World War: A Complete History*, Henry Holt, 1994, pp. xv, 540–541.

the First World War memorialize soldiers who were killed. Much less frequently remembered are the civilians who died, all those who, as described in another Sackville poem, "Quietly ... lie beneath your armies' feet."[54]

Margaret Sackville was the daughter of the 7th Earl De La Warr. During the war, she was a member of the Union of Democratic Control, an active pacifist, and a war poet; her collection *The Pageant of War* was published in 1916. One year earlier, writing in the suffragist magazine *Jus Suffragii*, Sackville stated, "For the first time, so far as I am aware ... the voice of organised womanhood finds expression" for women have "discovered the vital, easily ignored truth that man's business and woman's business cannot be separated—that any separation such as war creates is stultifying and ruinous."[55]

---

[54] From Sackville's poem "Victory."
[55] Margaret Sackville, *Jus Suffragii*, 1 Oct. 1915, p. 3, qtd. in *Fighting Forces, Writing Women: Identity and Ideology in the First World War,* by Sharon Ouditt, Routledge, 1994, p. 153,

May, 1915

Let us remember Spring will come again
To the scorched, blackened woods, where the wounded trees
Wait, with their old wise patience for the heavenly rain,
Sure of the sky: sure of the sea to send its healing breeze,
   Sure of the sun. And even as to these
     Surely the Spring, when God shall please,
   Will come again like a divine surprise
To those who sit to-day with their great Dead, hands in their hands, eyes in their eyes,
At one with Love, at one with Grief: blind to the scattered things and changing skies.

—Charlotte Mew

By May of 1915, the war that was to have been over by Christmas of 1914 had dragged into its tenth month. Poison gas was first used on the Western Front in April of 1915, and the list of dead and wounded grew to staggering numbers that spring following the Battle of Neuve Chapelle (March 1915), the 2nd Battle of Ypres (April 1915), the 2nd Battle of Artois (May–June 1915), and the start of the Gallipoli campaign (April 1915).

Charlotte May Mew was born in Bloomsbury in 1869. Three of her siblings died young, and two were institutionalized for mental illness. Most of her life, Mew struggled against poverty. She published only two volumes of poetry (one posthumously), but her work was appreciated by other writers, including H.D. (Hilda Doolittle), Virginia Woolf, and Siegfried Sassoon. Thomas Hardy praised Mew as "the least pretentious but undoubtedly the best woman poet of our day."[56] Tim Kendall, editor of *Poetry of the First World War* (2013), has said that Mew's poetry is "scandalously underappreciated."[57] In 1928, nine months after the sister with whom she was very close died of cancer, Mew committed suicide by drinking disinfectant. A 1953 review of Mew's *Collected Poems* opined, "There is a quality here which many good poets who are women have had in common—the presence of an emotion kept under restraint in daily life, and the absence of any wish to be striking and original."[58]

---

[56] Qtd. in *Lives of the Poets*, by Louis Untermeyer, Simon and Schuster, 1959, p. 656.
[57] Tim Kendall, "Charlotte Mew: May, 1915," *War Poetry*, 5 July 2011, web.archive.org/web/20190812182641/http://war-poets.blogspot.com/2011/07/charlotte-mew-may-1915.html.
[58] "Emotion in Restraint," *Times Literary Supplement*, no. 2707, 18 Dec. 1953, p. 814.

Any Englishwoman
May 1915

    England's in flower.
On every tree speared canopies unfold,
And sacred beauty crowns the lowliest weeds
Lifting their eager faces from the mould:
      Even in this hour
The unrelented pressure of the spring
Thrusts out new lovely life, unfaltering—
      Toward what deeds?
    What dreadful blossoming?

Ah, the red spines upon the curving briar,
      They tear the heart
        Great with desire
    And sick with sleepless pain
    For one that comes not again.
There's horror in the fragrance of the air,
Torment in this intolerable art.
    White petals on the pear!
      Yet, peering there,
I see beyond the rapture of young green
      And passion of pale fire
The glutton Death, who smiles upon the scene.

Last night there was a sudden wind that blew
    My joyful branches through.
Yesterday a rich blossom on the spray,
      To-day
All the sweet promise of life is vanished away:
Yea, of its ardent petals just a few
     White on the ground
       I found.
Bury them quick—I must not see them decay.

Others may know the triumph of the year
     And coming of the clear
Still days of autumn to redeem our grief.
For them the coloured bough, the noble sheaf:
      But I shall see

The petals that fell too soon from the blossoming tree,
    And the stain
There on the path, where they rest in the sorrowful rain.

—Evelyn Underhill

In 1916, a short piece titled "The Little Things: They Help One to Forget the War's Burden" appeared in the *Bristol Times and Mirror* on the feature page "Women and the Home":

> The little things, after all, are the great things. Let us, in this time of the nation's agony, these days of horror, anxiety, and breaking hearts, come back to some remembrance of the eternally beautiful little things. Surrounded by the Great War—great battleships, great armoured cars, great armies, let us spare a moment now and then for getting alone with the stars—just a moment's silent watching. You cannot think of rising prices, or overcrowded tramways, or wearying office-work, and see the pale Pleiades and a rising moon at the same time—thank God, the little things help us to forget! You can feel lonely and sad, perhaps, but it will not be a hopeless loneliness—you will be looking at something Eternal.[59]

Many searched for the comfort of the Eternal in the midst of "horror, anxiety, and breaking hearts."

Evelyn Underhill, the author of *Mysticism* (1911) and *The Path of Eternal Wisdom* (1912), was an established writer when war was declared. In 1916, Underhill published her second volume of poetry, *Theophanies*; a quotation from John Scotus Erigena appears on the title page: "Every visible and invisible creature is a theophany or appearance of God." The title's use of the plural attests to Underhill's conviction that God is not limited to a single manifestation, but instead is revealed in numerous, diverse, possibly even contradictory aspects of existence. Underhill's spiritual understanding was deeply shaken by the First World War; in a letter written in 1921 she confessed it was a time during which she "went to pieces."[60] Although she had supported the war at its start, in the interwar years, Underhill became increasingly committed to pacifism. In 1940, as war once again engulfed the world, Underhill wrote, "I am still entirely

---

[59] "Women and the Home, Fiction and Fashion: The Little Things," *Bristol Times and Mirror*, 15 Jan. 1916, p. 16.

[60] Evelyn Underhill, letter to Friedrich von Hügel, 21 Dec. 1921, qtd. in *Fragments from an Inner Life: The Notebooks of Evelyn Underhill*, edited by Dana Greene, Morehouse, 1993, p. 108.

pacifist and more and more convinced that the idea that this or any other war is 'righteous' or will achieve any creative result of a durable kind, is an illusion."[61] When she died in 1941, an obituary in the London *Times* recognized her as "one of the leading English writers on religious mysticism" and noted, "In poetry she was at her best when she wrote most simply."[62]

---

[61] Evelyn Underhill, letter to Fr. Curtis, C.R., Jan. 1940, qtd. in *The Life of Evelyn Underhill*, by Margaret Cropper, Skylight Paths, 2002, p. 234.
[62] "Obituaries: Mrs. E. Stuart Moore," *Times*, 18 June 1941, p. 7.

'I know the truth! Renounce all others!'

I know the truth! Renounce all others!
There's no need for anyone to fight.
For what? —Poets, generals, lovers?
Look: it's evening, look: almost night.

Ah, the wind drops, earth is wet with dew,
Ah, the snow will freeze the stars that move.
And soon, under the earth, we'll sleep too,
Who never would let each other sleep above.
   3rd October, 1915

—Marina Tsvetaeva, translated by A.S. Kline

The Battle of Tannenberg in August of 1914 nearly destroyed the Russian Second Army, and Russian troops continued to suffer greatly in 1915 due to severe shortages of weapons and munitions. Thousands of Russian recruits were not issued firearms, but instructed to take them from the dead at the first opportunity. In May of 1915, the combined forces of Austria-Hungary and Germany on the Eastern Front launched the Gorlice-Tarnow Offensive, and by August, an estimated 1.4 million Russian soldiers had been captured and sent to ill-equipped prisoner-of-war camps.[63] In September, the Russian army was forced to abandon its territories in Poland and was in full-scale retreat. Florence Farmborough, a British nurse with the Russian army wrote, "Bread, it was said, was growing scarce; in some parts famine already threatened to engulf the masses. The thousands of refugees swarming into the cities and towns were followed by pestilence and crime."[64]

Marina Tsvetaeva, regarded as one of the finest Russian poets of the twentieth century, was born in Moscow in 1892. Her father was a professor of Fine Arts at Moscow University, and her mother was a concert pianist, with strong family ties to Germany and Poland. Tsvetaeva's mother wished her to become a concert pianist and disparaged her daughter's writing. In later life, Tsvetaeva was to write, "After a mother like that, I had only one alternative: to become a poet."[65] Before her marriage to Sergei Efron in 1912, Tsvetaeva had traveled

---

[63] Martin Gilbert, *The First World War: A Complete History,* Henry Holt, 1994, p. 186.
[64] Farmborough, qtd. in *The First World War* by Martin Gilbert, p. 195.
[65] Marina Tsvetaeva, qtd. in *A Captive Spirit: Selected Prose of Marina Tsvetaeva,* edited by J. Marin King, Ardis, 1980, p. 276.

extensively in Europe, attending boarding schools in Germany and Switzerland and studying literature at the Sorbonne. When Russia declared war on Germany in 1914, her husband volunteered for the Russian army; she adopted a pacifist stance. Tsvetaeva composed "defiantly pro-German poems [that] she wrote and read in public during World War I."[66] In the aftermath of the October Revolution of 1917, Tsvetaeva found herself trapped in Moscow with her two daughters. Unable to leave the city, believing her husband to have been killed by the Bolsheviks, and with no family to assist her, she and her children struggled in abject poverty during the famine that followed. By 1919, Tsvetaeva felt she had no option but to place her young daughters (Alya, born in 1912, and Irina, born in 1917) in a state orphanage, hoping they could be fed. Alya survived, but Irina died of starvation in 1920.

Reunited with her husband in Berlin in 1922, Tsvetaeva continued to write poetry, but the family lived as impoverished exiles, moving from Berlin to Prague until eventually settling in Paris. By 1939, they had returned to Moscow, but under Stalin's regime, their lives were intolerable. On August 31, 1941, Tsvetaeva hanged herself; her husband was shot two months later, and their daughter Alya would spend sixteen years in Soviet prison camps. After Alya's release, she wrote an account of her family's life of unrelenting tragedy, *No Love without Poetry: The Memoirs of Marina Tsvetaeva's Daughter*. Writing of Tsvetaeva's poetry, Catherine Ciepiela has said that it "asks too much; her demands are embarrassing and improper; she 'makes one feel guilty' as one critic has phrased it ... She speaks, that is, as all human subjects would like to speak but dare not."[67]

---

[66] Simon Karlinsky, *Marina Tsvetaeva: The Woman, Her World, and Her Poetry*, Cambridge UP, 1986, p. 67.
[67] Ciepiela, "The Demanding Woman Poet," *PMLA*, May 1966, p. 430.

In Hospital

Under the shadow of a hawthorn brake,
   Where bluebells draw the sky down to the wood,
Where, 'mid brown leaves, the primroses awake
   And hidden violets smell of solitude;
Beneath green leaves bright-fluttered by the wing
Of fleeting, beautiful, immortal Spring,
I should have said, "I love you," and your eyes
Have said, "I, too...." The gods saw otherwise.

For this is winter, and the London streets
   Are full of soldiers from that far, fierce fray
Where life knows death, and where poor glory meets
   Full-face with shame, and weeps and turns away.
And in the broken, trampled foreign wood
Is horror, and the terrible scent of blood,
And love shines tremulous, like a drowning star,
Under the shadow of the wings of war.
        1916

—Edith Nesbit

Edith Nesbit, co-founder of the socialist Fabian society, is perhaps best known for her novel *The Railway Children*. In 1914, Nesbit edited a poetry collection she titled *Battle Songs*. In a note "To the Reader," she explains,

> I thought that our soldiers might like to have a book holding real songs about brave men and the splendid heroisms of war and I made this book as quickly as I could ... A good fight is a good fight and worthy of a place in song, if so be that the enemies are brave men fighting for a cause they believe to be just, not blackguards and barbarians making war on women, children, old men, and the wearers of the Red Cross.[68]

Nesbit's attitude toward the war appears to have been as changeable and complex as was her life; George Bernard Shaw, one of her lovers, described her as "audaciously unconventional."[69] Nesbit biographer Julia Briggs writes,

---

[68] Edith Nesbit, editor, *Battle Songs*, Max Goschen, 1914.
[69] George Bernard Shaw, qtd. in *A Woman of Passion: The Life of E. Nesbit*, by Julia Briggs, New Amsterdam, 1987, p. 86.

Edith was appalled by the war, and was constantly torn between her early, and ultimately Gallic, hatred of the Germans, and the painful recognition that they were human beings too. Her initial reaction was one of violent patriotism … In a letter to E.M. Forster she voiced such violent anti-German sentiment that he was quite shocked … [and] let their friendship lapse. Yet at the same time she was also taking active steps to prevent an old German friend of hers from being interned, and she rebuked [her friend] Alice sharply when she shouted and clapped at a German Zeppelin shot down in flames, sternly demanding whether she realized "that there are people being burned alive over there?"[70]

Eight years after the First World War had ended, Nesbit published *Many Voices*, a volume of poetry that included her war poems. "In Hospital," dated 1916, disputes the "splendid heroisms of war" that Nesbit had admired in 1914.

---

[70] Briggs, *A Woman of Passion*, p. 365.

Somme Film, 1916

There is no cause, sweet wanderers in the dark,
For you to cry aloud from cypress trees
To a forgetful world; since you are seen
Of all twice nightly at the cinema,
While the munition-makers clap their hands.

—C.H.B. Kitchin (1919)[71]

When the British Topical Committee for War Films sent cameramen Geoffrey Malins and John McDowell to the Western Front in late June of 1916, the committee did not intend to produce a full-length silent film of the war. The men were sent to the Somme to gather footage that could be used in newsreels to bolster home front morale. Malins and McDowell filmed scenes that include now-iconic images: the detonation of the mine at Hawthorn Ridge and the men of the 1st Battalion Lancashire Fusiliers gathered in a sunken lane, waiting the order to attack. But after viewing Malins' and McDowell's footage on July 12, the Wellington House Cinema Committee quickly decided to produce a war film. *Battle of the Somme*, the first full-length war documentary, opened in thirty-four London movie houses on August 21, 1916. One million people viewed the film in its first week, and after just six weeks, an estimated twenty million had seen the movie, nearly half the British population of forty-three million.[72] The film was shown in over 2,000 cinemas, with musical accompaniments that varied according to locale; in Dublin the film was "part of a variety programme including a singing comedienne and a one-legged dancer."[73] Across Great Britain, contemporary accounts state that audiences responded with "a mixture of pity and horror"; the *Daily Mail* reported that while watching a scene of soldiers attacking from their trenches, a woman cried out, "Oh God, they're dead."[74] Ian Beckett notes that the film's "flickering silent images transformed the public perception of the war, both at the time and for posterity."[75] In 2005, the documentary was chosen to be included in UNESCO's Memory of the World global register of key cultural artifacts.

---

[71] This version of the poem was published in Kitchen's *Curtains* (Blackwell, 1919). A slightly altered version was included in the 1920 publication *Oxford Poetry, 1919*, edited by T.W. Earp, Dorothy L. Sayers, and Siegfried Sassoon, Blackwell, 1920.
[72] Ian F.W. Beckett, *The Making of the First World War*, Yale UP, 2012, p. 100.
[73] Beckett, *The Making*, p. 98.
[74] Beckett, *The Making*, p. 100.
[75] Beckett, *The Making*, p. 105.

Clifford Henry Benn Kitchin witnessed the Battle of the Somme firsthand as a lieutenant with the 1/8 Royal Warwickshire regiment. His unit suffered devastating losses on the first day of the battle; of the 800 men of the regiment who attacked that day, 588 became casualties.[76] Kitchin himself was wounded in January of 1917 but survived the war. His younger brother, a pilot with the Royal Naval Air Service, died in an airplane crash in June of 1918. After the war, Kitchen turned to writing novels and achieved some success with the popular detective mystery *Death of My Aunt* (1929). When he died in 1967, an obituary in the *London Times* described him as "A man of uncompromising, and on occasions even uncomfortable, intellectual honesty, of wide erudition and of iridescent wit."[77]

---

[76] Robert David Williams, *A Social and Military History of the 1/8th Battalion, The Royal Warwickshire Regiment in the Great War,* 1999, U of Birmingham, Master's thesis, p. 69.

[77] "Mr. C.H. Kitchin: Dedicated Novelist." *London Times,* 4 Apr. 1967, p. 12.

The Ballad of Bethlehem Steel
or
The Need For Preparedness
A Tale of the Ticker
For the Public

A fort is taken, the papers say,
   Five thousand dead in the murderous deal.
A victory? No, just another grim day.
   But—up to five hundred goes Bethlehem Steel.

A whisper, a rumor, one knows not where—
   A sigh, a prayer from a torn heart rent—
A murmur of Peace on the death-laden air—
   But—Bethlehem Steel drops thirty per cent.

"We'll fight to the death," the diplomats cry.
   "We'll fight to the death," sigh the weary men.
As the battle roars to the shuddering sky—
   And— Bethlehem Steel has a rise of ten.

What matters the loss of a million men?
   What matters the waste of blossoming lands?
The children's cry or the women's pain?
   If—Bethlehem Steel at six hundred stands?

And so *we* must join in the slaughter-mill,
   We must arm ourselves for a senseless hate,
We must waste our youths in the murder drill—
   That Bethlehem Steel may hold its state.

—Grace Isabel Colbron (1915)

From 1914 to 1918, the Allied and Central Powers poured over 208 billion dollars into waging war.[78] Adjusted for inflation, the amount today would exceed 3.5 trillion dollars. Before the United States entered the war, many Americans wanted nothing to do with the conflict and hoped to remain neutral. Others, however, seized war-time opportunities to aggressively pursue profits. Celebrating those profits in May of 1916, Charles Schwab, president of Bethlehem Steel, addressed the executives of the American Iron and Steel Institute: "Boys, we are

---

[78] Horst Mendershausen, *The Economics of War,* Prentice-Hall, 1940, p. 305.

in a period of great prosperity. I wonder if any of us ever expected, anticipated or dreamed that we should ever see any such state of affairs as we see today ... Boys, may this prosperity continue."[79] Just how prosperous was Bethlehem Steel? In the months before war was declared in Europe, the company had struggled, operating at only 60 percent capacity and reducing workers' hours. But after securing military contracts from Russia, Britain, and France, Bethlehem Steel emerged as the leading US supplier of Allied ships, munitions, and ordnance. By end of 1917, "orders on hand at Bethlehem Steel were twenty times as great as at the end of 1913," and stock prices had risen from $30 to $600 a share.[80]

War profiteering was not unique to America. Companies in nearly every industrialized country sought to benefit from the war: Krupp (Germany), Renault (France), and Vickers (Britain) are some of the better-known examples. But the war-time ideal of sacrifice was challenged when not everyone seemed to accept an equal share of the sacrifice. In 1935, fearing the prospect of yet another world war, retired American General Smedley Butler accused those who had profited from the First World War:

> At least 21,000 new millionaires and billionaires were made in the United States during the World War. That many admitted their huge blood gains in their income tax returns. How many other war millionaires falsified their tax returns no one knows.
>
> How many of these war millionaires shouldered a rifle? How many of them dug a trench? How many of them knew what it meant to go hungry in a rat-infested dug-out? How many of them spent sleepless, frightened nights, ducking shells and shrapnel and machine gun bullets? How many of them parried the bayonet thrust of an enemy? How many of them were wounded or killed in battle?

Butler continues, "Beautiful ideals were painted for our boys who were sent out to die. This was the 'war to end wars.' This was the 'war to make the world safe for democracy.' No one told them that dollars and cents were the real reason. No one mentioned to them, as they marched away, that their going and their dying would mean huge war profits."[81]

American author and translator Grace Isabel Colbron was active in both the pacifist and suffragist movements. In her 1905 essay "Women and War," she argues that any country in which "the military ideal holds sway" will fail

---

[79] Kenneth Warren, *Bethlehem Steel: Builder and Arsenal of America*, U of Pittsburgh P, 2008, p. 105.
[80] Warren, *Bethlehem Steel*, pp. 103–106.
[81] Smedley D. Butler, *War Is a Racket*, pp. 13, 30.

to secure "the attainment of full legal and political rights for women." More specifically, she urges,

> Let American women think seriously on this matter of war and peace, on this question of imperialism and militarism. If our nation should by any unfortunate but highly improbable combination of circumstances take her place amid the army-ridden, land-stealing world powers, it would mean much more to the American woman than a succession of wars that would bereave her of her loved ones, or send them back to her crippled or afflicted with loathsome disease. It would mean for American woman as a sex the loss of much she has gained ... and it would place the goal of perfect political and legal equality she still desires far, far out of reach.[82]

Colbron's "The Ballad of Bethlehem Steel" was published in December of 1915 and reprinted in numerous newspapers and journals across the country throughout the next year. She gave a public reading of her anti-war ballad in January of 1916 at a Washington, DC, rally that protested the war and the Preparedness Movement.[83] Despite public protests, the American Congress declared war on Germany on April 6, 1917.

---

[82] Grace Isabel Colbron, "Women and War," *Advocate of Peace*, vol. 67, no. 4, Apr. 1905, p. 86.
[83] "To Read Original Poem: Miss Colbron Writes Ballad for Meeting against Preparedness," *Washington Evening Star*, 29 Jan. 1916, p. 10.

The Farmer, 1917

I see a farmer walking by himself
In the ploughed field, returning like the day
To his dark nest. The plovers circle round
In the gray sky; the blackbird calls; the thrush
Still sings—but all the rest have gone to sleep.
I see the farmer coming up the field,
Where the new corn is sown, but not yet sprung;
He seems to be the only man alive
And thinking through the twilight of this world.
I know that there is war behind those hills,
And I surmise, but cannot see the dead,
And cannot see the living in their midst—
So awfully and madly knit with death.
I cannot feel, but know that there is war,
And has been now for three eternal years,
Behind the subtle cinctures of those hills.
I see the farmer coming up the field,
And as I look, imagination lifts
The sullen veil of alternating cloud,
And I am stunned by what I see behind
His solemn and uncompromising form:
Wide hosts of men who once could walk like him
In freedom, quite alone with night and day,
Uncounted shapes of living flesh and bone,
Worn dull, quenched dry, gone blind and sick, with war;
And they are him and he is one with them;
They see him as he travels up the field.
O God, how lonely freedom seems to-day!
O single farmer walking through the world,
They bless the seed in you that earth shall reap,
When they, their countless lives, and all their thoughts,
Lie scattered by the storm: when peace shall come
With stillness, and long shivers, after death.

—Fredegond Shove

When Britain instituted mandatory conscription with the Military Service Act of 1916, conscientious objectors were required to apply to local tribunals to request exemption from military service. Often, those seeking exemption "were mocked and vilified by press and public, were ostracised by friends and family, sacked from jobs, imprisoned and physically brutalised. To most people, they were seen as shirkers, cowards, and even traitors."[84] Tribunals granted few exemptions: six million men served in the British military, yet only an estimated 16,000 were recorded as conscientious objectors. Despite their relatively small numbers, "the impact of these men on public opinion and on future governments was to be profound."[85] Margaret Brooks of the British Imperial War Museum writes, "To become a conscientious objector in 1916 was a difficult decision, which apparently involved rejecting the whole of conventional British society and everything it stood for."[86] Over one-third of conscientious objectors were imprisoned at least once, and many were assigned to non-military manual labor in support of the war effort.

Gerald Shove was a graduate of King's College at Cambridge, a close friend of the economist John Maynard Keynes, and a life-long pacifist. He met his future wife, the poet Fredegond Maitland, at a tea party in 1914, where the two spent the evening discussing the war. The couple became engaged the same week that Rupert Brooke, a Cambridge friend of Shove's, died on his way to Gallipoli. Although Gerald Shove likely would have been granted exemption from military service on medical grounds, he applied for conscientious objector status and was assigned to agricultural work. His wife Fredegond writes,

> the war was only then reaching its peak of horror and our life had suddenly grown very strenuous and anxious.
>
> We got out of bed when the alarm-clock said that it was five o'clock and Gerald uncomplaining set forth across the fields to his new work. He returned at dusk, but I used, of course, to walk over to the farm with packages of food and I used always to be terrified that he would collapse under the strain of the work.[87]

The "solemn and uncompromising form" of the solitary man in "The Farmer, 1917" likely describes Shove's husband, and the poem can be read as a comment on conscientious objectors.

Fredegond Shove was a cousin of Virginia Woolf and a niece by marriage of composer Ralph Vaughan Williams (he set four of her poems to music). She was also the first female poet included in the *Georgian Poetry* anthologies. Her work was selected for the 1918–1919 volume, chosen over the poetry of Charlotte Mew, Rose Macaulay, and Edith Sitwell, who had also been considered.

---

[84] Ann Kramer, *Conscientious Objectors of the First World War*, Pen and Sword, 2014, p. 1.
[85] Margaret Brooks, "Conscientious Objectors in Their Own Words," *Imperial War Museums*, 5 June 2018, web.archive.org/web/20190804022243/https://www.iwm.org.uk/history/conscientious-objectors-in-their-own-words.
[86] Brooks, "Conscientious Objectors."
[87] *Fredegond and Gerald Shove,* by Fredegond Shove, privately printed, 1952, p. 33.

Spreading Manure

There are fifty steaming heaps in the One Tree field,
    Lying in five rows of ten.
They must all be spread out ere the earth will yield
    As it should (and it won't, even then).

Drive the great fork in, fling it out wide;
    Jerk it with a shoulder throw.
The stuff must lie even, ten feet on each side,
    Not in patches, but level—so.

When the heap is thrown, you must go all round
    And flatten it out with the spade.
It must lie quite close and trim, till the ground
    Is like bread spread with marmalade.

The north-east wind cuts and stabs our breath;
    The soaked clay numbs our feet.
We are palsied, like people gripped by death,
    In the beating of the frozen sleet.

I think no soldier is so cold as we,
    Sitting in the Flanders mud.
I wish I was out there, for it might be
    A shell would burst, to heat my blood,

I wish I was out there, for I should creep
    In my dug-out, and hide my head.
I should feel no cold when they laid me deep
    To sleep in a six-foot bed.

I wish I was out there, and off the open land:
    A deep trench I could just endure.
But, things being other, I needs must stand
    Frozen, and spread wet manure.

—Rose Macaulay[88] (1919)

Britain's labor shortage during the First World War was critical: over three million men had left for military service, and women workers were desperately needed

---

[88] See also Macaulay's "Picnic."

to maintain the country's food supply. Numerous organizations attempted to recruit women for work on the land, and by 1917, the government realized the necessity of founding and funding a central organization, the Women's Land Army (WLA). By the end of the year, the WLA had placed over 23,000 "Land Girls," and although official records were either never kept or have been since destroyed, it is estimated that over a quarter of a million women volunteered for agricultural work. As the Land Army Song urged, "Come out of the towns and on to the downs, where a girl gets brown and strong; With swinging pace and morning face she does her work to song."[89]

Despite the need for women farm workers, resistance was high. A *London Telegraph* article published in May of 1916 reported, "At the Ryedale Agricultural Club, held at Helmsley, yesterday, Mr. Hebron said he could not get women workers for love or money. Women labour on the land was a farce. They were simply out on spooning expeditions, trying to catch husbands. (Laughter.) Women's place was at home."[90] Many doubted women's ability to capably accomplish farm tasks. Some with traditional values viewed the Land Girls' uniform trousers as disgraceful cross-dressing garments. An article in the *Sunday Mirror* argued that women were being ruined by "unwomanly" work: "It deforms their physical constitution ... It is man's work. It makes women into men."[91] In response, the WLA and its supporters created posters, poetry, and advertisements that celebrated the women's patriotic efforts and feminized the new roles in an attempt to change public attitudes. A 1918 appeal persuaded recruits, "Land labour may give you a few backaches, but it will also give you health, a complexion such as a fortune spent with beauty specialists would never beget, and happiness such as only comes from the knowledge that you are doing your full share to speed the day of Victory."[92]

Those wishing to join the WLA had to be over twenty years of age and were required to submit references, report for an interview, demonstrate their ability to read and write, and pass a physical exam. If accepted, each Land Army Girl signed a six-month or one-year contract, agreeing to be sent anywhere in the country that she was needed. She was typically paid between 20–25 shillings a week and charged 17 shillings/week for room and board. The *Women's Land Army Handbook* asked each recruit to pledge that she would "behave quietly,"

---

[89] "Land Army Song," *Women's Land Army L.A.A.S. Handbook,* Women's Branch Board of Agriculture and Fisheries, July 1919, p. 6.
[90] "Farmers and Women Workers," *London Telegraph,* 27 May 1916, p. 3.
[91] Qtd. in *Holding the Home Front,* by Caroline Scott, Pen and Sword, 2017, p. 114.
[92] Qtd. in *Holding the Home Front,* p. 132.

"secure eight hours' rest each night," "avoid entering the bar of a public house," "not smoke in public," and "never wear the uniform after work without her overall, nor walk about with her hands in her breeches pockets."[93] Formal training was scarce, but women were encouraged to send for leaflets on such topics as bee-keeping, thatching, implementing hygienic practices in the dairy, constructing pigsties, and treating ringworm in cattle. Land Girls worked nine to ten hours a day in all kinds of weather, often six days a week, at wages far below those of women who had volunteered for munitions or clerical work. As Carol Twinch notes in her book *Women on the Land*, "Theirs was a necessary but largely unspectacular heroism."[94]

Rose Macaulay, daughter of a Cambridge professor, volunteered with the WLA in 1916. She wrote to Irish writer Katharine Tynan on March 4, 1916, "I wish I could write poetry in these days; I somehow can't. The war seems to have killed all that; I can only just struggle with prose. I am trying to get through with a novel [*Non-Combatants and Others*], in moments snatched from nursing in a V.A.D. hospital and working on the land for 3d an hour."[95] Macaulay's only volume of war poetry, *Three Days,* was published in 1919. Katherine Mansfield said of Macaulay's writing, "it is not only her cleverness and wit which are disarming. It is her coolness, her confidence, her determination to say just exactly what she intends to say whether the reader will or no."[96]

---

[93] *Women's Land Army L.A.A.S. Handbook*, p. 6.
[94] Carol Twinch, *Women on the Land,* Lutterworth, 1990, p. 52.
[95] Qtd. in "Letters from Rose Macaulay to Katharine Tynan," by Martin Ferguson Smith, *English Studies*, vol. 99, no. 5, 2018, pp. 523–524.
[96] Katherine Mansfield, *Novels and Novelists,* Constable, 1930, p. 200.

I Sit and Sew

I sit and sew—a useless task it seems,
My hands grown tired, my head weighed down with dreams—
The panoply of war, the martial tread of men,
Grim faced, stern eyed, gazing beyond the ken
Of lesser souls, whose eyes have not seen Death,
Nor learned to hold their lives but as a breath—
But—I must sit and sew.

I sit and sew—my heart aches with desire—
That pageant terrible, that fiercely pouring fire
On wasted fields, and writhing grotesque things
Once men. My soul in pity flings
Appealing cries, yearning only to go
There in that holocaust of hell, those fields of woe—
But—I must sit and sew.

The little useless seam, the idle patch;
Why dream I here beneath my homely thatch,
When there they lie in sodden mud and rain,
Pitifully calling me, the quick ones and the slain?
You need me, Christ! It is no roseate dream
That beckons me—this pretty futile seam
It stifles me—God, *must* I sit and sew?

—Alice Moore Dunbar-Nelson (1920)

As Americans mobilized for war in 1917, political rallies, recruiting events, posters, and news editorials reminded them of why they were joining the bloodiest conflict the world had yet known: they were fighting to make the world safe for democracy. But an editorial appearing in the *New York Tribune* voiced the concerns of many Americans and challenged that premise: "Democracy implies equality of privilege and equal obligation of service. If we fight for this for the world in general we ought to be prepared to practise it among ourselves. At present we mingle democracy with discriminations. All the elements of our citizenship do not stand on the same level."[97] The editorial denounced inequities and harsh treatment that black soldiers regularly experienced.

---

[97] "Race Prejudice and the War," *New York Tribune*, 18 Nov. 1917, p. 2.

Black women who attempted to assist in the war effort were also the victims of prejudice. Hired for factory work at salaries considerably below those paid to white women performing the same jobs, black women were also frequently barred from volunteering as canteen and aid workers. Perhaps most concerning was the treatment of black nurses. W.C. Gorgas, the Army's Surgeon General, flatly refused the service of black nurses:

> Referring to your memorandum of February 12th, *relative to the appointment and training of colored nurses for colored soldiers*, at the present time *colored nurses are not being accepted for service in the Army Nurse Corps*, as there are *no separate quarters available for them* and *it is not deemed advisable to assign white and colored nurses to the same posts*.[98]

Emmett J. Scott, Special Advisor of Black Affairs to the Secretary of War, denounced the War Department's discriminatory policies:

> Waiving all discussion as to the matter of assigning white and colored nurses to the same posts or quarters, it is difficult for me to understand why some colored nurses have not been given an opportunity to serve. This vexing question is being put to me almost daily by colored newspaper editors, colored physicians, surgeons, etc., who are constantly bombarding my sector of the War Department, inquiring what has been done, and urging that something should be done in the direction of utilizing professionally trained and efficient colored nurses.[99]

Alice Dunbar-Nelson was a poet, playwright, journalist, and political activist (her first husband was the poet Paul Dunbar). During the First World War, she served on the Women's Committee of the Council of Defense and was active in the Circle of Negro War Relief, establishing a local chapter to provide assistance to black soldiers and their families.[100] Her war poem "I Sit and Sew" was first published in the *A.M.E. Church Review* in 1918. In 1920, Dunbar-Nelson's lengthy essay "Negro Women in War Work" appeared in *Scott's Official History of the American Negro in the World War*. She describes how "Into this maelstrom of war activity the women of the Negro race hurled themselves joyously. They asked no odds, remembered no grudges, solicited no favors, pleaded for no

---

[98] W.C. Gorgas, Surgeon General, 14 Feb. 1918, qtd. in *Scott's Official History of the American Negro in the World War,* edited by Emmett J. Scott, Homewood, 1919, p. 448.

[99] Emmet J. Scott to Dean F.P. Keppel, Office of the Secretary of War, 28 Feb. 1918, qtd. in *Scott's Official History,* p. 451.

[100] Sandra L. West, "Dunbar-Nelson, Alice (Alice Ruth Moore)," *Encyclopedia of the Harlem Renaissance,* edited by Aberjhani and Sandra L. West, Infobase, 2003, p. 93.

privileges. They came by the thousands, hands opened wide to give of love and service and patriotism."[101] And yet as Dunbar-Nelson acknowledges,

> The problem of the woman of the Negro race was a peculiar one ... There were separate regiments for Negro soldiers; should there be separate organizations for relief work among Negro women? If she joined relief organizations, such as the Red Cross Society, and worked with them, would she be assured that her handiwork would reach black hands on the other side of the world, or should she be great-hearted and give her service, simply for the sake of giving, not caring who was to be benefited?[102]

Dunbar-Nelson's essay asserts that black women "did all that could be done—all that they were allowed to do," but argues they were blocked from fully supporting their troops. Like Emmett J. Scott, she found the order excluding black nurses from overseas service deeply troubling: "Colored women since the inception of the war had felt keenly their exclusion from overseas service. The need for them was acute; their willingness to go was complete; the only thing that was wanted was authoritative sanction."[103] The African American community feared that without black nurses, black soldiers would receive inadequate medical care. Social codes forbidding intimacies between the races were likely to prevent white women from nursing black soldiers, and segregated hospital facilities were likely to offer substandard medical care. The concerns were real: during the war, black soldiers died at disproportionately higher rates due to segregated, poorly staffed hospitals.[104]

The poem "I Sit and Sew" testifies to the complex intersections of gender and race in the First World War. In the conclusion to her essay "Negro Women and War Work," Dunbar-Nelson praises black women for not only their war service, but their persistent hope in the face of discrimination: "She shut her eyes to past wrongs and present discomforts and future uncertainties. She stood large-hearted, strong-handed, clear-minded, splendidly capable, and did, not her bit, but her best, and the world is better for her work and her worth."[105]

---

[101] Alice Dunbar-Nelson, "Negro Women in War Work," *Scott's Official History of the American Negro in the World War*, p. 375.
[102] Dunbar-Nelson, "Negro Women in War Work," p. 376.
[103] Dunbar-Nelson, "Negro Women in War Work," pp. 377, 378.
[104] Emmett J. Scott, "Did the Negro Soldier Get a Square Deal?" *Scott's Official History of the American Negro in the World War*, pp. 429–430.
[105] Dunbar-Nelson, "Negro Women in War Work," p. 397.

To the Patriotic Lady across the Way

She wore a Liberty loan button
And above it a silken American flag,
And her knitting needles clicked
Through some soldier's sweater.
A youth came on the subway
And sat beside her—
A comely youth, neat, intelligent,
Yes, even respectable;
But his skin was black
And his lips were thick
And his nose was broad and flat.
She gathered her knitting needles together
In unseemly panic,
And as she fled, with disdainful nose, tip-tilted,
To the lower end of the car
I noticed that she wore a Liberty loan button
And a silken American flag—
And I do believe she thinks she's helping
To make the world safe for democracy.

—Zelda (Rose Pastor Stokes) (1917)

Less than six months after the United States entered the First World War, a deadly riot in Texas involving black soldiers, civilians, and local police left twenty-two dead and led to the largest murder trial in American history. In the summer of 1917, soldiers of the 24th US Infantry Regiment—which had originated with the Buffalo Soldier regiments of the West, who had served honorably in the Philippines and Mexico—were ordered from New Mexico to Texas. Assigned to guard the construction of Camp Logan, a new military installation, the soldiers arrived in Houston on July 28, 1917. Almost from the first, black soldiers were the targets of virulent racial discrimination that frequently extended to abuse and assault. Tensions escalated, and on August 23 when Private Alonzo Edwards came to the aid of a black woman whom he felt was the victim of police abuse, he was pistol-whipped and arrested. When a respected black Corporal, Charles Baltimore, tried to learn more about Edwards' imprisonment, he was also beaten. Attempting to flee, Baltimore was shot, captured, and imprisoned. At Camp Logan, false rumors of Baltimore's murder and of the advance of a white mob provoked black soldiers to arm themselves and march on Houston. They exchanged gunfire with police and civilians in a situation that soon spiraled out of control. By the end of the night, four black soldiers, a Mexican laborer, a black civilian, and sixteen whites were dead.[106]

The first of three military court martials charged sixty-three black soldiers with aggravated assault, mutiny, and murder, making it the largest murder trial in US history. The court appointed one man to defend the sixty-three accused: Major Harry S. Grier. A teacher of law at West Point, Grier was not a lawyer and had no trial experience. The verdicts were announced and sentences imposed in a closed session of the court on November 30, and on December 9, forty-one men were sentenced to life in prison, while thirteen were notified that they had been condemned to death.[107] On December 11, 1917, without public notice, the condemned men were hung and buried in graves marked only with the numbers 1–13. By the end of the three court martials, 118 men had been charged with serious crimes and of these, 110 were found guilty; 53 black soldiers were sentenced to life in prison, while 29 more were sentenced to death.[108] For the men of the 24th Infantry, "Wherever they had been sent, their race had never overtly been an issue. But on July 28, as they got to Houston, they found it was all that mattered."[109]

The poem "To the Patriotic Lady across the Way," authored by "Zelda," appeared in November of 1917 on the editorial page of the *New York Call*, a leading socialist newspaper. It was almost certainly written by journalist, activist, and socialist Rose Pastor Stokes; she had used the pen name Zelda at the start of her career as a writer for the *Jewish Daily* News.[110] In addition to writing editorials, poetry, and plays, Stokes was an activist who campaigned for women's suffrage, birth control, trade unions, and fair labor practices. When war broke out, she condemned profiteers and "rapidly became one of the most notorious women in America, an associate of Margaret Sanger, Emma Goldman and Elizabeth Gurley Flynn. In endless demand as a speaker on the lecture circuit, she was known to the public as 'The Red, Red Rose.'"[111] In March of 1918

---

[106] Robert V. Haynes, *A Night of Violence: The Houston Riot of 1917*, Louisiana State UP, 1976, pp. 167–170.

[107] Haynes, *A Night of Violence*, pp. 2–3.

[108] Mike Tolson, "The Ugly History of Camp Logan," *Houston Chronicle*, updated 21 Aug. 2017, web. archive.org/web/20190804024238/https://www.houstonchronicle.com/news/houston-texas/houston/article/The-ugly-history-of-Camp-Logan-11944840.php.

[109] Tolson, "The Ugly History."

[110] An article published in *The Call* on 26 May 1918 identifies "Zelda" as Rose Pastor Stokes: "Poverty and Brains Made a Socialist of Rose Pastor Stokes," by Pippa, p. 6.

[111] Patrick Renshaw, "Rose of the World: The Pastor-Stokes Marriage and the American Left, 1905–1925," *New York History*, Oct. 1981, vol. 62, no. 4, p. 417.

while on a lecture tour of the Midwest, Stokes attempted to correct a news report of one of her speeches, writing, "No government which is *for* the profiteers can also be for the people, and I am *for* the people while the government is for the profiteers."[112] She was arrested on three counts of sedition under the 1917 Espionage Act and charged with the "attempt to cause insubordination in the United States military forces," "obstruction of recruiting," and "conveying or making false reports interfering with either branch of the military service." An article in the *New York Call* reported that the US District Attorney accused Stokes of spreading "disloyal beliefs" and in his summary remarks charged, "She stands today as the most subtle, vicious German propagandist in America."[113] At her sentencing hearing, Stokes refuted the charges against her saying, "I am not conscious of committing any crime, your Honor, unless an ardent desire to serve the ends of social and economic justice, acclaimed as of the highest social value in times of peace, becomes an anti-social thing and a crime in time of war."[114] Although she was sentenced to ten years in jail, her conviction was reversed on appeal. Shortly after the war's end, in 1919 Rose Pastor Stokes helped to found the Communist Party of America, and in 1922, she attended the Comintern Congress in Moscow and Petrograd, where she delivered the minority report "on the Negro question in the United States."[115]

---

[112] *Kansas City Star,* 20 Mar. 1918, p.1.
[113] "Jury Finds Rose P. Stokes Guilty: Socialist Faces 60 Years Jail Sentence," *New York Call,* 25 May 1918, pp. 1–2.
[114] "Mrs. Stokes Sentenced to 10-Year Term," *New York Call,* 4 June 1918, pp. 1–2.
[115] Renshaw, "Rose of the World," p. 433.

Portrait of a Mother

Knit two and purl one;
Stir the fire, and knit again.
And oh, my son, my only son,
I think of you in wind and rain,
In rain and wind, 'neath fire and shell,
Going along the road to hell
On earth, in wind and rain,
My little son, my only son…
Knit two and purl one;
Stir the fire, and knit again.

Knit two and purl one;
Knit again, and stir the fire.
And oh, my son, my only son,
I work for you and never tire;
I never tire, but work and pray
Every hour of night and day.
Awake, asleep, I never tire,
My little son, my only son…
Knit two and purl one;
Knit again, and stir the fire.

Knit two and purl one;
Stir the fire, and knit again.
And oh, my son, for another's son
My hands are working. The wind and rain
Are shrill without. But you are gone
To a quiet land. I shall come anon
And find you, out of this wind and rain:
But I'm working now for another's son.
Knit two and purl one;
Stir the fire, and knit again.

—Violet Gillespie (1918)

During the war, both soldiers and civilians struggled to endure vast stretches of tense and tedious waiting. The sound of shelling and gunfire was the background music to life in the trenches. The clickety-clack of knitting needles played quietly in the daily lives of women who waited, and the sound could be heard in churches, rail stations, and tearooms, as well as at home by the fireside. Jane Tynan, lecturer at the University of the Arts London, explains, "Wartime knitting may have had a feminine image, but it was not timid. What started as a response to small gaps in uniform supply became a mass knitting frenzy, which made [the] government very nervous about the quirky, un-military garments reaching soldiers at the front." Tynan argues,

> Knitters were doing what the army could not: making a creative intervention in a difficult situation. The problem was that the success of mass war knitting projects highlighted army failures … On one hand, the mobility of knitting made it the perfect symbol of civilian enthusiasm for the war effort. On the other, when the passion to knit comforts brimmed over, it threatened to become an anti-establishment protest. The sheer scale of the effort, its anarchic spread nationally and internationally, gave wartime knitting political potential, with parallels in the craftist projects of today.
>
> To send something personal, and lovingly homemade, to a relative in real mortal danger, gave knitters the satisfaction of making a direct intervention, but crafting such personal items also meant contemplating fear and loss. This was not what the authorities wanted. Wartime knitting was supposed to be cheerful and optimistic, not dark and ponderous.[116]

Little is known of Violet Gillespie. She submitted ballads to a *Bookman* poetry competition in March of 1913, and in the list of commended writers she was identified as being from Forest Hill.[117] In 1918, Katharine Tynan reviewed Gillespie's *Poems of 1915*, writing, "she can make a song; her wistful and tender cadences will give joy to the lovers of poetry: she has her place, though a minor one, in the choir."[118]

---

[116] Jane Tynan, "Current Crafts Craze Echoes World War I Knitting Projects," *World War I Centenary Continuations and Beginnings*, 8 July 2014, web.archive.org/save/http://ww1centenary.oucs.ox.ac.uk/memoryofwar/crafts-craze-echoes-world-war-i-knitting-projects/.
[117] "Result of Competitions for February," *The Bookman*, Mar. 1913, p. 311.
[118] Katharine Tynan, "New Poetry," *The Bookman*, vol. 54, no. 321, June 1918, p. 104.

The Mourners

I look into the aching womb of night;
I look across the mist that masks the dead;
The moon is tired and gives but little light,
   The stars have gone to bed.

The earth is sick and seems to breathe with pain;
A lost wind whimpers in a mangled tree;
I do not see the foul, corpse-cluttered plain,
   The dead I do not see.

The slain I *would* not see... and so I lift
My eyes from out the shambles where they lie;
When lo! a million woman-faces drift
   Like pale leaves through the sky.

The cheeks of some are channelled deep with tears;
But some are tearless, with wild eyes that stare
Into the shadow of the coming years
   Of fathomless despair.

And some are young, and some are very old;
And some are rich, some poor beyond belief;
Yet all are strangely like, set in the mould
   Of everlasting grief.

They fill the vast of Heaven, face on face;
And then I see one weeping with the rest,
Whose eyes beseech me for a moment's space....
   Oh eyes I love the best!

Nay, I but dream. The sky is all forlorn,
And there's the plain of battle writhing red:
God pity them, the women-folk who mourn!
   How happy are the dead!

—Robert W. Service[119] (1916)

---

[119] See also Service's "Only a Boche."

Before the war, Canadian Robert W. Service was a best-selling writer, known for his rollicking, comic ballads of the Yukon, poems such as "The Shooting of Dan McGrew" and "The Cremation of Sam McGee." He was forty-one when the war began, and although he tried to enlist in the Seaforth Highlanders, he was rejected for medical reasons. Wanting to contribute to the war effort, Service became a war correspondent for Canadian newspapers while serving as an ambulance driver and stretcher-bearer. In early 1916, the *Ottawa Journal* published his account "At the Field Dressing Station during an Attack":

> Then again two mangled heaps are lifted in. One has been wounded by a bursting gun. There seems to be no part of him that is not burned, and I marvel that he lives. The skin of his breast is a blueish colour and cracked open in ridges. I am sorry I saw him. After this, when they put the things that once were men into my car I will turn away my head.[120]

Chief Canadian army censor Ernest J. Chambers commented, "the more I see of Robert W. Service's matter from the front, the more impressed I become that it is of a character to seriously interfere with recruiting in Canada."[121]

In the autumn of 1916, Service published his war poetry collection, *Rhymes of a Red Cross Man*, and dedicated it to his brother Albert, killed in August of 1916 while fighting in Belgium. *Rhymes of a Red Cross Man* became an instant bestseller, although critical reviews were mixed. Harriet Monroe, writing for *Poetry Magazine*, found the poems "poignant and sympathetic," but felt they lacked "the very heart-cry of the emotion,"[122] while the *Bookman* wrote, "No Canadian poet has a wider popularity with civilians and soldiers than Robert Service."[123] Although his rhyming narrative poetry spoke to the fears and feelings of those caught up in the First World War, a century later, Robert W. Service has been described as "one of the best known, best selling and critically most ignored English language writers of the twentieth century."[124]

---

[120] Robert W. Service in *Ottawa Journal*, 22 Jan. 1916, p. 2, qtd. in *Canadian Poetry from World War I*, edited by Joel Baetz, Oxford UP, 2009, p. 166.
[121] Qtd. in "All the News That Was Fit to Print," by Jeff Keshen, *Canadian Historical Review*, vol. 73, no. 3, 1992, p. 325.
[122] Harriet Monroe, "War Poems," *Poetry*, vol. 10, no. 5, Aug. 1917, p. 272.
[123] A. St. John Adcock, "Poets in Khaki," *Bookman*, vol. 55, Dec. 1918, p. 94.
[124] Edward J. Cowan, "The War Rhymes of Robert Service, Folk Poet," *Studies in Scottish Literature*, vol. 28, no. 1, 1993, p. 1.

When Will the War Be By?

'This year, neist year, sometime, never,'
  A lanely lass, bringing hame the kye,[125]
  Pu's at a flooer wi' a weary sigh,
An' laich, laich, she is coontin' ever[126]
  'This year, neist year, sometime, never
  When will the war be by?'

'Weel, wounded, missin', deid,'
  Is there nae news o' oor lads ava?
  Are they hale an' fere that are hine awa'?[127]
A lass raxed oot[128] for the list, to read—
  'Weel, wounded, missin', *deid*';
  An' the war was by for twa.[129]
        1916

—Charles Murray

The British War Office published its first casualty list on September 1, 1914, naming all soldiers reported killed, wounded, or missing. For nearly three years, a daily list was released, and several newspapers (e.g., *The Times* and *The Scotsman*) included the list in their publications until August 1917. At that time, newspapers halted publication of the lists, due to their length and the amount of space needed to report the names of casualties. His Majesty's Stationery Office assumed the task of printing the war casualty lists, selling them for three pence each. An estimated half-million Scots enlisted in the British army in the First World War; 125,000 of them died, never to return home.

    Charles Murray was perhaps the most popular Scots poet of his day. At a dinner held in his honor in 1912, the Master of Ceremonies praised Murray "for his service to local dialect and local literature … At a time when the vernacular was under a cloud, and might almost be described as moribund, in so far as it was tabooed and frowned upon by most of our educational mentors, he breathed new life into it."[130] Murray's writing was also praised for his skillful "delineation

---

[125] *bringing home the cows*
[126] *And softly, whispering, she is counting ever*
[127] *Are they strong and unbroken that are far away?*
[128] *reached out*
[129] *And the war was over for two*
[130] Alexander Mackie, qtd. in *Dinner in Honour of Charles Murray*, William Smith and Sons, 1913, p. 12.

of rural types of character" and for his observation of local people, described as "close and intimate ... conjoined with unfailing graphic force and brevity of expression."[131] In his remarks of thanks, Murray acknowledged, "I was raised upon Ramsay, Fergusson, and Burns, and the old Scots, and all my life as a boy I was taught to look out for quaint phrases, out of the way expressions, and to study and delight in the old, original characters of the countryside."[132] Explaining his decision to write in Scots dialect, Murray said, "the old dialect words have an aroma which is poetry itself; they are charged with hallowed associations to those who used them in their childhood, and go straight to the heart."[133]

Murray was a medical officer in the Boer War, and during the First World War he served as a lieutenant-colonel in the South African Defence Force (he was fifty when the war began in 1914).[134] In 1917, he published a volume of poetry written in Scots Doric dialect titled *A Sough O' War*. A *sough* refers to a deep sigh or strong breeze and can also refer to a song; in the glossary that accompanies the collection, *sough* is defined as a "rumour, sound of wind."[135] Murray dedicated his war poems "To a young sapper somewhere in France and to all in whatever airt upholding the fair name and honour of Scotland."

---

[131] Mackie, qtd. in *Dinner*, p. 14.
[132] Charles Murray, qtd. in *Dinner*, p. 22.
[133] Murray, qtd. in *Dinner*, pp. 17–18.
[134] St. John Adcock, editor, *The Bookman Treasury of Living Poets*, school ed. Part II, Hodder and Stoughton, 1927, p. 252.
[135] "Glossary," *A Sough O'War*, by Charles Murray, Constable, 1917, p. 56.

War Time

Young John, the postman, day by day,
In sunshine or in rain,
Comes down our road with words of doom
In envelopes of pain.

What cares he as he swings along
At his mechanic part,
How many times his hand lets fall
The knocker on a heart?

He whistles merry scraps of song,
What'er his bag contain—
Of words of death, of words of doom
In envelopes of pain.

—Mary E. Fullerton (1921)

It was the news no one wanted to hear; it was the knock at the door that everyone dreaded. Donald Overall was a young boy, but it was a morning he never forgot:

> I remember the day we heard very distinctly ... Mother and I were downstairs in the main hall when the doorbell rang. I was hiding behind her as she was handed an envelope. I remember she opened the letter immediately. I didn't know what it said, but she screamed and collapsed on the floor in a dead faint. I tried to wake her up; I didn't know what was wrong. I was holding on to her skirts and called out for help and an elderly couple who lived in a lower flat came out and comforted both of us. Mother came round slowly and they eventually got her upstairs into the bedroom. She was there for about ten days and it was while she was getting better, that she turned onto her side and said to me, 'Your father's dead, he won't come back. Now you are the man of the house, you must do things as best as you can.' And I said, 'Me, Mum?' I was five years old. That changed my life; it had to.[136]

Families learned of their loved one's death in a variety of ways: officers' next-of-kin received telegrams (Australian telegrams were pink), while families of other ranks typically were mailed an official form (British death notices were sealed in buff envelopes). Notification was slower during major offensives due to heavy casualties, and a fellow soldier might write the family if he saw a man killed or

---

[136] Richard van Emden, *The Quick and the Dead,* Bloomsbury, 2011, pp. 108–109.

found his body. Some families heard the news through word-of-mouth from a soldier on leave, and officers or chaplains might send a personal letter if they had the time.

Over 60,000 men from Australia died in the First World War, and an estimated one in four families mourned a son or husband who had been killed.[137] The bereaved lived thousands of miles from the battlefields where their loved ones had died, and so one of the only physical links with the dead was the envelope, letter, or telegram that brought the news.

Australian writer Mary E. Fullerton campaigned for women's rights and protested military conscription. "War Time" appeared in her collection *The Breaking Furrow* (1921), with other poems that condemned poverty and prejudice. In his history of Australian women writers, Dale Spender writes,

> Given that Mary Eliza Fullerton is acknowledged in H.M. Green's *History of Australian Literature* [1961], it could almost be said that here was one woman poet who had 'made it' into the literary canon—except of course that she rates no mention in the *Oxford History of Australian Literature,* or in Geoffrey Dutton's *Literature of Australia,* and she is not included in the *Oxford Anthology of Australian Literature.* Why she should have been omitted from these later surveys and selections is a matter for speculation, for it cannot be because she was unknown or that her work was without merit … Mary Fullerton wrote provocative polemic poetry which still makes its point today.[138]

---

[137] Bruce Scates, "Bereavement and Mourning (Australia)," *1914-1918 Online International Encyclopedia of the First World War,* encyclopedia.1914-1918, web.archive.org/web/20190901212344/https://www.online.net/article/bereavement_and_mourning_australia.

[138] Dale Spender, *Writing a New World: Two Centuries of Australian Women Writers,* Spinifex, 1988, p. 203.

Gone to the War

He's gone to the war, he's gone to the war,
I doan't care a rap if I see him noa more;
He lethered me reg'lar, Saturday night
When he collared his wages and allers got tight;
I'm sure I prefer to be single by far
Now he's gone to the war, now he's gone to the war.

His waages was thirteen and sixpence a week,
Wi' extry in harvest, but that was to seek
A cottage—nowt else—made up all our paay,
And when you've ten childer that's not much a daay;
He gev me nine shillings, it didn't goa far:
But now I have plenty—he's gone to the war.

A little bit more'n a shilling a daay
To feed 'em and cloathe 'em and bills for to paay;
The grocer he hated me going to shop,
And as for the butcher—we lived upon sop!
Water and bread, water and bread,
On plenty of water our childer was fed.

We was allers in debt 'coz we couldn't keep out,
Except at the pub, where noa credit's about;
If I wanted to find him I knawed where to goa:
He would be at the "Bull" wi' his mates in a row.
I slaaved at my work while he sung in the bar,
But I'm getting it back now he's gone to the war.

The sarjint popped in and he saw half a dozen—
Our Tom, Arthur Bates, Willie Jones and his cousin:
"There's plenty of vittles, and little to do,
"Wi' a suit of good cloathes and a medal or two":
They all joined together to have a last drink,
And that sarjint he snapped 'em afore they could wink.

He telled me about it: I said nowt the while,
I had to look solemn and try not to smile,
Because I should get—in the paper I seed—
Nearly two quid a week, and noa husband to feed!
"You can send me a quid and still save on the rest":

I nodded my head and said that would be best.

"Each week you can send it, I'll leave my address,
"And when the war's done I'll come back to you, Bess."
Soa off he went smiling to Lincoln, full sail,
Wi' cheering and shouting and plenty of ale;
I cried till he'd gone, then set off for to seek
The man what was handing out two quid a week.

Two quid a week! two quid a week!
Who wouldn't sell husbands for two quid a week?
Noa drink and noa bother, noa quarrelsome brutes
What's nasty and dirty and sleeps in their boots;
I pretended to cry, but I laughed in my cheek—
I'd swap forty husbands for two quid a week!

He come hoam on Sat'dy the colour of chalk,
They'd very nigh killed him to judge by his talk;
He'd marched and he'd sweated wi' noa chanch to shirk,
Not sin' he was born had he done soa much work;
He cried like a babby to get in the door,
And when it was Monday, he cried all the more.

He's gone to the war, he's gone to the war,
I shan't care a rap if I see him noa more;
Ten childer is plenty to take your attention,
Though sewing-machines is a useful invention;
I can buy owt I want wi' noa husband to keep,
I'm as happy as happy on two quid a week.

There's nobbut one trouble as troubles me now,
And that's how much longer them Germans can go;
They've stood it a year and my childer looks grand,
We've clothes and we've boots and we've money in hand.
If the war should stop now it would be moast distressing,
For one thing is certain: it's just been a blessing.

If anything happens I draw on a pension,
Not two quid a week, but it's still worth attention.
Of course, if the war would keep on a few years,
I shouldn't be bothering, then, wi' noa fears;

There would be enough saved to flit out of this Fen
And when Tom come home he could marry agen.

There niver was knawn such good times for to be,
Wi' two quid a week I'm in clover, you see.
Every now and agen Tom writes hoam for his quid—
Says he'll niver come back if I doan't do his bid!
But I shan't care a rap if I see him noa more,
He can stop where he is now he's gone to the war.

* * * *

But p'r'aps he'll improve now he's gone from his hoam,
And turn like he was when a-courtin' he come;
If that sarjint can straighten him into a lover,
I should long for the daay when the war would be over;
A sweetheart, a husband, a father, and more—
God knows I should welcome him hoam from the war.

—Bernard Samuel Gilbert (1915)

In commemorative tributes, soldiers of the First World War are nearly always remembered as heroes, but contemporary accounts are more likely to acknowledge the various natures and characters of those who served. In the memoir of his childhood, Clifford Dyment recalls a neighbor who visited his family shortly after they had received a letter informing them that his father had been killed:

> For some time my mother was too stunned by my father's death to think or do anything about our future ...
>
> A Mrs. Pryse called to see my mother the day after Captain Rushton's letter arrived. Mrs. Pryse told my mother that she would gladly give half her life to be in my mother's place. "Oh, how I envy you," she said. "If it were only my husband who had been killed instead of yours!" Every morning, Mrs. Pryse said, she looked for the welcome telegram of bad news, every night prayed that her husband would be killed next day.
>
> My mother was ill after this visit. She was shocked to know that bereavement was something that could be coveted. She was bewildered at the senselessness of an unwanted man surviving and a loved man dying. She was grieved at the cruelty that kept a hated man alive to be hated even more.[139]

---

[139] Clifford Dyment, *The Railway Game*, J.M. Dent, 1962, p. 29.

Bernard Samuel Gilbert was born in Billinghay, a Lincolnshire village on the edge of the fens. Gilbert worked in his family's seed merchant business until, at the age of thirty, he moved to Lincoln to pursue a career as a professional author, writing poems, novels, plays, political pamphlets, and news articles.[140] Andrew H. Jackson notes, "Gilbert's writings were frequently radical in their tone ... [expressing] his deep concern for the social conditions arising out of economic change."[141] In a 1914 news article for the *Lincolnshire Echo*, Gilbert defended his position on universal suffrage and women's rights: "It is not the wealthy widow wanting an equal voice with her groom, nor the political woman demanding a vote with a hatchet, but the wretched woman who waits outside the Public Houses, or starves with her children, that arouses my anger, and spurs my determination as a Suffragist."[142] During the war, Gilbert worked at the ministry of munitions in London. The forgotten "laureate of Lincolnshire"[143] published three volumes of dialect poetry during the war; many of his poems depict the home front struggles of working-class men and women.

---

[140] Andrew J.H. Jackson, "The Early Twentieth-Century Countryside of Bernard Samuel Gilbert: Lincolnshire Poet, Novelist, Playwright, Pamphleteer and Correspondent, 1911–1914," *Midland History*, vol. 41, no. 2, 2016.

[141] Andrew J.H. Jackson, "Civic Identity, Municipal Governance and Provincial Newspapers: The Lincoln of Bernard Gilbert," *Urban History*, vol. 42, no. 1, Feb. 2015, pp. 117, 118.

[142] Bernard Gilbert, qtd. in "Civic Identity," by Andrew J.H. Jackson, p. 119.

[143] Redfearn Williamson, "Introduction," *War Workers and Other Verses*, by Bernard Gilbert, Erskine Macdonald, 1916, p. 11.

Sic Transit—
(V.R., Died of Wounds, 2nd London General Hospital, Chelsea, June 9th, 1917)

I am so tired.
    The dying sun incarnadines the West,
And every window with its gold is fired,
    And all I loved the best
Is gone, and every good that I desired
    Passes away, an idle hopeless quest;
Even the Highest whereto I aspired
    Has vanished with the rest.
I am so tired.
        London, June 1917

—Vera Brittain[144]

In late spring of 1917, Voluntary Aid Detachment (VAD) nurse Vera Brittain resigned from her duties and returned from Malta to nurse Victor Richardson, a close friend of her brother and of her deceased fiancé, Roland Leighton. Richardson had been blinded and disfigured from wounds received in an attack on Arras in April of 1917. Shortly after learning of Richardson's injuries, Brittain had recorded in her diary, "I no longer expect things to go well for me; I don't know that I even ask that they shall. All I ask is that I may fulfil my own small weary part in this War in such a way as to be worthy of Them, who die & suffer pain."[145] She was prepared to devote herself to Richardson and serve as his caretaker for life, but his injuries worsened, and Victor Richardson died in early June. He was twenty-two when he died; Vera Brittain was twenty-three when she found herself mourning the death of yet another friend killed in battle.

"Sic Transit—" was written shortly after Richardson's death, its title alluding to the Latin phrase *Sic transit gloria mundi* (Thus passes the glory of the world). Brittain resumed her work as a VAD nurse, but her most significant part in the First World War was accomplished after the war was over. Her memoir *Testament of Youth,* published in 1933, is one of the classics of First World War literature.

---

[144] See also Brittain's "Perhaps."
[145] Vera Brittain, "April 18, 1917," *Chronicle of Youth,* William Morrow and Company, 1982, p. 339.

France
(To C. M. A. O.)

You also know
The way the dawns came slow
Over the railway stations out in France;
And you have seen the Drafts entrain
By the blurred lanterns in the rain,
And wept the True Romance.

You've also gone,
Dead tired, stumbling on,
Over the pavé when the day was born;
And weary beyond sleep lain down
And heard the clocks strike in the town,
Most young, and most forlorn.

And you have met
On lone roads in the wet
Field Batteries trotting North, and stood aside
And sent your heart with them to fight,
And ridden with them through the night
Until the pale stars died.

And you know too
How a man whistles through
The dark a line of some forgotten song;
You've seen the Leave Boat in, and then
Gone back to jest with broken men
Who once were swift and strong.

You know how black
The night sea tides surged back
On dock stones where the stretcher bearers knelt;
And how the fog greyed the men's lips
And the red crosses of the ships,
And how the searchlights wheeled.

You've woke to see
Death hurtle suddenly
On to the hut roofs when the Gothas[146] came;

---

[146] The *Gotha* was a German bomber aircraft.

> And watched a man by Love possessed
> Fight through to morning, and go West
> Whispering his Girl's name.
>
> Wherefore I know
> That you will serve also
> The living Vision men call Memory,
> And hold to the brave things we said,
> And keep faith with the faithful Dead—
> And speak of France with me.
>
> —May Wedderburn Cannan[147] (1919)

In her essay "War Service in Perspective," Vera Brittain describes the "barrier of indescribable experience" that the First World War erected between the men who had fought and the women who loved them. Soldier-poet Edmund Blunden wrote of that divide as an "impassable gulf," Edgell Rickword as "two incommunicable worlds," and Richard Aldington as "gesticulating across an abyss."[148] Soldiers found it difficult to talk about the war with others who hadn't been there; their poetry was one way of attempting to understand the Great War.

But what of the women who witnessed the war and were forever changed? "The single most characteristic feature of … women's experience of war was isolation," argues Gill Plain.[149] Female nurses, aid workers, ambulance drivers, and journalists worked on the borders of the combat zone, experiencing realities of total warfare that were incompatible with the propagandist information disseminated by official sources for those on the home front. Women volunteers who witnessed first-hand the effects of the war discovered that their experience estranged them from both noncombatants and soldiers, and cultural expectations of femininity severely constrained what they could discuss with others about what they had seen and done. In 1933, Edmund Blunden and Sylva Norman published their post-war memoir/novel *We'll Shift Our Ground,* an account of a couple who visit the battlefields of the war years after the Armistice. As Duncan, a veteran soldier, stares out over the old scenes, he begins to realize that Chloe "was not entirely an interloper and would rob no richness from the texture of his

---

[147] See also Cannan's "Since They Have Died" and "Paris, November 11, 1918."
[148] Qtd. in *The Great War and Women's Consciousness,* by Claire M. Tylee, Springer, 1989, pp. 54–55.
[149] Gill Plain, "'Great Expectations': Rehabilitating the Recalcitrant War Poets," *Feminist Review,* no. 51, Autumn 1995, p. 41.

thoughts." She reminds him, "It was *my* war, too ... although I never came here. All this, in a queer way, is my background; all the—emptiness of it."[150]

May Wedderburn Cannan volunteered in France at a railway canteen for British soldiers in 1915, returning to Paris in 1918 to work in the British intelligence office. She dedicated her poem "France" to her childhood friend Carola Mary Anima Oman, who worked for three years as a VAD nurse and in 1918 was assigned to care for the wounded near Boulogne.

---

[150] Edmund Blunden and Sylva Norman, *We'll Shift Our Ground,* Cobden-Sanderson, 1933, p. 126.

4

Making Sense of War

For some writers, patriotic love of their country and its values gave the war meaning; others looked to the tradition of heroic epics and believed that the First World War could inspire both nations and individuals to greatness. Reformers hoped that the war might usher in a better and more just world. But as some looked to the future with hope, others wrote of a more apocalyptic vision, seeing only meaningless death and wanton destruction. For many, the war was simply incomprehensible, an absurdity that defied rational explanation. At times, even the most articulate of writers admitted themselves hesitant to make definitive comments on the war and skeptical of those who did. And yet many of the most popular poems published during the war found meaning in transcendent belief, whether in religious faith, the regenerative powers of nature, or the sacrifice of the dead.

I Saw a Man This Morning[1]

I saw a man this morning
  Who did not wish to die:
I ask, and cannot answer,
  If otherwise wish I.

Fair broke the day this morning
  Upon the Dardanelles;
The breeze blew soft, the morn's cheeks
  Were cold as cold sea-shells.

But other shells are waiting
  Across the Ægean sea,
Shrapnel and high explosive,
  Shells and hells for me.

Oh hell of ships and cities,
  Hell of men like me,
Fatal second Helen,
  Why must I follow thee?

Achilles came to Troyland
  And I to Chersonese:
He turned from wrath to battle,
  And I from three days' peace.

Was it so hard, Achilles,
  So very hard to die?
Thou knowest and I know not—
  So much the happier I.

I will go back this morning
  From Imbros over the sea;
Stand in the trench, Achilles,
  Flame-capped, and shout for me.

—Patrick Shaw-Stewart (1920)

---

[1] This untitled poem was found in Shaw-Stewart's copy of A.E. Housman's *A Shropshire Lad*, with corrections and edits in Shaw-Stewart's handwriting.

In April of 1915, Patrick Shaw-Stewart sailed for Gallipoli with Rupert Brooke and others of their battalion. After Brooke's death from blood poisoning, Shaw-Stewart was one of the officers who assisted in the burial of his friend on the island of Skyros, taking charge of the graveside gun salute.[2] Before Brooke's death, anticipating the fight at Gallipoli, Shaw-Stewart had written, "It is the luckiest thing and the most romantic. Think of fighting in the Chersonese [the classical name for Gallipoli] ... or alternatively, if it's the Asiatic side they want us on, on the plains of Troy itself! I am going to take my Herodotus as a guidebook."[3] Although Shaw-Stewart survived the battle of Gallipoli, he was killed by an artillery shell on December 30, 1917, in fighting on the Western Front near Cambrai. An artillery officer who was with him reported,

> It was an exceptionally gallant death. It was in the early morning, about dawn; he [Shaw-Stewart] was going round his line; the Germans put up a barrage ... He was hit by shrapnel, the lobe of his ear was cut off and his face spattered so that the blood ran down from his forehead and blinded him for a bit. The gunner tried to make him go back to Battalion H.Q. to be dressed, but he refused, and insisted on completing his round. Very soon afterwards, a shell burst on the parapet, and a fragment hit him upwards through the mouth and killed him instantaneously.[4]

---

[2] Patrick Shaw-Stewart, letter of 25 Apr. 1915, qtd. in *Patrick Shaw-Stewart*, by Ronald Knox, William Collins, 1920, p. 126.
[3] Patrick Shaw-Stewart, letter of 24 Feb. 1915, qtd. in *Patrick Shaw-Stewart*, p. 112.
[4] Lord Alexander Thynne, qtd. in *Patrick Shaw-Stewart*, pp. 204–205.

A Meditation upon the Return of the Greeks

When in their long lean ships the Greek host weighed
Their splashing anchors, then they had much joy
For lovely Helen's sake to humble Troy...
Their first deed was the murder of a maid.[5]

Ten years from their pleasant land they stayed,
And after ten years, had they any joy?
They had old Helen, and they humbled Troy:
Were they at her lost loveliness dismayed?

Thinking of their lost Youth were they afraid?
Was Youth worth more than Helen—Helen of Troy?
Was it for this tired face they had spent joy?
For this tall, weary woman burnt a maid?

When on that quiet night the Greek host laid
Down their old dinted armour, had they any joy?

—Ivar Campbell

In the anthology *For Remembrance: Soldier Poets Who Have Fallen in the War* (1918), editor St. John Adcock arguably claims, "Not a hint of the war enters into the poems of Ivar Campbell."[6] Yet "A Meditation upon the Return of the Greeks" implicitly critiques the First World War, as Campbell borrows from ancient epics to question whether the sacrifices made in war are worth the cost. Campbell's allusions to the Greek epics differ from those made by most First World War poets for whom "Troy functioned ... as a powerful source of solace and as a guarantor of the worthiness of the present sacrifice."[7] With a strikingly different purpose, Campbell's references to the Trojan War in "A Meditation upon the Return of the Greeks" protest naïve idealism and suggest that the realities of war are neither noble nor glorious.

The grandson of the 8th Duke of Argyll, Ivar Campbell was a published writer before the war, his poetry appearing in the *Westminster Gazette* and *Country Life*. He loved exploring the Scottish countryside, writing, "Walking is a brave

---

[5] Iphigenia, daughter of Agamemnon, was sacrificed to appease the goddess Artemis.
[6] Arthur St. John Adcock, editor, *For Remembrance: Soldier Poets Who Have Fallen in the War*, rev. and enlarged ed., Hodder and Stoughton, 1920, p. 56.
[7] Elizabeth Vandiver, *Stand in the Trench, Achilles*, Oxford UP, 2010, p. 228.

thing ... a large thing, a dusty thing, an you will. But like the sea it touches Heaven."[8] Campbell served as an honorary attaché to the British Embassy in America, living in Washington, DC, and New Hampshire from the end of 1912 until March of 1914. Returning from America, he "told his friends of his desire to keep a book-shop in Chelsea. Here, under the name of Mr. John Cowslip he would sell not only books, but also drawings by modern artists ... [and] holly walking-sticks polished like ivory."[9] When war broke out in August of 1914, Campbell sought an army commission, but was rejected due to poor eyesight. Wanting to join the war effort, he learned to drive and volunteered with the American Red Cross Ambulance in France, while persistently reapplying to the British military. He was finally accepted on his third try and commissioned in early February of 1915 in the regiment of his clan, the Argyll and Sutherland Highlanders. He served on the Western Front until late November of 1915, when he was posted to Mesopotamia, arriving at Basra on Christmas Eve. Two weeks later, the 25-year-old second lieutenant was fatally wounded leading a charge against the Turks at Sheikh Sa'ad. Campbell died the next day on January 8, 1916.[10] His men buried him by the banks of the Tigris, but the location of his grave was lost; Campbell's name appears on the memorial to the missing at Basra. Reviewing his posthumously published *Poems* (1917), the *Times Literary Supplement* noted that just months before his death, Campbell "had mused on the grim prank played by war upon the idealist."[11]

---

[8] Ivar Campbell, *Poems*, A.L. Humphreys, 1917, p. 11.
[9] Guy Ridley, "Ivar Campbell," *Poems* by Ivar Campbell, p. 22.
[10] Ridley, "Ivar Campbell," pp. 26–27.
[11] "For Remembrance," *Times Literary Supplement*, no. 839, 14 Feb. 1918, p. 79.

A Litany in the Desert

I

On the other side of the Sangre de Cristo mountains there is a great welter of steel and flame. I have read that it is so. I know nothing of it here.

On the other side of the water there is terrible carnage. I have read that it is so. I know nothing of it here.

I do not know why men fight and die. I do not know why men sweat and slave. I know nothing of it here.

II

Out of the peace of your great valleys, America, out of the depth and silence of your deep canyons,

Out of the wide stretch of yellow corn-fields, out of the stealthy sweep of your rich prairies,

Out of the high mountain peaks, out of the intense purity of your snows,

Invigorate us, O America.

Out of the deep peace of your breast, out of the sure strength of your loins,

Recreate us, O America.

Not from the smoke and the fever and fret, not from the welter of furnaces, from the fierce melting-pot of cities;

But from the quiet fields, from the little places, from the dark lamp-lit nights—from the plains, from the cabins, from the little house in the mountains,

Breathe strength upon us:

And give us the young men who will make us great.

—Alice Corbin[12] (1918)

In her November 1914 essay "Poetry and War," *Poetry* magazine's assistant editor Alice Corbin Henderson wrote, "War has actually lost its illusion and its glamour … The American feeling about the war is a genuine revolt against war, and we have believed that *Poetry* might help to serve the cause of peace by encouraging the expression of this spirit of protest."[13] Most Americans

---

[12] The author used her maiden name (Alice Corbin) when writing poetry, but her married name (Alice Corbin Henderson) when writing prose.

[13] Alice Corbin Henderson, "Poetry and War," *Poetry*, vol. 5, no. 2, Nov. 1914, p. 83.

were initially against their country's involvement in the First World War, and American neutrality was frequently defended with references to George Washington's Farewell Address of 1796:

> Why quit our own to stand upon foreign ground? Why, by interweaving our destiny with that of any part of Europe, entangle our peace and prosperity in the toils of European Ambition, Rivalship, Interest, Humour or Caprice? 'Tis our true policy to steer clear of permanent Alliances, with any portion of the foreign world.[14]

By the time the United States entered the war in April of 1917, however, the mood of the country had shifted. Along with other prominent American writers, Corbin Henderson joined the Vigilantes, a writers' syndicate dedicated to composing and publishing patriotic writing in support of America's war effort. With over 300 members pledged to the organization, the Vigilantes included such well-known authors as Vachel Lindsay, Edwin Arlington Robinson, Ring Lardner, Edgar Lee Masters, and Amy Lowell (both Masters and Lowell, along with Henderson, withdrew their membership before the war ended).

Alice Corbin Henderson counted among her friends and close colleagues Ezra Pound and DH Lawrence; as an editor, she discovered and promoted the work of Carl Sandburg, Edgar Lee Masters, and Sherwood Anderson. Reviewing her 1921 collection, *The Red Earth: Poems of New Mexico*, Sandburg described Corbin's poetry as "clean and aloof as the high deliberate table-lands where it was written."[15]

---

[14] George Washington, qtd. in *A Sacred Union of Citizens: George Washington's Farewell Address and the American Character*, by Matthew Spalding and Patrick J. Garrity, Rowman and Littlefield, 1996, p. 186.

[15] Carl Sandburg, "Reviews: From New Mexico," *Poetry*, vol. 18, no. 3, June 1921, p. 157.

He Went for a Soldier

He marched away with a blithe young score of him
  With the first volunteers,
Clear-eyed and clean and sound to the core of him,
  Blushing under the cheers.
    They were fine, new flags that swung a-flying there,—
    Oh, the pretty girls he glimpsed a-crying there,
      Pelting him with pinks and with roses—
        Billy, the Soldier Boy!

Not very clear in the kind young heart of him
  What the fuss was about,
But the flowers and the flags seemed part of him—
  The music drowned his doubt.
    It's a fine, brave sight they were a-coming there
    To the gay, bold tune they kept a-drumming there,
      While the boasting fifes shrilled jauntily—
        Billy, the Soldier Boy!

Soon he is one with the blinding smoke of it—
  Volley and curse and groan:
Then he has done with the knightly joke of it—
  It's rending flesh and bone.
    There are pain-crazed animals a-shrieking there;
    And a warm blood stench that is a-reeking there;
      He fights like a rat in a corner—
        Billy, the Soldier Boy!

There he lies now, like a ghoulish score of him,
  Left on the field for dead:
The ground all round is smeared with the gore of him—
  Even the leaves are red.
    The thing that was Billy lies a-dying there,
    Writhing and a-twisting and a-crying there;
      A sickening sun grins down on him—
        Billy, the Soldier Boy!

Still not quite clear in the poor wrung heart of him
  What the fuss was about,
See where he lies—or a ghastly part of him—
  While life is oozing out:

There are loathsome things he sees a-crawling there;
There are hoarse voiced crows he hears a-calling there,
    Eager for the foul feast spread for them—
      Billy, the Soldier Boy!

How much longer, oh Lord, shall we bear it all?
 How many more red years?
Story it and glory it and share it all,
 In seas of blood and tears?
    They are braggart attitudes we've worn so long;
    They are tinsel platitudes we've sworn so long—
      We who have turned the Devil's Grindstone,
      Borne with the hell called War!

                                        —Ruth Comfort Mitchell (1916)

"Women were writing protest poetry before Sassoon and Owen," argues Nosheen Khan in *Women's Poetry of the First World War*.[16] The poem that prompts Khan's assertion is Mitchell's "He Went for a Soldier," written before America entered the First World War. It is likely that censorship would have prevented the poem's publication after April of 1917.

Born in California in 1882, Ruth Comfort Mitchell published *The Night Court and Other Verse* in 1916, dedicating the volume to her mother: "Because you made the freedom where it grew / My first small book goes, with my love, to you." A review in *The Century* praised her poetry for possessing "an art at once delicate and full of robust vigor," noting that it was "informed throughout by the modern spirit of communal sympathy and social purpose."[17] Mitchell's husband, Sanborn Young, became a California senator in 1925, and she joined him in politics, together working to legislate narcotic drugs and conserve wild animal populations. Her best-known novel, *Of Human Kindness,* is a defense of gentleman farmers, written in response to John Steinbeck's *The Grapes of Wrath*.

---

[16] Nosheen Khan, *Women's Poetry of the First World War,* UP Kentucky, 1988, p. 15.
[17] The Centurion, "October Books," *The Century,* vol. 92, Oct. 1916, p. 10.

War

Out in the dust he lies;
   Flies in his mouth,
Ants in his eyes…

I stood at the door
   Where he went out;
Full-grown man,
   Ruddy and stout;

I heard the march
   Of the trampling feet,
Slow and steady
   Come down the street;

The beat of the drum
   Was clods on the heart,
For all that the regiment
   Looked so smart!

I heard the crackle
   Of hasty cheers
Run like the breaking
   Of unshed tears,

And just for a moment,
   As he went by,
I had sight of his face,
   And the flash of his eye.

He died a hero's death,
   They said,
When they came to tell me
   My boy was dead;

But out in the street
   A dead dog lies;
Flies in his mouth,
   Ants in his eyes.

—Mary Gilmore (1917/1932)

In 1918 Gilmore donated the profits of her recently published volume of poetry, *The Passionate Heart*, to soldiers who had been blinded. However, her caustic poem "War" was not included in the volume. Although the poem had been published in *The Bulletin* in April of 1917,[18] it was not included in any of Gilmore's poetry collections until 1932, when it appeared in *Under the Wilgas* and was retitled "War." The poem's original title, "The Mother," emphasizes the war's devastating effect on civilians. Jacqueline Manuel, quoting another of Gilmore's poem, writes, "there has been comparatively little attention accorded the writing of civilian Australian women—those so-called ordinary women who would 'creep into bed in the dark and weep'[19] for those sons, husbands, lovers, fathers and friends who would never return."[20]

A journalist and socialist, Mary Gilmore campaigned to support better living conditions for indigenous peoples, children, and working women. When in 1962 she died at the age of ninety-seven, she was one of the most respected public figures in Australia: "If forcefulness of character and the indefatigable prose with which she had championed the causes of social reform, Australian identity and Australian writing played a considerable part in that reputation, her poetry was nonetheless an essential component."[21]

---

[18] Mary Gilmore, "The Mother," *The Bulletin*, 5 Apr. 1917, p. 3.
[19] These lines are from Mary Gilmore's poem "These Fellowing Men," *The Passionate Heart*, Angus and Robertson, 1918, p. 2.
[20] Jacqueline Manuel, "Australian Civilian Women's Poetic Responses to the First World War," *Journal of the Australian War Memorial*, no. 29, Nov. 1996, web.archive.org/web/20190805174149/https://www.awm.gov.au/articles/journal/j29/manuel.
[21] Jennifer Strauss, "Introduction," *The Collected Verse of Mary Gilmore, Volume One: 1887–1929*, U of Queensland P, 2004, p. xxvii.

War (Rhyfel)

Bitter to live in times like these.
While God declines beyond the seas;
Instead, man, king or peasantry,
Raises his gross authority.

When he thinks God has gone away
Man takes up his sword to slay
His brother; we can hear death's roar.
It shadows the hovels of the poor.

Like the old songs they left behind,
We hung our harps in the willows again.
Ballads of boys blow on the wind,
Their blood is mingled with the rain.

—Hedd Wyn (1918), translated by Gillian Clarke

An estimated 40,000 Welshmen died during the First World War.[22] One of those killed was the soldier Ellis Humphrey Evans, better known by his Welsh bardic name, Hedd Wyn. The phrase can be translated to mean *white, pure,* or *blessed peace,* and was inspired by the landscape of Evans' home in Trawsfynydd and the misty valleys of Meirionnydd. In early 1917 following the introduction of mandatory military conscription, Evans reluctantly joined the British army. He left the family farm and his shepherding duties to volunteer in place of a younger brother (he was the oldest of eleven children). During his brief time in France, Hedd Wyn wrote home, "Heavy weather, heavy soul, heavy heart. That is an uncomfortable trinity, isn't it?"[23] He arrived in France in June of 1917 and was dead by the end of the next month. Evans was killed on July 31, 1917, at Pilckem Ridge.[24] Simon Jones, a member of his company who survived, recalled in a 1975 interview,

> We started over Canal Bank at Ypres, and he was killed half way across Pilckem. I've heard many say that they were with Hedd Wyn and this and that, well I was

---

[22] John Davies, "The legacy of WW1," *BBC Wales History,* web.archive.org/save/www.bbc.co.uk/wales/history/sites/themes/periods/ww1_background.shtm.

[23] Ellis Evans, qtd. in *British Culture and the First World War,* by Toby Thacker, Bloomsbury, 2014, p. 161.

[24] 31,000 Allied soldiers were killed on July 31, 1917, among them the Irish poet Francis Ledwidge. Both Ledwidge and Evans are buried at Artillery Wood Cemetery.

with him as a boy from Llanuwchllyn and him from Trawsfynydd. I saw him fall and I can say that it was a nosecap shell in his stomach that killed him. You could tell that … He was going in front of me, and I saw him fall on his knees and grab two fistfuls of dirt …He was dying, of course …There were stretcher bearers coming up behind us, you see. There was nothing—well, you'd be breaking the rules if you went to help someone who was injured when you were in an attack.[25]

Less than six weeks after his death, on September 6, 1917, Hedd Wyn was announced as the winner of the Welsh National Eisteddfod's prestigious poetry chair. Learning that the poet had been killed in Flanders, presenters draped the chair in black. Since then the honor has been referred to as The Eisteddfod of the Black Chair. An anthology of Hedd Wyn's poetry, *Cerddi'r Bugail* (*The Shepherd's Poems*), was published posthumously in 1918, and the words *Y Prifardd Hedd Wyn* (The Chief Bard, Hedd Wyn) were added to the poet's headstone. Hedd Wyn's poetry can be found in cemeteries of the First World War on other men's gravestones: epitaphs on at least six graves in Belgium and France quote lines from his poem *Nid â'n Ango* (Not forgotten):*"Ei aberth nid â heibio,—ei wyneb / Annwyl nid â'n ango"* (His sacrifice will not be passed over / His dear face will not be forgotten).[26]

---

[25] Simon Jones, interview recorded by Robin Gwyndaf, St. Fagans National Museum of History, 26 Sept. 1975, "Welsh Bard Falls in the Battle Fields of Flanders," web.archive.org/web/20190619173343/https://museum.wales/articles/2007-04-25/Welsh-bard-falls-in-the-battle-fields-of-Flanders/.

[26] Clive Hughes, "Message in a Welsh Heart and an Irish Bottle," *Great War Forum*, 26 Jan. 2015, web.archive.org/web/20190619172548/https://www.greatwarforum.org/topic/223622-message-in-a-welsh-heart-and-an-irish-bottle/page/2/.

The Falling Leaves
November 1915

To-day, as I rode by,
I saw the brown leaves dropping from their tree
In a still afternoon,
When no wind whirled them whistling to the sky,
But thickly, silently,
They fell, like snowflakes wiping out the noon;
And wandered slowly thence
For thinking of a gallant multitude
Which now all withering lay,
Slain by no wind of age or pestilence,
But in their beauty strewed
Like snowflakes falling on the Flemish clay.

—Margaret Postgate[27]

Twenty-one years old when the war began, Margaret Postgate Cole recalls that at first, "I was not deeply affected by the war. I had no close ties of affection with anyone who had gone to it."[28] That changed when her younger brother Raymond refused to be drafted into the British army. She witnessed the outrage that was targeted at those who criticized the war or refused to be conscripted, how they were "booed and pelted, served with white feathers by excited young women,"[29] and threatened with prison or transport to the front lines. Cole writes that in 1916, "it needed a fair amount of courage to be a C.O."[30] Without a religious reason for his refusal to fight, nineteen-year-old Raymond Postgate was denied status as a conscientious objector and imprisoned. Margaret accompanied her brother to Oxford for his trial, and the experience shaped her views of war and politics for the rest of her life:

> when I walked away from the Oxford court room ... I walked into a new world, a world of doubters and protesters, and into a new war—this time against the ruling classes and the government which represented them, and *with* the working classes, the Trade Unionists, the Irish rebels of Easter Week, and all those who resisted their governments or other governments which held them

---

[27] Married in 1918, she also published under her married name, Margaret Postgate Cole.
[28] Margaret Cole, *Growing Up into Revolution*, Longmans, Green, 1949, p. 57.
[29] Cole, *Growing Up*, p. 51.
[30] Cole, *Growing Up*, p. 58.

down ... my intellectual conversion took place so easily that I cannot recollect even thinking about it; once the State had taken my brother it lost his sister's vote automatically.[31]

"The Falling Leaves" is one of the earliest anti-war poems written by a woman.

In 1911, Margaret Postgate won a scholarship to Girton College, Cambridge, where she earned a First Class honours in Classical Tripos and went on to teach classics at St. Paul's Girls' School. After her brother's trial, she became an active socialist, committed to "the abolition of all authority not based on reason and of all inequality based on prejudice or privilege of any kind."[32]

She left teaching for politics and accepted a full-time position at the Fabian Society Research Department, where she met George Douglas Howard Cole, an active member of the Fabian Society and a conscientious objector. They were married in 1918. After the war, Postgate Cole remained active in politics as a writer and lecturer, serving for thirteen years as an alderman on London City Council and campaigning in support of comprehensive education. She was honorary secretary of the Fabian Society from 1939 to 1953, and served as its president from 1962 until her death in 1980. Her only book of poetry was published in 1918, but she continued to write extensively on labour history and social issues. She was awarded Order of the British Empire (OBE) in 1965 for her work in education, and was created Dame of the British Empire (DBE) in 1970 for her lifetime achievements.

---

[31] Cole, *Growing Up*, pp. 59–60.
[32] Cole, *Growing Up*, p. 42.

Eastern Front (Im Osten)

The wrath of the people is dark,
Like the wild organ notes of winter storm,
The battle's crimson wave, a naked
Forest of stars.

With ravaged brows, with silver arms
To dying soldiers night comes beckoning.
In the shade of the autumn ash
Ghosts of the fallen are sighing.

Thorny wilderness girdles the town about.
From bloody doorsteps the moon
Chases terrified women.
Wild wolves have poured through the gates.

—Georg Trakl (1917), translated by Christopher Middleton

The war on the Eastern Front was as strategically important and as deadly as the battles waged in the West; even conservative estimates state that over 3.5 million soldiers and as many as two million civilians died. To describe the magnitude of destruction, many writers such as Trakl turned to apocalyptic imagery because "it suited the monumental scale of the war as well as bypassing the pointless discussion of who made what mistake at what moment to bring on catastrophe. Apocalypse is a judgment on a civilization as a whole, not on one or two incompetent leaders."[33]

Just months after the war began, Georg Trakl, a young Austrian poet and pharmacist, joined the Austro-Hungarian army as a medical officer and was posted to the province of Galicia (what is today part of the Ukraine and Poland). Before the war, Trakl had battled drug addiction and suicidal tendencies. What he witnessed on the Eastern Front inspired some of the most haunted poetry of the First World War. Trakl translator James Wright says, "patience is the clue to the understanding of Trakl's poems. One does not so much read them as explore them. They are not objects which he constructed, but quiet places at the edge of a dark forest where one has to sit still for a long time and listen very carefully."[34] It is believed that Trakl wrote "Eastern Front" shortly following the 1914 battle of

---

[33] Jay Winter, *Sites of Memory, Sites of Mourning*, Cambridge UP, 2014, p. 188.
[34] James Wright, "A Note on Trakl," *Twenty Poems of George Trakl*, translated by James Wright and Robert Bly, Sixties Press, 1961, p. 9.

Grodek. In the chaotic aftermath of the carnage, he had been assigned to care for nearly a hundred critically injured soldiers crowded into a barn. Alone with the wounded and dying, as night fell Trakl heard a gunshot and discovered that one of the sufferers had put a bullet in his own head. Seeking to escape the gruesome scene, Trakl fled outside, only to be confronted with the swinging corpses of civilians hanging from the trees. Shortly after, Trakl himself attempted suicide. He was diagnosed with dementia praecox (schizophrenia) and sent to a hospital near Krakow. Three weeks later, on November 3, 1914, Trakl fatally overdosed on cocaine. In a letter written just one year earlier, he had written, "It is a nameless unhappiness when one's world breaks in two."[35]

---

[35] Qtd. in *1910: The Emancipation of Dissonance,* by Thomas Harrison, U of California P, 1996, p. 45.

The Camp Follower

We spoke, the camp-follower and I.
About us was a cold, pungent odor—
Gun-powder, stale wine, wet earth, and the smell of thousands of men.
She said it reminded her of the scent
In the house of prostitutes she had lived in.
About us were soldiers—hordes of scarlet women, stupidly, smilingly giving up their bodies
To a putrid-lipped, chuckling lover—Death;
While their mistresses in tinsel whipped them on....
She spoke of a woman she had known in Odessa.
Owner of a huge band of girls,
Who had pocketed their earnings for years,
Only to be used, swindled and killed by some nobleman....
She said she thought of this grinning woman
Whenever she saw an officer brought back from battle, dead....
And I sat beside her and wondered.

—Maxwell Bodenheim (1914)

In his war memoir *Goodbye to All That,* Robert Graves tells of a young officer's visit to a brothel in Rouen, commenting "There were no restraints in France; these boys had money to spend and knew that they stood a good chance of being killed within a few weeks anyhow. They did not want to die virgins."[36] Richard Marshall writes that despite the fact that "Trench Foot has come to symbolise the squalor of the conflict in the popular imagination," soldiers were "more than five times as likely to end up in hospital suffering from Syphilis or Gonorrhoea."[37] An estimated 5 percent of soldiers serving in the British army during the war were infected with a venereal disease, and in 1915, the rate of infection for the Canadian Expeditionary Force was over 20 percent of their effective strength.[38] In research examining British soldiers' first-hand accounts of encounters with prostitution and brothels,

---

[36] Robert Graves, *Goodbye to All That,* Penguin, 1975, p. 195.
[37] Richard Marshall, "The British Army's Fight against Venereal Disease in the 'Heroic Age of Prostitution,'" *WW1C Continuations and Beginnings,* 25 Sept. 2012, web.archive.org/web/20190807204800/http://ww1centenary.oucs.ox.ac.uk/body-and-mind/the-british-army%e2%80%99s-fight-against-venereal-disease-in-the-%e2%80%98heroic-age-of-prostitution%e2%80%99.
[38] Marshall, "The British Army's Fight against Venereal Disease."

Clare Makepeace writes that prostitution was a commonplace aspect of the war about which little was written or discussed.[39] It was, however, the topic of soldiers' songs:

> Mademoiselle from Armentieres, parlez-vous,
> Mademoiselle from Armentieres, parlez-vous,
> You didn't have to know her long,
> To know the reason men go wrong!
> Hinky, dinky, parlez-vous!

"The Camp Follower" draws a connection between soldiers and prostitutes, but in actual practice, the two were treated very differently. Women were criminalized and blamed for the spread of venereal disease, and they bore the stigma of immorality. In England, the 1916 Defence of the Realm Act made it illegal for a prostitute to approach a man in uniform, and further legislation during the war gave police the right to medically examine any woman suspected of being a prostitute.[40] German laws and policies were similar:

> Any member of the military found to have a venereal disease was required to reveal the identity of any woman who might have transmitted the disease. Any woman accused of having sex with several men within a month—regardless of whether she accepted payment for this—could find herself a 'registered' prostitute after two warnings ... Here as elsewhere, the blame and punishment fell upon women rather than men.[41]

The historical record has preserved few if any first-hand accounts of prostitutes themselves.

Maxwell Bodenheim is associated with the early years of the Chicago Literary Renaissance. "The Camp Follower" was one of fourteen poems chosen for the November 1914 war poems issue of America's *Poetry* magazine. D.H. Lawrence complained to Harriet Monroe, the editor of *Poetry*, that the poem was "something for the nasty people of this world to batten on,"[42] but several years later, J.W. Cunliffe included "The Camp Follower" in his anthology *Poems of the Great War*.[43] Bodenheim arrived in New York City's Greenwich Village in 1915,

---

[39] Clare Makepeace, "Punters and Their Prostitutes: British Soldiers, Masculinity and *Maisons Tolérées* in the First World War," *What Is Masculinity?* edited by John H. Arnold and Sean Brady, Palgrave Macmillan, 2011, p. 413.
[40] Marshall, "The British Army's Fight against Venereal Disease."
[41] Susan R. Grayzel, *Women and the First World War*, Routledge, 2013, p. 72.
[42] Qtd. in "A Forgotten War Poem by D.H. Lawrence," by Ernest W. Tedlock, Jr., *Modern Language Notes*, vol. 67, no. 6, June 1952, p. 410.
[43] John William Cunliffe, editor, *Poems of the Great War*, Macmillan, 1916, p. 29.

where he "made a name for himself as a poet of great promise" among the avant-garde.[44] But he reveled in belligerent arguments, binge drinking, and scandal, and Bodenheim's reputation suffered. His friend Ben Hecht describes him as "more disliked, derided, denounced, beaten up, and kicked down more flights of stairs than any poet of whom I have ever heard or read," and recalls that "when in his cups, [he] contented himself with announcing, 'poetry is the impish attempt to paint the color of the wind.'"[45] Bodenheim had joined the army in 1909 at the age of seventeen, but was jailed and dishonorably discharged for "hitting a lieutenant over the head with his musket. The lieutenant had been ridiculing Private Bodenheim as a Jew."[46] When the United States entered the war in 1917, Bodenheim persuaded wealthy friends that he was a conscientious objector who had refused to register for the draft and was being hunted by military authorities. His sympathetic friends hid Bodenheim, housing and feeding him in luxury, until they learned from a recruiting officer of the author's ruse:

> "You're a bunch of fools … your poet friend Bodenheim registered for the service on the first day our office opened. Here's his card. Nobody's hunting for him. Your friend is ineligible for further Army service. He was dishonorably discharged after previous Army service in Texas. The United States Army has no interest in him whatsoever except to keep the daffy sonofabitch out of its ranks."[47]

Today, Bodenheim is chiefly remembered for the lurid circumstances surrounding his death. In 1954, destitute and ravaged by years of alcoholism, he and his wife were murdered in a New York City flophouse.

---

[44] John Strausbaugh, *The Village: 400 Years of Beats and Bohemians, Radicals and Rogues*, HarperCollins, 2013, p. 174.
[45] Ben Hecht, *Letters from Bohemia*, Hammond, 1965, pp. 107, 4.
[46] Hecht, *Letters*, p. 111.
[47] Hecht, *Letters*, p. 117.

The Other Side

There are not any, save the men that died,
Whose minds have probed into the heart of war.

Sometimes we stumble on a secret door
And listening guess what lies the other side.
Sometimes a moment's sudden pain
Flings back the veil that hangs between
Guessing and knowing; then lets it fall again
Before we understand what we have seen.

In and out everywhere,
Distorted in a twisted glass,
Fragmentary visions pass.
We try to fit them one with another,
Like a child putting a puzzle together,
When half the pieces are not there.

Out of a dim obscurity
Certain things stand plain and clear,
Certain things we are forced to see,
Certain things we are forced to hear.

A subaltern dying between the lines,
   Wondering why.
A father with nothing left of life
   But the will to die.

A young girl born for laughter and spring,
Left to her shame and loneliness.
What is one woman more or less
To men who've forgotten everything?

A thin line swinging forward to kill,
   And a man driven mad by the din.

Music-hall songs about "Kaiser Bill"
   And "the march through the streets of Berlin."

Grey-beards prattling round a fire
Of the good the war has done.

Three men rotting upon the wire;
And each of them had a son.

A soldier who once was fresh and clean
Lost to himself in whoring and drink,
Blind to what will be and what has been,
Only aware that he must not think.

In the pulpit a parson preaching lies,
Babbling of honour and sacrifice.

. . . .

Fragments flutter in and out,
Christ! what is it all about?
                Hampstead. March, 1917

                                      —Alec Waugh

By 1917, numerous people (known as Neverendians) believed that the war might last forever. One British officer used an elaborate mathematical formula of past battle gains to calculate that at its current rate, the war would continue for another 180 years.[48] Waugh's poem "The Other Side" suggests that the only way to comprehend the war was to die.

Alexander (Alec) Raban Waugh was the older brother of the British novelist Evelyn Waugh. Alec trained at the British Royal Military Academy at Sandhurst, and in 1917 was commissioned as a lieutenant in the Dorset Regiment. Posted to the Somme and Passchendaele, Waugh was captured near Arras on March 28, 1918, and spent the remainder of the war in German prison camps. In May of 1918, his war poetry collection, *Resentment,* was published in London. T.S. Eliot reviewed the volume, remarking that while the writing was "modern," it "would appear to have been influenced by some older person who admired Rupert Brooke. He [Waugh] is stark realism ... said to be very young, and to have written a novel. That is a bad beginning, but something might be made of him."[49] The *Bookman's* "Poets in Khaki" was more complimentary. Citing "Cannon Fodder" and "The Other Side," St. John Adcock wrote that Waugh's poems "strip the romance of war to the bone." In his review of forty-four soldier-poets, Adcock

---

[48] Paul Fussell, *The Great War and Modern Memory,* 1975, Oxford UP, 2000, pp. 71–72.
[49] T.S. Eliot, "Short Notices," *Egoist,* vol. 5, no. 7, Aug. 1918, p. 99. (Waugh's novel, *The Loom of Youth,* was a highly controversial and immensely popular account of his school days at Sherborne.)

included Waugh as one of "Three poets who I think do represent as faithfully and potently as any the later, essentially modern attitude towards war."[50] The two other writers singled out for this praise were Gilbert Frankau and Siegfried Sassoon.

---

[50] St. John Adcock, "Poets in Khaki," *Bookman*, vol. 55, Christmas 1918, p. 98.

A Letter from the Front

I was out early to-day, spying about
From the top of a haystack—such a lovely morning—
And when I mounted again to canter back
I saw across a field in the broad sunlight
A young gunner subaltern, stalking along
With a rook-rifle held at the ready and—
    would you believe it?—
A domestic cat, soberly marching behind him.

So I laughed, and felt quite well-disposed to the youngster,
And shouted out "The top of the morning" to him,
And wished him "Good sport!"—and then I remembered
My rank, and his, and what I ought to be doing;
And I rode nearer, and added, "I can only suppose
You have not seen the Commander-in-Chief's orders
Forbidding English officers to annoy their Allies
By hunting and shooting."
    But he stood and saluted
And said earnestly, "I beg your pardon, sir,
I was only going out to shoot a sparrow
To feed my cat with."

    So there was the whole picture—
The lovely early morning, the occasional shell
Screeching and scattering past us, the empty landscape—
Empty, except for the young gunner saluting,
And the cat, anxiously watching his every movement.

I may be wrong, and I may have told it badly,
But it struck *me* as being extremely ludicrous.

—Henry Newbolt (1918)

An estimated 500,000 cats were sent to the trenches of the First World War. They hunted the rats that infested soldiers' living quarters, were used to detect gas, and became mascots and companions for the troops. Some cats were even credited with saving men's lives.[51]

    John Henry Newbolt's conversational poem, lacking regular meter and rhyme, resembles a letter as nearly as a poem. It relates a simple anecdote and

---

[51] Sigmund Brouwer, *Innocent Heroes: Stories of Animals in the First World War,* Tundra, 2017, p. 34.

invites readers to make of it what they will. Born in 1862, Newbolt did not serve in the military, but was recruited by the British War Propaganda Bureau and appointed Controller of Telecommunications at the Foreign Office. Knighted in 1915, Newbolt is best remembered today for the poem, "Vitaï Lampada," which compares war to a competitive school sporting event. Its refrain, "Play up! play up! and play the game!" was used in First World War recruiting posters, but that poem was published in 1897. Newbolt grew to dislike both the poem and the attention he received from it, writing to his wife while on a 1923 speaking tour of Canada, "It's a kind of Frankenstein's Monster that I created thirty years ago and now I find it falling on my neck at every corner! In vain do I explain what is poetry: they roar for "Play up": they put it on their flags and on their war memorials and their tombstones: it's their National Anthem."[52]

Newbolt's last volume of poetry, *St. George's Day*, was published in 1918. In 1928 he edited *New Paths on Helicon*, an anthology of British poetry from the first quarter of the century. The collection offered only a limited selection of poetry from the war, and Newbolt explained in a note, "The War passed, and its detail ceased, for a time at any rate, to be of interest to a tired and harassed people."[53] *New Paths on Helicon* included poems by Siegfried Sassoon, Robert Nichols, and Herbert Read, but not Wilfred Owen. Four years earlier, Newbolt had explained in a letter to a friend,

> Much as I hate the idea of war and waste, and clearly as I see the obvious crash, still I imagine we are we, and if next time came, we should just shoulder it again. That's really what Sassoon said to me on Tuesday—he would go again, and if he then everybody. He has sent me Wilfred Owen's Poems with an Introduction by himself. The best of them I knew already—they are terribly good, but of course limited, almost all on one note ... Owen and the rest of the broken men rail at the Old Men who sent the young to die: they have suffered cruelly, but in the nerves and not the heart—they haven't the experience or the imagination to know the extreme human agony—'Who giveth me to die for thee, Absalom, my son, my son.' Paternity apart, what Englishman of fifty wouldn't far rather stop the shot himself than see the boys do it for him? I don't think these shell-shocked war poems will move our grandchildren greatly—there's nothing fundamental or final about them—at least they only put one figure into a very big equation, and that's not one of the unknown but one of the best known quantities.[54]

---

[52] Newbolt letter of 1 Mar. 1923, qtd. in *Playing the Game: A Biography of Sir Henry Newbolt*, by Susan Chitty, Quartet, 1997, p. 267.
[53] Henry John Newbolt, editor, *New Paths on Helicon*, Nelson, 1928, p. 393.
[54] Newbolt, letter to Alice Hylton, 2 Aug. 1924, qtd. in *Poetry of Henry Newbolt*, by Vanessa Furse Jackson, ELT, 1994, p. 161.

Singing "Tipperary"

We've each our Tipperary, who shout that haunting song,
And all the more worth reaching because the way is long;
You'll hear the hackneyed chorus until it tires your brain
Unless you feel the thousand hopes disguised in that refrain.

We've each our Tipperary—some hamlet, village, town,
To which our ghosts would hasten though we laid our bodies down,
Some spot of little showing our spirits still would seek,
And strive, unseen, to utter what now we fear to speak.

We've each our Tipperary, our labour to inspire,
Some mountain-top or haven, some goal of far desire—
Some old forlorn ambition, or humble, happy hope
That shines beyond the doubting with which our spirits cope.

We've each our Tipperary—near by or wildly far;
For some it means a fireside, for some it means a star;
For some it's but a journey by homely roads they know,
For some a spirit's venture where none but theirs may go.

We've each our Tipperary, where rest and love and peace
Mean just a mortal maiden, or Dante's Beatrice;
We growl a song together, to keep the marching swing,
But who shall dare interpret the chorus that we sing?

—William Kersley Holmes[55] (1915)

On August 13, 1914, British news correspondent George Curnock heard the Irish Connaught Rangers singing "It's a Long Way to Tipperary" as they arrived in Boulogne, France, and began their march toward the front lines. According to another reporter at the *Daily Mail*, Curnock's dispatch "made great play of the soldier's marching song, 'It's a long way to Tipperary,' and the Chief has given us orders to boom it, to print the music so that everybody shall know it. He says, thanks to Curnock's genius, we shall soon have everybody singing it."[56] Twenty years later, remembering his role in popularizing the song, Curnock wrote,

---

[55] See also Holmes's "The Soldier Mood."
[56] Tom Clarke, "Tuesday, August 18, 1914," *My Northcliffe Diary*, J.J. Little and Ives, 1931, pp. 55–56.

> The public at once took the song to heart ... By September 4 Bert Feldman, owner of the copyright of the song, was stating: "I'm printing 10,000 copies a day, which doesn't meet the demand. Guess we'll deafen the Kaiser with it before long." Two weeks later he [Feldman] was adding: "In America the song is making a great impression. France, Canada, Australia, India, and British Columbia are all vying with Great Britain for the song. The sales from present signs must approximate to two millions."[57]

The song's lyrics were translated into many languages, including French, Russian, German, Cornish, Hindustani, and Maori. Many related to the universal theme of dislocation:

> the song's premise of travelling a long way allowed it to be representative for any number of journeys made: New Zealanders or Australians leaving home for Egypt or West Indians arriving in Folkestone. The song's colonial undertones, the Irish 'Paddy' returning from metropolis to colony would be subverted by the mobilisations of war, which brought colonial troops to their hearts' desire in a 'Tipperary' that could be Egypt, Palestine, the Western Front and even Blighty.[58]

Lieutenant William Kersley Holmes published two volumes of war poetry: *Ballads of Field and Billet* (in which "Singing 'Tipperary'" appeared) and *More Ballads of Field and Billet*. The *Glasgow Herald* said of Holmes's poems, "They range from the grave to the humorous, from the realistic to the romantic, but something of the brightness of youth is in them all, something of that gallant gaiety which makes a jest of the discomforts of life, yet never thinks of life itself as a jest."[59]

---

[57] George C. Curnock, "Twenty Years Ago: The Immortal Story of 'Tipperary,'" *Daily Mail*, 11 Aug. 1934.

[58] Anna Maguire, "'It's a Long Way to Tipperary': Colonial Encounters with Music during the First World War," Taking British Music(s) Abroad: Soundscapes of the Imperial Message Study Day, 16 June 2015, King's College London, Conference Paper, pp. 2–3.

[59] Review qtd. in the *Dollar Magazine*, vol. 14, no. 54, June 1915, pp. 74–75 (a publication of Dollar Academy, Holmes's alma mater).

O Little David, Play on Your Harp

O Little David, play on your harp,
That ivory harp with the golden strings
And sing as you did in Jewry Land,
Of the Prince of Peace and the God of Love
And the Coming Christ Immanuel.
O Little David, play on your harp.

    A seething world is gone stark mad;
    And is drunk with the blood,
    Gorged with the flesh,
    Blinded with the ashes
    Of her millions of dead.
    From out it all and over all
    There stands, years old and fully grown,
    A monster in the guise of man.
    He is of war and not of war;
    Born in peace,
    Nurtured in arrogant pride and greed,
    World-creature is he and native to no land.
    And war itself is merciful
    When measured by his deeds.
    Beneath the Crescent[60]
    Lie a people maimed;
    Their only sin—
    That they worship God.
    On Russia's steppes
    Is a race in tears;[61]
    Their one offense—
    That they would be themselves.
    On Flanders plains
    Is a nation raped;
    A bleeding gift
    Of "Kultur's" conquering creed.[62]
    And in every land
    Are black folk scourged;

---

[60] A reference to the flag of the Ottoman Empire and the Armenian massacre.
[61] A reference to Russian pogroms that targeted Jews.
[62] A reference to German atrocities in Belgium.

Their only crime—
That they dare be men.

O Little David, play on your harp,
That ivory harp with the golden strings;
And psalm anew your songs of Peace,
Of the soothing calm of a Brotherly Love,
And the saving grace of a Mighty God.
O Little David, play on your harp.

—Joseph Seamon Cotter, Jr. (1918)

Over 350,000 black Americans joined the American Army during the First World War, but units were strictly segregated by race, with black soldiers assigned to hard labor and low-status jobs such as grave digging, exhumation, and reburial work. In the American Army of the First World War, racism was not only accepted, but often enforced. Few black units saw combat; an exception were those assigned to the French military, where they fought with bravery and distinction. In May of 1919, W.E.B. DuBois, author and co-founder of the National Association for the Advancement of Colored People (NAACP), shared with readers of *The Crisis* a secret memo that an American colonel had sent to the French Army in August of 1918. The colonel's memo exposes racist assumptions that were commonly held by US military officials:

> American opinion is unanimous on the "color question" and does not admit of any discussion.
>
> The increasing number of Negroes in the United States (about 15,000,000) would create for the white race in the Republic a menace of degeneracy were it not that an impassable gulf has been made between them.
>
> As this danger does not exist for the French race, the French public has become accustomed to treating the Negro with familiarity and indulgence.
>
> This indulgence and this familiarity are matters of grievous concern to the Americans. They consider them an affront to their national policy. They are afraid that contact with the French will inspire in black Americans aspirations which to them [the whites] appear intolerable.[63]

DuBois wrote that the memo "represents American and not French opinion and we have been informed that when the French Ministry heard of the distribution of this document among the Prefects and Sous-Prefects of France, they ordered such copies to be collected and burned."[64]

---

[63] Colonel J.L.A. Linard with the A.E.F. to the French Army, 7 Aug. 1918, qtd. in "Documents of the War," collected by W.E. Burghardt DuBois, "Secret Information Concerning Black American Troops," *Crisis*, May 1919, pp. 16–17.
[64] DuBois, "Secret Information Concerning Black American Troops," p. 16.

Joseph Seamon Cotter, Jr. is viewed as a "forerunner of the African American cultural renaissance of the 1920s," despite publishing only one book of poetry, *The Band of Gideon and Other Lyrics* (1918).[65] His poem "O Little David, Play on Your Harp" uses a well-known African American spiritual to frame the intersections of war, genocide, and racism (the spiritual was recorded in 1919 by Lieutenant Noble Sissle and Lieutenant James Reese Europe of the 369th Harlem Hellfighters). Cotter's poems were anthologized in James Weldon Johnson's *The Book of American Negro Poetry* (1922), in Countee Cullen's *Caroling Dusk* (1927), and in Hughes and Bontemps' *The Poetry of the Negro* (1949), but they did not appear in collections from the 1960s onward.[66] Cotter died of tuberculosis at the age of twenty-three; his one-act war play, *On the Fields of France,* was published posthumously in the *Crisis* in June of 1920.

---

[65] James Robert Payne, "Joseph Seamon Cotter, Jr.," *The Concise Oxford Companion to African American Literature,* edited by William L. Andrews, Frances Smith Foster, and Trudier Harris, Oxford UP, 2001, p. 90, *eBook Collection (ProQuest).*

[66] Julian Mason, "Who Was Joseph Seamon Cotter, Jr.?" *Southern Literary Journal,* vol. 23, no. 1, Fall 1990, pp. 104–106.

To the Memory of Some I Knew Who Are Dead and Who Loved Ireland

Their dream had left me numb and cold,
    But yet my spirit rose in pride,
Refashioning in burnished gold
    The images of those who died,
Or were shut in the penal cell.
    Here's to you, Pearse, your dream, not mine,
But yet the thought for this you fell
    Has turned life's waters into wine.

You who have died on Eastern hills
    Or fields of France as undismayed,
Who lit with interlinked wills
    The long heroic barricade,
You, too, in all the dreams you had,
    Thought of some thing for Ireland done.
Was it not so, Oh, shining lad,
    What lured you, Alan Anderson?

I listened to high talk from you,
    Thomas McDonagh, and it seemed
The words were idle, but they grew
    To nobleness by death redeemed.
Life cannot utter words more great
    Than life may meet by sacrifice,
High words were equaled by high fate,
    You paid the price. You paid the price.

You who have fought on fields afar,
    That other Ireland did you wrong
Who said you shadowed Ireland's star,
    Nor gave you laurel wreath nor song.
You proved by death as true as they,
    In mightier conflicts played your part,
Equal your sacrifice may weigh,
    Dear Kettle, of the generous heart.

The hope lives on age after age,
    Earth with its beauty might be won

For labour as a heritage,
      For this has Ireland lost a son.
   This hope unto a flame to fan
      Men have put life by with a smile,
   Here's to you, Connolly, my man,
      Who cast the last torch on the pile.

   You, too, had Ireland in your care,
      Who watched o'er pits of blood and mire,
   From iron roots leap up in air
      Wild forests, magical, of fire;
   Yet while the Nuts of Death were shed
      Your memory would ever stray
   To your own isle. Oh, gallant dead—
      This wreath, Will Redmond, on your clay.

   Here's to you, men I never met,
      Yet hope to meet behind the veil,
   Thronged on some starry parapet,
      That looks down on Innisfail,
   And see the confluence of dreams
      That clashed together in our night,
   One river, born from many streams,
      Roll in one blaze of blinding light.
               Dublin, December 17, 1917

                              —A.E. (George William Russell)

In the early months of the First World War, believing that their service would be rewarded by British acceptance of Irish Home Rule, many Irish volunteered to join the British Army. However, in the aftermath of the 1916 Easter Rising and the associated violence and repressive actions of the British Army, Irishmen who had chosen to fight with the British were commonly viewed as disloyal to Ireland. In December of 1917, speaking to this context of deeply divided loyalties, George William Russell, Irish nationalist, writer, and pacifist (known by the pseudonym A.E.), reworked his poem "Salutation," which had honored the 1916 rebels.[67] To the original poem, Russell added alternating stanzas that juxtaposed the sacrifice of leaders of the Easter Rising with the patriotism of

---

[67] Frances Flanagan, *Remembering the Revolution*, Oxford UP, 2015, p. 131.

Irish nationalists who had died fighting with the British Army in the First World War (he also removed the stanza that had honored Republican women). Under its new title, the poem repeated its call for unity among the people of Ireland. Russell's letter to the editor that accompanied "To the Memory" was titled "A New Nation," and Russell's editorial reiterated his belief that if the people of Ireland were to achieve greatness as a free nation, they must put aside their internal differences:

> And here I come to the purpose of my letter, which is to deprecate the scornful repudiation by Irishmen of other Irishmen, which is so common at present, and which helps to perpetuate our feuds. We are all one people. We are closer to each other in character than we are to any other race. The necessary preliminary to political adjustment is moral adjustment, forgiveness, and mutual understanding.[68]

The same week in which 488 Irish were killed in Dublin during the Easter Rising, 532 men of the Irish Division were gassed, bayoneted, shelled, and shot in attacks outside Hulluch in northern France.[69] Concluding his letter to the *Irish Times,* Russell wrote,

> I myself am Anglo-Irish, with the blood of both races in me, and when the rising of Easter Week took place all that was Irish in me was profoundly stirred, and out of that mood I wrote commemorating the dead. And then later there rose in memory the faces of others I knew who loved their country, but had died in other battles. They fought in those because they believed they would serve Ireland, and I felt these were no less my people. I could hold them also in my heart and pay tribute to them. Because it was possible for me to do so, I think it is possible for others; and in the hope that the deeds of all may in the future be a matter of pride to the new nation I append here these verses I have written.[70]

---

[68] Mr. George Russell ("A.E."), "Letters to the Editor: A New Nation," *Irish Times,* 19 Dec. 1917, p. 6.
[69] Ronan McGreevy, "Easter Week 1916: The Gassing of the Irish," *The Irish Times,* 15 Apr. 2016, web. archive.org/web/20190808165852/https://www.irishtimes.com/culture/heritage/easter-week-1916-the-gassing-of-the-irish-1.2611854.
[70] Russell ("A.E."), "Letters to the Editor: A New Nation," p. 6.

America at War

America,
If thy sons can go to war
Thinking—
If men democracy-trained can fight
And not glory in it
Or be afraid of it
But earnestly regret that war must be—
If they can follow thy banner
And know
That its red does not represent blood
But sunrise,
That its white
Is not death but deliverance,
That its stars
Are not pilots for warships
But makers of poetry—
O America,
Then shall democracy conquer
And war shall never more be.

—Gertrude Smith (1917)

In November of 1916, American President Woodrow Wilson was re-elected by a narrow margin after campaigning on the slogan "He kept us out of the war." Less than six months later, on April 2, 1917, Wilson called a special session of Congress, asking for a declaration of war. Wilson argued that Germany's unrestricted submarine warfare—showing no mercy even for hospital ships—demonstrated a "reckless lack of compassion or principle" and constituted "warfare against mankind." He condemned the German government's attempts to infiltrate American communities and government offices with spies, but mindful of the large number of German-Americans, Wilson assured the public, "We have no quarrel with the German people. We have no feeling towards them but one of sympathy and friendship. It was not upon their impulse that their Government acted in entering upon that war." Yet Wilson made it clear that American troops would be called upon to kill German soldiers, estimating that at least half a million men would be needed to join and strengthen the American army. The president urged Congress to declare war on Germany, proclaiming that the fight would be "for the ultimate peace of the world and for the liberation of its peoples ... The world must be made safe for democracy."[71] Four days later, Congress declared war on Germany, and many Americans responded with poetry.

Gertrude Smith was a student at Adelphi College; her poem "America at War" was included in the 1917 volume *Poets of the Future: A College Anthology*. The anthology's editor wrote, "The poems that I have selected for this anthology have all, at some point or other, filled me with joy. They have, either directly or indirectly, kept alive in me the faith that this world, despite the days of darkness and savagery that we are living through, is in the final analysis good and beautiful and true."[72] Smith's poem was also reprinted in the 1921 anthology *Poems of the War and the Peace*.[73] Other poems in that collection include Wilfred Owen's "Dulce et Decorum Est," Rupert Brooke's "The Soldier," Laurence Binyon's "For the Fallen," and Siegfried Sassoon's "Attack" and "Aftermath." "America at War" appears to be the only poem that Gertrude Smith published. She married, had children, served as vice president of the Vermont League of Women Voters, and seems to have disappeared from print.[74]

---

[71] Woodrow Wilson, *Why We Are at War: Messages to the Congress, January to April, 1917*, Harper and Brothers, 1917, pp. 40–61.
[72] Henry T. Schnittkind, "Introduction," *Poets of the Future: A College Anthology for 1916–1917*, edited by Henry T. Schnittkind, Stratford, 1917, p. x.
[73] Sterling Andrus Leonard, editor, *Poems of the War and the Peace*, Harcourt, Brace, 1921.
[74] "Mrs. John C. Oram Sr.," *New York Times*, 19 Dec. 1955, p. 27.

Violets—April 1915[75]

Violets from Plug Street Wood,
Sweet, I send you oversea.
(It is strange they should be blue,
Blue, when his soaked blood was red,
For they grew around his head:
It is strange they should be blue.)
Violets from Plug Street Wood
Think what they have meant to me—
Life and Hope and Love & You
(And you did not see them grow
Where his mangled body lay,
Hiding horror from the day;
Sweetest it was better so.)
Violets from oversea,
To your dear, far, forgetting land
These I send in memory,
Knowing You will understand.

—Roland Leighton

"Summer & trenches don't go together somehow," Roland Leighton wrote to his sweetheart, Vera Brittain, in April 1915.[76] Later that month, Roland wrote to Vera and described a discovery he had made while walking in Ploegsteert Wood (known to the British as "Plug Street Wood"). He had found "the body of a dead British soldier hidden in the undergrowth a few yards from the path." Leighton noted, "He must have been shot there during the wood-fighting in the early part of the War. The body had sunk down into the marshy ground so that only the tops of the boots stuck up above the soil. His cap & equipment beside him were half-buried & rotting away." Leighton ordered that the body be covered with dirt, "to make one grave more among the many in the wood."[77] The next day, Leighton started a poem, and while on leave that August (during which time the couple became engaged), he showed Vera the finished villanelle: "Violets—April

---

[75] The poem was included in *Boy of My Heart*, a tribute to Leighton published anonymously by his mother in 1916. The version included here is from Leighton's handwritten manuscript, *First World War Poetry Digital Archive*, web.archive.org/web/20190808172627/http://www.oucs.ox.ac.uk/ww1lit/collections/document/5653/5619.
[76] Roland Leighton, qtd. in *Chronicle of Youth*, by Vera Brittain, William Morrow, 1982, p. 176.
[77] Leighton, qtd. in *Chronicle of Youth*, p. 184.

1915." Vera's journal records, "I remembered how on that day he had written me a letter—he was then in Ploegsteert Wood—enclosing some violets from the top of his dug-out which he said he had just picked for me."[78]

By August of 1915, Leighton was having difficulties in finding beauty anywhere on the Western Front. He wrote to Vera, "I used to talk of the Beauty of War; but it is only War in the abstract that is beautiful. Modern warfare is merely a trade."[79] In September, his revised opinion of the war was even more direct:

> Let him who thinks War is a glorious, golden thing, who loves to roll forth stirring words of exhortation, invoking Honour and Praise and Valour and Love of Country with as thoughtless and fervid a faith as inspired the priests of Baal to call on their own slumbering deity, let him but look at a little pile of sodden grey rags that cover half a skull and a shin-bone and what might have been Its ribs, or at this skeleton lying on its side, resting half-crouching as it fell, perfect but that it is headless, and with the tattered clothing still draped round it; and let him realise how grand and glorious a thing it is to have distilled all Youth and Joy and Life into a foetid heap of hideous putrescence! Who is there who has known and seen who can say that Victory is worth the death of even one of these?[80]

Roland Leighton died of wounds on December 23, 1915. The inscription on his headstone at Louvencourt cemetery in France reads, "Goodnight though life and all take flight—Never goodbye." The lines are a reference to the poem "A Wink from Hesper ... " by W.E. Henley. Roland had shared the poem with Vera in a letter in May of 1915, describing how as he crossed the fields in the starlight, the poem came into his head: "Goodnight, sweet friend, goodnight! / Till life & all take flight / Never goodbye."[81] Roland again referenced the poem as he was returning to the Western Front after his August leave, sending a telegram to Vera that read, "Till we may live our roseate poem through," and a brief letter: "Nearly at Folkestone now. I am trying not to think of it, but the thought will come. Oh damn, I know it—

> Goodnight, sweet friend, goodnight!
> Till life and all take flight
> Never goodbye."[82]

---

[78] Brittain, *Chronicle of Youth*, p. 250.
[79] Roland Leighton, qtd. in *Testament of Youth*, by Vera Brittain, Virago, 2014, p. 150.
[80] Leighton, qtd. in *Testament of Youth*, p. 174.
[81] Leighton, qtd. in *Chronicle of Youth*, p. 191.
[82] Leighton, qtd. in *Chronicle of Youth*, p. 265.

High Barbary

The distant mountains' jagged, cruel line
Cuts the imagination as a blade
Of dove-grey Damascene. In many a raid
Here Barbary pirates drave the ships of wine
Back to Sicilian harbours, harried kine,
Pillaged Calabrian villages and made
The land a desolation; here they played
On Glamour's passioned gamut at Lust's sign.

Saracens, Moors, Phoenicians—all the East,
Franks, Huns, Walloons,[83] the pilgrims of the Pope,
All, all are gone. The clouds are trailing hence;
So goes to Benediction some proud priest
Sweeping the ground with broidered golden cope.
—Go, gather up the fumes of frankincense.

—James Howard Stables (1916)

The First World War extended far beyond the Western Front: some of the fiercest fighting occurred at sea, on Turkish beaches in the Gallipoli Campaign, in Galicia on the Eastern Front, in the high Alps between Italy and Austria-Hungary, in the Middle East, and in Africa. *Barbary* is the historic name given to the coast of North Africa, and gazing out over an alien landscape, the poem's speaker finds that his imagination has been cut as with "a blade / Of dove-grey Damascene." Damascus steel was famous for its use in swords and knives, but when used as an adjective, "Damascene" refers to a moment of insight that transforms one's beliefs and attitudes: an epiphany.

"High Barbary" was written by J. Howard Stables and published in his book of poetry, *The Sorrow That Whistled*. The son of a vicar, Stables left his studies at Christ Church, Oxford to enlist early in the war with the Hampshire Regiment. He was later commissioned in the Indian Army Reserve of Officers and served with the 15th Gurkha Rifles in India, Northeastern Pakistan, and Mesopotamia (what is now modern Iraq). He died at age twenty-one in a battle near Baghdad in early 1917. Wounded and left behind when the British troops withdrew, Stables has no known grave; his name is listed on the Basra Memorial to the

---

[83] French-speakers of Belgium.

missing in modern Iraq. Because of modern wars and tensions in that country, the entire memorial was moved in 1997 from its original location to the middle of what became a major battleground during the first Gulf War. A 1916 review of Stables' volume of poetry remarks,

> "The Sorrow that Whistled" is an unusual little book, as suits with its name. The writer, whom one takes to be young, revels in Eastern colour and fragrance. He can do something quite good and simple, such as "While Scouring Linen." On the other hand, he can do something extremely bad, as in the "Thoughts of a Refugee." Yet there is here a promise, and, not unconnected with it, indications that J.H. Stables is a young soldier. There could be no better school for a young poet who wants to shed the faults of youth than the trenches.[84]

---

[84] Katharine Tynan, "War Poets and Others," *The Bookman*, Oct. 1916, p. 22.

Epiphany Vision

This is the night of a Star.
Dusk grow window and wall;
A Cross unseen floats red o'er the wrack of war;
Silences fall
In the house where the wounded are.

"Good-night to all!"
Then I pause awhile by the open door, and see
Their patient faces, pale through the blue smoke-rings,
On the night of Epiphany....
But who are these, who are changed utterly,
Wearing a look of Kings?

Brothers, whence do ye come?
Royal and still, what Star have ye looked upon?
—"From hill and valley, from many a city home
We came; we endured till the last of strength was gone,
Over the narrow sea.
But what of a Star? We have only fought for home
And babes on the mother's knee."
(Their silence saith.)

—Brothers, what do ye bring
To the Christ Whom Kings adored?—"We cannot tell.
We might have fashioned once some simple thing;
Once we were swift, who now are very slow;
We were skilled of hand, who bear the splint and the sling.
We gave no thought to Pain, in the year ago,
Who since have passed through Hell.
But what should we bring Him now—we, derelicts nigh past mending?"

(Frankincense, myrrh and gold;
Winds His choristers, worlds about His knee....
Hath He room at all in His awful Treasury
For the gifts our Kings unfold
That can ne'er be told?)

This is the night of a Star.
This is the long road's ending

They are sleeping now; they have brought their warrior best
To the Lord their God Who made them;
And lo! He hath repaid them
With rest.—
This is the night of a Star.
The laugh that rings through torment, the ready jest,
Valour and youth, lost hope, and a myriad dreams
Splendidly given—
He hath taken up to the inmost heart of Heaven.
And now—while the night grows cold, and the ward-fire gleams—
You may guess the tender Smile as He walketh hidden
In the place where His Wise Ones are.

—Mary-Adair Macdonald (1917)

British Voluntary Aid Detachment (VAD) nurse Mary-Adair Macdonald left her home in Lyndhurst, Hampshire, to join the VAD in September of 1915, and she served until May of 1918 at various hospitals in England.[85] A small pamphlet of her poetry was published in 1917 and dedicated to the nurses of England, Scotland, Ireland, and the Empire who have "nourished the wounded and soothed many a dying soldier." Her poem "In the Ward" describes the women who tended the "maimed and pale," the nurses who served as "handmaids of your pain."[86]

---

[85] "Miss Mary-Adair Macdonald." *British Red Cross,* web.archive.org/web/20190620155546/https://vad.redcross.org.uk/Card?fname=mary+&sname=macdonald&id=140468.
[86] Mary-Adair Macdonald, "In the Ward," *From a V.A.D. Hospital: Three Poems,* W. Speaight and Sons, 1917.

At Bethlehem—1915

The travellers are astir—
Bearing frowns for incense,
Scorns for myrrh.

War flings its sign afar—
There's blood upon the Manger,
Blood upon the Star.

Dear Lord!
Who fain would find the Saviour
Find the Sword.

—Egbert T. Sandford

During the First World War, the Bible "was a central and resonant force. It consoled and inspired, and its language was an intrinsic part of everyday as well as literary speech."[87] The poem "At Bethelehem—1915" offers an unusual retelling of Christ's birth. Rather than use the Christian narrative to find meaning in the deaths of the war or provide comfort in the promise of redemption and the afterlife, the poem prophesies an unsettling vision of violence. The Magi of Matthew's gospel come not to worship but to sow discord; the gifts they bring are scorn and blood. Sandford re-envisions the Christmas nativity as no less than a cataclysmic invasion; his poem has more in common with W.B. Yeats's "The Second Coming," written in 1919, than with most religious poetry written during the First World War.

Egbert T. Sandford, a government-employed warehouse manager at Plymouth, described himself as "just an ordinary working man," and said that the primary aim of his poetry was to "take the common things of life and weave them into song."[88] His chief literary influences were the poets William Blake and Francis Thompson, and he credited a literary class at Blackheath for having given him the encouragement and inspiration to write. A reviewer said of Sandford's poetry, "His quality is a spiritual fervor ... he has imagination and a fiery sincerity, and his best work is therefore sure of its place, whether many eyes or few see it there."[89]

---

[87] Jane Potter, "The Great War Poets," *The Blackwell Companion to the Bible in English Literature*, edited by Rebecca Lemon et al., Blackwell, 2008, p. 681.

[88] Sandford, qtd. in "Introduction," by S. Gertrude Ford, *Brookdown and Other Poems*, 2nd ed., Erskine Macdonald, 1916, p. 9.

[89] Review from *The Tablet*, in front matter of *Brookdown and Other Poems*, 2nd ed.

Veni, Sancte Spiritus! (Deit, Spered Santel!)[90]
A Song of welcome to the New Year

I

Now in the one thousand nine hundred and fourteenth year after Christ was born in the stable;
Like the Poor man's face all at once against the windows of the worldly rich at their wild dancing;
Like the three words on the wall, when Belshazzar made his great feast;
Like a moon of grief and terror, blinding each day's sun with its savage splendour,
Over every contemptible horizon of the Strumpet Europe,
The blood-face of War!
And before that terrible Star every star fell back, cast into the depths of night;
And all works ceased, until the Great Work should be wrought;
And men fixed their eyes upon fields of carnage, the place of celebration of a great Mystery, a transcendental Sacrifice,
The Mass whose celebrant is Fire, its unexampled music the gun, the Mass whose victim they call the son of man.

IV

I sleep no more. There is a voice, in the winter night, calling to me, a strange voice;
A strong voice, and harsh, a voice accustomed to command: such a voice rings agreeably in young men's ears;
(And it is no woman's voice, nor that mermaid voice that haunts the Celtic sea);
A voice that none can disobey: War, howling at the frontiers.
I will obey. Soon I shall be with my brothers, a soldier following soldiers.
Soon I shall be among the slaughter…What signs are on my brow? New year, shall I see your end?
But it is of no account! Sooner, or later, when the hour to approach the Father sounds, I shall go with gladness. Jesus shall comfort our mothers.
Be blessed, new year, even should, among your three hundred and sixty-five days, there be my last!
Be blessed! For more than one hundred years have passed over this land and known only the anger of God, but you shall witness His mercies.
You shall see banished beliefs return, the wings of victory spread again, under the beating flag of France, and our country exalted for evermore;

---

[90] The poem is composed of seven sections; all of sections I and IV are included here. The poem in its entirety can be read in *French Poems of the Great War*, translated by Ian Higgins, Saxon Books, 2016, pp. 40–45.

You shall see my Brittany free at last, and her language held in honour, as it was when her knights were alive to defend her.

New year, year of war! Be blessed, even should you bring, wrapped in the folds of your cloak, next to springtime for the world, death for me.

What is the death of one man, or one hundred, the death of one hundred thousand men, if our country only live, if the race still live…

When I die, say the prayers and bury me like my fathers, my face set towards the enemy,

And ask nothing for me of my Redeemer, except the last place in His Paradise…

Paris, January 1915

—Yann-Ber Kalloc'h, translated by Ian Higgins

Yann-Ber Kalloc'h (in French, Jean-Pierre Calloc'h) was a French soldier and Breton nationalist who wrote primarily in the Vannetais dialect of Breton. In January of 1916, Kalloc'h wrote to a friend,

> Certainly, after the war, something will have to be done for Brittany and its language. If I must die in my boots, here or there before the end, one of my greatest sorrows in dying will be that I will be unable to join others in rallying under the Breton flag. But may the will of God be fulfilled. He does not need anyone to raise up Brittany.[91]

Kalloc'h was also a devout Catholic who viewed the First World War as God's punishment on the wicked and as a herald of the coming apocalypse, in which only the faithful of Ireland and Brittany would be welcomed into Paradise. "Veni, Sancte Spiritus!" includes multiple references to the biblical apocalypse as described in the Revelation of St. John; it was the last poem Kalloc'h wrote before being sent to the frontline trenches.[92] The poem's title "Veni, Sancte Spiritus!" can be translated "Come, Holy Spirit" and refers to a thirteenth-century chanted hymn of the Catholic liturgy used during Pentecost. Sung in Latin, the song names the Holy Spirit as the "Greatest Comforter," who bestows peace in the midst of struggle and death.

Kalloc'h was killed by shellfire in April of 1917 at the bois d'Urvillers, near St. Quentin. His poems were published posthumously in 1921 in the collection

---

[91] Kalloc'h to Achille Collin, 31 Jan. 1916, *A Genoux: Lais Bretons* by Jean-Pierre Calloc'h, French translation by Pierre Mocaër, Plon-Nourrit et Cie, 1921, p. 225 (my trans.).

[92] Antony Heulin, *La mort dans l'oeuvre de Yann-Ber Kalloc'h et Loeiz Herrieu*, 2014, U of Rennes, PhD dissertation, p. 489.

Ar en deulin (*A Genoux* or *Kneeling*). In a letter dated August 4, 1916, Kalloc'h wrote to a friend,

> Now many fall and will fall in these fields. If my turn comes to sleep forever, to buy the victory of my brothers with my blood, do not pity me; it is good to die thus. Remember that I will have fallen ... for the deliverance of our Earth and for the Beauty of the World ... and then for the Glory of Brittany![93]

At the war's end, a petition was brought before the Versailles Peace Conference, requesting that Breton history and the Breton language be taught in Brittany. Although the petition had 800 signatures, including those of Marshall Foch and other influential French bishops and politicians, France vetoed the discussion of the Breton question: "For the victors, the fate of minorities in former enemy territory was more important than the clearly expressed aspirations of minorities at home."[94]

---

[93] Kalloc'h to A.M. Lucien Douay, 4 Aug. 1916, *A Genoux*, pp. 226–227 (my trans.).
[94] Meic Stephens, *Linguistic Minorities in Western Europe,* Gomer, 1976, p. 373.

Solomon in All His Glory

Still I see them coming, coming,
  In their ragged broken line,
Walking wounded in the sunlight,
  Clothed in majesty divine.

For the fairest of the lilies,
  That God's summer ever sees,
Ne'er was clothed in royal beauty
  Such as decks the least of these.

Tattered, torn, and bloody khaki,
  Gleams of white flesh in the sun,
Raiment worthy of their beauty,
  And the great things they have done.

Purple robes and snowy linen
  Have for earthly kings sufficed,
But these bloody sweaty tatters
  Were the robes of Jesus Christ.

—Geoffrey Studdert Kennedy (1920)

As the war dragged on, many in Britain grew to resent Church of England clergy who enthusiastically supported the war and encouraged others to enlist while they remained safe in their pulpits. The Bishop of London, Arthur Winnington-Ingram, was one of the most fervent war promoters, and his hatred of Germany was so vociferous that even Prime Minister Asquith described the bishop's rhetoric as "jingoism of the shallowest kind."[95] However, approximately 3,000 of the 25,000 Church of England clergy did enlist and accompany troops to the front as military chaplains; they were likely as diverse as the men they served. Some were scorned, others were loved.

Geoffrey Studdert Kennedy is one of the best-known British chaplains of the First World War; his war-time nickname "Woodbine Willie" was earned from his practice of offering cigarettes to wounded and dying soldiers as he attended to their physical and spiritual needs. He was awarded the Military Cross for conspicuous gallantry in 1917, when during an attack at Messines Ridge, he risked his life to cross a heavily shelled area to procure morphine for the

---

[95] Alan Wilkinson, *The Church of England in the First World War,* Lutterworth, 2014, p. 70.

wounded and to attend to and retrieve injured soldiers from No Man's Land. In his 1918 collection of essays, *The Hardest Part*, Studdert Kennedy writes, "Beside the wounded tattered soldier who totters down to this dressing-station with one arm hanging loose, an earthly king in all his glory looks paltry and absurd."[96] The war converted the military chaplain to pacifism, and in his 1919 essay "God in History," Studdert Kennedy writes,

> War is only glorious when you buy it in the *Daily Mail* and enjoy it at the breakfast-table. It goes splendidly with bacon and eggs. Real war is the final limit of damnable brutality, and that's all there is in it. It's about the silliest, filthiest, and most inhumanly fatuous thing that ever happened. It makes the whole universe seem like a mad muddle. One feels that all talk of order and meaning in life is insane sentimentality.[97]

Disputing those who defended God-ordained warfare, Studdert Kennedy reasoned, "Men are driven to the conclusion that war is the will of the Almighty God. If it is true, I go morally mad. Good and evil cease to have any meaning. If anything is evil, war is." He concluded, "War is the crucifixion of God, not the working of His will."[98]

---

[96] Geoffrey Studdert Kennedy, "God in the Bible," *The Hardest Part*, Hodder and Stoughton, 1919, pp. 71–72.
[97] Geoffrey Studdert Kennedy, "God in History," *The Hardest Part*, Hodder and Stoughton, 1919, p. 32.
[98] Studdert Kennedy, "God in History," pp. 35, 44.

To My Daughter Betty, the Gift of God
(Elizabeth Dorothy)

In wiser days, my darling rosebud, blown
To beauty proud as was your mother's prime,
In that desired, delayed, incredible time,
You'll ask why I abandoned you, my own,
And the dear heart that was your baby throne,
To dice with death. And oh! they'll give you rhyme
And reason: some will call the thing sublime,
And some decry it in a knowing tone.
So here, while the mad guns curse overhead,
And tired men sigh with mud for couch and floor,
Know that we fools, now with the foolish dead,
Died not for flag, nor King, nor Emperor,
But for a dream, born in a herdsman's shed,
And for the secret Scripture of the poor.
the field, before Guillemont, Somme, September 4, 1916

—Thomas M. Kettle

As the Royal Dublin Fusiliers prepared to join the fight at the Battle of the Somme in September of 1916, a 36-year-old father wrote a poem and dedicated it to his three-year-old daughter, Elizabeth. The poem's title, "The Gift of God," recalls both the soldier's daughter and the Christ Child born in the stable shed. The poem's author, Lieutenant Thomas Kettle, had served as an Irish member of Parliament and was a highly respected barrister, journalist, orator, and scholar.

A few months earlier in July of 1916, Kettle had written to his wife, Mary Sheehy Kettle (who was loved by the adolescent James Joyce and believed to be the model for both the young female character in the short story "Araby" and Miss Ivors in "The Dead"), "What impresses and moves me above all is the amazing faith, patience and courage of the men. To me it is not a sort of looking-down-on but rather a looking-up-to appreciation of them. I pray and pray and am afraid!—they go quietly and heroically on. God bless them and make me less inferior to them."[99] A few weeks later, Kettle wrote his wife,

---

[99] Tom Kettle, letter 24 July 1916, qtd. in *War Letters of Fallen Englishmen*, edited by Laurence Housman, E.P. Dutton, 1930, p. 167.

If God spares me I shall accept it as a special mission to preach love and peace for the rest of my life. If He does not, I know now in my heart that for anyone who is dead but who has loved enough, there is provided some way of piercing the veils of death and abiding close to those whom he has loved till that end which is the beginning. I want to live, too, to use all my powers of thinking, writing and working to drive out of civilization this foul thing called war and to put in its place understanding and comradeship.[100]

In his last letter to Mary, he prepared his wife for the worst:

The long-expected is now close to hand. I was at Mass & Communion this morning at 6 o.c., the camp is broken up, and the column is about to move. It is no longer indiscreet to say that we are to take part in one of the biggest attacks of the war. Many will not come back. Should that be God's design for me you will not receive this letter until afterwards. I want to thank you for the love and kindness you spent and all but wasted on me. There was never in all the world a dearer woman or a more perfect wife and adorable mother. My heart cries for you and Betty whom I may never see again. I think even that it is perhaps better that I should not see you again. God bless and keep you! If the last sacrifice is ordained think that in the end I wiped out all the old stains. Tell Betty her daddy was a soldier and died as one. My love, now at last clean will find a way to you.[101]

Four days after writing "To My Daughter Betty, the Gift of God," Kettle and his men were ordered over the top in an assault on the German lines. He was shot nearly immediately, and a friend wrote, "he only lasted about one minute, and he had my crucifix in his hands. Then Boyd took all the papers and things out of Tom's pockets in order to keep them for Mrs. Kettle, but poor Boyd was blown to atoms in a few minutes. The Welsh Guards buried Mr. Kettle's remains."[102] Tom Kettle's body was never found; his name is inscribed on the British monument to the missing at Thiepval. A reviewer for the *Times Literary Supplement* wrote of Kettle's posthumously published poetry, "He fought the Germans for a dream, as he had fought England for a dream; and however uncomfortable it may be for the politicians and rulers of the Empire when this power is expended upon politics, this heroic dreaming is the source of all good Irish literature."[103]

---

[100] Tom Kettle, letter 10 Aug. 1916, qtd. in *War Letters*, p. 167.
[101] Tom Kettle to Mary Kettle, letter 3 Sept. 1916, University College Dublin, UCDA LA34/402 Papers of Tom Kettle.
[102] Sean Boyne, *Emmet Dalton: Somme Soldier, Irish General, Film Pioneer*, Merion, 2015, p. 26.
[103] "Mr. T.M. Kettle's Poems," *Times Literary Supplement*, no. 785, 1 Feb. 1917, p. 56.

'Since they have Died'

Since they have died to give us gentleness,
And hearts kind with contentment and quiet mirth,
Let us who live give also happiness
And love, that's born of pity, to the earth.

For, I have thought, some day they may lie sleeping
Forgetting all the weariness and pain,
And smile to think their world is in our keeping,
And laughter come back to the earth again.
February 1916

—May Wedderburn Cannan[104]

One of the most-anthologized First World War poems written by a woman is Cannan's "Rouen." Her poem "'Since They Have Died'" recalls the epitaph composed by John Maxwell Edmonds: "When you go home, tell them of us, and say / 'For your to-morrow these gave their to-day.'"[105]

May Wedderburn Cannan served in France for four weeks at a military railway canteen in 1915. Volunteers were trained to offer soldiers encouragement and sympathy, and the experience likely forged in Cannan a strong emotional tie between love and pity, both for the new recruits headed to the front lines and for the wounded being evacuated. "'Since They Have Died'" describes the love that the dead have inspired as a love that is "born of pity." But perhaps the best-known statement on war and pity was written in 1918 by Wilfred Owen in the draft preface to his poetry collection:

> This book is not about heroes. English poetry is not yet fit to speak of them.
> Nor is it about deeds, or lands, or anything about glory, honour, might, majesty, dominion, or power, except War.
> Above all I am not concerned with Poetry.
> My subject is War, and the pity of War.
> The Poetry is in the pity.[106]

---

[104] See also Cannan's "France" and "Paris, November 11, 1918."
[105] J.M. Edmonds, *Twelve War Epitaphs*, Ashendene, 1920.
[106] Wilfred Owen, "Preface," *The Poems of Wilfred Owen,* edited by Jon Stallworthy, Hogarth, 1988, p. 192.

The Gift of India

Is there aught you need that my hands withhold,
Rich gifts of raiment or grain or gold?
Lo! I have flung to the East and West
Priceless treasures torn from my breast,
And yielded the sons of my stricken womb
To the drum-beats of duty, the sabers of doom.

Gathered like pearls in their alien graves
Silent they sleep by the Persian waves,
Scattered like shells on Egyptian sands,
They lie with pale brows and brave, broken hands,
They are strewn like blossoms mown down by chance
On the blood-brown meadows of Flanders and France.

Can ye measure the grief of the tears I weep
Or compass the woe of the watch I keep?
Or the pride that thrills thro' my heart's despair,
And the hope that comforts the anguish of prayer?
And the far sad glorious vision I see
Of the torn red banners of Victory?

When the terror and tumult of hate shall cease
And life be refashioned on anvils of peace,
And your love shall offer memorial thanks
To the comrades who fought in your dauntless ranks,
And you honour the deeds of the deathless ones
Remember the blood of thy martyred sons!
    August 1915

—Sarojini Naidu

An estimated 1.4 million Indian troops served in the British army in the First World War, the largest contribution made by any of the British Empire's colonies. Santanu Das writes, "In a grotesque reversal of Joseph Conrad's novelistic vision, hundreds of thousands of non-white men were voyaging to the heart of whiteness, as it were, to witness 'The horror! The horror!' of Western warfare."[107] Nearly 75,000 Indians died on foreign fields and over 70,000 were wounded; one badly injured Indian sepoy wrote, "This is not war. It is the ending

---

[107] Santanu Das, "Introduction," *Race, Empire and First World War Writing*, Cambridge UP, 2011, p. 4.

of the world."[108] Serving on the Western Front, as well as in Mesopotamia and Gallipoli, Indian troops were vitally important to Britain's war effort, and many volunteered in hopes of gaining recognition for India's political independence.

Sarojini Naidu, known as the nightingale of India, was renowned for her poetry and her skills as an orator. She campaigned on behalf of women's suffrage, the peaceful co-existence of religious traditions, and Indian independence. In 1919, Naidu served as India's Home Rule Ambassador to England. A close associate and friend of Mahatma Gandhi since before the First World War, Naidu was elected president of the Indian National Congress in 1925 and governor of the Indian state of Uttar Pradesh in 1947 (the first Indian woman to serve in both positions). She devoted her life to her country, writing in the "Foreword" to her volume of poetry *The Broken Wing*,

> In the radiant and far-off yesterdays of our history it was the sacred duty of Indian womanhood to kindle and sustain the hearth-fires, the beacon-fires and the altar-fires of the nation.
>
> The Indian woman of to-day is once more awake and profoundly alive to her splendid destiny as the guardian and interpreter of the Triune Vision of national life—the Vision of Love, the Vision of Faith, the Vision of Patriotism.
>
> Her renascent consciousness is everywhere striving for earnest expression in song or speech, service or self-sacrifice, that shall prove an offering not unworthy of the Great Mother in the eyes of the world that honour her.
>
> Poignantly aware of the poverty of my gift, I still venture to make my offering with joined palms uplifted in a Salutation of Song.
>
> Sarojini Naidu, Hyderabad, Deccan, 1916[109]

---

[108] Das, "Introduction," p. 4.
[109] Sarojini Naidu, "Foreword," *The Broken Wing: Songs of Love, Death, and Destiny, 1915–1916*, John Lane, 1917, p. 7.

In the Ypres Sector

You have left beauty here in everything,
And it is we that are both deaf and blind.
By coarse grass mounds here the small crosses rise
Sunk sideways in the ditch, or low inclined
Over some little stream where waters sing
By shell holes blue with beauty from the skies.

Even the railway cutting has kind shade
And colour, where the rusty wire is laid
Round the soft tracks. Because you knew them thus
The dark mouthed dug-outs hold a light for us.
And here each name rings rich upon our ears
Which first we learnt with sorrow and with tears.

—Carola Oman[110] (1919)

Describing a dead soldier's body, British soldier-poet Richard Aldington writes that some aspects of the Western Front were "More beautiful than one can tell."[111] Carola Oman, a British VAD nurse, describes the beauty she also saw in the landscape and suffering of war.

The daughter of an Oxford historian, Carola Oman's earliest ambition was to be a writer. But although Oman's mother "acknowledged her daughter's creative powers, she believed that Carola's excitable temperament made it prudent to keep her close to home."[112] Volunteering as a VAD nurse in 1916, Oman served at Felstead House Auxiliary Hospital in Oxford until she was accepted for foreign service in April of 1917. She was posted to various hospitals in England, including the Russian hospital in London, before being sent to France in September of 1918, where she served at Boulogne and Wimereux until January of 1919. Her first book, *The Menin Road and Other Poems*, was published later that year.

---

[110] See also Oman's "Unloading Ambulance Train" and "To the Survivors."
[111] Richard Aldington, "Soliloquy II." *War and Love (1915–1918)*, Four Seas, 1919, p. 55.
[112] Mark Bostridge, "Oman, Carola Mary Anima," *Oxford Dictionary of National Biography*, 4 Oct. 2007, Oxford UP, DOI: http://dx.doi.org/10.1093/ref:odnb/71516.

5

Remembering the Dead

War elegies, often highly personal, remember husbands, sons, friends, farmers, students, artists, writers—those whose humor, kindnesses, absurdities, and talents were lost forever. Some writers found solace in recalling happy memories before the war; others were haunted by survivor's guilt or the prospect of a desolate future. The staggering losses led many to attempt to communicate with the dead; numerous poems of the First World War are peopled with ghosts and the imagined return of those who have died, or they envision a future in which all are reunited in the afterlife. Still other writers lament that the dead will be forgotten, or respond with disbelief and denial. Remembering those who died did not require acceptance of the loss.

Let Us Tell Quiet Stories of Kind Eyes

Let us tell quiet stories of kind eyes
   And placid brows where peace and learning sate:
Of misty gardens under evening skies
   Where four would walk of old, with steps sedate.

Let's have no word of all the sweat and blood,
   Of all the noise and strife and dust and smoke
(We who have seen Death surging like a flood,
   Wave upon wave, that leaped and raced and broke).

Or let's sit silently, we three together,
   Around a wide hearth-fire that's glowing red,
Giving no thought to all the stormy weather
   That flies above the roof-tree overhead.

And he, the fourth, that lies all silently
   In some far-distant and untended grave,
Under the shadow of a shattered tree,
   Shall leave the company of the hapless brave,

And draw nigh unto us for memory's sake,
   Because a look, a word, a deed, a friend,
Are bound with cords that never a man may break,
   Unto his heart for ever, until the end.

—Geoffrey Bache Smith (1918)

In the summer of 1916, a young lieutenant on the Western Front learned that one of his closest friends had died on the first day of the Somme. He wrote, "something has gone crack ... I don't feel a member of a little complete body now ... I feel a mere individual."[1] The officer was J.R.R. Tolkien, and his grief and sense of dislocation were prompted by the death of Robert Gilson. Tolkien and Gilson, together with Christopher Wiseman and Geoffrey Bache Smith, had formed Tolkien's "first fellowship." The four were schoolmates at King Edward's School in Birmingham, and beginning in 1911, the boys met regularly in the school's library and at Barrow's, the tea shop of a local department store. Calling

---

[1] J.R.R. Tolkien, letter to Geoffrey Smith, 12–13 Aug. 1916, qtd. in *Tolkien and the Great War*, by John Garth, Houghton Mifflin, 2003, p. 176.

themselves the TCBS (Tea Club and Barrovian Society), the friends discussed their ambitions for shaping a better world through literature and art.² The First World War interrupted their plans, and all four enlisted in military service: Wiseman in the navy, and Tolkien, Gilson, and Smith with the British Army. Only Wiseman and Tolkien would survive the war.

Anticipating a dangerous night patrol mission in early February of 1916, Smith had written to Tolkien about death and friendship:

> my chief consolation is, that if I am scuppered to-night—I am off on duty in a few minutes—there will still be left a member of the great TCBS to voice what I dreamed and what we all agreed upon. For the death of one of its members cannot, I am determined, dissolve the TCBS. Death is so close to me now that I feel— and I am sure you feel, and all the three other heroes feel, how impuissant it is. Death can make us loathsome and helpless as individuals, but it cannot put an end to the immortal four! ...
>
> Yes, publish ...
>
> May God bless you, my dear John Ronald, and may you say the things I have tried to say long after I am not there to say them, if such be my lot.³

After learning of Gilson's death in July of 1916, Geoffrey Bache Smith wrote "Let Us Tell Quiet Stories of Kind Eyes." Six months after Gilson's death, in early December of 1916, Geoffrey Bache Smith was struck by shrapnel from an exploding artillery shell. Although his wounds were not initially thought serious (while waiting to be transported to the casualty clearing station, Smith smoked a cigarette and wrote a reassuring letter to his mother),⁴ gas gangrene set in, and two days later he died.

In 1918, J.R.R. Tolkien wrote an introductory note to Smith's posthumously published book of poetry, *A Spring Harvest*, and when Tolkien published *The Hobbit* in 1937, he sent copies to "some friends and relations, including ... the mother of his dear friend Geoffrey Bache Smith, who had died in battle over twenty years before."⁵ Robert Quilter Gilson is buried at Bécourt; Geoffrey Bache Smith lies at Warlincourt Halte British cemetery.

---

² Garth, *Tolkien and the Great War*, pp. 58–59.
³ Geoffrey Smith, letter to Tolkien, 3 Feb. 1916, qtd. in *Tolkien and the Great War*, pp. 118–119.
⁴ Garth, *Tolkien and the Great War*, p. 211.
⁵ Colin Duriez, *J.R.R. Tolkien: The Making of a Legend*, Lion Books, 2012, p. 158.

Féri Bekassy[6]

We, who must grow old and staid,
Full of wisdom, much afraid,
In our hearts like flowers keep
Love for you until we sleep.

You the brave, and you the young
You of a thousand songs unsung,
Burning brain, and ardent word,
You the lovely and absurd.

Say, on that Galician plain
Are you arguing again?
Does a trench or ruined tree
Hear your—'O, I *don't* agree!'

We, who must grow staid and old,
Full of caution, worn and cold,
In our hearts, like flowers keep
Your image, till we also sleep.
1915

—Frances Cornford

A Hungarian scholar and poet who had begun studies at Cambridge in 1911, Ferenc Békássy left his university friends to join the Austro-Hungarian army soon after war was declared. Shortly before riding to the Eastern Front, in a letter dated May 1915, Békássy wrote to Noel Olivier, a young woman both he and Rupert Brooke had courted:

> I am going to the front in five days' time, and am already feeling quite detached from everything … I'm going gladly, I know it's very worth taking the risk, and I am sure to get something good out of the war unless I die in it. It's part of 'the good life' just now, that I should go: and the sooner one gives up the idea that the world can be made better than it is, the better. I daresay one can make it happier, but then happiness isn't the main point, is it?[7]

---

[6] Originally published under the title "Feri Dead 1915" in *Different Days* (1928), the poem was slightly revised in later editions. The version included here appears in Cornford's *Collected Poems* (1954).
[7] Ferenc Békássy, letter to Noel Olivier, qtd. in *The Alien in the Chapel,* edited by George and Mari Gömöri, Skyscraper, 2016, pp. 184–185.

Békássy's war poem "1914" can be found in this anthology; he was killed in action on June 25, 1915, just days after arriving at the Eastern Front.

Frances Cornford, granddaughter of Charles Darwin, was a Cambridge friend of Békássy's. She was also a friend of Rupert Brooke's, and they exchanged and discussed their poetry in the years before the war.[8] In 1959 Cornford was awarded the Queen's Medal for Poetry; perhaps her best known work is one of her earliest, "To a Fat Lady Seen from a Train" (a poem she sought to distance herself from for most of her life).[9] Siegfried Sassoon said of her writing, "Much as I admired her, I did feel that she was too intense, analytic and cultured for me. That vibrant voice of hers had a quality of academic aloofness about it."[10] In the introduction to Cornford's *Selected Poems,* Jane Dowson notes that readers may miss the depths of Cornford's poetry as they "take the simplicity at face value and miss the undertow," for nearly all of Cornford's work is infused with a "sense of the impermanence of all human relationships."[11]

---

[8] Hugh Cornford, "Frances Cornford 1886–1960," *Frances Cornford: Selected Poems,* edited by Jane Dowson, Enitharmon, 1996, p. xxxi.
[9] Jane Dowson, "Introduction," *Frances Cornford: Selected Poems,* edited by Jane Dowson, Enitharmon, 1996, pp. xiii, xx.
[10] Siegfried Sassoon, qtd. in "Introduction," by Dowson, p. xix.
[11] Dowson, "Introduction," pp. xv, xvi.

Telling the Bees
(For Edward Tennant)

Tell it to the bees, lest they
Umbrage take and fly away,
   That the dearest boy is dead,
Who went singing, blithe and dear,
By the golden hives last year.
   Curly-head, ah, curly-head!

Tell them that the summer's over,
Over mignonette and clover;
   Oh, speak low and very low!
Say that he was blithe and bonny,
Good as gold and sweet as honey,
   All too late the roses blow!

Say he will not come again,
Not in any sun or rain,
   Heart's delight, ah, heart's delight!
Tell them that the boy they knew
Sleeps out under rain and dew
   In the night, ah, in the night!

—Katharine Tynan (1918)

Folklore holds that when a member of a village dies, the bees must be told or they will desert the local hive. As Peter Stanford explains in *How to Read a Graveyard*, "The origins [of the belief] are obscure: some say bees are traditional symbols of fertility, and so instinctively flee death, others that they used to have a role in some cultures in carrying souls into the afterlife, while their honey was a symbol of the divine, or even heaven."[12] There are various customs for telling the bees: hanging black crepe about the hive so that the bees join in the mourning ceremonies, leaving them funeral biscuits dipped in wine, or visiting the hive and whispering the names of the dead.[13]

   Irish writer Katharine Tynan was a close associate of W.B. Yeats and leading member of the Irish Literary Revival. She dedicated the poem "Telling the Bees"

---

[12] Peter Stanford, *How to Read a Graveyard,* A and C Black, 2013, p. 164.
[13] Hattie Ellis, *Sweetness and Light: The Mysterious History of the Honeybee,* Harmony, 2004, pp. 136–138.

to nineteen-year-old Edward Tennant, known to his family and friends as "Bim." One of the nearly 100,000 British men killed during the four-month Battle of the Somme, Tennant was shot by a German sniper on September 22, 1916, while he himself was on a night-time sniping mission. In his last letter to his mother, dated September 20, Tennant wrote,

> To-night we go up to the last trenches we were in, and tomorrow we go over the top ... I went to a service on the side of a hill this morning, and took the Holy Communion afterwards, which always seems to help one along, doesn't it? ... I feel rather like saying 'If it be possible, let this cup pass from me,' but the triumphant finish 'nevertheless not what I will, but what Thou willest,' steels my heart and sends me into this battle with a heart of triple bronze.[14]

After his death, a private who served under him wrote to Tennant's mother, offering condolences and recalling, "When danger was greatest, his smile was loveliest."[15]

---

[14] Edward Tennant, letter 20 Sept. 1916, qtd. in *Edward Wyndham Tennant: A Memoir*, by Pamela Glenconner, John Lane, 1919, pp. 234, 235.
[15] Private S.A., undated letter, qtd. in *Edward Wyndham Tennant*, p. 242.

In Memoriam
Private D. Sutherland killed in Action in the German Trench, May 16, 1916, and the Others who Died

So you were David's father,
And he was your only son,
And the new-cut peats are rotting
And the work is left undone,
Because of an old man weeping,
Just an old man in pain,
For David, his son David,
That will not come again.

Oh, the letters he wrote you,
And I can see them still,
Not a word of the fighting,
But just the sheep on the hill
And how you should get the crops in
Ere the year got stormier,
And the Bosches have got his body,
And I was his officer.

You were only David's father,
But I had fifty sons
When we went up in the evening
Under the arch of the guns,
And we came back at twilight—
O God! I heard them call
To me for help and pity
That could not help at all.

Oh, never will I forget you,
My men that trusted me,
More my sons than your fathers',
For they could only see
The little helpless babies
And the young men in their pride.
They could not see you dying,
And hold you while you died.

Happy and young and gallant,
They saw their first-born go,

But not the strong limbs broken
And the beautiful men brought low,
The piteous writhing bodies,
They screamed, "Don't leave me, Sir,"
For they were only your fathers
But I was your officer.

—Ewart Alan Mackintosh[16] (1917)

The night of May 16, 1916, Lieutenant Ewart Alan Mackintosh's actions earned him the Military Cross for conspicuous gallantry.[17] As he led his Seaforth Highlanders in a raid on German trenches near Arras, sixteen were men wounded, two seriously. Mackintosh carried one of the wounded, nineteen-year-old Private David Sutherland, over 100 yards through German trenches with enemy troops in close pursuit. Sutherland died of his wounds, however, before he could be carried across No Man's Land. His body had to be left behind. David Sutherland is one of the nearly 35,000 men commemorated on the Arras Memorial to the Missing.

In August of 1916, Mackintosh himself was badly wounded at High Wood. Evacuated to England to recover, he was afterwards assigned as a training officer near Cambridge. While in England, he met and fell in love with Elizabeth Sylvia Marsh, a Quaker VAD nurse. They became engaged and planned to marry after the war, but by October of 1917, Mackintosh was back with the Seaforths on the Western Front. The last verses of his poem "To Sylvia," dated October 20, 1917, explain his determination to return to France:

God knows—my dear—I did not want
To rise and leave you so,
But the dead men's hands were beckoning
And I knew that I must go.

The dead men's eyes were watching, lass,
Their lips were asking too,
We faced it out and payed the price—
Are we betrayed by you?

The days are long between, dear lass,
Before we meet again,

---

[16] See also Mackintosh's "In No Man's Land."
[17] "2nd. Lt. (temp. Lt.) Ewart Alan Mackintosh, 1/5 Bn., Sea. Highrs., T.F.," *Supplement to the London Gazette*, 24 June 1916, p. 6299.

Long days of mud and work for me,
For you long care and pain.

But you'll forgive me yet, my dear,
Because of what you know,
I can look my dead friends in the face
As I couldn't two months ago.[18]

Mackintosh was killed by a sniper during the Battle of Cambrai on November 21, 1917. His last words were addressed to the men of a Lewis gun team near his position, advising them "to keep their heads down."[19] The last two lines of Mackintosh's poem "A Creed" are carved on the Scottish American Memorial in Edinburgh's Princes Street Gardens: "If it be life that waits I shall live for ever unconquered, / If death I shall die at last strong in my pride and free."[20]

---

[18] E.A. Mackintosh, "To Sylvia," *War the Liberator,* John Lane, 1918.
[19] Roderick McLennan, as told to grandson Kenny, "The Death of Ewart Alan Mackintosh," *NQ Higher Scottish History,* web.archive.org/web/20190623202826/http://www.sath.org.uk/edscot/www.educationscotland.gov.uk/higherscottishhistory/impactofthegreatwar/perspective/poems.html.
[20] E.A. Mackintosh, *A Highland Regiment,* John Lane, 1917.

At the Front (An der Front)

The countryside is desolate. The fields look tear-stained.
A grey cart is going along an evil road.
The roof has slipped off a house.
Dead horses lie rotting in pools.

The brown lines back there are trenches.
On the horizon a farm is taking its time to burn.
Shells explode, echo away—pop, pop pauuu.
Cavalrymen disappear slowly in a bare copse.

Clouds of shrapnel burst open and fade away. A defile[21]
Takes us in. Infantrymen are halted there, wet and muddy.
Death is as much a matter of indifference as the rain which is coming on.
Who cares about yesterday, today, or tomorrow?

And the barbed wire runs across the whole of Europe.
The forts sleep gently.
Villages and towns stink out of their terrible ruins.
Like broken dolls the dead lie between the lines.
    —Wilhelm Klemm (1915), translated by Patrick Bridgwater

On the Western Front, soldiers lived with the dead; they ate near them, slept with them, endured their stench, and gazed across No Man's Land at a landscape littered with decaying bodies. Allyson Booth uses the term "corpsescapes" to describe the fact that "Trench soldiers in the Great War inhabited worlds constructed, literally, of corpses."[22] Often, the mental demands of confronting death and carnage on this scale were overwhelming.

The best-known physician-poet of the war is Canadian John McCrae, author of "In Flanders Fields"; few know of German physician-poet Wilhelm Klemm. An American reviewer compared Klemm's work to that of Walt Whitman in *Drum-taps* and named Klemm as one of two "young artists who preferred emphasizing the realities of war to boasting their 'Vaterlandsliebe [Patriotism].'"[23] In 1915,

---

[21] A narrow pass through which soldiers can advance only in single file or a narrow column.
[22] Allyson Booth, *Postcards from the Trenches: Negotiating the Space between Modernism and the First World War*, Oxford UP, 1996, p. 50.
[23] Alec W.G. Randall, "German Poets and the War," *The Living Age*, vol. 289, no. 3745, 15 Apr. 1916, p. 189.

serving as a doctor with the German army in Flanders, Klemm published his first volume of poetry, *Gloria! War Poems from the Field* (*Gloria! Kriegsgedichte aus dem Feld*). The epigraph that introduces the collection is from Goethe: "Alles vergängliche ist nur ein Gleichnis" (Everything is only a parable). From the field hospital where he operated, Klemm wrote to his wife, "War can be so dreadful that one longs for the bullet which will free one from all the tension and misery—to some extent this is the secret which makes the men able to endure such indescribable suffering."[24] In another poem, "Evening at the Front," Klemm writes, "Oh questing bullet, when will you come to me?"[25] Klemm survived the war, dying in Wiesbaden in 1968. Two of his four sons were killed in the Second World War.

---

[24] Wilhelm Klemm, qtd. and translated in *The German Poets of the First World War*, by Patrick Bridgwater, St. Martin's, 1985, p. 177.

[25] From "Evening at the Front," qtd. and translated in *The German Poets*, p. 179.

To L.H.B. (1894–1915)

Last night for the first time since you were dead
I walked with you, my brother, in a dream.
We were at home again beside the stream
Fringed with tall berry bushes, white and red.
"Don't touch them: they are poisonous," I said.
But your hand hovered, and I saw a beam
Of strange, bright laughter flying round your head
And as you stooped I saw the berries gleam.
"Don't you remember? We called them Dead Man's Bread!"
   I woke and heard the wind moan and the roar
Of the dark water tumbling on the shore.
Where—where is the path of my dream for my eager feet?
By the remembered stream my brother stands
Waiting for me with berries in his hands ...
"These are my body. Sister, take and eat."
         1916.

—Katherine Mansfield

On October 6, 1915, one week after spending leave in England with his sister and just one week before his sister's birthday, Leslie Heron Beauchamp died in Ploegsteert Wood, near Messines, Belgium. Known to his family as "Chummie," Beauchamp was instructing troops in the use of grenades when one malfunctioned, killing him and a nearby officer.[26] Beauchamp's sister, New Zealand author Katherine Mansfield, was devastated by the loss, writing in her journal, "though he is lying in the middle of a little wood in France and I am still walking upright and feeling the sun and the wind from the sea, I am just as much dead as he is. The present and the future mean nothing to me."[27] She increasingly turned to memories of the past and their shared childhood in New Zealand. Leslie became a ghostly Muse for his sister: "When I am not writing I feel my brother calling me and he is not happy. Only when I write or am in state of writing—a state of 'inspiration'—do I feel that he is calm."[28]

---

[26] "Accidental death by grenade detonation of 2nd Lt Leslie Beauchamp and Sergeant J Holden," 7 Oct. 1915, National Archives at Kew, WO 339/35941.
[27] Katherine Mansfield, Nov. 1915, *Journal of Katherine Mansfield*, edited by J. Middleton Murry, 1974, p. 38.
[28] Katherine Mansfield, "13 Feb. 1916," *Journal*, p. 45.

Mansfield channeled her grief into stories and poems, as her notebooks from early 1916 reveal:

> Now—now I want to write recollections of my own country .... till I simply exhaust my store. Not only because it is "a sacred debt" that I pay to my country because my brother and I were born there, but also because in my thoughts I range with him over all the remembered places ... But all must be told with a sense of mystery, a radiance, an afterglow, because you, my little sun of it, are set. You have dropped over the dazzling brim of the world. Now I must play my part.[29]

Katherine Mansfield died in 1923 at the age of thirty-four.

---

[29] Katherine Mansfield, "22 Jan. 1916," *Journal*, pp. 43–44.

To John[30]

O heart-and-soul and careless played
    Our little band of brothers,
And never recked the time would come
    To change our games for others.
It's joy for those who played with you
    To picture now what grace
Was in your mind and single heart
    And in your radiant face.
Your light-foot strength by flood and field
    For England keener glowed;
To whatsoever things are fair
    We know, through you, the road;
Nor is our grief the less thereby;
    O swift and strong and dear, good-bye.

—William Grenfell (1917)

Ettie Grenfell, Baroness Desborough, lost two of her sons in just over two months. Her eldest, Julian, died on May 26, 1915; his younger brother Gerald William Grenfell, known to the family as Billy, was killed in Belgium on July 30, 1915, less than a mile from where his brother had been wounded. Both sons wrote poems: Julian, best known for "Into Battle," is one of the sixteen British war poets commemorated in Westminster Abbey. His younger brother Billy's only published war poem appeared in the 1917 anthology *The Muse in Arms*. A brief note acknowledges that the poem was contributed to the anthology by Billy's parents after his death. The younger Grenfell's poem was written in response to the death of John Manners, killed on September 1, 1914, when his platoon failed to receive the order to retreat. Manners' body has never been found; his name is listed on the La Ferté-sous-Jouarre memorial to the Missing of the Marne. Billy Grenfell was also killed in action: his name is listed among the missing on the Menin Gate in Ypres, Belgium.

---

[30] The title is footnoted in the *Muse in Arms* publication: "The Hon. John Manners."

Soldier-Poet
To Francis Fowler Hogan

I think at first like us he did not see
The goal to which the screaming eagles flew;
For romance lured him, France, and chivalry;
But Oh! Before the end he knew, he knew!
And gave his first full love to Liberty,
And met her face to face one lurid night
While the guns boomed their shuddering minstrelsy
And all the Argonne glowed with demon light.
And Liberty herself came through the wood,
And with her dear, boy lover kept the tryst;
Clasped in her grand, Greek arms he understood
Whose were the fatal lips that he had kissed—
Lips that the soul of Youth has loved from old—
Hot lips of Liberty that kiss men cold.

—Hervey Allen (1921)

The largest battle in the history of the American Army is the Meuse-Argonne Offensive, lasting from September 26 to November 11, 1918. Over 1.2 million American soldiers were involved; 26,277 men were killed and 95,786 were wounded. Edward G. Lengel writes, "No single battle in American military history, before or since, even approaches the Meuse-Argonne in size and cost, and it was without question the country's most critical military contribution to the Allied cause in the First World War. And yet, within a few years of its end, nobody seemed to realize that it had taken place."[31]

Hervey Allen, a National Guard soldier from Pittsburgh, Pennsylvania, never made it to the Argonne forest. Gassed, burned, wounded by shrapnel, and suffering the effects of shell shock from the attack at Fismette, he was evacuated to a military hospital in August of 1918. Allen's memoir, *Toward the Flame*, is considered one of the best American combat memoirs of the First World War. Shortly before his part in the war ended, Allen met at the front with his close friend Francis (Frank) Hogan, a fellow Pittsburgher and aspiring poet. The men talked briefly before Allen rejoined his unit. Allen remembers, "I had an impulse to take Frank with me, but I only shook hands with him … I never saw him again. He was a brilliant and promising poet."[32]

---

[31] Edward G. Lengel, *To Conquer Hell*, Henry Holt, 2008, p. 4.
[32] Hervey Allen, *Toward the Flame*, George H. Doran, 1926, p. 77.

Frank Hogan was twenty-one when he died in the Argonne, just weeks before the fighting ended. His mother had his body returned to the United States, and he was reburied on August 13, 1921, in Pittsburgh's Homewood Cemetery. Hogan's poem "Fulfilled" was written while he was fighting in France: "Think not that my life has been futile, / Nor grieve for an unsaid word, / For all that my lips might never sing / My singing heart has heard."[33]

---

[33] From Francis F. Hogan, "Fulfilled," *Carnegie Tech War Verse*, edited by Haniel Long, Carnegie Institute of Technology, 1918, p. 21.

Victory

I watched it oozing quietly
  Out of the gaping gash.
The lads thrust on to victory
  With lunge and curse and crash.

Half-dazed, that uproar seemed to me
  Like some old battle-sound
Heard long ago, as quietly
  His blood soaked in the ground.

The lads thrust on to victory
  With lunge and crash and shout.
I lay and watched, as quietly
  His life was running out.

—Wilfrid Wilson Gibson[34] (1915)

Wilfrid Gibson did not write from first-hand experience of the war, but instead drew inspiration from news accounts and soldiers' stories. He repeatedly tried to volunteer for the army, but was rejected four times, until he eventually succeeded in being accepted as a private in the Motor Transport Corps. Gibson later served as a medical officer's clerk, but was never sent abroad. He published his war poetry collection *Battle* in 1915, explaining to Robert Frost that he viewed the book as a protest against the war, "however feeble and ineffectual."[35] Years later as the Second World War engulfed Europe, Gibson wrote to friend and fellow-poet Laurence Binyon, "War … is to me a business of innumerable personal tragedies: the tendency to think in abstract causes seems to me liable to callous the souls of even the best of men."[36]

---

[34] See also Gibson's "Retreat."
[35] Wilfrid Gibson letter to Robert Frost, 18 Nov. 1915, qtd. in "'War Is a Business of Innumerable Personal Tragedies': Wilfrid Gibson, Elizabeth Gibson Cheyne and the First World War," by Judy Greenway, *Dymock Poets and Friends,* no. 15, 2016, p. 51.
[36] Wilfrid Gibson letter to Laurence Binyon, 10 Oct. 1941, qtd. in "'War Is a Business,'" p. 44.

The Son

I found the letter in a cardboard box,
Unfamous history. I read the words.
The ink was frail and brown, the paper dry
After so many years of being kept.
The letter was a soldier's, from the Front—
Conveyed his love, and disappointed hope
Of getting leave. 'It's cancelled now,' he wrote.
'My luck is at the bottom of the sea.'

Outside, the sun was hot; the world looked bright;
I heard a radio, and someone laughed.
I did not sing, or laugh, or love the sun.
Within the quiet room I thought of him,
My father killed, and all the other men
Whose luck was at the bottom of the sea.

—Clifford Dyment (1937)

Many First World War poems were written by friends, sweethearts, fathers, mothers, and sisters of men who had left to fight; fewer were written by the children of soldiers. Two such poems were written by men whose fathers served with the Lancashire Fusiliers. Ted Hughes wrote "Six Young Men" nearly forty years after the First World War had ended. Hughes himself had no memory of the war; he was born in 1930, twelve years after Armistice Day. Clifford Dyment was just four when his father died; his poem "The Son" was published nineteen years later in 1937.

William Dyment, Clifford's father, was born on September 15, 1888, in Llancarfan. He married Bessie Riding on October 20, 1912, in the Registry Office in Newport. As a young man, William Dyment had wanted to see the world, and so with no money to finance his adventures, he signed on as a ship's carpenter. He possessed "that romantic touch of the rascal so helpful to success in this world."[37] Recounting a childhood memory before the war, Clifford Dyment recalls his boyish fascination with the cows that passed their home in Caerleon-upon-Usk and his own desperate wish for a tail to swish and flick. He cried inconsolably one day until his father returned from work:

---

[37] Clifford Dyment, *The Railway Game: An Early Autobiography*, J.M. Dent, 1962, p. 16.

> He took me in his arms and held me high above the limestone slabs of the floor, on a level with his face. His soft, dreamy, sad eyes looked deeply into mine. Immediately, as though by some power of paternal divination, he knew what I wanted. He put me down, went to the tool chest he kept in a black hole under the stairs, took out a coil of rope, frayed the end with his knife to make a tuft, and knotted it around my waist ... and after dinner, I wobbled about the back garden on hands and knees, mooing.[38]

By 1916 William Dyment had left his cabinetry business for essential war work on the Great Western Railway; in May of 1917, he joined the Royal Engineers. Clifford remembers the morning his father left the family: "He caught me up in his arms and hugged me and my face was hurt by one of his new buttons ... 'Lift me up on your soldier,' I asked my father."[39]

William Dyment wrote home regularly, letting his family know that he had received their packages—"Only the rather crumbly shortbread was broken"—but most often writing about leave and his hopes of returning home for a visit: "The leave I mentioned in my earlier letters as being likely has been cancelled. Twice that has happened already. Truly, my luck seems at the bottom of the sea. I must stop now. Forgive the gloomy tone of the last sentence—life is as pleasant as it can be here on the whole, but I was so looking forward to leave."[40] And a bit later William wrote his wife,

> there is a good chance of leave soon ... Real Dyment luck that would be!
>
> I want to come dearly to see you, darling, and yet I feel I shall be unhappy when I do because I shall be thinking all the time of going back ... Sometimes I feel I would rather stay out here with no leaves at all until the whole terrible business is over—and then come home to stay for good. What a wonderful day that will be![41]

William Dyment was transferred to the 17th Battalion Lancashire Fusiliers and described his new job as "an excellent one. I am with the officers and do mending [carpentry] jobs for them ... They want to recommend me for a commission. They press me, say I am just the right sort of chap, but I keep on saying No. I prefer to be just what I am—not what is called a temporary gentleman."[42] In his last letter to his wife, he assured her, "There is no need to be anxious about me,

---

[38] Dyment, *Railway Game*, pp. 10–11.
[39] Dyment, *Railway Game*, p. 18.
[40] Dyment, *Railway Game*, pp. 21, 20–21.
[41] Dyment, *Railway Game*, p. 22.
[42] Dyment, *Railway Game*, p. 25.

dear. Really, I am very comfortable in this new job, which is just right for me. It is so much better here than where I was before in the support lines. It is very quiet here."[43]

The next letter the family received was from William Dyment's commanding officer:

> Dear Mrs. Dyment,
> It is my unpleasant duty to have to write and tell you that your husband has been killed in action ... We were being shelled at H.Q. and he was mending my table when a piece of shell hit him on the head and killed him instantly. We all feel his loss tremendously ... I know how you and his kiddies will feel it but you will I know be a little consoled to know that we all thought him just as fine a fellow as you did.[44]

William Clifford Dyment was killed on May 22, 1918, and is buried at the Varennes Military Cemetery. In 1919–1920, when British military cemeteries were erecting permanent markers to commemorate Commonwealth war dead, relatives were contacted and asked if they wished to purchase a brief epitaph inscription for their loved one's headstone (limited to sixty-six characters). Records indicate that a letter was sent to William Dyment's next of kin, B. Dyment, in Nottingham. Next to William's name is noted, "No Reply."

---

[43] Dyment, *Railway Game*, pp. 27–28.
[44] W.O. Rushton, letter qtd. in *Railway Game*, p. 28.

Out in a Gale of Fallen Leaves

Out in a gale of fallen leaves,
Where the wind blows clear through the rain-soaked trees,
Where the sky is torn betwixt cloud and blue
And the rain but ceases to fall anew:
And dead leaves, in bud on your April flight,
Will whisper your name to the wind to-night
And the year is dying in which you died
And I shall be lonely this Christmas-tide.
Hyde Park, October 1917

—Marian Allen

"Love is stronger than death" reads the epitaph on the headstone of Captain Arthur Tylston Greg, buried at Jussy Communal cemetery in France. Shortly after war was declared in August of 1914, Arthur Greg left his law studies at Oxford and joined the British Army. Serving with the Cheshire Regiment near Ypres, Belgium, in the spring of 1915, he was seriously wounded after being shot in the jaw. After recovering from his injuries, Greg rejoined the military and applied to the Royal Flying Corps. By April of 1917, he had been certified as a pilot and returned to France to join the No. 55 Squadron. Less than one month later, on April 23, 1917, as they returned from a bombing mission, Arthur Greg's squadron was attacked by German aircraft. It is likely that among the German pilots was Hermann Göring, the First World War ace who would survive to establish the Gestapo and command the Luftwaffe in the Second World War.[45] Greg's plane was shot down, and although he crash-landed near St. Quentin, both he and his observer died of their wounds.

In 1918, Arthur Greg's sweetheart, Marian Allen, published a volume of poetry, *The Wind on the Downs*. "Out in a Gale of Fallen Leaves" was written six months after Greg's death. In another poem from *Wind on the Downs* titled "And What Is War?" Marian Allen attempts to answer the question:

The sound of laughing voices disappearing,
  The marching of a thousand eager feet,
Passing, ever passing out of hearing,
  Echoing, ever echoing down the street;
A sudden gust of wind, a clanging door,
  And then a lasting silence—that is war.

Marian Allen went on to write and illustrate books for children; she returned to Oxford where she died in 1953. She never married.

---

[45] "Arthur Tylston Greg," *Cross and Cockade International Forum,* web.archive.org/web/20190624181932/https://www.crossandcockade.com/forum/forum_posts.asp?TID=58.

XX.
Jo's Requiem

He had the plowman's strength
in the grasp of his hand:
He could see a crow
three miles away,
and the trout beneath the stone.
He could hear the green oats growing,
and the south-west wind making rain.
He could hear the wheel upon the hill
when it left the level road.
He could make a gate, and dig a pit,
and plough as straight as stone can fall.
And he is dead.

—Ernest Rhys[46] (1918)

First published in *The Leaf Burners*, "Jo's Requiem" appeared in Ernest Rhys's poetry collection as the last poem in a series of twenty related dramatic lyrics entitled "The Tommiad." The title of the verse sequence is a play on the *Iliad*, suggesting an epic dedicated to British Tommies, the name given to British infantry soldiers. But Rhys was a Welsh writer, and the title may also be a play on the Welsh word *tommi*, "to spread dung" or "to bespatter with dirt." "Jo's Requiem" was retitled "Lost in France" as early as 1945 in the British anthology *Soldiers' Verse*. For a while, the poem's two titles appeared together, with "Lost in France" as the main title and "Jo's Requiem" as the subtitle. In recent publications, the poem's subtitle has disappeared altogether. "Lost in France" was chosen for display on the London Underground in 2014 as one of the poems marking the centenary of the First World War commemorations. The altered title no longer suggests a tribute to a single, knowable man, but presents the poem as a more abstract commentary on the dead of the war.

---

[46] See also Rhys's "The Leaf Burners."

Anzac Cove

There's a lonely stretch of hillocks:
   There's a beach asleep and drear:
There's a battered broken fort beside the sea.
There are sunken trampled graves:
   And a little rotting pier:
And winding paths that wind unceasingly.

There's a torn and silent valley:
   There's a tiny rivulet
With some blood upon the stones beside its mouth.
There are lines of buried bones:
   There's an unpaid waiting debt:
There's a sound of gentle sobbing in the South.
       January, 1916

—Leon Gellert

The Gallipoli campaign officially ended on January 9, 1915, when the last of the British forces withdrew from the Turkish peninsula. The battle had lasted nearly a year, and neither side could claim a clear victory: in total, over 100,000 men died, and more than 230,000 were wounded. In May 1916, just five months after the last troops had left Helles, the *London Telegraph* featured the news story "Anzacs in France," characterizing Gallipoli as a heroic tragedy and describing survivors as "hard fellows ... [with] Homeric fighting qualities."[47]

Leon Gellert survived Gallipoli. The Australian writer had enlisted with the 10th Battalion just eighteen days after Britain declared war on Germany and landed at Anzac Cove on April 25, 1915, but shrapnel wounds, dysentery, and blood poisoning ended his war. Gellert was evacuated from the Dardanelles, and due to his injuries and epileptic symptoms, was discharged from the military in June of 1916. His war poetry collection, *Songs of a Campaign*, was published in 1917. A reviewer for the *Times Literary Supplement* wrote,

> The relentless common sense of the Australian fighting man who cares little for battle honours or even the ancient ceremonial of Army life (such as saluting) is often apparent in his verse ... Mr. Gellert has succeeded in singing what Australia has been thinking of the great crimson page in the book of her adventurous living between the sea and a desert.[48]

---

[47] Philip Gibbs, "Anzacs in France," *London Telegraph*, 10 May 1916, p. 8.
[48] "An Australian Soldier Poet," *Times Literary Supplement*, no. 848, 18 Apr. 1918, p. 181.

To One Dead

A blackbird singing
On a moss upholstered stone,
Bluebells swinging,
Shadows wildly blown,
A song in the wood,
A ship on the sea.
The song was for you
And the ship was for me.

A blackbird singing
I hear in my troubled mind,
Bluebells swinging
I see in a distant wind.
But sorrow and silence,
Are the wood's threnody,
The silence for you
And the sorrow for me.

—Francis Ledwidge[49] (1917)

An Irish nationalist, Francis Ledwidge joined the British Army in October of 1914 to defend Ireland and further the cause of Irish Home Rule. With the 10th Irish Division, he fought at Gallipoli and was injured in Serbia. Known as the "Poet of the Blackbird," Ledwidge lived to see only one volume of his poetry published: *Songs of the Fields* (1915). In the spring of 1916, Ledwidge was on leave, passing through Manchester on his way home to Ireland, when he received news of the 1916 Easter Rising and the execution of his friend, fellow poet, and Easter Rising leader, Thomas MacDonagh. Ledwidge extended his stay in Ireland without permission, spoke out in favor of the Easter Rising, and was court-martialed upon his return to the Western Front. Although he continued to serve with the British Army and was eventually promoted to the rank of lance corporal, the events of the First World War and the Easter Rising intensified Ledwidge's allegiance to Ireland, and in his writings, the Irish countryside is poignantly imagined as a symbol of hope and peace. In early 1917, he wrote to Irish poet Katharine Tynan, "If I survive the war, I have great hopes of writing

---

[49] See also Ledwidge's "Home."

something that will live. If not, I trust to be remembered in my own land for one or two things which its long sorrow inspired."⁵⁰

During the summer of 1917, Ledwidge waited for the publication of his second volume of poetry, *Songs of Peace,* as his unit prepared for another major battle on the Western Front. In one of his last letters to Tynan, Ledwidge reminisced about Ireland and home:

> I would give £100 for two days in Ireland with nothing to do but ramble on from one delight to another. I am entitled to a leave now, but I'm afraid there are many before my name in the list. Special leaves are granted, and I have to finish a book for the autumn. But, more particularly, I want to see again my wonderful mother, and to walk by the Boyne to Crewbawn and up through the brown and grey rocks of Crocknaharna. You have no idea of how I suffer with this longing for the swish of the reeds at Slane and the voices I used to hear coming over the low hills of Currabwee. Say a prayer that I may get this leave, and give as a condition my punctual return and sojourn till the war is over. It is midnight now and the glow-worms are out. It is quiet in camp, but the far night is loud with our guns bombarding the positions we must soon fight for.⁵¹

On July 31, 1917, the first day of the battle of Passchendaele, Francis Ledwidge and five other men of the Royal Inniskilling Fusiliers were killed by a stray artillery shell that landed behind the lines. Ledwidge is buried at Artillery Wood Cemetery in Belgium; his grave is only steps away from that of the Welsh poet Hedd Wyn, who also died that day.

---

[50] Ledwidge letter to Tynan, 6 Jan. 1917, qtd. in *Francis Ledwidge: A Life of the Poet,* by Alice Curtain, Martin Brian, and O'Keefe, 1972, p. 170.
[51] Ledwidge letter to Tynan, 10 July 1917, qtd. in *Francis Ledwidge,* p. 186.

1914

He went without fears, went gaily, since go he must,
And drilled and sweated and sang, and rode in the heat and dust
Of the summer; his fellows were round him, as eager as he,
While over the world the gloomy days of the war dragged heavily.

He fell without a murmur in the noise of battle; found rest
'Midst the roar of hooves on the grass, a bullet struck through his breast.
Perhaps he drowsily lay; for him alone it was still,
And the blood ran out of his body, it had taken so little to kill.

So many thousand lay round him, it would need a poet, maybe,
Or a woman, or one of his kindred, to remember that none were as he;
It would need the mother he followed, or the girl he went beside
When he walked the paths of summer in the flush of his gladness and pride,

To know that he was not a unit, a pawn whose place can be filled;
Not blood, but the beautiful years of his coming life have been spilled,
The days that should have followed, a house and a home, maybe,
For a thousand may love and marry and nest, but so shall not he.

When the fires are alight in the meadow, the stars in the sky,
And the young moon drives its cattle, the clouds graze silently,
When the cowherds answer each other and their horns sound loud and clear,
A thousand will hear them, but he, who alone understood, will not hear.

His pale poor body is weak, his heart is still, and a dream
His longing, his hope, his sadness. He dies, his full years seem
Drooping palely around, they pass with his breath
Softly, as dreams have an end—it is not a violent death.

My days and the world's pass dully, our times are ill;
For men with labour are born, and men, without wishing it, kill.
Shadow and sunshine, twist a crown of thorns for my head!
Mourn, O my sisters! singly, for a hundred thousand dead.

—Ferenc Békássy[52]

All but forgotten outside his native Hungary, Ferenc Békássy was a student at King's College, Cambridge, before the war. A close friend of John Maynard

---

[52] See also Cornford's "Féri Bekassy."

Keynes, Békássy competed with Rupert Brooke for the affections of Noel Olivier, the daughter of Baron Olivier and the cousin of Laurence Olivier. When war was declared in August of 1914, Keynes helped Békássy return to Austria-Hungary, where he enlisted as a Hussar. Battling against Russian troops on the Eastern Front, Békássy was killed on June 25, 1915, just days after arriving at the front lines. He was twenty-two years old. A volume of his poetry, *Adriatica and Other Poems*, was published in 1925 by Virginia and Leonard Woolf. In the book's preface, a close friend wrote of Békássy, "His lovable qualities his friends will not forget; and they cannot matter to the world. Such traits are common—in obituaries at least."[53]

In his own death, Ferenc Békássy has been remembered "singly" at King's College, Cambridge. Although he died in the same war as his Cambridge classmates, Békássy fought with the Central Powers, aligning himself with his native Hungary, England's enemy. Because of this, "The commemoration of Ferenc Békássy's death in action was never going to be straightforward for King's College. His attachment to the place and his many friends there pulled in one direction; the grief for the other men killed while serving on the opposing side pulled in another."[54] In 1920, the British families of those who had lost their sons in the war, led by the father of Charles Sorley (another poet killed in the war), protested Békássy's inclusion on the King's College Chapel Roll of Honour. His name was omitted from the list. As a compromise proposed by John Maynard Keynes, in 1921 Békássy's name was inscribed on another wall of King's chapel, where he is listed simply as a "Pensioner."

---

[53] F.L. Lucas, "Preface," *Adriatica and Other Poems* by Ferenc Békássy, Hogarth, 1925, p. v.
[54] Peter Jones, "Epilogue—The Alien in the Chapel," *The Alien in the Chapel*, edited by George and Mari Gömöri, Skyscraper, 2016, p. 237.

Red Cross

I remember a moonless night in a blasted town,
And the cellar-steps with their army-blanket-screen,
And the stretcher-bearers, groping and stumbling down
To the Red Cross struggle with Death in the ill-lit scene.

There, entering-in, I saw, at a table near,
A surgeon tense by a man who struggled for breath.
A shell, that shattered above us, rattled the gear,
The dying one looked at me, as if I were Death.

He died, and was borne away, and the surgeon wept;
An elderly man, well-used, as one would have thought
To western war and the revels that Death then kept:
Why weep for one when a million ranked as naught?

He said, "We have buried heaps since the push began.
From now to the Peace we'll bury a thousand more.
It's silly to cry, but I could have saved that man
Had they only carried him in an hour before."

—John Masefield (1939)

John Masefield, the second-longest serving poet laureate of the UK (1930–1967), was thirty-four when the war began in August of 1914. Just one month earlier, he had entertained Rupert Brooke as a house guest, the two men reading poetry and walking the Berkshire Downs together. An established writer, Masefield responded to the outbreak of war almost immediately with the poem "August 1914." Published in the *English Review* that September, it recalls the men who, departing for war,

> Then sadly rose and left the well-loved Downs,
> And so by ship to sea, and knew no more
> The fields of home, the byres, the market towns,
> Nor the dear outline of the English shore,
>
> But knew the misery of the soaking trench,
> The freezing in the rigging, the despair
> In the revolting second of the wrench
> When the blind soul is flung upon the air ...[55]

[55] John Masefield, "August 1914," *English Review*, Sept. 1918, pp. 145–147.

Masefield had initially attempted to join the army but was rejected for medical reasons, and so he joined the reserves. He served briefly at the front as a medical orderly and later as a war historian, writing *Gallipoli* (1916), *The Old Front Line* (1917), and *The Battle of the Somme* (1919). Samuel Hynes in *A War Imagined* asserts that although John Masefield had "the fullest experience of war" of all the Georgian poets, "'August 1914' is the only war poem that Masefield published."[56] (Hynes does not categorize Masefield's 1917 sonnets memorializing the life and death of Rupert Brooke as war poems). But Masefield's lack of poetic output during the war wasn't for lack of trying: "The pocket notebook that he carried during his walking tours of the Somme contains drafts of more than a dozen poems of which four or five refer in some way to the war," yet these were never completed nor published.[57] Masefield himself later explained,

> When the war began, I wrote some verses, called *August, 1914* ... Some other verses were written in the first months of the war, including some of the sonnets; but that was the end of my verse-writing. Perhaps, when the war is over and the mess of the war is cleaned up and the world is at some sort of peace, there may be leisure and feeling for verse-making.[58]

Masefield's poem "Red Cross" was published in *The Queen's Book of the Red Cross* in 1939, a book intended to raise funds during the Second World War for "the great work of mercy on the battlefield."[59] The poem draws from Masefield's first-hand experience over twenty years earlier. In September of 1916, he had written to his wife while accompanying the volunteer American Field Service Ambulance that was attached to the French army,

> They asked me to come down into the Poste; so I went.
> On the operating table a French soldier lay dying, & was even then in the article of death. His legs had been shattered by a torpedo, & they had amputated them, but he had lost too much blood to live. A little company stood about him, one man to fan him, a doctor holding his pulse & watching his face, one or two others standing by, ready to do anything, all very alert, efficient, & full of feeling. They had a saline injection going. 'We did what we could,' one of the men said, in good English, 'but he was too far gone,' in fact the man died half a

---

[56] Samuel Hynes, *A War Imagined*, Bodley Head, 1990, p. 32.
[57] Hynes, *A War Imagined*, p. 32.
[58] John Masefield, "Preface," *The Poems and Plays of John Masefield: Volume One Poems*, Macmillan, 1920, p. viii.
[59] *The Queen's Book of the Red Cross*, Hodder and Stoughton, 1939, p. 29.

minute after I reached him. He was a tall, thin man of about 27, a man of some refinement, by his hands.[60]

Masefield was a witness not only to death, but to the mutilation and carnage of the battlefields. In another letter to his wife, he described the horrors:

> We went into a wood, which we will call Chunk-of-Corpse-Wood, for its main features were chunks of corpse, partly human, partly trees. There was a cat eating a man's brain, & such a wreck of war as I never did see, & the wounded coming by, dripping blood on the track, & one walked on blood or rotten flesh, & saw bags of man being carried to the grave. They were shoveling parts of men into blankets.[61]

Canadian soldier Amos William Mayse wrote to his wife, "I am sure that if spared I shall wake often with the horror of it all before me & I shall not want to talk much about it either."[62] What other soldiers found difficult to talk about, Masefield found difficult to shape into poetry. "Red Cross" is Masefield's delayed war poem, published over two decades after his experiences of the First World War.

---

[60] John Masefield to his wife, 24 Sept. 1916, in *John Masefield's Letters from the Front, 1915–1917*, edited by Peter Vansittart, F. Watts, 1985, p. 148.
[61] Masefield to his wife, 22 Oct. 1916, *Letters*, p. 194.
[62] Amos William Mayse, letter to Betty and children, 23 June 1917, *Canadian Letters and Images Project*, Stephen Davies, Project Director, web.archive.org/save/https://www.canadianletters.ca/content/document-9835.

Only a Boche

We brought him in from between the lines: we'd better have let him lie;
For what's the use of risking one's skin for a *tyke* that's going to die?
What's the use of tearing him loose under a gruelling fire,
When he's shot in the head, and worse than dead, and all messed up on the wire?

However, I say, we brought him in. *Diable!* The mud was bad;
The trench was crooked and greasy and high, and oh, what a time we had!
And often we slipped, and often we tripped, but never he made a moan;
And how we were wet with blood and with sweat, but we carried him in like our own.

Now there he lies in the dug-out dim, awaiting the ambulance,
And the doctor shrugs his shoulders at him, and remarks, "He hasn't a chance."
And we squat and smoke at our game of bridge on the glistening, straw-packed floor,
And above our oaths we can hear his breath deep-drawn in a kind of snore.

For the dressing station is long and low, and the candles gutter dim,
And the mean light falls on the cold clay walls and our faces bristly and grim;
And we flap our cards on the lousy straw, and we laugh and jibe as we play,
And you'd never know that the cursed foe was less than a mile away.
As we con our cards in the rancid gloom, oppressed by that snoring breath,
You'd never dream that our broad roof-beam was swept by the broom of death.

Heigh-ho! My turn for the dummy hand; I rise and I stretch a bit;
The fetid air is making me yawn, and my cigarette's unlit,
So I go to the nearest candle flame, and the man we brought is there,
And his face is white in the shabby light, and I stand at his feet and stare.
Stand for a while, and quietly stare: for strange though it seems to be,
The dying Boche on the stretcher there has a queer resemblance to me.

It gives one a kind of a turn, you know, to come on a thing like that.
It's just as if I were lying there, with a turban of blood for a hat,
Lying there in a coat grey-green instead of a coat grey-blue,
With one of my eyes all shot away, and my brain half tumbling through;
Lying there with a chest that heaves like a bellows up and down,
And a cheek as white as snow on a grave, and lips that are coffee brown.

And confound him, too! He wears, like me, on his finger a wedding ring,
And around his neck, as around my own, by a greasy bit of string,

A locket hangs with a woman's face, and I turn it about to see:
Just as I thought... on the other side the faces of children three;
Clustered together cherub-like, three little laughing girls,
With the usual tiny rosebud mouths and the usual silken curls.
"Zut!" I say. "He has beaten me; for me, I have only two,"
And I push the locket beneath his shirt, feeling a little blue.

Oh, it isn't cheerful to see a man, the marvellous work of God,
Crushed in the mutilation mill, crushed to a smeary clod;
Oh, it isn't cheerful to hear him moan, but it isn't that I mind,
It isn't the anguish that goes with him, it's the anguish he leaves behind.
For his going opens a tragic door that gives on a world of pain,
And the death he dies, those who live and love, will die again and again.

So here I am at my cards once more, but it's kind of spoiling my play,
Thinking of those three brats of his so many a mile away.
War is war, and he's only a Boche, and we all of us take our chance;
But all the same I'll be mighty glad when I'm hearing the ambulance.
One foe the less, but all the same I'm heartily glad I'm not
The man who gave him his broken head, the sniper who fired the shot.

No trumps you make it, I think you said? You'll pardon me if I err;
For a moment I thought of other things.... *Mon Dieu! Quelle vache de guerre.*
—Robert W. Service[63] (1916)

Robert W. Service, known as "the Canadian Kipling," was one of the most popular poets during the war. Volunteering as an ambulance driver at the front, Service also penned accounts of his experiences that were published in Canadian newspapers. In an article titled "R.W. Service Shelled to Shelter, Hides on Hill of a Hundred Horrors," he describes arriving at an aid station where he is told of "two men wounded, by a grenade. There is a third, but we want you to wait a little for him. We think he is dying." When the aid station comes under attack from German shellfire, Service crawls beneath his ambulance, seeking shelter. His narrative continues,

> "Every shell-scream is an interrogation; the answer—what?" ... Then the doctor hails me from his shelter.
> "Ah, the Boches will have their little joke. This place is not quite safe. You must not stay here too long."

---

[63] See also Service's "The Mourners."

I agree. It is not exactly the place I would choose for a picnic. I am not lingering just for the fun of the thing. I am waiting for a man to die. (In my heart I believe I wish he'd hurry up and do it.)

When the shelling stops, Service drives the two wounded men away from the front-line aid post, but he confesses, "I cannot help looking back. There, a corrugated line against the sky is the German trench, more silent, more deserted, more innocent-looking than ever."[64]

---

[64] Robert W. Service, "R.W. Service Shelled to Shelter, Hides on Hill of a Hundred Horrors," *Toronto Daily Star*, 11 Dec. 1915, qtd. in *Canadian Poetry from World War I*, edited by Joel Baetz, Oxford UP, 2009, pp. 162–163.

"Glad That I Killed Yer"
A modern song of Lamech

Hear my voice; hearken unto my speech: for I have slain a man.—Genesis iv.23.

Glad that I killed yer—
  It was you or me:
    Our bayonets locked,
  And then I pulled mine free;
    My heart beat like to burst;
    But Gawd, I got in first—
Glad that I killed yer!

Glad that I killed yer,
  Though you are so young:
    How still you lie
  With both your arms outflung:
    There's red blood on your hair—
    Well, what the Hell I care?—
Glad that I killed yer!

Glad that I killed yer—
  You're my enemy;
    I had to hate—
  And you—you hated me;
    You mightn't be to blame—
    I killed yer just the same—
Glad that I killed yer!

Glad that I killed yer—
  That's the game o' war;
    But for my luck
I'd lie just like you are;
    Your blood is on my hand—
    Surely you understand
I *had* to kill yer?

Glad that I killed yer—
  Yet I can't forget
    The look you gave me
  When we turned—and met—
    Why do you follow me with staring eye?

Was it so difficult a thing to die—
Gawd! when *I* killed yer?

Glad that I killed yer—
  Yet I'm sorry, too,
    For those will wait
  So long at home for you:
    I have a mother living down at Bow—
    Thank Gawd for this that yours will never know
'Twas I that killed yer!

Glad that I killed yer—
  It was you or me:
    It does seem strange,
  But it had got to be.
    My heart beat like to burst,
    But Gawd, I got in first—
Glad that I killed yer!

—Joseph Lee (1917)

In 1930, Willibald Hanner, a German veteran, delivered an address to German business leaders recalling his experiences of the First World War:

> We know and feel, that the war didn't only have external effects. It did not just change the map of the world, it changed the soul of human beings. We ourselves cannot entirely sense the enormous impact of the war on the human spirit, because we were part of it … we who lived through this inferno can never be free from it … And I know: we will carry all this with us to our graves. The war is our fate; it has torn our lives."[65]

Poetry was one vehicle for coping with the psychological traumas of the war. In several of his poems, British soldier Joseph Lee revisits memories of men who died at his hands:

The Bullet

Every bullet has its billet;
  Many bullets more than one:
God! Perhaps I killed a mother
  When I killed a mother's son.

—Joseph Lee (1916)

---

[65] Willibald Hanner, qtd. in *Bitter Wounds: German Victims of the Great War, 1914-1939*, by Robert Weldon Whalen, Cornell UP, 1984, pp. 181-182.

A journalist and poet before the war, Joseph Johnston Lee was nearly forty when he enlisted with Dundee's 4th Battalion of the Black Watch. He fought in battles at Festubert, Neuve Chapelle, Aubers Ridge, and Loos. During the Battle of Cambrai, Lee was taken prisoner by the Germans, and his account of the experience, *A Captive at Carlsruhe and Other German Prison Camps*, was published after the war. Remembering his first day as a prisoner of war, Lee writes, "How illogical is war! This very morning as we entered the first village in which German troops were billeted, we found them waiting to serve us, with outset tables on which were clean glasses and pitchers of clear water!"[66]

Lee was one of the more popular of the trench poets during the war; his two volumes of war poetry were illustrated with his sketches from the front. A reviewer in the *London Spectator* praised his poetry, writing,

> Of the verse that has come straight from the trenches, the *Ballads of Battle*, by Lance-Corporal Joseph Lee, of the Black Watch, are among the very best. In him the "Jocks" have found a true interpreter. The horror, the exultation, the weariness, and the humour of trench warfare are here, and at the back of it all the vision of "the little croft beneath the Ben."[67]

Lee returned to a career in journalism, dying in Dundee in 1949.

---

[66] Joseph Lee, *A Captive at Carlsruhe*, John Lane, 1920, p. 16.
[67] "Literary Supplement: War Time Poems," *London Spectator*, 7 Oct. 1916, p. 19.

Hallow-e'en, 1915

Will you come back to us, men of our hearts, to-night
In the misty close of the brief October day?
Will you leave the alien graves where you sleep and steal away
To see the gables and eaves of home grow dark in the evening light?

O men of the manor and moated hall and farm,
Come back to-night, treading softly over the grass;
The dew of the autumn dusk will not betray where you pass;
The watchful dog may stir in his sleep but he'll raise no hoarse alarm.

Then you will stand, not strangers, but wishful to look
At the kindly lamplight shed from the open door,
And the fire-lit casement where one, having wept you sore,
Sits dreaming alone with her sorrow, not heeding her open book.

Forgotten awhile the weary trenches, the dome
Of pitiless Eastern sky, in this quiet hour
When no sound breaks the hush but the chimes from the old church tower,
And the river's song at the weir,—ah! then we will welcome you home.

You will come back to us just as the robin sings
Nunc Dimittis[68] from the larch to a sun late set
In purple woodlands; when caught like silver fish in a net
The stars gleam out through the orchard boughs and the church owl flaps his
    wings.

We have no fear of you, silent shadows, who tread
The leaf-bestrewn paths, the dew-wet lawns. Draw near
To the glowing fire, the empty chair,—we shall not fear,
Being but ghosts for the lack of you, ghosts of our well-beloved dead.

—Winifred M. Letts

The First World War saw a dramatic surge in spiritualism, and in a desperate wish to communicate with the dead, many of the grieving turned to Ouija boards, mediums, and séances.[69] One-hundred years later, one of the most publicized

---

[68] A Christian hymn typically sung at evening worship services. Chanted in Latin, the words are from Simeon's song of praise at seeing the Christ child: "Lord, now let your servant depart in peace according to your word, for my eyes have seen your salvation."

[69] Suzie Grogan, *Shell Shocked Britain: The First World War's Legacy for Britain's Mental Health,* Pen and Sword, 2014, p. 132.

centenary commemorations of the First World War was Jeremy Deller's public art event "We're Here Because We're Here." On July 1, 2016, groups of men dressed as First World War soldiers walked the streets of Great Britain in silence. Appearing in shopping malls, train stations, and parks, the "ghost soldiers" did not speak, except for occasionally joining together to sing the trench song "We're Here Because We're Here." Deller was inspired by researching what he described as "the phenomenon in Britain during the war of women, mainly, seeing their dead loved ones in the street, just catching a glimpse of someone on a bus or through a shop window, thinking it was their husband, or their brother, or their son … So it was as if the project had already happened during the war; people had already seen the dead in the streets."[70]

Winifred Letts was an Anglo-Irish writer who served as a VAD and a masseuse for wounded soldiers. In 1916, she published her collection of war poetry *Hallow-e'en and Poems of the War*. She lived to be ninety years old; her obituary in the *Irish Times* noted, "She was not a great poet. But great poets are few. She was a good poet. And very good poets are not so many."[71]

---

[70] Jeremy Deller, qtd. in *Jeremy Deller: We're Here Because We're Here*, BBC 4 documentary, 13 Nov. 2016, web.archive.org/web/20190809212922/https://www.bbc.co.uk/programmes/b083bk7n.
[71] Monk Gibbon, "Winifred Letts: An Appreciation," *Irish Times*, 17 June 1972, p. 5.

His Latch-Key

("I am sending you all my keys except the latch. That I will keep, so that some day, when I get leave, I may walk in on you unexpectedly and give you a surprise."
—*In a letter from the Front.)*

And long … long … long we waited
For the sound that would tell he was here,
For the sound that would tell us our vigil was o'er,
And our hearts need be anxious no more,—
For that sweetest of sounds that could fall on the ear
Of those who had lived on the knife-edge of fear,—
The sound of his key in the door;—
The sound of all sounds that could bring back life's cheer,
And comfort our hearts that were sore.
O the ears of our souls strained as never before,
For that sound of all sounds that our joy would restore,—
The sound of his key in the door.

And we said, "We shall know when our boy's on the way."
And we said, "We shall know when he's near."
His step we shall catch while it's still far away,
And with it an end to our fear."
"But," we said,—"we will wait for his key in the door,
For the sound that shall tell us our waiting is o'er,—
For the joy of its rattle, so gallant and gay,
As we've heard it so often of yore.
O yes, we shall know ere he reaches the door,
For his guardian angel will fly on before
To tell us he's on the way."

And so we waited, by night and by day,
For the sound that would all our long waiting repay,—
For the sound of his key in the door.

But now,—
Well …. "All's Well!" …. but we're waiting no more
For the sound of his key in the door.
It lies with him there in his lowly grave,
Out there at the Front, where his all he gave
Our lives and the Soul of Life to save,
And our hopeful vigil is o'er.

For now it is he who is waiting for us,
On the other side of The Door;
And Another stands with him there, waiting for us,
And the sound of *our* key in That Door.

—John Oxenham (1917)

The best-selling poet of the First World War was John Oxenham, the pen name of William Arthur Dunkerley, a teacher and the mayor of Worthing, a seaside town in Sussex. Published editions of Oxenham's war poetry sold over seven million copies, and he donated the profits to "various Funds for the Wounded."[72] His poems were immensely popular with both soldiers and their loved ones. Dunkerley was sixty-one when the war began in 1914, and although he visited the Western Front in November of 1917, he never served in the military. Shortly after the end of the war, a New Zealand newspaper wrote, "Mr. Oxenham's verse must have given solace and comfort to many a war-weary and sorrow-laden soul during the four long, dreary years of conflict."[73] Although Oxenham's war poems are rarely included in modern anthologies, a 1918 review appearing in the *Bookman* explains his appeal to readers of his time:

> The verse of Mr. Oxenham is sincere, unaffected, and unpretentious in its treatment of the common sentiments and aspirations of an unsophisticated humanity; much of it is devotional; and all of it gives the impression of having been written without effort. Not the slightest element of mystery attaches to its widespread success. Simplicity is its key-note, and superficially it appears to be utterly devoid of literary artifice ... the absence of obscure passages and recondite allusions has no doubt contributed to the overwhelming success of the verses with people who, as a rule, are not poetry readers.[74]

---

[72] David Hodge, "John Oxenham," *The Bookman*, vol. 53, no. 317, Feb. 1918, p. 147.
[73] "Books of the Day," *Dominion*, vol. 12, no. 293, 6 Sept. 1919, p. 11.
[74] David Hodge, "John Oxenham," pp. 286–287.

To the Dead

Since in the days that may not come again
The sun has shone for us on English fields,
Since we have marked the years with thanksgiving,
Nor been ungrateful for the loveliness
Which is our England, then tho' we walk no more
The woods together, lie in the grass no more,
For us the long grass blows, the woods are green,
For us the valleys smile, the streams are bright,
For us the kind sun still is comfortable
And the birds sing: and since your feet and mine
Have trod the lanes together, climbed the hills,
Then in the lanes and on the little hills
Our feet are beautiful for evermore.
And you—O if I call you, you will come,
Most loved, most lovely faces of my friends
Who are so safely housed within my heart,
So parcel of this blessed spirit land
Which is my own heart's England, so possest
Of all its ways to walk familiarly
And be at home, that I can count on you,
Loving you so, being loved, to wait for me,
So may I turn me in, and by some sweet
Remembered pathway find you once again.
Then we can walk together, I with you,
Or you, or you along some quiet road,
And talk the foolish, old, forgivable talk,
And laugh together: you will turn your head,
Look as you used to look, speak as you spoke,
My friend to me, and I your friend to you.
Only when at the last, by some cross-road
Our longer shadows, falling on the grass,
Turn us back homeward, and the setting sun
Shines like a golden glory round your head,
There will be something sudden and strange in you.
Then you will lean, and look into my eyes,
And I shall see the bright wound at your side,
And feel the new blood flowing to my heart,
Your blood, beloved, flowing to my heart,

And I shall hear you speaking in my ear—
O not the old, forgivable, foolish talk,
But flames, and exaltations, and desires,
But hopes, and comprehensions, and resolves,
But holy, incommunicable things
That like immortal birds sing in my breast,
And, springing from a fire of sacrifice,
Beat with bright wings about the throne of God.
—Gerald Caldwell Siordet (1915/c.1918)[75]

"To the Dead" relies for much of its meaning on its religious allusions. The central action of the poem echoes the story of Christ's appearance to his friends on the road to Emmaus immediately after His resurrection; the poem's images of flames and fire allude to the presence of the Holy Spirit at Pentecost, and when the poem describes the travelers' feet as "beautiful for evermore," it references Isaiah 52:7: "How beautiful upon the mountains are the feet of him who brings good news, who publishes peace."

Gerald Caldwell Siordet (known to his family as "Jack") was an unlikely soldier. Tall and thin, he was an aspiring artist, critic, and poet. Friends with John Singer Sargent, Glyn Philpot, and Jane Morris (wife of artist William Morris), Siordet also tutored the young Aldous Huxley, preparing him for entry to Oxford. In September of 1914, Siordet volunteered as a soldier, leaving his artistic ambitions and his work as an ivories cataloguer at the Victoria and Albert Museum.[76] He was commissioned as an officer with the 13th Battalion of The Rifle Brigade. The War Memorial book of Balliol College, Oxford, Siordet's alma mater, records,

> though he seemed little suited, either in physique or in temperament, for a soldier's life, he was probably happier as a soldier than he had ever been before. Both in his poems which he wrote during this period, and in the drawings which were found in his notebooks, there is evidence to show how finely his mind was touched by his new experience.[77]

Siordet's military career was marked by devoted concern for the men under his command: he was wounded at the Somme and awarded a Military Cross for

---

[75] "To the Dead" was published in the *London Times* on 30 Nov. 1915 under the pen name Gerald Caldwell; this version is from Siordet's undated volume of poetry.
[76] Biographical information is taken from James Caldwell Ritchie, *Gerald Caldwell Siordet (1885–1917) Artist and Poet,* Hurtwood, 2017.
[77] Ritchie, "Annex 2: The Balliol College War Memorial Book 1914–1919," *Siordet*, p. 54.

conspicuous gallantry in a failed attack that killed one of his closest friends, Geoffrey Smith. After recovering from his injuries, Siordet was posted to join the Mesopotamia Expeditionary Force in January 1917. He wrote to his younger sister, Vera, that on his ship to the Middle East he was "accused of being a Socialist by the Quartermaster for suggesting that while we [the officers] had 6 courses at Dinner and 4 at Luncheon the men had a right to have something better than meat with maggots in it for their dinner."[78] After a month in Mesopotamia, Siordet wrote home, "There is no sense of moral right to help one along in this part of the war—the Turk is a most gallant and chivalrous enemy and no one wishes him ill."[79]

Despite assuring his sister, "Please don't be anxious. I don't think fighting out here is anything as bad as in France,"[80] Siordet was killed on February 9, 1917, leading an attack on the Turkish position near Kut al-Amara. After his death, his family received with his personal effects a letter from an officer who had never met Siordet, but who had assumed command of the 13th Rifle Brigade on the Western Front after Siordet was evacuated from the Somme. Captain E.R. Wedemeyer wrote to thank Siordet for sending "numerous parcels ... containing all kinds of jolly good things for the men." Wedemeyer wrote to Siordet, the former officer of the Rifle Brigade, "There are not many of the old 13th left. I'm afraid the last show took most of them,"[81] and he expressed sincere gratitude for Siordet's continued efforts, even from a distance, to provide for the men of his former unit. It is likely that Siordet was killed before receiving the letter. His name appears on the Basra Memorial to the missing in Iraq.

---

[78] Siordet, letter to Vera Siordet, 5 Jan. 1917, qtd. in Ritchie, p. 91.
[79] Siordet, letter to Ruth Scott, 6 Feb. 1917, qtd. in Ritchie, p. 95.
[80] Siordet, letter to Vera, 5 Jan. 1917, qtd. in Ritchie, p. 92.
[81] E.R. Wedemeyer, letter to Siordet, 3 Jan. 1917, qtd. in Ritchie, p. 110.

Perhaps—
(To R.A.L. Died of Wounds in France, December 23rd, 1915)

Perhaps some day the sun will shine again,
    And I shall see that still the skies are blue,
And feel once more I do not live in vain,
    Although bereft of You.

Perhaps the golden meadows at my feet
    Will make the sunny hours of Spring seem gay,
And I shall find the white May blossoms sweet,
    Though You have passed away.

Perhaps the summer woods will shimmer bright,
    And crimson roses once again be fair,
And autumn harvest fields a rich delight,
    Although You are not there.

Perhaps some day I shall not shrink in pain
    To see the passing of the dying year,
And listen to the Christmas songs again,
    Although You cannot hear.

But, though kind Time may many joys renew,
    There is one greatest joy I shall not know
Again, because my heart for loss of You
    Was broken, long ago.
        1st London General Hospital, February 1916

—Vera Brittain[82]

In December of 1915, Vera Brittain, a young VAD nurse just shy of her twenty-second birthday, eagerly awaited a visit from her fiancé, Roland Aubrey Leighton. In the last week of November, Roland had written to Vera from his dugout in the trenches:

> Through the door I can see little mounds of snow that are the parapets of trenches, a short stretch of railway line, and a very brilliant full moon. I wonder what you are doing. Asleep, I hope—or sitting in front of a fire in blue and white striped pyjamas? I should so like to see you in blue and white pyjamas.[83]

---

[82] See also Brittain's "Sic Transit—."
[83] Roland Leighton, "To Vera Brittain," 26 Nov. 1915, qtd. in *Letters from a Lost Generation*, edited by Alan Bishop and Mark Bostridge, Abacus, 2004, p. 189.

On December 17, Vera received a message from Roland suggesting he might get his wish to see her: "Shall be home on leave from 24th Dec.–31st. Land Christmas Day."[84] That Christmas Eve, Vera worked with other nurses filling soldiers' stockings with candy and nuts, and the following morning, she attended Christmas communion at the hospital chapel, where she knelt to "thank whatever God there be for Roland and for all my love and joy."[85] She then caught a train to Brighton, where she waited for her fiancé's arrival. The next day, she found herself with time on her hands:

> I walked along the promenade, and looked at the grey sea tossing rough with white surf-crested waves, and felt a little anxiety at the kind of crossing he had had. But at any rate he should be safely in England by this time, though he probably has not been able to send me any message to-day owing to the difficulties of telephones and telegrams on Sunday & Christmas Day combined.[86]

On Monday December 27, she received news of Roland:

> I had just finished dressing when a message came to say that there was a telephone message for me. I sprang up joyfully, thinking to hear in a moment the dear dreamed-of tones of the beloved voice.
>
> But the telephone message was not from Roland but from Clare [his mother]; it was not to say that Roland had arrived, but that instead had come this telegram, sent on to the Leightons by Mr. Burgin, to whom for some time all correspondence sent to Lowestoft had been readdressed:
>
> T223. Regret to inform you that Lieut. R.A. Leighton 7th Worcesters died of wounds December 23rd. Lord Kitchener sends his sympathy."[87]

On his last day of duty before leave, Leighton had volunteered to lead his men into No Man's Land to repair wire in front of their trench. He was hit by German machine gun fire, severely wounded in the stomach and spine. Carried by stretcher to a hospital clearing station, Roland died the next evening.

On New Year's Eve, Vera wrote her last diary entry for 1915:

> This time last year He was seeing me off on Charing Cross Station after *David Copperfield*—and I had just begun to realise I loved Him. To-day He is lying in the military cemetery at Louvencourt—because a week ago He was wounded in action, and had just 24 hours of consciousness more and then went "to sleep

---

[84] Vera Brittain, *Testament of Youth*, 1933, Virago, 2014, p. 207.
[85] Vera Brittain, *Chronicle of Youth*, William Morrow, 1982, p. 296.
[86] Brittain, *Chronicle of Youth*, p. 296.
[87] Brittain, *Chronicle of Youth*, p. 296.

in France." And I who in impatience felt a fortnight ago that I could not wait another minute to see Him, must wait till all Eternity. All has been given me, and all taken away again—in one year.

So I wonder where we shall be—what we shall all be doing—if we all still *shall* be—this time next year.[88]

Friends attempted to comfort Brittain, telling her that time would heal, but she recalls,

I resented the suggestion bitterly; I could not believe it, and did not even want it to be true. If time did heal I should not have kept faith with Roland, I thought, clinging assiduously to my pain, for I did not then know that if the living are to be of any use in this world, they must always break faith with the dead.[89]

Perhaps this reflection in Brittain's memoir, written in 1933, is in response to the challenge issued in John McCrae's poem "In Flanders Fields."

---

[88] Brittain, *Chronicle of Youth*, pp. 296–297.
[89] Brittain, *Testament of Youth*, p. 221.

New Year, 1916

Those that go down into silence…[90]

There is no silence in their going down,
   Although their grave-turf is not wet with tears,
Although Grief passes by them, and Renown
   Has garnered them no glory for the years.

The cloud of war moves on, and men forget
   That empires fall. We go our heedless ways
Unknowing still, uncaring still, and yet
   The very dust is clamorous with their praise.

—Ada M. Harrison

"New Year, 1916" considers the complex intersections of silence and war. The UK and Commonwealth nations' tradition of keeping two minutes of silence on Remembrance Sunday was first observed at 11:00 a.m. on November 11, 1919, on the first anniversary of the Armistice that ended the war. The suggestion came from Sir Percy Fitzpatrick, a South African author and politician whose eldest son had been killed in December of 1917. While visiting Cape Town in 1918, Fitzpatrick had been moved by the city's daily ceremony of the Two-Minute Pause, during which all work, movement, and talk were suspended. As the first anniversary of the Armistice approached, Fitzpatrick wrote a memorandum to War Cabinet minister Lord Milner, proposing a period of silence like that which he had observed in Cape Town, when "Silence, complete and arresting, closed upon the city—the moving, awe-inspiring silence of a great Cathedral where the smallest sound must seem a sacrilege … Only those who have felt it can understand the overmastering effect in action and reaction of a multitude moved suddenly to one thought and one purpose."[91] The proposal was accepted by the Cabinet, approved by King George V, and publicized in newspapers on November 7, 1919, as "a personal request from the King."[92] An editorial in London's *Daily Herald* commented,

> You are asked to be silent for two minutes to-day, to be silent and pause in your labours, to remember this day and this hour last year …

---

[90] An allusion to Psalm 115:17: "The dead praise not the Lord, neither any that go down into silence."
[91] Sir Percy Fitzpatrick, qtd. in *The Silence of Memory: Armistice Day 1919–1946*, by Adrian Gregory, Berg, 1994, p. 9.
[92] Gregory, *The Silence of Memory*, p. 11.

What will you remember and what will you forget? You will remember, mothers, the gay sons you have lost; wives, you will think of the husbands who went out in the mist of the winter morning—the mist that sent cold chills round the heart—never to come back. And brothers will think of brothers and friends of friends, all lying dead today under an alien soil.

But what will you forget? The crime that called these men to battle ... The war that was to end war and in reality did not?..

Make the most of this day of official remembrance. By the sacred memory of those lost to you, swear to yourself this day at 11 o'clock, that never again, God helping you, shall the peace and happiness of the world fall into the murderous hands of a few cynical old men.[93]

The two-minute Silence remains one of the most enduring rituals of memory associated with the First World War. Attempting to explain its power, Joanna Scutts writes,

Was the Silence a ritual of prayer by another name? It tended to be seen as such in America, where it never caught on nationally out of fear that at its base, the moment of silence was an attempt to smuggle religion into the public sphere. At the same time, the Cenotaph and its ceremonies were not securely Christian either. The church was often wary of the power of Armistice Day as a kind of folk observance, as an attempt to commune with the dead. Its power, however, lay in its absence of nationalist or religious dogma ... Amid all the competing narratives, however, the most powerful remained that two-minute silence, in which a prayer could be offered, or a mute protest lodged, and where no government or church could intrude.[94]

Ada May Harrison was born in South Africa, but studied modern and medieval literatures at Cambridge's Newnham College from 1918 to 1921. After the war she wrote children's books, many illustrated by her husband, the artist Robert Sargent Austin. During the Second World War, Harrison compiled and edited *Grey and Scarlet: Letters from the War Areas by Army Sisters on Active Service.*

---

[93] *Daily Herald,* 11 Nov. 1919, p. 1, qtd. in *The Silence of Memory,* p. 12.
[94] Joanna Scutts, "Stop All the Clocks," *Lapham's Quarterly,* 11 Nov. 2014, web.archive.org/save/https://www.laphamsquarterly.org/roundtable/stop-all-clocks.

Reported Missing....

My thought shall never be that you are dead:
Who laughed so lately in this quiet place.
The dear and deep-eyed humour of that face
Held something ever living, in Death's stead.
Scornful I hear the flat things they have said
And all their piteous platitudes of pain.
I laugh! I laugh!—For you will come again—
This heart would never beat if you were dead.
The world's adrowse in twilight hushfulness,
There's purple lilac in your little room,
And somewhere out beyond the evening gloom
Small boys are culling summer watercress.
Of these familiar things I have no dread
Being so very sure you are not dead.

—Anna Gordon Keown (1917)

The bodies of over 70,000 British and Commonwealth men were never found after the battle of the Somme, and nearly 55,000 remained missing in action after battles in the Ypres Salient. Just outside the city of Verdun, the Douaumont Ossuary contains the bones of over 130,000 French and German soldiers who were never identified. Historians estimate that over three million soldiers who died in the First World War have no known grave.[95] Men were lost in collapsed tunnels that exploded during mining operations or buried in trenches after heavy artillery fire; others drowned and disappeared in the deep mud of No Man's Land; still others received injuries so severe that they couldn't be identified, men who were obliterated by the weapons of modern warfare. Allyson Booth has examined the "problem of corpselessness" in the First World War as it relates to "civilians' experience of disembodied death," noting that the term 'Missing' would be understood in very different ways by men at the front who had seen what happened to bodies hit by shellfire as compared to the very different meaning assigned to the word by "a frantic mother clinging to the ordinary verbal distinction between 'missing' and 'dead.'"[96]

Anna Gordon Keown wrote poetry, plays, and novels. *Time* magazine named her post-war novel *The Cat Who Saw God* as their Book of the Week selection

---

[95] Neil Hanson, *Unknown Soldiers: The Story of the Missing of the First World War*, Alfred A. Knopf, 2006, p. xiv.
[96] Allyson Booth, *Postcards from the Trenches*, Oxford UP, 1996, pp. 29–30.

in November of 1932, writing, "Late great Emperor Nero takes possession of the body of a cat, settles down with an English spinster. Amusing in the English manner."[97] Siegfried Sassoon wrote the foreword to Keown's *Collected Poems* (1954), observing, "It will be apparent to any informed reader that the voice heard in these poems has not been influenced by the modernities of the past thirty years" and adding, "It must be added that there is much variety in this volume, from which the inward radiance of the writer's temperament continually emerges. It should be enjoyed by those who have failed to get sustenance from symbolist mystification, and whose ears are attuned to the traditional music of the past."[98]

---

[97] "Books of the Week," *Time*, 13 Nov. 1932.
[98] Siegfried Sassoon, "Foreword," *Collected Poems*, Anna Gordon Keown, Caravel, 1953, pp. 9–10.

An Epilogue[99]

I. The Fluke

For two years you went
Through all the worst of it,
Men fell around you, but you did not fall.
On the Somme when the air was a sea
Of contesting flashes and clouds of smoke,
Your gunners fell fast but you got never a scratch.
And once when you watched from a village tower
(At Longueval, was it?) between our guns and theirs
As men fought in the houses below,
A shell from an English battery came
And tore a hole in the tower below you,
But you were not hurt and remained observing.

And now,
A casual shell has come
And pierced your head,
And the men who were with you, uninjured,
Carried you back,
And you died on the way.

IV. The Landscape

You said, that first winter,
That the landscape around Ypres
Reminded you of Chinese paintings:
The green plain, striped with trenches,
The few trees on the plain,
And the puffs of smoke sprinkled over the plain.
You said, when the war was over,
That you would record that green desolation
In flat colours and lines
As a Chinese artist would.
That is what you were going to do.
The plain is still there.

—J.C. Squire (1917/1922)

---

[99] Both "The Fluke" and "The Landscape" belong to the five-part poem "An Epilogue," published in Squire's *Poems: Second Series* (1922). The author's preface states, "the group called *An Epilogue* should have been dated 1917."

John Collings Squire and William Hammond Smith met while at Blundell's School when they were students, sometime between 1901 and 1903. The friendship continued beyond their early school years; both men attended Cambridge University (Squire at St. John's and Smith at Sidney Sussex). Smith went on to study art at the Slade School of Fine Art, and Squire assumed the duties of literary editor at the *New Statesman*. When war broke out, Squire was deemed unfit for military service due to poor eyesight, while Smith enlisted in the Royal Field Artillery. Stationed on the Western Front, Smith saw action at Festubert, Hohenzollern Redoubt, Hill 60, Zillebeke, Ploegsteert, the Somme, Longueval, Lorette Ridge, High Wood, Butte de Warlencourt, and Arras. He survived some of the most ferocious fighting of the war, but was killed on April 12, 1917. With his battery in a support position, Smith was assigned to an observation post behind the lines. Leaving cover to gain a better view of the action, he was struck in the head by a stray shell splinter, carried back to the dressing station, and died within an hour. He was thirty-one.[100]

In addition to "An Epilogue," Squire remembered his friend William Smith in "To a Bull-dog (W.H.S., Capt. [Acting Major] R.F.A.; killed April 12, 1917)," a poem addressed to Smith's dog, Mamie, who had been left in Squire's care. Although many modern critics find the poem overly sentimental and even "excruciatingly maudlin,"[101] during the war and in the years following, it was one of Squire's most anthologized poems, described by critics of the time as "oddly affecting,"[102] and "strangely moving."[103] A 1919 review asserted, "Few of the 'in memoriam' poems of the war touch the heart as does that poem, *To a Bulldog*, with its moving close."[104] Here are the poem's final stanzas:

> And though you run expectant as you always do
>   To the uniforms we meet,
> You'll never find Willy among all the soldiers
>   In even the longest street,
>
> Nor in any crowd; yet, strange and bitter thought,
>   Even now were the old words said,

---

[100] Biographical information on Smith from "Smith, William Hammond," *Tonbridge at War*, web.archive.org/web/20190623213503/http://tonbridgeatwar.daisy.websds.net/Authenticated/ViewDets.aspx?RecID=343&TableName=ta_factfile.

[101] George Walter, "Loose Women and Lonely Lambs: The Rise and Fall of Georgian Poetry," *British Poetry, 1900–50*, edited by Gary Day and Brian Docherty, St. Martin's, 1995, p. 27.

[102] "Poets and Poetry," *The Spectator*, 3 Apr. 1920.

[103] Iolo A. Williams, *Poetry To-Day*, Herbert Jenkins, 1927, p. 101.

[104] Robert Lynd, "Mr. J.C. Squire," *Old and New Masters*, Scribner, 1919, p. 209.

If I tried the old trick and said "Where's Willy?"
   You would quiver and lift your head,

And your brown eyes would look to ask if I were serious,
   And wait for the word to spring.
Sleep undisturbed: I shan't say *that* again,
   You innocent old thing.

I must sit, not speaking, on the sofa,
   While you lie asleep on the floor;
For he's suffered a thing that dogs couldn't dream of,
   And he won't be coming here any more.[105]

---

[105] J.C. Squire, *Poems, First Series*. Martin Secker, 1918, p. 95.

Elegy on the Death of Bingo, Our Trench Dog
By the Trench Bard

Weep, weep, ye dwellers in the delvèd earth,
Ah, weep, ye watchers by the dismal shore
Of No Man's Land, for Bingo is no more;
He is no more, and well ye knew his worth,
For whom on bully-beefless days were kept
Rare bones by each according to his means,
And, while the Quartermaster-Sergeant slept,
The elusive pork was rescued from the beans.
He is no more, and, impudently brave,
The loathly rats sit grinning on his grave.

Him mourn the grimy cooks and bombers ten,
The sentinels in lonely posts forlorn,
The fierce patrols with hands and tunics torn,
The furtive band of sanitary men.
The murmuring sound of grief along the length
Of traversed trench the startled Hun could hear;
The Captain, as he struck him off the strength,
Let fall a sad and solitary tear;
'Tis even said a batman passing by
Had seen the Sergeant-Major wipe his eye.

The fearful fervour of the feline chase
He never knew, poor dog, he never knew;
Content with optimistic zeal to woo
Reluctant rodents in this murky place,
He never played with children on clean grass,
Nor dozed at ease beside the glowing embers,
Nor watched with hopeful eye the tea-cakes pass,
Nor smelt the heather-smell of Scotch Septembers,
For he was born amid a world at war
Although unrecking what we struggled for.

Yet who shall say that Bingo was unblest
Though all his Sprattless[106] life was passed beneath

---

[106] Spratt's was the first company to mass-produce dog biscuits.

The roar of mortars and the whistling breath
Of grim, nocturnal heavies going west?
Unmoved he heard the evening hymn of hate,
Unmoved would gaze into his master's eyes.
For all the sorrows men for men create
In search of happiness wise dogs despise,
Finding ecstatic joy in every rag
And every smile of friendship worth a wag.

—Edward de Stein[107] (1919)

The pilots of the Lafayette Escadrille kept two lion cubs (Whiskey and Soda); the 2nd Battalion of the Welsh Regiment had a goat (Taffy IV); the South African 3rd Transvaal Regiment awarded a baboon named Jackie the rank of private; Australians took a koala to war with them, and the American 102nd Infantry Regiment proudly boasted the most decorated dog of the First World War, Sergeant Stubby, who participated in seventeen engagements and was wounded twice. At least sixteen million animals served in the war, assisting in military efforts.[108] The role of horses in the First World War has received increased attention since the 1982 publication of Michael Morpurgo's novel *War Horse* (as well as the release of the award-winning play and movie based on the book), but other animals also played a critical part. Camels, elephants, mules, donkeys, canaries, pigeons, cats, and dogs were used to transport supplies, detect gas attacks, send messages, hunt rats, rescue the wounded, scout enemy territory, and keep watch as sentries. Even slugs contributed to the war effort: their high sensitivity to mustard gas helped alert men in the trenches.[109]

Just as importantly, animals provided comfort and companionship, reminding soldiers of home and life before the war. Many units had mascots, and soldiers often smuggled pets with them or adopted stray animals they found at the front. Cats were popular for their prowess in killing the millions of rats that swarmed the trenches, but for many soldiers, dogs were fondly regarded as man's best friend. It is estimated that over 100,000 military dogs accompanied the German

---

[107] See also de Stein's "Envoie."
[108] Rômulo Romeu Nóbrega Alves and Raynner Rilke Duarte Barboza, "What about the Unusual Soldiers? Animals Used in War," *Ethnozoology: Animals in Our Lives*, edited by Rômulo Romeu Nóbrega Alves and Ulysses Paulino Albuquerque, Academic Press, 2017, p. 324.
[109] Alves and Barboza, "Animals," p. 332.

and French armies.¹¹⁰ But animals also became targets and casualties of war, and countless died in the line of duty.

Before the war, Edward de Stein was known at Magdalen College, Oxford, for "his wit and skill as a raconteur."¹¹¹ He served with the British military from 1914 to 1920, attaining the rank of Temporary Captain with the King's Royal Rifle Corps and of Temporary Major with the Machine Gun Corps. Published in 1919, his *Poets in Picardy* is a collection of parodies and poems. De Stein writes in the preface,

> The rhymes contained in this volume were all jotted down in France during 1916, 1917, and 1918, either in the trenches, in billets, or in the more dignified purlieus of staff offices.
>
> Any merit that may be found in them is due to the influence of that wonderful spirit of light-heartedness, that perpetual sense of the ridiculous which, even under the most appalling conditions, never seemed to desert the men with whom I was privileged to serve and which indeed seemed to flourish more freely in the mud and rain of the front-line trenches.

De Stein's entry in the Oxford Dictionary of National Biography states that he was a poet and astute businessman, as well as an accomplished watercolourist, pianist, fisherman, and gardener—a man who was "skilled at tapestry work" as well as being "an excellent shot." He was knighted for his work during the Second World War with the Ministry of Supply, and with his sister, he deeded ownership of Lindisfarne Castle on Holy Island to the National Trust.¹¹² He died in 1965.

---

[110] United States Department of the Air Force, "Section A—A History of Military Working Dogs," *USAF Military Working Dog Program*, 18 Dec. 1973, p. 1-1.
[111] John Orbell, "Stein, Sir Edward Adolphe Sinauer de," *Oxford Dictionary of National Biography*, 23 Sept. 2004, DOI: doi.org/10.1093/ref:odnb/32793.
[112] Orbell, "Stein, Sir Edward Adolphe Sinauer de," *Oxford Dictionary of National Biography*.

6

Aftermath

A mix of emotions anticipated and accompanied the Armistice, and the effects of the war lasted long after hostilities ceased. Poems celebrated the joys of homecoming and grieved for those who would never return. Many greeted the war's end with relief, but were less optimistic regarding the prospects for a lasting peace. Survivors were confronted with the complex task of shaping and commemorating the legacy of the First World War.

November Eleventh

We stood up and we didn't say a word,
It felt just like when you have dropped your pack
After a hike, and straightened out your back
And seem just twice as light as any bird.

We stood up straight and, God! but it was good!
When you have crouched like that for months, to stand
Straight up and look right out toward No-Man's-Land
And feel the way you never thought you could.

We saw the trenches on the other side
And Jerry, too, not making any fuss,
But prob'ly stupid-happy, just like us.
Nobody shot and no one tried to hide.

If you had listened then I guess you'd heard
A sort of sigh from everybody there,
But all we did was stand and stare and stare,
Just stare and stand and never say a word.

—Hilmar R. Baukhage (1919)

After 1,568 days, the First World War ended on the eleventh hour of the eleventh day of the eleventh month of 1918. And yet on the last morning of the war, over 2,700 men died on the Western Front. As early as August of 1918, German General Ludendorff had informed his staff that Germany could not win the war, and in late September, Generals Ludendorff and Hindenburg agreed that they must seek an armistice. The Kaiser was informed on September 30, and on October 4, German officials contacted American President Woodrow Wilson, asking for terms based on his Fourteen Points. Turkey agreed to peace terms on October 30, and Austria-Hungary sought an armistice on November 3, but the German delegation didn't meet to discuss an armistice with the French until late in the evening of November 7. By now, rumors of peace were everywhere.

Many Allied generals were not in favor of a negotiated peace; their armies were finally making gains, and they wished to pursue the fight, pushing their advantage to force Germany's unconditional surrender. In the railway carriage at Compiègne, the German delegation had very little room to negotiate and were forced to accept nearly all terms imposed by the Allies, including the provision that within fourteen days, they would evacuate and return all occupied territory and cede their rights to Alsace-Lorraine. The Armistice was finally signed at 5:10 a.m. on the morning of November 11 and took effect less than six hours later. Along the Western Front, German troops celebrated during the night of November 10, shooting off flares and rockets. On the morning of November 11, a 5:40 a.m. radio broadcast from the Eiffel Tower announced the upcoming peace, and London received the news before 6:00 a.m.

Although nearly everyone knew in advance that the war was over, even the most conservative estimates acknowledge that casualties from both sides on the war's last day reached nearly 11,000. At least 2,738 men died on November 11 in attacks on German positions that had already been ceded to the Allies. As Joseph E. Persico explains,

> Putting these losses into perspective, in the June 6, 1944, D-Day invasion of Normandy, nearly twenty-six years later, the total losses were reported at 10,000 for all sides. Thus the total Armistice Day casualties were nearly 10 percent higher than those on D-Day. There was, however, a vast difference. The men storming the Normandy beaches were fighting for victory. Men dying on Armistice Day were fighting in a war already decided.[1]

It is nearly impossible to imagine the anxiety of the men who had survived and knew the end was only hours away. German soldier Georg Bücher had fought on the Western Front since 1914. He recalls,

> It was all the harder for us since we knew the end could not be far off ... We ducked at the sound of every explosion—which we had never bothered to do before. The old hands fought for the deepest, safest dug-outs and did not scruple to leave to the young recruits the hundred and one things which were risky ... The thought of an attack was more terrifying to them than to the young soldiers who were still so inexperienced, so touchingly helpless, yet in spite of everything, so willing.[2]

American officer Harry G. Rennagel, writing to his family, remembers his unit's astonishment at learning they were to attack on that last morning. When a shell exploded near him at 10:55 a.m., he was spared, but discovered five of his men had been hit:

> One fatally injured, hole near heart, two seriously injured and the other two badly hurt. We took care of the injured men and then I knelt beside the lad whose eyes had such a look of sorrow that my eyes filled with tears.

---

[1] Joseph E. Persico, *Eleventh Month, Eleventh Day, Eleventh Hour*. Random House, 2004, pp. 378–379.
[2] Qtd. in *Eleventh Month*, by Persico, p. 322.

> "What is it old man?" I asked.
>
> "Lieutenant, I'm going fast. Don't say I'll get better, you know different and this is a pretty unhappy time for me. You know we all expected things to cease to-day, so I wrote my girl, we were to be married when I returned, and my folks that I was safe and well and about my plans, and now—by some order I am not going home."
>
> "A glance at my watch, 11.05. I looked away and when I looked back — he had gone for The Highest Reward. I can honestly tell you I cried and so did the rest."[3]

In the trenches, it was the silence that deafened after years of exploding shells and rattling machine guns. American artillery officer Captain Bob Casey writes,

> *Eleven A.M.*—The silence is oppressive. It weighs in on one's eardrums.
>
> We have lived and had our being in din since we left the Foret de la Reine. There seems to be something uncanny—unnatural in the all-enveloping lack of sound ... The air is full of half-forgotten sounds: the rustling of dead leaves, the organ tone of wind in the tree tops, whispers through the underbrush, lazy echoes of voices in the road.
>
> With all is a feeling that it can't be true ... We cannot comprehend the stillness.[4]

Captain Harry Truman, the future US president, recalls, "It was so quiet it made me feel as if I'd suddenly been deprived of my ability to hear,"[5] and Connell Albertine of the 26th Yankee Division records, "We ran out into No-Man's Land and stood there, stunned by the quiet, a quietness we had never before experienced."[6] It was hard to celebrate the peace without remembering those who would never return home. Capturing the sober mood, British Lieutenant Patrick Campbell writes, "I felt excited, and happy, but in an uncertain subdued way. I did not want to shout or to drink; there was nothing to drink anyway. I wanted to be with my friends, but none of those of my own age were left in the brigade."[7]

---

[3] Qtd. in *History of Buffalo and Erie County, 1914–1919*, 2nd ed., edited by Daniel J. Sweeney, Committee of One Hundred, 1920, p. 316.
[4] Anonymous (Robert J. Casey), *The Cannoneers Have Hairy Ears*, J.H. Sears, 1927, pp. 329–330.
[5] Qtd. in *Eleventh Month*, p. 352.
[6] Connell Albertine, *Yankee Doughboy*, Branden, 1968, p. 234.
[7] Qtd. in *No Man's Land*, by John Toland, Doubleday, 1980, p. 577.

Hilmar R. Baukhage, author of "November Eleventh," graduated from the University of Chicago in 1911 and afterwards studied at the Sorbonne and the University of Bonn. Fluent in French and German, Baukhage enlisted in the US Army in May of 1918. Serving as a second lieutenant with the Field Artillery, he was also a writer for the American military newspaper, *The Stars and Stripes*, and he covered the Versailles Peace Conference in 1919. After the war, he became one of America's most trusted broadcast journalists—using only his last name and the tag line, "Baukhage Talking." He was the first to broadcast live from the White House, covering the Japanese bombing of Pearl Harbor, and from Berlin, he broadcast Hitler's invasion of Poland in 1939.[8]

---

[8] Charles Kupfer, *Indomitable Will*, Bloomsbury, 2012, p. 103; Edward Bliss, *Now the News: The Story of Broadcast Journalism*, Columbia UP, 2010, p. 57.

Paris, November 11, 1918
For G.A.H.

Down on the boulevards the crowds went by,
The shouting and the singing died away,
And in the quiet we rose to drink the toasts,
Our hearts uplifted to the hour, the Day:
The King—the Army—Navy—the Allies—
England—and Victory.—
And then you turned to me and with low voice
(The tables were abuzz with revelry),
'I have a toast for you and me,' you said,
And whispered 'Absent,' and we drank
Our unforgotten Dead.
    But I saw Love go lonely down the years,
    And when I drank, the wine was salt with tears.

—May Wedderburn Cannan[9] (1919)

As the church bells of Shrewsbury rang out on November 11, 1918, announcing the end of the war, a telegram was delivered to an address on Monkmoor Road. While others celebrated, Tom and Susan Owen received the news that their son Wilfred had been killed just one week before peace was declared.[10] For all who had lost friends, sons, husbands, brothers, and sweethearts, news of the Armistice was bittersweet. The war had ended, but the long and lonely work of adjusting to a world irrevocably changed by grief and loss had just begun.

On the morning of the Armistice, 25-year-old May Wedderburn Cannan was at her desk in the British War Office located in Paris. As acting head of the women's Espionage Section in Paris (a branch of MI5), Cannan recalls that day:

> I was called into the Colonel's room "to take some notes from the telephone" … A voice, very clear, thank God, said "Ready?" and began to dictate the Terms of the Armistice. They muttered a bit crowding round me and I said fiercely "Oh, shut up, I can't *hear*" and the skies didn't fall.
>
> I wrote in my private short-long-hand and half my mind was in a prayer that I should be able to read it back. I could feel my heart thumping and hear the silence in the room round me. When the voice stopped I said mechanically "understood" and got up.

---

[9] See also Cannan's "France" and "Since They Have Died."
[10] *Wilfred Owen*, by Guy Cuthbertson, Yale UP, 2014, p. 293.

> I made four copies of what I had written and took them in and went back to my little office staff and told them. I can't remember much what we said: I can only remember being so cold, and crying, and trying not to let the others see.[11]

Cannan dedicated "Paris, November 11, 1918" to "G.A.H." Although the individual's identity is uncertain, Cannan's account of her time in France frequently mentions "G.," a co-worker in the British War Office and fellow lodger at a Paris boarding house. The two women became friends, and in her autobiography, Cannan describes the evening of the Armistice and her return to the small hotel they shared:

> The Pension produced some champagne at dinner and we drank the loyal toast. And then across the table G. lifted her glass to me and said "Absent". I did not know her story nor she mine, but I drank to my friends who were dead and to my friends who, wounded, imprisoned, battered, shaken, exhausted, were alive in a new, and a terrible world.[12]

Bevil Quiller-Couch, Cannan's fiancé, survived some of the bloodiest battles of the Western Front, only to die in Germany in February of 1919, a victim of the Spanish influenza pandemic.

---

[11] May Wedderburn Cannan, *Grey Ghosts and Voices*, Roundwood, 1976, p. 135.
[12] Cannan, *Grey Ghosts and Voices*, p. 136.

Remembrance Day

Some one was singing
    Up a twisty stair,
  A fragment of a song,
    One sweet, spring day,
When twelve o'clock was ringing,
    Through the sunny square—

"There was a lad baith frank and free,
Cam' doon the bonnie banks o' Dee
Wi' tartan plaid and buckled shoon,
An' he'll come nae mair to oor toon."—

"He dwells within a far countree,
Where great ones do him courtesie,
They've gien him a golden croon,
An' he'll come nae mair to oor toon"—

No one is singing
  Up the twisty stair.
Quiet as a sacrament
  The November day.

Can't you hear it swinging,
    The little ghostly air?—
  Hear it sadly stray
    Through the misty square,
In and out a doorway,
    Up a twisty stair—
Tartan plaid and buckled shoon,
He'll come nae mair to oor toon.

                              —Marion Angus (1922)

On the fields of battle, unnatural quiet marked the end of the war. But silence was experienced by those on the home front as well, a stillness that echoed with absence and stretched forward through the years. Describing the poetry of Scottish writer Marion Angus, one reviewer wrote, "To read her verse is like sitting in an empty room where fingers tap on the window pane, and outside the house, something passes on noiseless feet."[13]

---

[13] Winifred Duke, "Women Poets of Today," *Glasgow Herald,* 15 Jan. 1936, p. 8, qtd. in *The Singing Lass,* Aimée Chalmers, Polygon, 2006, p. 16.

Born in 1865, Marion Angus was raised in Arbroath and was devoted to the language, landscape, and people of Northeast Scotland. She was a writer for nearly all her life, but her first volume of poetry wasn't published until 1922 when she was in her fifties. During the war, Angus volunteered at Stobs, a military camp for civilian internees and prisoners of war; by 1916, it housed over 4,500 men. She worked in the dining hall there and at the nearby YMCA recreation hut for British troops near the Stobs rail station.[14] Her nephew recalls that she was "much exhausted by this work, with its long hours and harsh conditions, but she spoke after it with the greatest respect and admiration for the ordinary private soldiers, and their simple good sense and kindliness."[15] Many of her poems rework the traditional Scottish ballad form, intermingling past and present, Scots and English, to suggest the fragmentary and interpreted nature of time, history, and experience. When she died in 1946, Marion Angus was credited as being "one of the most distinctive voices of the modern Scots revival,"[16] all the more remarkable because "To have been Scottish and a woman and a poet in the first third of this [twentieth] century was to have been marginal in three ways."[17]

---

[14] Katherine Gordon, editor, *Voices from Their Ain Countrie*, Association for Scottish Literary Studies, 2006, p. 8; Chalmers, *The Singing Lass*, p. 27.

[15] W.S. Angus, qtd. in *Voices from Their Ain Countrie*, p. 8.

[16] "Death of Marion Angus Scots Vernacular Poet," *Arbroath Guide*, 24 Aug. 1946, qtd. in *The Singing Lass*, p. 54.

[17] Dorothy Porter [McMillan], "Scotland's Songstresses," *Cencrastus*, vol. 25, Spring 1987, p. 48, qtd. in *The Singing Lass*, p. 65.

Victory, whose calm gaze… (Victoire aux calmes yeux…)

Victory, whose calm gaze defends the just,
Who clenched your fist and fought your way through hell—
Despite the shed blood, the betrayal of the trust
And strength of youth into pain and debility,
Despite the scabbing rust of suffering
That clogs and ruts every turn along the way,
I would proclaim your august divinity,
Could I not see, in your other fist,
Like ancient medals in dusty display,
Those human faces rubbed away.

—Anna de Noailles (1920), translated by Ian Higgins

The Allied forces had won the war, but few believed that the treaties signed at Versailles in 1919 would be able to guarantee a lasting peace. France's economy and much of her land lay in ruins, and 25 percent of its young men between the ages of eighteen and twenty-seven had died in the war.[18] For all nations involved, the number of dead and wounded was nearly incomprehensible, and the losses "meant incalculable impoverishment of the belligerents' national strength to the detriment of leadership, energy, initiative and working skill. The impoverishment would be perpetuated in future generations. This, among all the other debits, was the most grievous price imposed by the war."[19]

Comtesse Anna de Noailles was one of the most famous French writers and cultural figures of the early twentieth century. Admired by Colette, Cocteau, and Proust, she was a leading figure in the pre-war literary salons of Paris. On the day that Archduke Franz Ferdinand was assassinated in Sarajevo, an article in the *New York Times* praised her talents: "At present, a Rumanian, the Countess of Noailles, has undisputed possession of the scepter of French poetry, which she has enriched with new accents."[20] Her writing earned her "immense popularity among readers of all classes and levels of sophistication."[21] During the war, de Noailles' husband fought with the French army, and she volunteered as a *marraine de guerre*,[22] sending letters and care packages to French soldiers.[23]

---

[18] Robert Gerwarth, *The Vanquished*, Farrar, Straus and Giroux, 2017, p. 172.
[19] John Williams, *The Other Battleground*, Henry Regnery, 1972, p. 288.
[20] Max Nordau, "Though Our Men Figure Largely in European Literature, Our Women Have Failed to Inspire," *New York Times*, 28 June 1914, p. SM5.
[21] Catherine Perry, *Persephone Unbound: Dionysian Aesthetics in the Works of Anna de Noailles*, Bucknell UP, 2003, p. 19.
[22] See in this volume "Regiments (Régiments)."
[23] Geert Buelens, *Everything to Nothing*, translated by David McKay, Verso, 2015, pp. 196–197.

Thirty-four of her war poems were published in her collection *Les Forces éternelles* (1920). In 1921, the French Academy awarded de Noailles the Grand Prix de Littérature, and she was selected as the first woman to be admitted to the Royal Belgian Academy. She received the French Légion d'honneur in 1930, and 10,000 mourners attended her state funeral in 1933. Today, most of her books are out of print; only limited texts have been translated into English, and her writing "has virtually disappeared from the French cultural memory."[24]

---

[24] Perry, *Persephone Unbound*, p. 15.

To the Survivors

They are all given back to you—
Midsummer Warwick woods, at night;
The still
Vision of Sherborne from the hill
Under a sudden rainbow; flight
Of virgin winds above the faithful downs;
The towns
Of Yorkshire; docks that breathe
Old witcheries with smoke and copper dusk;
And morning mists that wreathe
The pale
Towers of Canterbury; and the husk
Of ruined Porchester; the vale
Of Gloucester; Cotswold walls
Loose-stoned and low; waterfalls
Of northern Devon; all the patched
Wonder of field and casual pool, and thatched
Unventilated cottages. By us
Four years avoided, ransomed now, again
(And four times richer thus)
They come; and all this pain
Is past. Can you believe it true?
They are all given back again to you.
   Oxford Magazine, Dec. 1918

—Carola Oman[25]

Like Siegfried Sassoon's poem "Everyone Sang," Oman's "To the Survivors" expresses a communal sense of wonder. The war is over, and the journey home has perhaps never been so tenderly imagined. The English landscape that featured so largely in the imagination of British soldiers is listed in all its variety, as if marking stops on a pilgrimage. David Reynolds writes in *The Long Shadow*,

> The French evoked their homeland through villages, churches, and the values of *civilisation;* German writers also focused on their cultural heritage but often celebrated their cities and industry. Where English poets were unusual was in defining their country so intensely through its countryside ... For many during

---

[25] See also Oman's "Unloading Ambulance Train" and "In the Ypres Sector."

the Great War, both in Britain and at the front, the "civilization" for which they fought therefore boiled down to a profound if nebulous love of home, often expressed in pastoral idiom ... Man and nature ravaged in Flanders fields; man and nature in harmony in an idealized England—the war's meaning lay somewhere in the gap.[26]

Carola Oman's first book, *The Menin Road and Other Poems*, was published in 1919 following her three years of service at home and abroad as a volunteer VAD nurse. In 1922, she married Gerald Foy Ray Lenanton, a war veteran; the marriage was childless due to Lenanton's war injuries.[27] Oman continued to write after the war, authoring over thirty books. Her historical fiction novels were influenced by her friend Georgette Heyer, but she is best known for her erudite historical biographies. Oman's prize-winning work on Lord Admiral Nelson "still stands as the benchmark against which modern biographies of Nelson may be judged."[28] For her contributions to the arts, she was appointed CBE (Commander of the Most Excellent Order of the British Empire) in 1957.

---

[26] David Reynolds, *The Long Shadow*, W.W. Norton, 2014, pp. 186, 190.
[27] Mark Bostridge, "Oman, Carola Mary Anima," *Oxford Dictionary of National Biography*, 4 Oct. 2007, Oxford UP, DOI: http://dx.doi.org/10.1093/ref:odnb/7156.
[28] Bostridge, "Oman, Carola Mary Anima."

The Extra

Sheltered and safe we sit.
Our chairs are opposite;
We watch the warm fire burn
In the dark. A log I turn.
Across the covered floor
I hear the quiet hush
Of muffled steps; the brush
Of skirts;—then a closing door.
Close to you and me
The clock ticks quietly.

I know that we exist
Two entities in Time.
Our vital wills resist
Enclosing night; our thoughts
Command a Truth above
All fear, in knowing Love.

But a voice in the street draws near;
A wordless blur of sound
Breaks like a flood around:
"Trust not your hopes, for all are vain,
Trust not your happiness and pain,
Trust not your storehouses of grain,
Trust not your strength on land or sea,
Trust not your loves that come and go,
Trust only the hate of the unknown foe,—
War is the one reality."

Are we awake or dreaming?
On the hearth, the ashes are gleaming.

Listen, dear:
The clock ticks on in the quiet room,
It's all a joke, a poor one, too.
Or else I'm mad! This can't be true?
I light the lamp to lift the gloom.
My world's too good for such a doom.
One fact, if nothing else, I know,
I'll die sooner than have it so!

—Gladys Cromwell (1919)

One of the most sensational news stories of January 1919 was the double suicide of twin sisters who had volunteered with the Red Cross as nurses and canteen workers. The women were the wealthy daughters of a New York City businessman, and one was a published poet. Following the tragedy, Harriet Monroe of *Poetry* magazine wrote,

> The toll of our heroic soldier dead does not complete the list of those who have given their lives in the cause of liberty ... The self-drowning of the twin sisters Gladys and Dorothea Cromwell should not be called suicide, but the tragic result of over-strain due to months of contact with the dark realities of war ... Thus her fellow-poets of America are entitled to inscribe the name of Gladys Cromwell on their honor-roll, just under those of Alan Seeger, Joyce Kilmer and the other poet-heroes who died in battle.[29]

The Cromwell twins were born in November of 1885, and at their father's death in 1914, Gladys and Dorothea each inherited a fortune. Exceptionally close, the sisters sought opportunities to use their talents and money to help others, for "A delicate humility made them feel debtors to life."[30] The war provided the sisters with the opportunity to volunteer as aid workers, and they enrolled in the Canteen Service of the Red Cross, sailing for France in January of 1918. Stationed at Chalons for eight months, they were favorites of the French soldiers, who often laughed at their inability to tell the identical twins apart. Harriet Rogers, an administrator at Chalons, praised the women: "They are angels who not only do first-class work on day and night service, but also find time to visit the soldiers in the French hospitals and to befriend the little French refugee children. Everybody loves them and admires their efficiency and courage in real danger."[31] Working long shifts, often under enemy fire, Gladys and Dorothea began to suffer "from the exhaustion that is so acute to those who have never known physical labour; yet no one suspected until the end came that for many months they had believed their work a failure, and their efforts futile."[32]

In September of 1918, the sisters requested a transfer to an American Evacuation Hospital, stating that they longed to work with "our own boys." But already under severe strain, they were haunted by what they encountered near the front. In the biographical note to Cromwell's poems, Anne Dunn writes,

> In the diaries they left, signs of mental breakdown begin to show as early as October. After the Armistice, when they returned to Chalons as guests, they

---

[29] Harriet Monroe, "A Gold Star for Gladys Cromwell," *Poetry*, vol. 13, no. 6, Mar. 1919, pp. 326–327.
[30] Anne Dunn, "Biographical Note," *Poems*, by Gladys Cromwell, Macmillan, 1919, p. 114.
[31] "Praise the Dead Cromwell Twins," *Boston Globe*, 30 Jan. 1919, p. 3.
[32] Dunn, "Biographical Note," p. 115.

showed symptoms of nervous prostration, but years of self-control and consideration for others made them conceal the black horror in which they lived—the agony through which they saw a world which they felt contained no refuge for beauty and quiet thought. In such a world they conceived they had no place.[33]

After the Armistice, their brother urged them to return to America, and the sisters arranged to sail on the *SS La Lorraine* from Bordeaux. On the night of January 19, 1919, a sentry on the deck of the *Lorraine* was the only one who saw the women calmly walk to the ship's rail, then quickly climb over and plunge into the water. By the time the captain of the *Lorraine* could be notified, the ship had traveled five miles beyond the place the Cromwell sisters were last seen.

Their double suicide provoked widespread public debate concerning the mental effects of war work on women volunteers. In a *New York Times* front-page article, Mrs. Edward Shearson, a passenger on the ship from which the sisters jumped, was quoted as saying, "It is my belief that all American women should come home as soon as possible. Conditions are such that they can be released and all, especially young women, should be brought back. Their work is finished. They are tired and nervous."[34] Gladys's and Dorothea's bodies were recovered, and they were buried in France with military honors. The French Government awarded them the Croix de Guerre and the Médaille de la Reconnaissance française. Gladys Cromwell's posthumously published *Poems* won the Poetry Society of America prize in 1920.

---

[33] Dunn, "Biographical Note," p. 116.
[34] "Brings Story of Cromwell Tragedy," *New York Times,* 29 Jan. 1919, p. 6.

Recall-Up (Rappel)

Suppose, all at once,
Blood were to bead
From mahoganies
And walls and hangings
In your drawing-rooms?

Suppose, in the night, all at once
The lamps bled,
Lights like wounds?
Or your rugs swelled and
Exploded, like bellies of dead horses?

Suppose the violins
Took up
The tears of the men,
The last refrain of the men
With exploded skulls across every plain on the globe?

Suppose your diamonds, your bright diamonds,
Now were only eyes
Madness-filled
All round you, in the night,
All at once?

What would you tell of life
To a skeleton, suddenly there,
Stock-still, bone-bare,
Its only mark
A Military Cross?

—Marcel Sauvage (1919), translated by Ian Higgins

The English term *shell shock* originated in the First World War; the French called it *commotional syndrome, war neurosis, battle hypnosis,* or *obusite* (from the word for *artillery shell*). Some French physicians simply labeled the condition *hysteria*, a term with a history that "also served to humiliate soldiers."[35] French soldiers suffering from the trauma of the war struggled against cultural stigmas associated with psychiatric wounds:

[35] Gregory M. Thomas, *Treating the Trauma of the Great War: Soldiers, Civilians, and Psychiatry in France 1914–1940*, Louisiana State UP, 2009, pp. 20–21.

mental illness was still too closely tied to degenerates and drunks. While an amputee could easily be touted as a hero, a chronically confused soldier was not a model veteran ... The mentally alienated veterans sequestered in asylums were considered *les morts vivants*—"the living dead." They were survivors of the war, but they were as good as dead to their families, who saw them rarely and could no longer count on them for financial or emotional support ... Even those who escaped institutionalization were seen to inhabit a realm that was somewhere short of truly living.[36]

Marcel Sauvage was nearly nineteen when the war interrupted his medical studies in Paris. Serving as a stretcher bearer at the Somme, Sauvage was seriously injured and gassed while recovering the wounded. A French newspaper commended his courage, describing him as a *"brancardier d'un dévouement absolu"* (stretcher bearer of absolute devotion).[37] Sauvage's war poems were written between 1916 and 1920; the title of his poem "Recall-Up" (*Rappel*) carries a double meaning, suggesting in French both the action of summoning the troops and that of remembering.

---

[36] Thomas, *Treating the Trauma*, pp. 125–126.
[37] "A L'Ordre de Jour," *Bulletin des Ecrivains de 1914–1915–1916–1917*, no. 32, June 1917, p. 2.

Saturdays

Now has the soljer handed in his pack,
    And "Peace on earth, goodwill to all" been sung;
I've got a pension and my ole job back—
    Me, with my right leg gawn and half a lung;
But, Lord! I'd give my bit o' buckshee[38] pay
    And my gratuity in honest Brads[39]
To go down to the field nex' Saturday
    And have a game o' football with the lads.

It's Saturdays as does it. In the week
    It's not too bad; there's cinemas and things;
But I gets up against it, so to speak,
    When half-day-off comes round again and brings
The smell o' mud an' grass an' sweating men
    Back to my mind—there's no denying it;
There ain't much comfort tellin' myself then,
    "Thank Gawd, I went *toot sweet* an' did my bit!"

Oh, yes, I knows I'm lucky, more or less;
    There's some pore blokes back there who played the game
Until they heard the whistle go, I guess,
    For Time an' Time eternal. All the same
It makes me proper down at heart and sick
    To see the lads go laughing off to play;
I'd sell my bloomin' soul to have a kick—
    But what's the good of talkin', anyway?

—E.W. Pigott (1920/1922)[40]

Perhaps the best-known British football story of the First World War is that of the men of the London Irish Rifles who dribbled a ball across No Man's Land under enemy fire as they attacked the German lines at Loos in 1915. What is less well-known is the plight of soldiers who returned from the war, unable to ever again join in a game of football. An estimated eight million veterans returned home disabled: in Britain, 750,000 of those were permanently disabled,

---

[38] buckshee: something extra obtained for free (first known use 1919).
[39] Brads = slang term for £1 notes issued between 1914 and 1928, when Sir John Bradbury was Secretary to the Treasury.
[40] When first published in *Punch* on 28 Jan. 1920, the poem was unattributed. When republished in *Poems of Punch 1909–1920*, E.W. Pigott was named as the author. Although it is difficult to determine more about the author's identity, the Imperial War Museum's *Lives of the First World War* lists a Lieutenant Edward William Pigott, who served with the London and East Lancashire Regiments.

and 1.5 million veterans in Germany suffered the permanent physical effects of the war.[41] As Deborah Cohen explains, "More than any other group, disabled veterans symbolized the First World War's burdens. Long after the Armistice, the sight of empty sleeves tucked into pockets recalled 'sad memories of the war and its longdrawn suffering.' For the disabled themselves, as one veteran explained, the Great War 'could never be over.'"[42]

Over 41,000 British veterans of the First World War suffered the amputation of one or more limbs; in Germany the number of war amputees totaled over 65,000.[43] In the aftermath of the war, the economic plight of veterans with disabilities was particularly acute as widespread social unrest spread and unemployment rose. In Britain, the maximum pension awarded to veterans with disabilities in 1920 was 40 shillings per week, a sum far below what was needed to support a man, much less a family (e.g., unskilled builders earned 84 shillings/week, coal miners between 99 and 135 shillings/week[44]). Disability review boards assessed the extent to which veterans were disabled, and they awarded the full 40 shillings only to those who were determined to have experienced 100 percent disability, specifically defined as

> Loss of two or more limbs, loss of an arm and an eye, loss of a leg and an eye, loss of both hands or all fingers and thumbs, loss of both feet, loss of a hand or a foot, total loss of sight, total paralysis, lunacy, wounds or disease resulting in a man being permanently bedridden, wounds to internal organs or head involving total permanent disability, very severe facial disfigurement.

Those with legs amputated at the hip were assessed as 80 percent disabled and received 32 shillings per week, while a man with a leg amputated below the knee was determined to be 50 percent disabled and entitled to receive only 20 shillings a week.[45] As Thomas Kelly of Dunbartonshire, formerly a sergeant in the British Army, wrote to his government,

> There was not so much red-tape to go through in August, 1914, when the country was crying for men and I left a good job to join the soldiers, but now when I am a maimed and not fit for manual labour, this country has no further use for us. Yet it was to be a country fit for heroes to live in.[46]

---

[41] Deborah Cohen, *The War Come Home,* U of California P, 2001, pp. 1, 4.
[42] Cohen, *The War Come Home,* p. 2.
[43] Joanna Bourke, *Dismembering the Male,* U of Chicago P, 1996, p. 33; Robert Weldon Whalen, *Bitter Wounds,* Cornell UP, 1984, p. 55.
[44] "War and Impairment: The Social Consequences of Disablement," UNITE and UK Disability History Month, Nov./Dec. 2014, p. 3, web.archive.org/web/20190629232803/https://ukdhm.org/v2/wp-content/uploads/2014/09/UK-Disability-history-month-2014-Broadsheet.pdf.
[45] Ministry of Pensions leaflet, qtd. in *Dismembering the Male,* p. 66.
[46] Thomas Kelly letter, The National Archives of the UK, LAB 2/1195/TDS2884/1919.

The Mascot Speaks

They say I can't go back with him,
  They say we dogs are banned.
They told him that. They didn't think
  That I could understand.

I've had him pretty near a year,
  Since I was just a pup.
I used to be a sort of bum,
  And then—he picked me up.

We've slept together in the rain,
  And snow, too, quite a lot.
Cold nights we kept each other warm,
  Some days we ate—some not.

Once he went to the hospital.
  I followed. They said, "No."
He swore a lot and told the doc
  Unless I stayed, he'd go.

He's going to go home pretty soon
  And leave me here—oh well—
I wonder if dogs have a heav'n?
  I know we've got a hell.

—Rags (1919)

America was one of the few countries that did not officially use dogs in the First World War, yet American newspapers and magazines regularly carried sentimental narratives about dogs who served, giving them names and human characteristics, so that dogs became "vessels for patriotism."[47] Alison Laurence argues that the American popular press frequently valorized dogs for their service, implying that dogs had earned the right "to be treated as any human brother in arms."[48] The cover of the American Red Cross magazine for April 1918 presented a dramatic illustration entitled "The Wounded Comrade," which depicted an American soldier carrying a wounded dog to safety in the midst of battle. Laurence argues, "The public's insistence upon protecting dogs may

---

[47] Alison G. Laurence, "Patriot, Pet, and Pest: America Debates the Dog's Worth during World War I," 2013, U of New Orleans, Master's thesis, p. 18.
[48] Laurence, "Patriot, Pet, and Pest," pp. 18–19.

have been in direct response, even if a subconscious one, to the war itself," a way both of deflecting attention from the brutality, violence, and massive numbers of men who had been killed and of attempting "to spare life during a time of rapid acclimation to the reality of global casualties."[49]

But in a post-war Europe ravaged by hunger and deprivation, few could afford sympathy for animals. British policy decreed that only those horses owned by officers were to be guaranteed transport home: the fate of the remaining horses and mules depended on their age and physical condition. The prime stock—85,000 animals—were returned to the UK; of these, 70 percent were sold to farmers, and the others were retained by the British military. The majority of the army's horses and mules remained on the continent, sold to either to farmers or slaughterhouses.[50] Dogs fared little better: as the French army demobilized, they destroyed nearly all of the 15,000 dogs in service, and "the vast quantities of dogs used by the British, Germans, Italians, and Russians faced the same fate."[51] Stephen Johnston argues, "Millions of animals have been killed in the name of country—not despite the patriotic love professed for them, but precisely because of it."[52]

"The Mascot Speaks" was published in March of 1919 in the American military newspaper *The Stars and Stripes*. The poem was purportedly authored by "Rags," the name of one of the most popular and celebrated dogs of the First World War. Rags was a homeless stray, found on the streets of Paris by Jimmy Donovan, a sergeant with the 1st Division Signal Corps. On numerous occasions, Rags assisted Donovan and his men, carrying messages and locating wounded soldiers between the lines. On October 2, 1918, during the Meuse-Argonne offensive, Rags carried a critical message that saved lives and allowed his unit to take their objective. Just one week later, Rags and Donovan were seriously wounded by shellfire. Sharing a stretcher, they were evacuated to a field hospital on an officer's orders: "Tell them the dog is to get the same treatment as a soldier."[53] In the military hospital, Rags slept under Donovan's bed for weeks and was allowed to accompany him on an ambulance train destined for the French port of Brest. There, Donovan was carried aboard a ship bound for

---

[49] Laurence, "Patriot, Pet, and Pest," p. 39.
[50] "What Happened to the Horses When the War Ended?" *World War One BBC*, audio transcript, web.archive.org/web/20190704000811/https://bam.files.bbci.co.uk/bam/live/content/zqn9xnb/transcript.
[51] Michael G. Lemish, *War Dogs*, Brassey's, 1999, p. 29.
[52] Stephen Johnston, "Animals in War: Commemoration, Patriotism, Death," *Political Research Quarterly*, vol. 65, no. 2, June 2012, p. 359.
[53] Qtd. in *From Stray Dog to World War I Hero*, by Grant Hayter-Menzies, Potomac Books, 2015, p. 48.

America, but Rags was forbidden passage. The dog was left "sitting by himself on the edge of the dock in Brest, before him a ship he could not board, beyond it an ocean he could not cross, and behind him a city he didn't know, where his only option was to return to the life of a stray … Given his battlefield injuries, it is likely he would not have survived very long."[54] Rags was saved by an officer who recognized him and smuggled him aboard. The dog was then assisted by a "Rags committee," whose members ensured that, upon his arrival in New York, the dog was smuggled past military and immigration authorities to join Donovan on a train headed to Chicago and nearby Fort Sheridan. Once again, Rags loyally stayed by Donovan in hospital, keeping vigil until Donovan died in 1919. Adopted by another soldier and his family, Rags participated in 1st Division parades and reunions and was the subject of a 1930 biography. He died in 1936 and was buried with military honors in Aspin Hill pet cemetery outside Washington, DC.

---

[54] Hayter-Menzies, *From Stray Dog,* p. 52.

The Heart of the World

In the heart of the world is the call for peace.
   Up-surging symphonic roar.
'Tis ill of all clashings; it seeks release
   From fetters of greed and gore.
The winds of the battlefields echo the sigh
   Of hero souls slumbering deep;
Who gave all they had and now dreamlessly lie
   Where the bayonets sent them to sleep.

Peace for the wealthy; peace for the poor;
Peace on the hillside and peace o'er the moor.

In the heart of the world is the call for right;
   For fingers to bind up the wound,
Slashed deep by the ruthless harsh hand of might
   When Justice is crushed to the ground.
'Tis ill of the fevers of fear of the strong—
   Of jealousies—prejudice—pride—
Is there no ideal that's proof against wrong?
   Man asks of the man at his side.

Right for the lowly; right for the great.
Right all to pilot to happiness' gate.

In the heart of the world is the call for love.
   White heart—Red—Yellow—and Black.
Each face turns to Bethlehem's bright star above,
   Tho' wolves of self howl at each back.
The whole earth is lifting its voice in a prayer
   That nations may learn to endure,
Without killing and maiming, but doing what's fair
   With a soul that is noble and pure.

Love in weak peoples; love in the strong.
Love that will banish all hatred and wrong.

In the heart of the world is the call of God.
   East—West—and North—and South.
Stirring, deep-yearning, breast-heaving call for God
   A-tremble behind each mouth.

> The heart's ill of torments that rend men's souls.
>   Skyward lift all faiths in hope.
> Across all the oceans the evidence rolls
>   Refreshing all life's arid slopes.
>
> *God in the highborn; God in the low.*
> *God calls us, world-brothers. Hark ye! and know.*
>
> —Joshua Henry Jones, Jr. (1919)

When America entered the war, many African Americans joined the US Army, believing that military service would help them gain them full citizenship rights, including both social and political equality. Yet although "World War I assaulted far more of the hierarchical structures of privilege than its participants had ever expected,"[55] African American soldiers returned home to heightened racial tensions and an increase in mob violence. Social and political unrest exploded in the Red Summer of 1919. A report prepared for the US Congress identified thirty-eight race riots in towns and cities across America in the nine-month period from January through October, with "Forty-three negroes, four white men lynched from Jan. 1 to Sept. 14 [1919]."[56] W.E.B. DuBois's editorial "Returning Soldiers" appeared in *The Crisis* in May of 1919. He reminded readers of the sacrifice that black troops had made in fighting "for America and her highest ideals," but lamented the violence and degradation of on-going racism:

> This country of ours, despite all its better souls have done and dreamed, is yet a shameful land.
>   *It lynches.*
>   And lynching is barbarism of a degree of contemptible nastiness unparalleled in human history. Yet for fifty years we have lynched two Negroes a week, and we have kept this up right through the war.[57]

Two years later, *Contemporary Poetry of the Negro* was published, and its editor, Robert T. Kerlin wrote, "In the poetry which the Negro is producing to-day there is a challenge to the world ... The World War, in which the Negroes gave liberally, patriotically, heroically, of their blood and treasure for democracy, quickened dying hopes and begot new aspirations."[58] Kerlin cited Joshua Henry

---

[55] Stephen Kern, *The Culture of Time and Space 1880–1918,* Harvard UP, 2003, p. 301.
[56] "For Action on Race Riot Peril," *New York Times,* 5 Oct. 1919, p. 10.
[57] W.E.B. DuBois, "Returning Soldiers," *The Crisis,* May 1919, pp. 13,14.
[58] Robert T. Kerlin, *Contemporary Poetry of the Negro,* Hampton Normal and Agricultural Institute, 1921, pp. 17–18.

Jones, Jr.'s "The Heart of the World" as one of the best literary examples of these new hopes. When Jones published his 1919 book of poetry, he footnoted the title of "The Heart of the World," explaining that the poem had been "Inspired by the speech of President Woodrow Wilson at Boston on his return from the first sittings of the peace conference in 1919."[59]

Joshua Henry Jones, Jr. graduated from Brown University in 1903. A journalist, poet, and novelist, he was also Boston's poet laureate, writing the lyrics to the city's official song, "Dear Old Boston." Jones died in Boston in 1955.

---

[59] Joshua Henry Jones, Jr., *The Heart of the World*, Stratford, 1919, p. 1.

The Dead (Les Morts…)

The widows' veils
In the wind
All blow the one way.

And the mingling tears
Of the million sorrows riverwards
All flow the one way.

Rank by rank, shoulder to shoulder
The bannerless, unhating dead,
Hair plastered down with clotted blood,
The dead all lie the one way.

In the single clay, where unendingly
The dying and the coming worlds make one,
The dead today are brothers, brow to brow,
Doing penance for the same defeat.

Oh, go clash, divided sons,
And tear Humanity asunder
Into vain tatters of land—
The dead all lie the one way;

For in the earth there remains
But one homeland and one hope,
Just as for the Universe there is
But one battle and one victory.

—René Arcos (1919), translated by Ian Higgins

Situated on the Chemin des Dames, the village of Cerny-en-Laonnois was completely destroyed during repeated battles fought there during the First World War. After the war, the site was designated a *zone rouge*, an area so environmentally damaged as to be unfit for human habitation. Where the village once stood, thousands of bodies were buried. Today, visitors find one of the most unusual cemetery configurations on the Western Front: a French and a German military cemetery adjoin one another, meeting in one corner where no fences, walls, or boundaries separate the two cities of the dead. Here is the final resting place of 5,150 French, 7,526 German, and 54 Russian soldiers. Only half of those buried at Cerny-en-Laonnois are identified; the rest lie in mass graves or ossuaries. Nearby memorials are dedicated to the 1st Loyal North Lancashire Regiment (part of the British Army known as the "Old Contemptibles") and the 38th African Infantry Division, which included troops from Morocco, Tunisia, and Algeria. Following the Second World War, a memorial chapel was privately built at the site "to further the reconciliation of people by the memory of their sons killed on opposing sides of the battlefield."[60]

French soldier and poet René Arcos was injured early in the war, but returned to the Western Front as an anti-war correspondent for the *Chicago Daily News*. A year after the war ended, he published his poetry collection *Le Sang des autres (The Blood of Others)*. In 1923, Arcos became editor-in-chief of the newly published literary magazine *Europe*. In its inaugural issue, he wrote,

> We speak of Europe because our vast peninsula, between the East and the New World, is the crossroads where civilizations meet. But it is to all peoples that we address ourselves … in the hope of helping to dispel the tragic misunderstandings that currently divide humanity … It is urgent that we learn to look higher than all the interests, the passions, and the egoisms of individuals and ethnicities. There can be no victory won by man against man.[61]

---

[60] Etienne Verkindt, "Cerny-en-Laonnois: la Chapelle-Mémorial et les cimetières français et allemande," *Le Chemin des Dames*, web.archive.org/web/20190701193235/https://www.chemindesdames.fr/fr/le-chemin-des-dames/visiter/les-lieux-de-memoire/les-principaux-sites/cerny-en-laonnois-la-chapelle.

[61] René Arcos, "Patrie Européenne," *Europe*, no. 1, Feb. 1923, pp. 110, 113 (my trans.).

Reconciliation

When all the stress and all the toil is over,
And my lover lies sleeping by your lover,
With alien earth on hands and brows and feet,
  Then we may meet.

Moving sorrowfully with uneven paces,
The bright sun shining on our ravaged faces,
There, very quietly, without sound or speech,
  Each shall greet each.

We who are bound by the same grief for ever,
When all our sons are dead may talk together,
Each asking pardon from the other one
  For her dead son.

With such low, tender words the heart may fashion,
Broken and few, of pity and compassion,
Knowing that we disturb at every tread
  Our mutual dead.

—Margaret Sackville[62] (1916)

In the aftermath of the war, women's pacifist organizations were among the strongest voices calling not merely for peace, but for reconciliation. The first international Women's Peace Congress had met in 1915 during the war. More than 1,300 women from twelve countries attended, working for women's rights and an end to the war (the convention emerged from the International Congress of Women).[63] At the war's end, the organization reformed as the Women's International League for Peace and Freedom (WILPF) and sought to counterbalance the views of those presiding over the Paris Peace Conference: "When the women of the WILPF met in Zurich in May 1919, the desire for solidarity at the women's conference was in stark contrast to the official Versailles gathering, where the German delegation was treated as beneath contempt."[64] At Versailles, German delegates were forced to accept sole responsibility for the

---

[62] See also Sackville's "A Memory."
[63] The majority of suffragists were not pacifists, but instead attempted to distance themselves from the peace movement, fearing that any association with pacifists would label them as unpatriotic and damage their efforts to earn voting privileges.
[64] Alison Fell and Ingrid Sharp, *The Women's Movement in Wartime: International Perspectives, 1914-1919*, Springer, 2007, p. 14.

war, but in Zurich, the German attendees were welcomed. At the meeting of the WILPF, those from Allied nations were shocked by the changes the war had inflicted on their sisters: "Some [German delegates] had been present four years earlier at the Hague, and the change in them was pitiful. Scarred and shrivelled by hunger and privation, they were scarcely recognizable."[65] The women of the WILPF believed it was critical to shape public attitudes as well as political policies, and in support of such efforts, German representatives urged educators "to rid their classrooms of books that celebrated war and replace them with histories of other countries," while American members pressured Congress for reductions in the armed forces and military spending.[66]

Margaret Sackville was the first president of the British Poetry Society and an early member of another pacifist organization, the Union of Democratic Control (UDC). Formed in 1914 to oppose the war, the UDC claimed 650,000 members by 1917 (including affiliations),[67] and Sackville was one of twelve women who served on the UDC's General Council. Her brother Lieutenant Gilbert Sackville was killed on December 16, 1915; Sackville wrote "Reconciliation" shortly after. The poem appeared in her 1916 collection, *The Pageant of War*, about which one reviewer said, "The bitterest recrimination in this book is not against the Prussian, but against those who deny the possibility of a permanent peace, those who of old 'poisoned Socrates' and crucified Christ."[68] In the preface to Sackville's *Selected Poems* (1919), Wilfrid Scawen Blunt writes, "Her war poems are not mere experiments in realism, but genuine laments for the pity of such things, the ugliness of rage and the waste of what is noblest."[69]

---

[65] Jill Liddington, *The Road to Greenham Common*, Syracuse UP, 1991, p. 136.

[66] Erika Kuhlman, *Reconstructing Patriarch of the Great War: Women, Gender, and Postwar Reconciliation between Nations*, Palgrave Macmillan, 2008, pp. 118–119, 124.

[67] "Union of Democratic Control (UDC)," *Encyclopedia of British and Irish Political Organizations*, edited by Peter Barberis, John McHugh, and Mike Tyldesley, A and C Black, 2000, p. 1224.

[68] "Pax Ventura," *Times Literary Supplement*, no. 748, 18 May 1916, p. 233.

[69] Wilfrid Scawen Blunt, "Preface," *Selected Poems*, by Margaret Sackville, Constable, 1919, p. vii.

Everything's looted, betrayed and traded

Everything's looted, betrayed and traded,
Black death's wing's overhead.
Everything's eaten by hunger, un-sated,
So why does a light shine ahead?

By day, a mysterious wood, near the town,
Breathes out cherry, a cherry perfume.
By night, on July's sky, deep, and transparent,
New constellations are thrown.

And something miraculous will come
Close to the darkness and ruin,
Something no-one, no-one, has known,
Though we've longed for it since we were children.

—Anna Akhmatova (1922), translated by A.S. Kline

In Russia, the monumental scale of death, famine, and disease that had accompanied three years of participation in the First World War gave rise to a national mood of despair. By 1917, the number of Russian soldiers who were injured, dead, missing, or held as prisoners of war was approaching five million men. The situation on the home front was equally bleak: over 400,000 Russian civilians were killed as a result of military action in the First World War, and another 730,000 died due to famine and disease.[70] When the Russian Revolution began on March 8, 1917, few doubted the Great War's role in the unrest that led to the eventual overthrow of Russia's monarchist government. One year later, in early March of 1918, the new Bolshevik government signed the treaty of Brest-Litovsk with the Central Powers and withdrew from the war. The terms of the treaty "dispossessed Russia of territories amounting to nearly one-quarter of the area of European Russia, and inhabited by one-third of Russia's total population."[71] Yet the end of the war in Russia did not mean peace, for the deaths of the two million soldiers killed in the First World War "was eclipsed by the nine to fourteen million fatalities over the next five years as a result of the civil war and its concomitant epidemics and famines."[72]

---

[70] Vadim Erlichman, *Poteri narodonaseleniya v XX veke* [*Population Losses in the Twentieth Century*], 2004 and "Military Casualties World War Estimated," Statistics Branch, GS, War Department, 25 Feb. 1924.
[71] Francis A. March, *History of the World War,* United Publishers, 1919, p. 456.
[72] David Reynolds, *The Long Shadow,* W.W. Norton, 2013, p. 205.

Russian poet Anna Akhmatova published "Everything's looted, betrayed and traded" in 1922. Four years earlier in January of 1918, she had spoken with her friend Boris Anrep on the eve of his departure from Russia. As they discussed the Bolshevik October Revolution of 1917, Anrep recalls, "She was excited and said we must expect more changes in our lives. The same thing's going to happen that occurred in France during the Revolution, but maybe even worse."[73] Akhmatova's decision to remain in Russia and bear witness to the cataclysmic changes would prove costly. By the end of 1921, her former husband, Nikolay Gumilyov, had been executed by the Soviets, and over the next decades, many of her friends were silenced, exiled, imprisoned, or murdered. The poem "Everything's looted, traded, betrayed," appeared in the collection *Anno Domini MCMXXI*, the last book Akhmatova published before her works were censored and banned by the Soviet government—a ban that lasted, with only a handful of limited exceptions, until the late 1950s. A 1924 review of her writing in the *London Times Literary Supplement* reported, "It has been said that the success of her poetry among the wide public was mainly due to the fact that each poem of hers is a concentrated novel—a psychological novel compressed to eight or twelve lines."[74] Joseph Brodsky, the Russian writer who was mentored by Akhmatova and later himself exiled from the country, named her "the Keening Muse," noting that many of her lyrical poems were underpinned with "the note of controlled terror."[75] In his essay remembering Akhmatova and her work, Brodsky writes, "At certain periods of history it is only poetry that is capable of dealing with reality by condensing it into something graspable, something that otherwise couldn't be retained by the mind."[76]

---

[73] Boris Anrep, qtd. in "Anna Akhmatova: The Stalin Years," by Roberta Reeder, *New England Review*, vol. 18, no. 1, 1997, pp. 108–109.
[74] "Anna Akhmatova," *Times Literary Supplement*, no. 1192, 20 Nov. 1924, p. 746.
[75] Joseph Brodsky, "The Keening Muse" in *Less than One: Selected Essays*, by Joseph Brodsky, Farrar, Straus and Giroux, 1986, p. 41.
[76] Brodsky, "The Keening Muse," p. 52.

The Other Possibility (Die andere Möglichkeit)

If we had won the war with waving
of flags and roaring, if we had,
then Germany would be past saving,
then Germany would have gone mad.

One would attempt to make us tame
like savage tribes that one might mention.
We'd leave the sidewalk if a sergeant came
and stand attention.

If we had won the war of late
we'd be in a proud and headstrong state
and press in bed in our dreams
our hands to our trouser seams.

Women must bear, each woman serves
a child a year. Or calaboose.
The state needs children as preserves,
and it swills blood like berry juice.

If we had won the war, I bet
that heaven would be national,
the clergy would wear epaulets,
God be a German general.

Trenches would take the place of borders.
No moon, insignia instead.
An emperor would issue orders.
We'd have a helmet and no head.

If we had won, then everyone
would be a soldier; the entire
land would be run by goon and gun,
and all around would be barbed wire.

On order, women would throw twins,
for men cost hardly more than stone,
and above all one cannot win
a war with guns alone.

> Then reason would be kept in fetters,
> accused and always on the spot.
> And wars would come like operettas.
> If we had won the last war—but
> we were in luck and we did not.
>
> —Erich Kästner (1930), translated by Walter Kaufmann

In his multi-volume novel *November 1918,* German author Alfred Döbler describes the return to Berlin of Germany's defeated army:

> And then came the sight that caused many in the crowd to weep. Men as well as women, moved by a feeling of humanity's common fate, remembering the long war and all the dead.
>
> Did the people see the troops? They were looking at the long war, at victories and at the defeats. Before them a piece of their own life was marching past, with wagons and horses, machine-guns and cannons.[77]

The old life was gone, never to be recovered, but perhaps nowhere was this more evident and mourned than in Germany. An estimated two million German soldiers died in the war, and Germans on the home front endured years of hunger and disease. The German national debt, which stood at 5 billion marks in 1913, had soared to 153 billion marks by the war's end.[78] Richard Bessel notes, "Post-war German governments, whatever their political complexion, faced the task not of how 'to bring culture and prosperity to the working people' but of how, in effect, to distribute poverty."[79] The Versailles Treaty assigned Germany and its allies blame for the damages caused by their war of "aggression,"[80] and in 1921, the Allies presented Germany with the bill for reparations: 132 billion gold marks. In practice the figure was adjusted to 50 billion marks over thirty-six years—still an enormous sum.[81] British economist John Maynard Keynes protested that the terms of peace were in actuality a "policy of reducing Germany to servitude for a generation" thereby causing "the decay of the whole civilised

---

[77] Alfred Döblin, qtd. in *Germany after the First World War,* by Richard Bessel, Oxford UP, 2002, p. v.
[78] Philipp Blom, *Fracture: Life and Culture in the West, 1918-1938,* Basic Books, 2015, p. 75.
[79] Bessel, *Germany after the First World War,* p. 102.
[80] Article 231 of the treaty specified: "The Allied and Associated Governments affirm and Germany accepts the responsibility of Germany and her allies for causing all the loss and damage to which the Allied and Associated Governments and their nationals have been subjected as a consequence of the war imposed upon them by the aggression of Germany and her allies."
[81] David Reynolds, *The Long Shadow: The Legacies of the Great War in the Twentieth Century,* W.W. Norton, 2014, p. 131.

life of Europe."[82] A German official labeled the reparations as "the continuation of the war by other means."[83]

Erich Kästner fought in the First World War as a young artillery gunner, an experience that shaped his pacifist views. His best-known work, the children's novel *Emil and the Detectives,* was published in 1929 and has been translated into over fifty-five languages. Kästner's satiric poem "The Other Possibility" appeared in his 1930 poetry collection *Ein Mann gibt Auskunft* (*A Man Gives Information*). Three years later, Kästner stood in Berlin's Opernplatz square and watched as a mob of over 40,000 people burned the books of fourteen undesirable authors. Karl Marx, Sigmund Freud, and Erich Maria Remarque were among the banned authors—as was Kästner himself, who had chosen not to flee Germany, but to remain and chronicle events. During the Second World War, he was refused admission to the compulsory Nazi writers' association and interrogated several times by the Gestapo. His career never recovered from the self-censorship required for his personal survival. Shortly before Kästner's death in 1974, his friend Marcel Reich-Ranicki described him as "Germany's most hopeful pessimist," writing that "he belonged to the moralists who are at the same time jesters."[84]

---

[82] John Maynard Keynes, *Economic Consequences of the Peace,* Macmillan, 1919, p. 209.
[83] Reynolds, *The Long Shadow,* p. 133.
[84] Marcel Reich-Ranicki, "The Poet of Little Freedom: An Essay about Erich Kästner from 1974," *Literaturkritik.de*, no. 8, Aug. 2014, web.archive.org/web/20190920195813/https://literaturkritik.de/id/19563.

High Wood[85]

"Ladies and gentlemen, this is High Wood,
Called by the French, Bois des Fourneaux.
The famous spot which in Nineteen Sixteen,
July, August, September, was the scene
Of long and bitterly contested strife,
By reason of its high commanding site.
Observe the effect of shell-fire on the trees
Standing and fallen; here is wire; this trench,
For months inhabited, twelve times changed hands;
(They soon fall in), used later as a grave.
It has been said on good authority
That in the fighting for this patch of wood
Were killed somewhere about eight thousand men,
Of whom the greater part were buried here,
This mound on which you stand being...
                              Madame, please.
You are requested kindly not to touch
Or take away the Comp'ny's property
As souvenirs: you'll find we have on sale
A large variety, all guaranteed.
As I was saying, all is as it was,
This is an unknown British officer;
The tunic having lately rotted off.
Please follow me—this way... the *path* sir, *please*,
The ground which was secured at great expense
The company keeps absolutely untouched,
And in that dug-out (genuine) we provide
Refreshments at a reasonable rate.
You are requested not to leave about
Paper or ginger-beer bottles, or orange-peel,
There are waste-paper baskets at the gate."

— John Stanley Purvis / Philip Johnston (1918)

Covering an area approximately one-tenth of a square mile (or about seventy-five acres), High Wood saw some of the fiercest fighting of the Somme. Over

---

[85] The poem as it appears here was first published in *The Nation* (1918) without a title. The title used here was given the poem in its first book publication: Guy Chapman's *Vain Glory* (1937).

8,000 British and German men were killed in attacks on the wood between July and September of 1916. Nearly two decades later, Lieutenant Colonel Graham Hutchinson, who had commanded the 33rd Battalion Machine Gun Corps in the bloody struggle for the area, visited the site. He writes, "Passing through High Wood in August, 1934, I found trunks of trees, one of them at the eastern corner, so familiar, standing, pitted with shrapnel and machine-gun bullets. And everywhere throughout the Wood, scarcely concealed by undergrowth, were steel helmets, rifle barrels, quantities of bombs, boots, and the remains of all kinds of equipment."[86]

In the years immediately following the Armistice, hundreds of thousands had "rushed to the scene of war," and by January of 1920, Michelin had published 850,000 copies of battlefield guidebooks.[87] For visitors to battlefields and cemeteries,

> The meaning of the visit ultimately depended upon the travellers' memory of wartime experiences, whether these occurred at the front, were experiences of bereavement, or centred on his or her imagined vision of the war. These journeys were not passive activities. Tourists and pilgrims assumed that at particular places and moments it was possible to renew, recreate or capture something of the war and the experiences which defined it.[88]

Others believed that tours of the war zones attracted ghoulish souvenir hunters and trivialized the conflict. A 1927 article in the *Ypres Times* lamented,

> In they come with a rattle and a clatter through the Menin Gate, all packed together in huge char-à-bancs, and after a raucous voiced guide has pointed out the very obvious Cloth Hall ruins, they are whirled away again to one of the show places, perhaps Hill 60, and when they get back home they think they have seen Ypres and the Salient, and perhaps begin to wonder what all the fuss was about.[89]

Thanatourism examines the entangled ethics and economics of "dark tourism" sites, asking, "Is it possible that some death sites have become the locations (or, even, excuses) for service industries supplying conveniently-spaced watering-holes, lavatories and retail outlets designed to intervene in the journeys made by visitors through our heritages and landscapes"?[90] Today, High Wood is privately

---

[86] Graham Seton Hutchinson, *Pilgrimage*, Rich and Cowan, 1935, p. 58.
[87] David W. Lloyd, *Battlefield Tourism: Pilgrimage and the Commemoration of the Great War in Britain, Australia and Canada, 1919–1939*, Berg, 1998, pp. 29, 103.
[88] Lloyd, *Battlefield Tourism*, p. 1.
[89] E.F. Williams, "Ypres Calling," *Ypres Times*, Apr. 1927, qtd in *Battlefield Tourism*, p. 42.
[90] Malcolm Foley and John Lennon, *Dark Tourism: The Attraction of Death and Disaster*, Cengage, 2000, p. 5.

owned and forbidden to visitors; it has never been fully cleared of unexploded munitions nor the bodies of the thousands of men who died and were buried there.

The *Nation* published "High Wood" in February of 1918 as an untitled poem attributed to "Philip Johnston (B.E.F.)"; the poem was reprinted in *Reedy's Mirror* the following month, titled "Personally Conducted" and also attributed to Johnston. The first book to publish the poem appears to be Guy Chapman's *Vain Glory* (1937), a collection of first-hand accounts of the war. Chapman titled the poem "High Wood," altered its punctuation and wording, and changed the spelling of the author's name to "Johnstone." In 1968, after the death of John Stanley Purvis, his sister wrote to an admirer of Philip Johnston's poetry and revealed that Purvis's war poetry had been published under that pseudonym.[91] In 2009, Miss Purvis's claim of her brother's identity as Philip Johnston/Johnstone was confirmed when a war-time notebook was discovered in the Borthwick Institute's papers of John Stanley Purvis. Purvis's war-time journal contains handwritten poems, among them "High Wood," which he titled in his notebook "The Tourist's Complete Guide to the Battlefields, High Wood" and dated "Humbercamp, 2-6-17." Lieutenant Purvis wrote "High Wood" over one year before the war ended, anticipating the aftermath.

John Stanley Purvis fought with the 5th Battalion Yorkshire Regiment (Green Howards) at the Somme and was wounded on September 15, 1916, in the final attack on High Wood. Wylly's regimental history of the Green Howards reports that by the time the 5th Battalion was relieved on September 19, 4 officers and 48 men of other ranks had been killed; 11 officers and 162 others had been wounded, and 27 men were missing (a total of 252 casualties).[92] Less than a year later, Purvis's younger brother, Captain George Bell Purvis, was killed near Ypres on June 8, 1917. Purvis survived the war and resumed his job as a history teacher at Cranleigh School in Surrey. He was ordained in 1933 and returned to his native Yorkshire, where he was appointed as the Archivist to the Archbishop and Diocese of York in 1939, later becoming the Canon of York Minister. He is best known for his translation of the York Mystery Plays.

---

[91] Ernest Raymond, *Good Morning, Good People,* Cassell, 1970, pp. 46–47.
[92] H.C. Wylly, *The Green Howards in the Great War,* Green Howards, 1926, p. 156.

Envoie[93]

How shall I say good-bye to you, wonderful, terrible days,
If I should live to live and leave 'neath an alien soil
You, my men, who taught me to walk with a smile in the ways
Of the valley of shadows, taught me to know you and love you, and toil
Glad in the glory of fellowship, happy in misery, strong
In the strength that laughs at its weakness, laughs at its sorrows and fears,
Facing the world that was not too kind with a jest and a song?
What can the world hold afterwards worthy of laughter or tears?
—Edward de Stein (1919)

---

[93] From the French, *a sending forth,* specifically, *the action of sending forth a poem, the concluding part of a poetical composition.*

Primary Sources

A.E. (George William Russell). "To the Memory of Some I Knew Who Are Dead and Who Loved Ireland." *Irish Times*, 19 Dec. 1917, p. 6.

Akhmatova, Anna. *Anno Domini MCMXXI*. Petropolis, 1922.

Akhmatova, Anna. "Everything's looted, betrayed and traded." Translated by A.S. Kline. *Poets of Modernity: Anna Akhmatova*, web.archive.org/web/20191113221451/https://www.poetsofmodernity.xyz/POMBR/Russian/Akhmatova.php.

Alchin, Gordon (*see also* Observer, R.F.C.). *Oxford and Flanders*. B.H. Blackwell, 1916.

Allen, Hervey. *Toward the Flame*. George H. Doran, 1926.

Allen, Hervey. *Wampum and Old Gold*. Yale UP, 1921.

Allen, Marian. *The Wind on the Downs*. Arthur L. Humphreys, 1918.

Angus, Marion. *The Lilt and Other Verses*. D. Wyllie and Sons, 1922.

Apollinaire, Guillaume. *Selected Poems*. Translated by Martin Sorrell. Oxford UP, 2015.

Apollinaire, Guillaume. *Tendre comme le souvenir*. Gallimard, 1952.

Arcos, René. *Le Sang des autres: Poèmes: 1914–1917*. A. Kundig, 1919.

Arcos, René. "The Dead." *French Poems of the Great War*, edited and translated by Ian Higgins, Saxon Books, 2016, pp. 148–149.

Ball, Hugo. "Dance of Death, 1916." Translated by Edmund Potts, *The Project: A Socialist Journal*, web.archive.org/web/20191107154912/http://www.socialistproject.org/international/into-the-dance-of-death-german-artistic-and-cultural-responses-to-the-first-world-war/.

Ball, Hugo. "Totentanz 1916." *Der Revoluzzer*, vol. 2, no. 1, Jan. 1916.

Baukhage, Hilmar R. and C. Leroy Baldridge. *I Was There with the Yanks on the Western Front 1917–1919*. G.P. Putnam's Sons, 1919.

Békássy, Ferenc. *Adriatica and Other Poems*. Hogarth, 1925.

Benemann, Maria Dobler. "Visé (After a Letter from the Field)." *Lines of Fire: Women Writers of World War I*, edited and translated by Margaret R. Higonnet, Plume, 1999, pp. 484–485.

Benemann, Maria Dobler. *Wandlungen*. Verlag der Weissen Bücher, 1915.

Bodenheim, Maxwell. "The Camp Follower." *Poetry*, vol. 5, no. 2, Nov. 1914, p. 65.

Borden, Mary. *The Forbidden Zone*. William Heinemann, 1929.

Brittain, Vera. *Chronicle of Youth: The War Diary 1913–1917*, edited by Alan Bishop with Terry Smart, William Morrow, 1982.

Brittain, Vera. *Testament of Youth*. 1933. Virago, 2014.

Brittain, Vera. *Verses of a V.A.D.* Erskine Macdonald, 1918.

Brooke, Rupert. *The Collected Poems of Rupert Brooke: With a Memoir*. Sidgwick and Jackson, 1918.

Calloc'h, Jean-Pierre (*see also* Kalloc'h, Yann-Ber). *A Genoux: Lais Bretons* [*Ar en deulin*]. French translation by Pierre Mocaër, Plon Nourrit et Cie, 1921.

Calloc'h, Jean-Pierre (*see also* Kalloc'h, Yann-Ber). "Veni, Sancte Spiritus!" *French Poems of the Great War*, edited and translated by Ian Higgins, Saxon Books, 2016, pp. 40–45.

Cammaerts, Émile. *Belgian Poems: Chants Patriotiques et Autres Poèmes par Émile Cammaerts*. Translated by Tita Brand-Cammaerts, John Lane, 1915.

Campbell, Ivar. *Poems*. A.L. Humphreys, 1917.

Cannan, May Wedderburn. *Grey Ghosts and Voices*. Roundwood, 1976.

Cannan, May Wedderburn. *In War Time*. Blackwell, 1917.

Cannan, May Wedderburn. *The Splendid Days*. Blackwell, 1919.

Colbron, Grace Isabel. "The Ballad of Bethlehem Steel." *The Public: A Journal of Democracy*, vol. 18, 10 Dec. 1915, pp. 1198–1199.

Cole, Margaret Postgate. *Growing Up into Revolution*. Longmans, Green, 1949.

Cole, Margaret Postgate (*see also* Margaret Postgate). *Margaret Postgate's Poems*. George Allen and Unwin, 1918.

Corbin, Alice. "Litany in the Desert." *War Poems from the Yale Review*, Yale UP, 1918, pp. 43–44.

Cornford, Frances. *Collected Poems*. Cresset, 1954.

Cornford, Frances. *Different Days*. Hogarth, 1928.

Cotter, Joseph S., Jr. *The Band of Gideon and Other Lyrics*. Cornhill, 1918.

Coulson, Leslie. *From an Outpost and Other Poems*. Erskine Macdonald, 1917.

Cromwell, Gladys. *Poems*. Macmillan, 1919.

de Noailles, Anna. *Les Forces éternelles*. Arthème Fayard, 1920.

de Noailles, Anna. "'Victory, whose calm gaze …'" *French Poems of the Great War*, edited and translated by Ian Higgins, Saxon Books, 2016, p. 168.

de Stein, Edward. *The Poets in Picardy*. John Murray, 1919.

Delarue-Mardrus, Lucie. "Regiments." *French Poems of the Great War*, edited and translated by Ian Higgins, Saxon Books, 2016, p. 47.

Delarue-Mardrus, Lucie. *Souffles de Tempête*. Eugène Fasquelle, 1918.

Dobell, Eva. *Bunch of Cotswold Grasses*. Arthur H. Stockwell, 1919.

Down, Oliphant. *Poems*. Gowans and Gray, 1921.

Dunbar-Nelson, Alice. "I Sit and Sew." *The Dunbar Speaker and Entertainer*, edited by Alice Moore Dunbar-Nelson, J.L. Nichols, 1920, p. 145.

Dyment, Clifford. *The Railway Game: An Early Autobiography*, J.M. Dent, 1962.

Dyment, Clifford. *Straight or Curly?* J.M. Dent, 1937.

Eassie, Robert M. *Odes to Trifles and Other Rhymes*. John Lane, 1917.

Europe, James Reese, Noble Sissle and Eubie Blake. "On Patrol in No Man's Land." M. Witmark and Sons, 1919. Sheet music.

Ford, Ford Madox (Ford Madox Hueffer). *On Heaven, and Poems Written on Active Service*. John Lane, 1918.

Frankau, Gilbert. *The City of Fear and Other Poems*. Chatto and Windus, 1917.

Fullerton, Mary E. *The Breaking Furrow*. Sydney J. Endacott, 1921.
Garnier, Noël. *Le Don de ma Mére*. Ernest Flammarion, 1920.
Garnier, Noël. "Still Raining …" *French Poems of the Great War*, edited and translated by Ian Higgins, Saxon Books, 2016, p. 120.
Gellert, Leon. *Songs of a Campaign*. Angus and Robertson, 1917.
Gibson, Wilfrid Wilson. *Battle*. Elkin Mathews, 1915.
Gibson, Wilfrid Wilson. *Friends*. Elkin Mathews, 1916.
Gilbert, Bernard. *Gone to the War and Other Poems*. J.W. Ruddock, 1915.
Gilbert, Bernard. *War Workers and Other Verses*. Erskine Macdonald, 1916.
Gillespie, Violet. "Portrait of a Mother." *Poetry Review*, vol. 9, no. 2, Mar./Apr. 1918, p. 112.
Gilmore, Mary. *The Passionate Heart*. Angus and Robertson, 1918.
Gilmore, Mary. *Under the Wilgas*. Robertson and Mullens, 1932.
Granier, Albert-Paul. *Cockerels and Vultures*. Translated by Ian Higgins, Saxon Books, 2014.
Granier, Albert-Paul. *Les Coqs et les Vautours*. 1917. Des Equateurs, 2008.
Grenfell, William. "To John." *The Muse in Arms*, edited by E.B. Osborn, John Murray, 1917, p. 139.
Guiterman, Arthur. *Song and Laughter*, E.P. Dutton, 1929.
Harrison, Ada M. "New Year, 1916." *Cambridge Poets 1914–1920*, edited by Edward Davison, Heffer, 1920, p. 106.
Harvey, Frederick William. *A Gloucestershire Lad at Home and Abroad*. Sidgwick and Jackson, 1916.
Herbert, A.P. *The Bomber Gipsy and Other Poems*. Methuen, 1918.
Herbert, A.P. *Half-Hours at Helles*. Blackwell, 1916.
Herbert, A.P. *The Secret Battle*. Methuen, 1919.
Hodgson, William Noel. *Verse and Prose in Peace and War*. Smith, Elder, 1916.
Hogan, Francis F. "Fulfilled." *Carnegie Tech War Verse*, edited by Haniel Long, Carnegie Institute of Technology, 1918, p. 21.
Holmes, W. Kersley. *Ballads of Field and Billet*. Alexander Gardner, 1915.
Holmes, W. Kersley. *More Ballads of Field and Billet*. Alexander Gardner, 1915.
"Home Is Where the Pie Is." *Yanks: A.E.F. Verse*. G.P. Putnam's Sons, 1919, pp. 14–15.
Horne, Cyril Morton. *Songs of the Shrapnel Shell, and Other Verse*. Harper and Brothers, 1916.
H.S.S. (Hugh Stewart Smith). *Verses*. [publisher not identified], [1916?].
Hueffer, Ford Madox (*see also* Ford Madox Ford). *On Heaven, and Poems Written on Active Service*. John Lane, 1918.
Johnston, Philip (John Stanley Purvis). "High Wood" [originally untitled]. *The Nation*, vol. 22, no. 20, 16 Feb. 1918, p. 618.
Jones, Joshua Henry, Jr. *The Heart of the World*. Stratford, 1919.
Kalloc'h, Yann-Ber (*see also* Jean-Pierre Calloc'h). *A Genoux: Lais Bretons* [*Ar en deulin*]. French translation by Pierre Mocaër, Plon Nourrit et Cie, 1921.

Kalloc'h, Yann-Ber (*see also* Jean-Pierre Calloc'h). "Veni, Sancte Spiritus!" *French Poems of the Great War*, edited and translated by Ian Higgins, Saxon Books, 2016, pp. 40–45.
Kästner, Erich. *Ein Mann gibt Auskunft*. Deutsche Verlags-Anstalt, 1930.
Kästner, Erich. "The Other Possibility." *Twenty-five German Poets*, edited and translated by Walter Kaufmann, W.W. Norton, 1975, p. 291.
Keown, Anna Gordon. "Reported Missing." *Poetry Review*, vol. 8, no. 6, Nov. 1917, p. 343.
Kettle, T.M. *Poems and Parodies*. Talbot, 1916.
Kitchin, C.H.B. *Curtains*. Blackwell, 1919.
Klemm, Wilhelm. "At the Front." *The German Poets of the First World War*, edited and translated by Patrick Bridgwater, St. Martin's, 1985, p. 180.
Klemm, Wilhelm, *Gloria! Kriegsgedichte aus dem Feld*. Albert Langen, 1915.
Ledwidge, Francis. *Last Songs*. Herbert Jenkins, 1918.
Ledwidge, Francis. *Songs of Peace*. Herbert Jenkins, 1917.
Lee, Joseph. *Ballads of Battle*. John Murray, 1916.
Lee, Joseph. *A Captive at Carlsruhe*. John Lane, 1920.
Lee, Joseph. *Work-a-Day Warriors*. John Murray, 1917.
Leighton, Roland. "Violets—April 1915." *First World War Poetry Digital Archive*, web.archive.org/web/20190808172627/http://www.oucs.ox.ac.uk/ww1lit/collections/document/5653/5619.
Leighton, Roland. "Violets from Plug Street Wood." *Boy of My Heart*, Hodder and Stoughton, 1916, p. 66.
Letts, Winifred M. *Hallow-e'en and Poems of the War*. John Murray, 1916.
Lichtenstein, Alfred. *Gedichte und Geschichten*. Edited by Kurt Lubasch, Georg Müller, 1919.
Lichtenstein, Alfred. *The Prose and Verse of Alfred Lichtenstein*. Translated by Sheldon Gilman, Robert Levine, and Harry Radford, Xlibris, 2000.
Lissauer, Ernst. "A Chant of Hate against England." Translated by Barbara Henderson. *New York Times*, 15 Oct. 1914, p.12.
Lissauer, Ernst. "Hassgesang gegen England." *Worte in die Ziet: Flugblätter 1914 von Ernst Lissauer*, vol. 1, Otto Hapke, 1914, pp. 1–2.
Lowell, Amy. *Pictures of the Floating World*. Macmillan, 1919.
M.G. "Camouflage." *Yanks: A.E.F. Verse*. G.P. Putnam's Sons, 1919, pp. 52–53.
Macaulay, Rose. *Non-combatants and Others*. 1916. Methuen, 1986.
Macaulay, Rose. *Three Days*. Constable, 1919.
Macdonald, Mary-Adair. *From a V.A.D. Hospital: Three Poems*. W. Speaight and Sons, 1917.
MacGill, Patrick. *The Great Push*. Herbert Jenkins, 1916.
MacGill, Patrick. *Soldier Songs*. Herbert Jenkins, 1917.
Mackay, Helen. *Journal of Small Things*. Duffield, 1917.
Mackay, Helen. *London, One November*. Duffield, 1916.

Mackintosh, Ewart Alan. *A Highland Regiment*. John Lane, 1917.
Mackintosh, Ewart Alan. *War the Liberator*. John Lane, 1918.
Manning, Frederic. *Eidola*. John Murray, 1917.
Manning, Frederic. *The Middle Parts of Fortune*. Piazza, 1929. Penguin, 1990.
Mansfield, Katherine. *Poems*. Constable, 1923.
Masefield, John. "August 1914." *English Review*, Sept. 1914, pp. 145–147.
Masefield, John. *John Masefield's Letters from the Front, 1915–1917*, edited by Peter Vansittart, F. Watts, 1985.
Masefield, John. "Red Cross." *The Queen's Book of the Red Cross*. Hodder and Stoughton, 1939, p. 29.
Mew, Charlotte. *The Rambling Sailor*, Poetry Bookshop, 1929.
Mitchell, Ruth Comfort. *The Night Court and Other Verses*. Century, 1916.
Murray, Charles. *A Sough O'War*. Constable, 1917.
Naidu, Sarojini. *The Broken Wing: Songs of Love, Death, and Destiny, 1915–1916*. John Lane, 1917.
Nesbit, Edith, editor. *Battle Songs*. Max Goschen, 1914.
Nesbit, Edith. *Many Voices*. Hutchinson, 1922.
Newbolt, Henry. *Admirals All and Other Verses*. Elkin Matthews, 1897.
Newbolt, Henry. *St. George's Day and Other Poems*. John Murray, 1918.
Observer, R.F.C. (Gordon Alchin). *Oxford and Flanders*. B.H. Blackwell, 1916.
Oman, Carola. *The Menin Road and Other Poems*. Hodder and Stoughton, 1919.
Oxenham, John. *The Vision Splendid*. Methuen and Company, 1917.
Parker, Dorothy. "The Lovely Leave." *The Portable Dorothy Parker*, Viking, 1944, pp. 21–40.
Parker, Dorothy. *Sunset Gun*, Boni and Liveright, 1928.
Parker, Harry L. "Left Behind." *The Stars and Stripes*, 14 Mar. 1919, p. 4.
Péret, Benjamin. *Je ne mange pas de ce pain-là*. Editions Surréalistes, 1936.
Péret, Benjamin. "Little Song of the Maimed." *Collected Verse Translations*, by David Gascoyne, edited by Alan Clodd and Robin Skelton, Oxford UP, 1970, p. 61.
Philipps, Colwyn. *Colwyn Erasmus Arnold Philipps*. Smith, Elder, 1915.
Pigott, E.W. "Saturdays." *Poems from Punch 1909–1920*, Macmillan, 1922, pp. 234–235.
Pope, Jessie. *Jessie Pope's War Poems*. Grant Richards, 1915.
Postgate, Margaret (Margaret Postgate Cole). *Margaret Postgate's Poems*. George Allen and Unwin, 1918.
Purvis, John Stanley (*see also* Philip Johnston). "High Wood" [originally untitled]. *The Nation*, vol. 22, no. 20, 16 Feb. 1918, p. 618.
Rags. "The Mascot Speaks." *The Stars and Stripes*, 21 Mar. 1919, p. 4.
Rawnsley, Hardwicke Drummond. "Going to the Front." *A Treasury of War Poetry: British and American Poems of the World War, 1914–1919*, 2nd series, edited by George Herbert Clarke, Houghton Mifflin, 1919, p. 137.
Read, Herbert. *The Cult of Sincerity*. Faber and Faber, 1968.
Read, Herbert. *Naked Warriors*. Art and Letters, 1919.

Rhys, Ernest. *The Leaf Burners and Other Poems*. J.M Dent, 1918.

Rickword, Edgell. *Behind the Eyes*. Sidgwick and Jackson, 1921.

Rickword, Edgell. "War and Poetry: 1914–1918 (1940)." *Edgell Rickword: Literature in Society*, edited by Alan Young, Carcanet, 1978, pp. 137–156.

Roberts, Charles G.D. *New Poems*. Constable and Company, 1919.

Rostand, Edmond. "Burning Beehives." *French Poems of the Great War*, edited and translated by Ian Higgins, Saxon Books, 2016, pp. 20–23.

Rostand, Edmond. *Le Vol de la Marseillaise*. Charpentier et Fasquelle, 1919.

Russell, George William (*see also* A.E.). "To the Memory of Some I Knew Who Are Dead and Who Loved Ireland." *Irish Times*, 19 Dec. 1917, p. 6.

Sackville, Margaret. *The Pageant of War*. Simpkin, Marshall, Hamilton, Kent, [1916].

Sandford, J. Egbert. *Brookdown and Other Poems*. 2nd ed., Erskine Macdonald, 1916.

Sauvage, Marcel. *Quelques choses*. Édition de La Veilleuse, 1919.

Sauvage, Marcel. "Recall-Up." *French Poems of the Great War*, edited and translated by Ian Higgins, Saxon Books, 2016, p. 169.

Schnack, Anton. "Standing To." *The German Poets of the First World War*, edited and translated by Patrick Bridgwater, St. Martin's, 1985, pp. 189–190.

Schnack, Anton. *Tier rang gewaltig mit Tier*. E. Rowohlt, 1920.

Service, Robert W. *Rhymes of a Red Cross Man*. Barse and Hopkins, 1916.

Shaw-Stewart, Patrick. "I Saw a Man This Morning." *Patrick Shaw-Stewart*, by Ronald Knox, William Collins, 1920, pp. 159–160.

Shove, Fredegond. *Dreams and Journeys*. Blackwell, 1918.

Simpson, Henry Lamont. *Moods and Tenses*. Erskine Macdonald, 1919.

Sinclair, May. *A Journal of Impressions in Belgium*. Hutchinson, 1915.

Sinclair, May. "After the Retreat." *The Egoist*, vol. 2, no. 5, 1 May 1915, p. 77.

Siordet, Gerald Caldwell. *Gerald Caldwell Siordet*. [Privately printed], [1918?].

Smith, Geoffrey Bache. *A Spring Harvest*. Erskine Macdonald, 1918.

Smith, Gertrude. "America at War." *Poets of the Future: A College Anthology for 1916–1917*, edited by Henry T. Schnittkind, Stratford, 1917, p. 154.

Smith, Hugh Stewart. "On the Plains of Picardy." *A Deep Cry*, edited by Anne Powell, Palladour Books, 1993, pp. 119–120.

Smith, Hugh Stewart (*see also* H.S.S.). *Verses*. [publisher not identified], [1916?].

Squire, J.C. *Poems: First Series*. Martin Secker, 1918.

Squire, J.C. *Poems: Second Series*. Hodder and Stoughton, 1922.

Stables, J. Howard. *The Sorrow That Whistled*. Elkin Mathews, 1916.

Stokes, Rose Pastor (*see also* Zelda). "To the Patriotic Lady across the Way." *The New York Call*, 20 Nov. 1917, p. 8.

Studdert Kennedy, Geoffrey. *The Hardest Part*. Hodder and Stoughton, 1919.

Studdert Kennedy, Geoffrey. *More Rough Rhymes of a Padre*. Hodder and Stoughton, 1920.

Trakl, Georg. *Die Dichtungen*. Kurt Wolff, 1917.

Trakl, Georg. "Eastern Front." *Georg Trakl: A Profile*, edited by Frank Graniano and translated by Christopher Middleton, Logbridge-Rhodes, 1983, p. 69.

Trent, K.L. "A Digger's Disillusion." *New Zealand at the Front*. Cassell, 1918, pp. 112–113.
Trotter, Bernard Freeman. *A Canadian Twilight and Other Poems of War and of Peace*. McClelland, Goodchild and Stewart, 1917.
Tsvetaeva, Marina. "I know the truth! Renounce all others!" Translated by A.S. Kline, *Marina Tsvetaeva: Twenty-Four Poems*, www.poetryintranslation.com/PITBR/Russian/Tsvetaeva.php#anchor_Toc254018896.
Tsvetaeva, Marina. *Neizdannoye: Stikhi, teatr, proza* (*Unpublished Works: Poetry, Drama, Prose*). Paris, YMCA Publishers, 1976, p. 85.
Tynan, Katharine. *Herb o' Grace: Poems in War-Time*. Sidgwick and Jackson, 1918.
Underhill, Evelyn. *Theophanies: A Book of Verses*. J.M. Dent, 1916.
Ungaretti, Giuseppe. *Il porto sepolto*. Stabilmento Tipografico Friulano, 1916.
Ungaretti, Giuseppe. "Vigil." *Stand*, translated by Jonathan Griffin, vol. 11, no. 4, 1970, p. 60.
van Beek, Theodore. "After the 'Offensive.'" *English Review*, Apr. 1919, pp. 276–277.
Vernède, Robert Ernest. *Letters to His Wife*. W. Collins Sons, 1917.
Vernède, Robert Ernest. *War Poems and Other Verses*. William Heinemann, 1917.
Waterhouse, Gilbert. *Rail-head and Other Poems*. Erskine Macdonald, 1916.
Waugh, Alec. *Resentment*. Grant Richards, 1918.
West, Arthur Graeme. *The Diary of a Dead Officer*. George Allen and Unwin, [1918?].
White, Donald S. "The Boys Who Live in the Ground." *Songs from the Trenches: The Soul of the A.E.F*, edited by Herbert Adams Gibbons, Harper and Brothers, 1918, pp. 175–176.
Wickersham, J. Hunter. "The Raindrops on Your Old Tin Hat." *American Legion Weekly*, vol. 2, no. 33, 10 Sept. 1920, p. 3.
Widdemer, Margaret. *The Old Road to Paradise*. Henry Holt, 1918.
Wilson, T.P. Cameron. *Magpies in Picardy*. The Poetry Bookshop, 1919.
Wilson, T.P. Cameron. *Waste Paper Philosophy, to Which Has Been Added Magpies in Picardy*. George H. Doran, 1920.
Wyeth, John Allan. *This Man's Army: A War in Fifty-Odd Sonnets*. 1929. U of South Carolina P, 2008.
Wyn, Hedd. *Cerddi'r Bugail*. William Lewis, 1918.
Wyn, Hedd. "War." Translated by Gillian Clarke. *Ten Poems from Wales: Fourteen Centuries of Verse*, edited by Gillian Clarke, Candlestick, 2013, p. 7.
Zelda (Rose Pastor Stokes). "To the Patriotic Lady across the Way." *The New York Call*, 20 Nov. 1917, p. 8.

Further Reading

Adcock, A. St. John. *For Remembrance: Soldier Poets Who Have Fallen in the War*, rev. and expanded ed. Hodder and Stoughton, 1920.
Andrews, Clarence Edward, editor. *From the Front: Trench Poetry*. D. Appleton, 1918.
Bagshaw, F.B., R.M. Eassie and W.M. Scanlon, editors. *A Christmas Garland from the Front*. George Pulman and Sons, 1915.
Brereton, Frederick, editor. *An Anthology of War Poems*. Collins, 1930.
Bridgwater, Patrick. *The German Poets of the First World War*. St. Martin's, 1985.
Buddies: A Sequel to Yanks: A Book of Verse. Eastern Supply Company, 1921.
Buelens, Geert. *Everything to Nothing: The Poetry of the Great War, Revolution and the Transformation of Europe*. Verso, 2015.
Chapman, Guy, editor. *Vain Glory: A Miscellany of the Great War 1914–1918*. Cassell, 1937.
Clarke, George Herbert, editor. *A Treasury of War Poetry*. Houghton Mifflin, 1917.
Clarke, George Herbert, editor. *A Treasury of War Poetry*, 2nd series. Houghton Mifflin, 1919.
Cornebise, Alfred E., editor. *Doughboy Doggerel: Verse of the American Expeditionary Force 1918–1919*. Ohio UP, 1985.
Cross, Tim, editor. *The Lost Voices of World War I: An International Anthology of Writers, Poets and Playwrights*. Bloomsbury, 1988.
Cunliffe, J.W., editor. *Poems of the Great War*. Macmillan, 1916.
Das, Santanu, editor. *The Cambridge Companion to the Poetry of the First World War*. Cambridge UP, 2013.
Davison, Edward, editor. *Cambridge Poets 1914–1920*. Heffer, 1920.
Eaton, W. D., editor. *Great Poems of the World War*. T.S. Denison, 1922.
Edwards, Mabel C. and Mary Booth, editors. *The Fiery Cross: An Anthology*. Grant Richards, 1915.
Foxcroft, Frank, editor. *War Verse*. Thomas Y. Crowell, 1918.
Fussell, Paul. *The Great War and Modern Memory*. 1975. Oxford UP, 2000.
Gardner, Brian, editor. *Up the Line to Death: The War Poets 1914–1918*. Methuen, 1964.
Gibbons, Herbert Adams, editor. *Songs from the Trenches: The Soul of the A.E.F.* Harper and Brothers, 1918.
Goldie, David and Roderick Watson, editors. *From the Line: Scottish War Poetry 1914–1945*. Glasgow Association for Scottish Literary Studies, 2014.
Hibberd, Dominic and John Onions, editors. *Poetry of the Great War: An Anthology*. Macmillan, 1986.

Hibberd, Dominic and John Onions, editors. *The Winter of the World: Poems of the First World War*. Constable, 2007.

Higgins, Ian, editor and translator. *French Poems of the Great War*. Saxon Books, 2016.

Higonnet, Margaret R., editor and translator. *Lines of Fire: Women Writers of World War I*, Plume, 1999.

Holman, Carrie Ellen, editor. *In the Day of Battle: Poems of the Great War*. William Briggs, 1916.

Hynes, Samuel. *A War Imagined: The First World War and English Culture*. Atheneum, 1990.

Kendall, Tim, editor. *Oxford Handbook of British and Irish War Poetry*. Oxford UP, 2007.

Kendall, Tim, editor. *Poetry of the First World War: An Anthology*. Oxford UP, 2014.

Khan, Nosheen. *Women's Poetry of the First World War*. UP of Kentucky, 1988.

Leonard, Sterling Andrus, editor. *Poems of the War and the Peace*. Harcourt, Brace, 1921.

Lewis-Stempel, John. *Where Poppies Blow*. Weidenfeld and Nicolson, 2016.

Lloyd, Bertram, editor. *The Paths of Glory: A Collection of Poems Written during the War*. Allen and Unwin, 1919.

Lloyd, Bertram, editor. *Poems Written during the Great War, 1914–1918*. Allen and Unwin, 1918.

Long, Haniel, editor. *Carnegie Tech War Verse*. Carnegie Institute of Technology, 1918.

Moore, T. Sturge, editor. *Some Soldier Poets*. Grant Richards, 1919.

Newman, Vivien, editor. *Tumult and Tears: The Story of the Great War through the Eyes and Lives of Its Women Poets*. Pen and Sword, 2016.

Nichols, Robert, editor. *Anthology of War Poetry, 1914–1918*. Nicholson and Watson, 1943.

Noakes, Vivien, editor. *Voices of Silence: The Alternative Book of First World War Poetry*. Sutton, 2006.

O'Prey, Paul, editor. *Counter-Wave: Poetry of Rescue in the First World War*. Dare-Gale, 2018.

Osborn, E.B., editor. *The Muse in Arms: A Collection of War Poems*. John Murray, 1917.

Parsons, I.M., editor. *Men Who March Away: Poems of the First World War*. Chatto and Windus, 1965.

Powell, Anne, editor. *A Deep Cry: A Literary Pilgrimage to the Battlefields and Cemeteries of First World War British Soldier-Poets Killed in Northern France and Flanders*. Palladour, 1993.

Reilly, Catherine W. *English Poetry of the First World War: A Bibliography*. George Prior, 1978.

Reilly, Catherine W., editor. *Scars upon My Heart: Women's Poetry and Verse of the First World War*. Virago, 1981.

Roberts, David, editor. *We Are the Dead: Poems and Paintings from the Great War, 1914–1918*. Red Horse, 2012.

Roussel, Anna Whittaker, editor. *Cease Firing: Fifty Poems of the New Peace*. John C. Winston Company, 1930.
Scott, Emmett J. *Scott's Official History of the American Negro in the World War*, Homewood, 1919.
Silkin, Jon, editor. *The Penguin Book of First World War Poetry*. 2nd ed., Penguin, 1979.
Stallworthy, Jon, editor. *Anthem for Doomed Youth: Twelve Soldier Poets of the First World War*. Constable, 2002.
Stephen, Martin, editor. *Never Such Innocence: A New Anthology of Great War Verse*. Buchan and Enright, 1988.
Stout, Earl Jonathan, editor. *Daybreak of Peace: A Collection of Appropriate Verse for Use in the Observance of Armistice Day*. F.A. Owen, 1926.
Taylor, Martin, editor. *Lads: Love Poetry of the Trenches*. Constable, 1989.
Trotter, Josephine, editor. *Valour and Vision*. Longmans, Green and Company, 1920.
Van Wienen, Mark W., editor. *Rendezvous with Death: American Poems of the Great War*. U of Illinois P, 2002.
Walter, George, editor. *In Flanders Fields: Poetry of the First World War*. Allen Lane, 2004
Walter, George, editor. *The Penguin Book of First World War Poetry*. Penguin, 2006.
Winter, Jay. *Sites of Memory, Sites of Mourning*. Cambridge UP, 1995.
Yanks: A.E.F. Verse. G.P. Putnam's Sons, 1919.
Ziv, Frederic W., editor. *The Valiant Muse*. G.P. Putnam's Sons, 1936.

Index of Poets, Translators, and Poems

Following the name of each poet, an abbreviation appears identifying national affiliation(s): America (US), Australia (AU), Austria-Hungary (AH), Belgium (B), Canada (C), France (F), Germany (G), Great Britain (GB), India (IN), Ireland (IR), Italy (IT), New Zealand (NZ), Russia (R), and South Africa (SA).

A.E. [George William Russell] (IR)
    To the Memory of Some I Knew Who Are Dead and Who Loved Ireland 257
Akhmatova, Anna (R)
    Everything's looted, betrayed and traded 369
Alchin, Gordon (GB)
    A Song of the Air 78
Allen, Hervey (US)
    Soldier-Poet 296
Allen, Marian (GB)
    from *And What Is War?* 302
    Out in a Gale of Fallen Leaves 302
Angus, Marion (GB)
    Remembrance Day 346
Anonymous (US)
    Home is Where the Pie Is 152
Apollinaire, Guillaume (F)
    Nothing Much 99
Arcos, René (F)
    The Dead 365

Ball, Hugo (G)
    Dance of Death 1916 34
Baukhage, Hilmar R. (US)
    November Eleventh 340
Békássy, Ferenc (AH)
    1914 307
Benemann, Maria Dobler (G)
    Visé 177
Bodenheim, Maxwell (US)
    The Camp Follower 244
Borden, Mary (US, GB)
    The Hill 82
    The Song of the Mud 42

Brand-Cammaerts, Tita (trans.)
    New Year's Wishes to the German Army (Cammaerts) 170
Bridgwater, Patrick (trans.)
    At the Front (Klemm) 291
    Standing To (Schnack) 96
Brittain, Vera (GB)
    Perhaps— 325
    Sic Transit— 222
Brooke, Rupert (GB)
    Fragment 18

Calloc'h, Jean-Pierre [Yann-Ber Kalloc'h] (F)
    Veni, Sancte, Spiritus! 269
Cammaerts, Émile (B)
    New Year's Wishes to the German Army 170
Campbell, Ivar (GB)
    A Meditation upon the Return of the Greeks 230
Cannan, May Wedderburn (GB)
    Paris, November 11, 1918 344
    France 223
    'Since they have Died' 276
Clarke, Gillian (trans.)
    War (Wyn) 238
Colbron, Grace Isabel (US)
    The Ballad of Bethlehem Steel 196
Cole, Margaret Postgate [Margaret Postgate] (GB)
    The Falling Leaves 240
Corbin, Alice (US)
    A Litany in the Desert 232
Cornford, Frances (GB)
    Féri Bekassy 284

Cotter, Joseph Seamon, Jr. (US)
   O Little David Play on Your Harp 254
Coulson, Leslie (GB)
   The Rainbow 58
Cromwell, Gladys (US)
   The Extra 352

de Noialles, Anna (F)
   Victory, whose calm gaze ... 348
de Stein, Edward (GB)
   Elegy on the Death of Bingo, Our Trench Dog 335
   Envoie 377
Delarue-Mardrus, Lucie (F)
   Regiments 172
Dobell, Eva (GB)
   Gramophone Tunes 89
Down, William Oliphant (GB)
   Picardy Parodies No. 2 (W.B. Y--ts) 122
Dunbar-Nelson, Alice Moore (US)
   I Sit and Sew 204
Dunkerley, William Arthur (GB)
   His Latch-Key 320
Dyment, Clifford (GB)
   The Son 299

Eassie, Robert (C)
   Selections from "Alphabet of Limericks" 126
   Selections from "Rhymes from a New Nursery" 126
Europe, James Reese (US)
   On Patrol in No Man's Land 27

Ford, Ford Madox [Ford Madox Hueffer] (GB)
   Albade 137
Frankau, Gilbert (GB)
   Ammunition Column 85
Fullerton, Mary E. (AU)
   War Time 216

Garnier, Noël (F)
   Still Raining ... 46
Gascoyne, David (trans.)
   Little Song of the Maimed (Péret) 93
Gellert, Leon (AU)
   Anzac Cove 304
Gibson, Wilfrid Wilson (GB)
   Retreat 110
   Victory 298
Gilbert, Bernard Samuel (GB)
   Gone to the War 218
Gillespie, Violet (GB)
   Portrait of a Mother 210
Gilman, Sheldon, Robert Levine, and Harry Radford (trans.)
   Prayer before Battle (Lichtenstein) 107
Gilmore, Mary (AU)
   War 236
Granier, Albert-Paul (F)
   Fever 105
   War Song 31
Grenfell, William (GB)
   To John 295
Griffin, Jonathan (trans.)
   Vigil (Ungaretti) 38
Guiterman, Arthur (US)
   Pershing at the Front 129

Harrison, Ada M. (SA, GB)
   New Year, 1916 328
Harvey, Frederick William (GB)
   Cricket: The Catch 56
Henderson, Barbara (trans.)
   Hymn of Hate/A Chant of Hate against England (Lissauer) 166
Herbert, A.P (GB)
   Beaucourt Revisited 67
   The Bathe 73
Higgins, Ian (trans.)
   Burning Beehives (Rostand) 161
   Fever (Granier) 105
   Recall-Up (Sauvage) 355
   Regiments (Delarue-Mardrus) 172
   Still Raining ... (Garnier) 46
   The Dead (Arcos) 365
   Veni, Sancte, Spiritus! (Kalloc'h) 269
   Victory, whose calm gaze ... (de Noailles) 348
   War Song (Granier) 31
Higonnet, Margaret R. (trans.)
   Visé (Benemann) 177
Hodgson, William Noel (GB)
   Back to Rest 63
Holmes, William Kersley (GB)
   Singing "Tipperary" 252
   The Soldier Mood 154

Horne, Cyril Morton (IR)
   from *Aftermath* 41
   The Moles 40
Hueffer, Ford Madox [Ford Madox Ford] (GB)
   Albade 137

Johnston, Philip [John Stanley Purvis] (GB)
   High Wood 374
Jones, Joshua Henry, Jr. (US)
   The Heart of the World 362

Kalloc'h, Yann-Ber [Jean-Pierre Calloc'h] (F)
   Veni, Sancte, Spiritus! 269
Kästner, Erich (G)
   The Other Possibility 371
Kaufman, Walter (trans.)
   The Other Possibility (Kästner) 371
Keown, Anna Gordon (GB)
   Reported Missing 330
Kettle, Thomas M. (IR)
   To My Daughter Betty, the Gift of God 274
Kitchin, C.H.B. (GB)
   Somme Film, 1916 194
Klemm, Wilhelm (G)
   At the Front 291
Kline, A.S. (trans.)
   Everything's looted, betrayed and traded (Akhmatova) 369
   I know the truth! Renounce all others! (Tsvetaeva) 190

Ledwidge, Francis (IR)
   Home 118
   To One Dead 305
Lee, Joseph (GB)
   "Glad That I Killed Yer" 315
   The Bullet 316
Leighton, Roland (GB)
   Violets—April 1915 262
Letts, Winifred M. (GB, IR)
   Hallow-e'en, 1915 318
Lichtenstein, Alfred (G)
   Prayer before Battle 107
Lissauer, Ernst (G)
   Hymn of Hate (A Chant of Hate against England) 166

Lowell, Amy (US)
   September. 1918 150

M.G. (US)
   Camouflage 144
Macaulay, Rose (GB)
   Picnic 147
   Spreading Manure 201
Macdonald, Mary-Adair (GB)
   Epiphany Vision 266
MacGill, Patrick (IR)
   A Lament 124
   Sing Me to Sleep 125
   The Star-Shell 61
Mackay, Helen (US)
   Quinze Vingt 91
Mackintosh, Ewart Alan (GB)
   In Memoriam 288
   In No Man's Land 25
   from *To Sylvia* 289
Manning, Frederic (AU)
   Relieved 69
   The Face 101
Mansfield, Katherine (NZ)
   To L.H.B. (1894–1915) 293
Masefield, John (GB)
   from *August 1914* 309
   Red Cross 309
Mew, Charlotte (GB)
   May, 1915 186
Middleton, Christopher (trans.)
   Eastern Front (Trakl) 242
Mitchell, Ruth Comfort (US)
   He Went for a Soldier 234
Murray, Charles (GB)
   When Will the War Be By? 214

Naidu, Sarojini (IN)
   The Gift of India 277
Nesbit, Edith (GB)
   In Hospital 192
Newbolt, Henry (GB)
   A Letter from the Front 250

Oman, Carola (GB)
   In the Ypres Sector 279
   To the Survivors 350
   Unloading Ambulance Train 87

Oxenham, John (GB)
  His Latch-Key 320

Parker, Dorothy (US)
  Penelope 175
Parker, Harry L. (US)
  Left Behind 132
Péret, Benjamin (F)
  Little Song of the Maimed 93
Philipps, Colwyn (GB)
  There is a healing magic in the night (Release) 112
Pigott, E.W. (GB?)
  Saturdays 357
Pope, Jessie (GB)
  To a Taube 80
Postgate, Margaret [Margaret Postgate Cole] (GB)
  The Falling Leaves 240
Potts, Edmund (trans.)
  Dance of Death (Ball) 34
Purvis, John Stanley [Philip Johnston] (GB)
  High Wood 374

Rags (US)
  The Mascot Speaks 359
Rawnsley, Hardwicke Drummond (GB)
  Going to the Front 164
Read, Herbert (GB)
  Fear (III.) 103
Rhys, Ernest (GB)
  Jo's Requiem (XX.) 303
  The Leaf Burners 158
Rickword, Edgell (GB)
  Trench Poets 36
Roberts, Charles G.D. (C)
  Going Over 116
Rostand, Edmond (F)
  Burning Beehives 161
Russell, George William [A.E.] (IR)
  To the Memory of Some I Knew Who Are Dead and Who Loved Ireland 257

Sackville, Margaret (GB)
  A Memory 184
  Reconciliation 367
Sandford, Egbert T. (GB)
  At Bethlehem—1915 268
Sauvage, Marcel (F)
  Recall-Up 355

Schnack, Anton (G)
  Standing To 96
Service, Robert W. (C)
  Only a Boche 312
  The Mourners 212
Shaw-Stewart, Patrick (GB)
  I Saw a Man This Morning 228
Shove, Fredegond (GB)
  The Farmer, 1917 199
Simpson, Henry Lamont (GB)
  Going In 75
Sinclair, May (GB)
  After the Retreat 181
Siordet, Gerald Caldwell (GB)
  To the Dead 322
Smith, Geoffrey Bache (GB)
  Let Us Tell Quiet Stories of Kind Eyes 282
Smith, Gertrude (US)
  America at War 260
Smith, Hugh Stewart (GB)
  On the Plains of Picardy 120
  from *The Incorrigibles: Written from the Front to a Friend* 121
Sorrell, Martin (trans.)
  Nothing Much (Apollinaire) 99
Squire, J.C. (GB)
  "An Epilogue": The Fluke (I.) 332
  "An Epilogue": The Landscape (IV.) 332
  from *To a Bull-dog* 333
Stables, James Howard (GB)
  High Barbary 264
Stokes, Rose Pastor [Zelda] (US)
  To the Patriotic Lady across the Way 207
Studdert Kennedy, Geoffrey (GB)
  Solomon in All His Glory 272

Trakl, Georg (AH)
  Eastern Front 242
Trent, K.L. (NZ)
  A Digger's Disillusion 50
Trotter, Bernard Freeman (C)
  A Kiss 134
Tsvetaeva, Marina (R)
  I know the truth! Renounce all others! 190
Tynan, Katharine (IR)
  Telling the Bees 286

Underhill, Evelyn (GB)
   Any Englishwoman 187
Ungaretti, Giuseppe (IT)
   Vigil 38

van Beek, Theodore (SA, GB)
   After the "Offensive" 65
Vernède, Robert Ernest (GB)
   To C.H.V. 139

Waterhouse, Gilbert (GB)
   Bivouacs 114
Waugh, Alec (GB)
   The Other Side 247
West, Arthur Graeme (GB)
   The Night Patrol 22
White, Donald S. (US)
   The Boys Who Live in the Ground 48
Wickersham, John Hunter (US)
   The Raindrops on Your Old Tin Hat 141
Widdemer, Margaret (US)
   Homes 179
Wilson, Theodore Percival Cameron (GB)
   During the Bombardment 53
Wyeth, John Allan (US)
   Night Watch 98
   Picnic: Harbonnières to Bayonvillers 71
   The Transport 20
Wyn, Hedd (GB)
   War 238

Zelda [Rose Pastor Stokes] (US)
   To the Patriotic Lady across the Way 207

Index of Poem Titles and First Lines

The exact punctuation of first lines as it appears in the poems is not necessarily duplicated here. Excerpted poems are marked with an asterisk, and the poem's title and the first line quoted in this anthology appear in this index.

1914 307

A blackbird singing 305
A burst of sudden wings at dawn 118
A Chant of Hate against England 166
A Digger's Disillusion 50
A fort is taken, the papers say 196
A girl's voice in the night troubled my heart 116
A grim gray tribute of memory 41
A house marked Ortskommandantur—a great 71
A Kiss 134
A Lament 124
A leaping wind from England 63
A Letter from the Front 250
A Litany in the Desert 232
A Meditation upon the Return of the Greeks 230
A Memory 184
A Song of the Air 78
A star-shell holds the sky beyond 61
A thick still heat stifles the dim saloon 20
A whole night long 38
Above the valley, rich and fair 80
After the "Offensive" 65
After the Retreat 181
*Aftermath** 41
Albade 137
All those boys who have left 172
America 260
America at War 260
Ammunition Column 85
An Epilogue: The Fluke (I.) 332
An Epilogue: The Landscape (IV.) 332
And long ... long ... long we waited 320
And though you run expectant as you always do* 333

*And What Is War?** 302
Any Englishwoman 187
Anzac Cove 304
At Bethlehem—1915 268
At the Front 291
*August 1914** 309
Autumn and dusk—a band far off plays *I* 98

Back to Rest 63
Beaucourt Revisited 67
Bitter to live in times like these 238
Bivouacs 114
Broken, bewildered by the long retreat 110
Burning Beehives 161

Camouflage 144
Come friend and swim. We may be better then 73
Cricket: The Catch 56

Dame Death is joyously dancing 31
Dance of Death 1916 34
Down on the boulevards the crowds went by 344
During the Bombardment 53

Eastern Front 242
Elegy on the Death of Bingo, Our Trench Dog 335
England's in flower 187
Envoie 377
Epiphany Vision 266
Every bullet has its billet 316
Everything's looted, betrayed and traded 369
Everything's looted, betrayed and traded 369

Fear (III.) 103
Fear is a wave 103
Féri Bekassy 284
Fever 105
For two years you went 332
For us, foot-slogging sadly, it is clear 121
Fragment 18
France 223
French and Russian, they matter not 166
Fritzie-Witzie sat on a bomb 126
From the top of the hill I looked down on the beautiful, the gorgeous, the super-human and monstrous landscape of the superb exulting war 82

"Glad That I Killed Yer" 315
Glad that I killed yer 315
God knows—my dear—I did not want* 289
Going In 75
Going Over 116
Going to the Front 164
Gone to the War 218
Gramophone Tunes 89

Hallow-e'en, 1915 318
He had the plowman's strength 303
He marched away with a blithe young score of him 234
He Went for a Soldier 234
He went without fears, went gaily, since go he must 307
He's gone to the war, he's gone to the war 218
Heartbeat, heartbeat, why the rush 105
High Barbary 264
High Wood 374
His Latch-Key 320
Home 118
Home is where the heart is 152
Home is Where the Pie Is 152
Homes 179
How like the dead we look, in the glisten 46
How many d'you reckon we've killed 99
How pleasing: straight away, they burned some beehives 161
How shall I say good-bye to you, wonderful, terrible days 377
Hymn of Hate 166

I am only a cog in a giant machine, a link of an endless chain 85
I am so tired 222
I found the letter in a cardboard box 299
I got a letter from 132
I had no heart to march for war 164
I knew a man, he was my chum 36
I know the truth! Renounce all others! 190
I know the truth! Renounce all others! 190
I look into the aching womb of night 212
I remember a moonless night in a blasted town 309
I Saw a Man This Morning 228
I saw a man this morning 228
I see a farmer walking by himself 199
I shall go into death as into a doorway filled with summer coolness, the scent of hay, and cobwebs: I shall never return 96
I Sit and Sew 204
I sit and sew—a useless task it seems 204
I strayed about the deck, an hour, to-night 18
I think at first like us he did not see 296
I wandered up to Beaucourt; I took the river track 67
I was out early to-day, spying about 250
I watch the white dawn gleam 58
I watched it oozing quietly 298
I will arise and go now, and go to Picardy 122
I wish that every hour of life 170
I wish the sea were not so wide 124
I've been in a trench for fifteen days 40
If I could only see again 181
If we had won the war with waving 371
In Hospital 192
In Memoriam 288
In No Man's Land 25
In Somecourt Wood, in Somecourt Wood 114
In the heart of the world is the call for peace 362
In the pathway of the sun 175
In the Ypres Sector 279
In wiser days, my darling rosebud, blown 274
Into the siding very wearily 87
Is there aught you need that my hands withhold 277

Jack and Bill, they stuck it till 126
Jo's Requiem (XX.) 303

Knit two and purl one 210

Ladies and gentlemen, this is High Wood 374
Last night for the first time since you were dead 293
Left Behind 132
Lend me your arm 93
Let us remember Spring will come again 186
Let Us Tell Quiet Stories of Kind Eyes 282
Let us tell quiet stories of kind eyes 282
Little Song of the Maimed 93

May, 1915 186
My thought shall never be that you are dead 330

New Year, 1916 328
New Year's Wishes to the German Army 170
Night Watch 98
Nothing Much 99
November Eleventh 340
Now has the soljer handed in his pack 357
Now in the one thousand nine hundred and fourteenth year after Christ was born in the stable 269

O heart-and-soul and careless played 295
O Little David, Play on Your Harp 254
O Little David, play on your harp 254
On Patrol in No Man's Land 27
On the other side of the Sangre de Cristo mountains 232
On the Plains of Picardy 120
On the Plains of Picardy 120
Only a Boche 312
Out in a Gale of Fallen Leaves 302
Out in a gale of fallen leaves 302
Out in the dust he lies 236
Out of the smoke of men's wrath 101
Over the top! The wire's thin here, unbarbed 22

Paris, November 11, 1918 344
Penelope 175

Perhaps some day the sun will shine again 325
Perhaps— 325
Pershing at the Front 129
Picardy Parodies No. 2 (W.B. Y--ts) 122
Picnic 147
Picnic: Harbonnières to Bayonvillers 71
Portrait of a Mother 210
Prayer before Battle 107

Quinze Vingt 91

Recall-Up 355
Reconciliation 367
Red Cross 309
Regiments 172
Release 112
Relieved 69
Remembrance Day 346
Reported Missing 330
Retreat 110

Saturdays 357
Selections from "Rhymes from a New Nursery" 126
Selections from an "Alphabet of Limericks" 126
September. 1918 150
She kissed me when she said good-bye 134
She wore a Liberty loan button 207
Sheltered and safe we sit 352
Sic Transit— 222
Since in the days that may not come again 322
'Since they have Died' 276
Since they have died to give us gentleness 276
Sing Me to Sleep 125
Sing me to sleep where bullets fall 125
Singing "Tipperary" 252
Smoke-black the air, the city in rubble 177
So we die, we die 34
So you were David's father 288
Soldier-Poet 296
Solomon in All His Glory 272
Some one was singing 346
Some sing the glory of the war 48
Somme Film, 1916 194
Spreading Manure 201
Standing To 96

Still I see them coming, coming 272
Still Raining 46
Suppose, all at once 355

Tell it to the bees, lest they 286
Telling the Bees 286
The Ballad of Bethlehem Steel 196
The Bathe 73
The Boys Who Live in the Ground 48
The Bullet 316
The Camp Follower 244
The countryside is desolate. The fields look tear-stained 291
The Dead 365
The distant mountains' jagged, cruel line 264
The Extra 352
The Face 101
The Falling Leaves 240
The Farmer, 1917 199
The General came in a new tin hat 129
The Gift of India 277
The Heart of the World 362
The hedge on the left, and the trench on the right 25
The Hill 82
from *The Incorrigibles: Written from the Front to a Friend** 121
The lamplight's shaded rose 179
The Leaf Burners 158
The little girls are singing, "Rin! Ron! Rin!" 137
The Mascot Speaks 359
The mist hangs low and quiet on a ragged line of hills 141
The Moles 40
The Mourners 212
The Night Patrol 22
The Other Possibility 371
The Other Side 247
The Rainbow 58
The Raindrops on Your Old Tin Hat 141
The Soldier Mood 154
The Son 299
The Song of the Mud 42
The sound of laughing voices disappearing* 302
The Star-Shell 61
The Transport 20

The travellers are astir 268
The troops are singing fervently, each for himself 107
The widows' veils 365
The wrath of the people is dark 242
Their dream had left me numb and cold 257
Their last sight was the red sight of battle 91
Then sadly rose and left the well-loved Downs* 309
There are fifty steaming heaps in the One Tree field 201
There are not any, save the men that died 247
There is a healing magic in the night 112
There is a healing magic in the night 112
There is no cause, sweet wanderers in the dark 194
There was a brave girl of Nieppe 126
There was a sweet thing at Olhain 126
There was a young fellow of Vimy 126
There was a young hero of Aire 126
There was no sound at all, no crying in the village 184
There's a lonely stretch of hillocks 304
They are all given back to you 350
They say I can't go back with him 359
They tell us tales of camouflage 144
This afternoon was the colour of water falling through sunlight 150
This is the end of it, this the cold silence 65
This is the night of a Star 266
This is the song of the mud 42
This is the song of the Plane 78
This year, neist year, sometime, never 214
Those that go down into silence 328
Through the long ward the gramophone 89
from *To a Bull-dog** 333
To a Taube 80
To C.H.V. 139
To John 295
To L.H.B. (1894–1915) 293
To My Daughter Betty, the Gift of God 274
To One Dead 305
from *To Sylvia** 289
To the Dead 322

*To the Memory of Some I Knew Who Are
    Dead and Who Loved Ireland* 257
To the Patriotic Lady across the Way 207
To the Survivors 350
To-day, as I rode by 240
Trench Poets 36

Under the shadow of a hawthorn brake
    192
Under two oak trees 158
Unloading Ambulance Train 87

Veni, Sancte, Spiritus! 269
Victory 298
Victory, whose calm gaze ... 348
Victory, whose calm gaze defends the just
    348
Vigil 38
Violets—April 1915 262
Violets from Plug Street Wood 262
Visé 177

War [Out in the dust he lies] 236
War [Bitter to live in times like these] 238
War Song 31
War Time 216
We are weary and silent 69
We brought him in from between the
    lines: we'd better have let him lie 312
We lay and ate sweet hurt-berries 147

We spoke, the camp-follower and I 244
We stood up and we didn't say a word
    340
We went down to the lake 75
We were eating chip potatoes underneath
    the April stars 154
We, who must grow old and staid 284
We've each our Tipperary, who shout that
    haunting song 252
Weep, weep, ye dwellers in the delvèd
    earth 335
What did we know of birds? 53
What shall I bring to you, wife of mine
    139
What's the time, nine, all in line 27
When all the stress and all the toil is over
    367
When I first thought of enlisting 50
When in their long lean ships the Greek
    host weighed 230
When Will the War Be By? 214
Whizzing, fierce, it came 56
Will you come back to us, men of our
    hearts, to-night 318

You also know 223
You have left beauty here in everything
    279
You said, that first winter 332
Young John, the postman, day by day 216